NOWHERE AT HOME

*Letters from Exile of
Emma Goldman and
Alexander Berkman*

EDITED BY
Richard and Anna Maria Drinnon

SCHOCKEN BOOKS · NEW YORK

Library of Congress Cataloging in Publication Data

Goldman, Emma, 1869–1940.
  Nowhere at home.

  1. Anarchism and anarchists—United States—
Correspondence, reminiscences, etc. I. Berkman,
Alexander, 1870–1936. II. Title.
HX844.G615   1974   320.5'7   73-91346

For all exiles,
external and internal

Acknowledgments

IN the interwar years, especially following Hitler's rise to power, those in flight from repression and terror frequently paused long enough in Amsterdam to drop off their personal and group archives. Their deposits at the International Institute of Social History make it today one of the great good places in the world for the study of radical and social movements. Our collection of letters comes thus most fittingly from manuscript holdings so largely built up by exiles. We are deeply grateful to the Director, Professor Fr. de Jong Edz., to Deputy Director Ch. B. Timmer, and to the staff for permission to go through the Goldman–Berkman Archives once again, to photocopy letters and copies of letters, and then to have the results published. Our obligation is all the greater since the Institute has an impressive list of source-material publications under its own imprint. And we are particularly indebted to Mr. Rudolf de Jong of the Institute's anarchist section for making our most recent stay in Amsterdam so pleasant, for reading the collection at an early stage, and for his many valuable suggestions. Thanks to him and his associates, our return to Amsterdam was like coming home again.

Ian Ballantine, Emma Goldman's present literary executor, graciously gave us permission to publish the exchanges of his great-aunt and Alexander Berkman.

Although this is first and foremost a collection of Goldman and Berkman letters, eight of those that appear below were written by their friends. For permission to publish individual letters or for their help in trying to locate literary executors, we wish to thank the following: Arthur Leonard Ross, Emma Goldman's counselor and Frank Harris's executor; Irma Duncan Rogers, Isadora Duncan's protégée and friend; and Paula Scott, Evelyn Scott's daughter-in-law.

Several letters in Part One were originally the property of Ellen Kennan, a libertarian teacher who was for many years a friend of Emma

Goldman. These letters, along with many others, are presently in the possession of her cousin, Esther Brack, of Modesto, California. We ran off copies of those we now publish, along with the others, and presented the lot to the International Institute. Since they have now been added to the other papers in the Goldman–Berkman Archives, we have not bothered to indicate the separate provenance of the few that appear below. We do record here our appreciation to Ms. Brack and to librarian Zoia Horn, our good friend, for bringing these letters to our attention.

Finally, our debt to Mollie Steimer and Senya Flechine is special. Living presently in Cuernavaca, Mexico, they have patiently tolerated our long distance queries about Yiddish phrases, supplied photographs and directed us to others, and helped with the identification of individuals. Fellow exiles of Emma Goldman and Alexander Berkman, they are still managing, somehow, to live their principles in strange lands with "nowhere to go." They have our admiration and thanks.

Contents

Illustrations appear after pp. 63 and 187.

Introduction

Back in France. Soon again requested
to leave. Expelled again and again. Must
get off the earth, but am still here.
Nowhere to go, but awaiting the next order.

Alexander Berkman

It is only now, when most of my friends
have gone by the board and when I myself
feel so cast out, pursued by the furies
and nowhere at home, that the love
of the few friends [left] has begun
to stand out more beautifully than ever.

Emma Goldman

For all men who say *yes* lie; and all men
who say *no*,—why they are in the happy condition
of the judicious unencumbered travelers
in Europe; they cross the frontiers into
Eternity with nothing but a carpet-bag,
—that is to say, the Ego. Whereas those *yes*-gentry,
they travel with heaps of baggage, and, damn them!
they will never get through the Custom House.

Herman Melville

IN late 1931 Emma Goldman assured Alexander Berkman she had been writing faithfully:

> Got your letter of the 14th [of December] with enclosures. I don't see why you should have been anxious. I wrote you the 9th, again the 13th, with a postcard between. And again the 14th. It seems to me I keep writing to you all the time. Anyhow I am glad you still care about your old sailor suffi-ciently to be anxious if you do not hear every day. May you never cease to be that.
>
> Dear heart, do you know what I keep busy with? Writing endless letters to America. . . . Yesterday I worked over a letter to Arthur [Leonard Ross] in answer to four of his. I wrote ten pages. You can imagine how long it took me to do that. Besides, other letters to the States which had to be gotten out before this rotten old year is done with. I still have about fifteen to do. Fact is, I did not budge out of my [Paris] apartment all week. I will never make a good or rapid typist. I hate it and I grow ill if I keep long at the machine. My old neck and spine do not bear up under much strain. That's how I keep busy. I know it is useless labor. But it is the only link in my life, to keep in touch with our friends in America. And so I keep at it.

Keep at it she did, writing letter after letter to friends in America while managing somehow to send almost daily dispatches to her old comrade. Never ceasing to be eager to hear from her when they were separated, Berkman replied almost as frequently as she wrote.

The mail is terribly important to banished men and women like Alexander Berkman and Emma Goldman: For them the postman never need ring twice. Uprooted persons by definition, exiles yearn to hear from family, comrades, editors, publishers, lawyers, acquaintants. Has a favorite brother, ill for so long, finally died? Will someone explain why a hitherto faithful correspondent writes only perfunctory notes? Does the silence of another old friend mean he has fallen off the face of the earth?

Did the corrected galley proofs actually get to a distant editor? If so, what egregious liberties is he taking with them? And where is the check for the advance? Questions breed more questions, submerge in the mails, and frequently fail to surface: "So much gets lost in the French mails," Berkman complained to Emma in 1927. "That package sent to me at St. Tropez, you remember. . . . I investigated it and found that the package reached the American Express here and was sent by them to the Paris post office to be sent to St. Tropez and then and there it disappeared." Still, however frustrated by what they have not received, exiles go on rising each morning to wait on the postman. Conceivably, though this would be most rare good luck, he may bring word of a revolution at home that has banished the banishers; much more likely would be the next best news he could hand them: the regime that condemned them to wander in foreign lands has fallen from power.

Political exiles have always tried to contribute to this end and perforce have worked through the mails. Herzen, Bakunin, and Kropotkin, for example, sought to undermine the Czar by sending their books, periodicals, manifestoes, and suggestions to their Russian confederates. In an essay "The Tragedy of the Political Exiles," which appeared in the *Nation* on October 10, 1934, Emma Goldman pointed out that, no matter how great the suffering of these and other pre-World War I exiles, "they had their faith and their work to give them an outlet. They lived, dreamed, and labored incessantly for the liberation of their native lands. They could arouse public opinion in their place of refuge against the tyranny and oppression practiced in their country, and they were able to help their comrades in prison with large funds contributed by the workers and liberal elements in other parts of the world." But the war for democracy and the rise of left and right dictatorships, she argued, had ended an era when rebels could find asylum in a number of countries and had relative freedom of movement: Now "tens of thousands of men, women, and children have been turned into modern Ahasueruses [Wandering Jews], forced to roam the earth, admitted nowhere. If they are fortunate enough to find asylum, it is nearly always for a short period only; they are always exposed to annoyance and chicanery, and their lives made a veritable hell." Berkman was a leading case in point, though what she said applied to herself as well. Yet, utterly unwilling to accept this tragic turn of events, she kept at her "endless letters to America." It was by no means a useless labor.

The endlessness of her correspondence was almost literal fact. Our guess is that she must have written some two hundred thousand letters, notes, postcards, and wires—all referred to here under the generic term *letters*—in her lifetime.* She could thus say with little exaggeration that

---

* Dan H. Laurence, Bernard Shaw's editor, estimates that the playwright wrote a quarter of a million letters. Emma must have written almost as many, though a large number of course were lost or destroyed or confiscated—much of her correspondence to 1917, for

friends had returned "veritable mountains of letters" for her to use in writing *Living My Life* (1931). Beginning in the 1920s, she multiplied their already awesome number by broadcasting carbon copies to a wide circle of correspondents. As she explained to novelist Evelyn Scott:

> I am delighted to know, dearest mine, you like my scheme of sending carbon copies of letters to my different friends. I began this method really to save labor because I find much typing sheer torture besides being a rotten typist. And now it has become a habit. I am glad to say most of my correspondents are enthusiastic about it. . . .
>
> I have been hard at work making some order among my papers, mss., lecture notes, and letters. My dear, it was a job. You see, I am always so rushed while on tour to the last moment that I never can afford the time to put everything in order. I did it here [in St. Tropez]. Would you believe it, my correspondence alone would take about ten volumes. Sasha [Berkman] insists I'll be punished good and hard when I come before my maker for having been such a prolific letter writer. I must say I find it infinitely easier to express myself in letters than in books. My thoughts come easier though not always worthwhile.

In her reply Ms. Scott remarked on the colossal undertaking of sorting a correspondence which "must in itself constitute a marvelous record of radical thought in our age. Your letters are to me not only exceptionally fluent but stirring in those thoughts 'worthwhile.' I have wondered at your aversion to writing books when the written word, as your correspondence shows, is so easily at your command."

Letters became Emma Goldman's medium primarily because she was an exile and because in them the gap between the written and the spoken word was at its narrowest. A short stride over the gap enabled her to express her great strength as a speaker and conversationalist: It was as though she were responding to an earnest questioner after a lecture or having her say after a fine meal in someone's apartment. She spoke with directness and intensity from the current edge of her thinking, feeling, experiencing—and not incidentally therewith effectively revoked the official edict of separation from all she held dear. This "proclivity to spread myself in letters," for which she was chided by Berkman and others, meant that her distant friends had access to her continuous present and to her self-revelation of different aspects of character to different correspondents. Her letters gave them immediate data on how she was living her life and were in a sense invitations to live as much of it as they could with her. The end result made her seem, with the touch of irony detected by anarchist historian Max Nettlau, a figure out of an earlier letter-writing society: "In letters happily,

---

instance, was scooped up by federal raiders and carried behind the walls of the U.S. Department of Justice. For a discussion of those papers that survived and came to rest in various archives, see the "Bibliographical Essay" in Richard Drinnon, *Rebel in Paradise: A Biography of Emma Goldman* (New York: Bantam Books, 1973).

though tiptop up to date otherwise," he wrote in 1929, "you are eighteenth century, doing honor to the good old art of letter writing, which the wire and telephone have strangled, and this is a good thing, as a thoughtful way of communication by letters is an intellectual act of value of its own, which rapid talk, etc., cannot replace in its essence. . . ."

In his still ridiculously neglected *Prison Memoirs of an Anarchist* (1912), Alexander Berkman had expressed acute psychological and political insights through a style of unusual simplicity and suppleness. As editor of *Mother Earth*, Emma Goldman's monthly, and later of his own *Blast*, he went on to demonstrate that he was in some respects a more able, practiced writer than she. Yet his surviving correspondence, considered as a whole, is less impressive than hers and this rather surprising contrast calls for a few words of explanation. It was partly due to his temperament, which was less outgoing than Emma's, and to the many years in prison, which fed his reluctance to reveal inner feelings even to intimate friends. Moreover, a man without a passport, repeatedly subject to deportation orders, and forever at the beck and call of the authorities, he was understandably less ready to disclose all in writing. In 1928 he wrote Emma, for instance, that he had destroyed a certain letter, adding: "I destroy most letters, except those on business or such as have reference to matters which might in the future serve as data etc. There are many deportations here now, and with some of those people my address might be found—the government has it anyhow, and so searches are always possible, and it is no use keeping personal letters." Finally, Berkman was less vitally interested in expressing himself in letters than Emma, for he refused to consider ever returning to America. Now if the expatriate differs from the exile mainly in that he *chooses* not to go home again, Berkman became in this sense more the expatriate, while Emma's yearning for repatriation marked her as always the exile.* Put more directly, letters to and from home meant less for him because home meant less.

But these distinctions have a way of becoming misleading when they become too tidy. In fact some of Berkman's letters showed that he cared deeply what happened to his American correspondents and that he had not really relinquished all hope for the libertarian cause there. He was frequently stung by Emma into writing, if only in self-defense, eloquent and emotionally moving replies to her questions and arguments. Their letters indeed constitute a marvelous record of radical thought. Therein they noted their ongoing reflections on the repression and terror in post-Revolutionary Russia, the lot of exiles and refugees on the Continent, the reaction in England, the Sacco-Vanzetti case and other events in the United States, the rise to power of the Nazis in Germany, the appeal of

---

* Mary McCarthy argues persuasively for this distinction in "A Guide to Exiles, Expatriates, and Internal Emigrés," *New York Review of Books*, XVIII (March 9, 1972), 4–8.

dictatorship for the masses, and the like. Their continuing dialogue about things that mattered produced a "double, yet separate correspondence," to borrow Samuel Richardson's formulation, which was remarkable in its sweep and depth, frankness, and, not least, loving concern.

2

One day this correspondence should be published in its entirety. Meanwhile its very richness presents special problems of selection: Why these particular letters and not others? Why not a greater or a lesser number? Should they appear in the usual chronological order? Or should we attempt to gather them into topical units? Our answers to these questions may be more readily understood if we explain how this volume came to be.

Over a decade ago the senior (in years) editor used the Berkman–Goldman letters as a framework for a biography of Emma Goldman. Their correspondence then posed some critically important questions: What was an appropriate response of Western radicals to the Soviet Union? Could anarchism cope with the problem of violence? How might men and women learn to establish decent relationships? And how might exiled revolutionaries live their beliefs? Stripping away the descriptive and analytical flesh from these questions as they appeared in the biography and using our notes as guides to the whole body of their correspondence, we retraced our steps to the archives and to those letters that had provided the skeleton of the earlier study. We then had the most important letters photocopied; from these four hundred and forty copies we later chose some as more significant than others, eliminated the latter, and cut some of the irrelevancies from the former. Our method has amounted to a kind of willful perversity, tantamount to the unwriting of a book, and can only be justified by the results: If we have carried out our editorial chores with a measure of success, the reader will find that the two sides of the correspondence collected here already constitute a biography of sorts, the lives of Emma Goldman and Alexander Berkman in their letters.

Collections of letters are usually strung on a simple chronological thread for good reason: By their nature such communications are hard to classify. Correspondents only occasionally discuss a single topic. Some letters contain passages on all the topics under consideration: Should they appear and, if so, where? Others obviously fit a particular category but contain passages on themes discussed elsewhere: Should these repetitions be cut? Even a selection of letters that are entirely of a piece may give a misleading view of the writer. Thus when Emerson edited some of Thoreau's letters to demonstrate his friend's "most perfect piece of stoicism," Sophia Thoreau held the edition dishonest in that it contained none of her brother's "tokens of natural affection." Furthermore, excising these tokens destroys the unity of a letter; worse still, snippets can form a composite almost as lacking in fidelity as those redistributed passages of certain nineteenth-century editors. Nevertheless, recognizing these dangers, we still have chosen a topical organization for the five parts of *Nowhere at Home,* but have arranged the letters chronologically within each part—readers primarily concerned with chronology should not find it unbearably difficult to hop from part to part in pursuit of letters from a particular year or years. Happily some of their letters are almost completely given over to a theme; excerpts from others are usually direct responses to earlier queries or assertions and at all events are clearly identified as sections from particular letters. Excisions are always marked by the usual ellipsis dots. In Part Five, "Living the Revolution," we have presented the reader with as many whole letters as space would allow: Especially there he or she can become acquainted with the relatively trivial, homely details of their everydays.

Emma spelled and typed atrociously and proved it once and for all by rendering the adverb as "atrotiously." As she sat at her machine, parsnips came out "parsnaps," cushions as "cussions," trash as "thrash," array as "erray," practical habitually appeared as "practicle," and octopus even surfaced as "octiebus." In 1931 she wrote Berkman about the irritating habits of a mutual friend, adding: "Of course I gave him a peace of my mind." When the man apologized, "it was impossible to be angry with him though he certainly goes on one's nerves." The crisis of a feminine friend struck her as mere whim, knowing as she did "all these sexual obheavals of the American women." In fact, the lives of these women were pitiably empty, she held, "and so they make a mountain of every little molehead." Her typing was no less idiosyncratic. In 1925, for instance, she wrote Berkman a long letter from London, starting out by inserting her first page at an angle, so that the text leaned heavily over the right margin, and finishing by typing to the very bottom of the legal-sized sheet, whereupon her lines commenced an eerie diagonal course: "Look at this rotten crooked letter, will you?" she asked Berkman. "Try as I may I can never get it quite straight. There must be something crooked in my make up somewheres, don't you XXX think?" And try as she might, the letters still "jomped." In 1934 she responded to Berkman's twitting with a wry plea for indulgence:

> Have a heart, dearest, old Pal. How can you be so cruel to tease me about my typing? Gawd knows I am already sickeningl y conscious of it. What is more I think I am getting worse instead of better. This is the more inexplaninable because I am not so lacking in other respects.Except spelling.That is another strange complex. I suppose there is no help for me on this or the other world.

To reproduce these vagaries of spelling, punctuation, spacing, and typography, all duly witnessed by swarms of *sics*, would be rank pedantry. We have therefore "normalized" spellings, mostly hers, corrected their obvious typographical errors, regularized punctuation, silently eliminated most abbreviations, and blocked and formalized their salutations and closes. Our overriding concern has been the interests and needs of the general reader, but we have not presumed to keep from him those idioms that are slightly awry. It strikes us as refreshing, anyhow, to imagine someone "making a mountain out of a molehead," another wanting "to eat the pie and have it at the same time," or to think of those pseudo-radical women who gave Emma "a pain in a soft spot." American English was after all not their native tongue, as Emma's spelling in a favorite saying forcibly reminds us: "Every little bit helps, said the old lady who pie pied in the sea."

Marks and flaws in the photocopies we have had to use may have misled us on occasion. Still, we might have misread originals for the same reasons and did find onionskin carbons sometimes more readable when photocopied. No point would be served, in our opinion, by indicating in each instance whether our copy is of an original or of a carbon. As our acknowledgments indicate, all the letters or carbon copies we reproduce are at the International Institute of Social History in Amsterdam. Doubtful passages and dates and incomplete letters are indicated by warnings in brackets or in the notes. To keep the latter at a minimum, we ask the reader to turn to the index for data, when known, on an unidentified individual on the first appearance of his name. In the headings appear the initials of Alexander Berkman and Emma Goldman; these are followed by the date and, when known, the place of writing. Thus: *AB TO EG, December 20, 1933, NICE.* Following the complimentary closes, finally, their initials in brackets indicate, in the absence of a note marking an incomplete original, that we are reproducing a carbon copy.

No doubt our choices among and from the letters of Alexander Berkman and Emma Goldman have not infrequently been misguided and sometimes simply unwise. But the reader may be certain of one thing: At no point did we feel obliged to keep from him those details "too intimate to publish." If not for other reasons, it would have been too absurd to repress matters from lives dedicated to forthright expression. When Emma was preparing to write her autobiography in 1928, for instance, attorney Arthur Leonard Ross advised her to exclude her role in Berkman's attempt to assassinate Henry Clay Frick:

> A bourgeois president of a bourgeois country could no more see in the story the humane promptings of a girlish heart than I can see Vesuvius from my office window. . . . Should you entertain any illusions concerning your reentry into the Promised Land, remember that whatever vestige of hope there is will be dissipated by the publication of the story. Your guilt of

complicity in a crime would be established against you pro confesso, and the actual purchase and delivery of the deadly weapon is the overt act.

Emma's reply merits quoting at length:

> Dear Arthur, I appreciate deeply your interest in my autobiography and in my chances of a possible return to the States. But it will be out of the question to consider your suggestion of eliminating the story. . . . There are numbers of reasons why I could not possibly do that. The principal being that my connection with Berkman's act and our relationship is the leitmotif of my forty years of life [since]. As a matter of fact it is the pivot around which my story is written. You are mistaken if you think that it was only "the humane promptings of a girlish heart" which impelled my desperate act contained in the story. It was my religiously devout belief that the end justifies all means. The end, then, was my ideal of human brotherhood. If I have undergone any change it is not in my ideal. It is more in the realization that a great end does not justify *all* means. . . .
>
> After all, forty years have passed since that intense and tragic event. I do not think that even the stupid 100% American government would hold this against me, especially as one of us has paid a price in blood and tears. But even if that should be the case, I would rather never again have the opportunity of returning than to eliminate what represents the very essence of my book.

The final sixteen years of their relationship represents the very essence of this collection. As editors we have undertaken no less than to emulate their openness about its ups and downs.

3

A short while ago a newspaper photograph showed a "draft dodger" in Toronto holding a biography of Emma before his face to hide his identity. The other day at a New York demonstration, the EMMA GOLDMAN BRIGADE of radical feminists marched boldly down Fifth Avenue behind a red-and-black banner bearing her name. In the spring of 1973 students at Hunter College organized a "Self Liberation Conference" to discuss Berkman and other anarchists, with music provided by the Death City Survivors. A few months ago two new editions of Berkman's classic *Prison Memoirs* came out within weeks of each other. The issues of his *Blast* and of Emma's *Mother Earth* were recently reprinted. Publishers have also brought out soft-cover editions of her *Anarchism and Other Essays* (orig. 1911), of *My Disillusionment in Russia* (orig. 1923, 1925), and of her autobiography *Living My Life*. What a columnist recently observed about Emma on the editorial page of the Washington *Post* (February 23, 1973) might also have been said of Berkman: "Her ideas of fifty years ago, bouncing back at us in history's echo chamber, are in a language which has had to wait half a century for translation." Why? And why their astonishing contemporaneity?

In those distant days of high patriotism and the Red Scare, when Emma Goldman and Alexander Berkman were sent packing back past the Statue of Liberty, their strictures against the omnicompetent state struck all but a handful of libertarians as subversive foreign nonsense. Conservatives, liberals, and mainstream radicals were in perfect agreement on the need for centralization, unity, big nations. Herbert Hoover conservatives championed "rugged individualism," but proceeded to build up the U.S. Department of Commerce and corporate bureaucracies. Franklin Roosevelt liberals expressed concern over civil liberties, but never wavered in their confidence that more agencies and more statutes, along with scientific management, would guarantee the freedom of individuals. And the Old Left, "progressive" by definition, also embraced integral nationalism and unrestrained industrialism, asking only that the managerial elites be staffed by socialists or communists. Everybody agreed that the good life could and would be achieved through the increased application of centrally directed technology. No one or almost no one proposed transcending the given reality or even suggested ways of asking the right questions about political and technological processes that were destroying the last possibilities of individuality and community. No one, left, right or center, in short, posed a compelling challenge to the nearly universal habit of reading history with centralist prejudices.

Yet as the twentieth century rolled on these *yes*-gentry cut ever more ridiculous figures: As though history were poking a little malicious fun at them for defying her processes, they were repeatedly let down by the "progress" they celebrated. The gas ovens, saturation bombing, Hiroshima, napalm, colonized minorities at home and colonial wars abroad all helped unmask centralist prejudices for what they were—apologies for systems of domination and repression. Man as Master (of many other men) used the nation state to slaughter more tens of millions of human beings: the war in Southeast Asia alone killed at last reckoning a million Indochinese and fifty thousand young Americans. With the publication of the Pentagon Papers, Americans learned that they had been consistently lied to about the origins of the war and that their leaders had almost certainly committed major war crimes. Meanwhile, Man as Conqueror (of nature) increased the Gross National Product by escalating his violations of the earth. The two processes converged in Vietnam with a destruction of lives and land justly labeled "ecocide."

By the 1960s events themselves had thus helped translate the ideas of these two anarchists and gave them meaning for a generation in search of a politics of vision (and survival). Liberation movements of students, women, gays, and ethnic minorities produced an inchoate New Consciousness, a "counterculture" that could appreciate their pioneering struggles against war, racism, sexism, and injustice, and could draw on their example to carry out latter-day anarchistic experiments in radical journalism, forming communes, establishing free schools and clinics, homesteading; the communication over the generations was almost as direct as that suggested by the short step from the title of Emma's *Mother Earth* to that of the ecology-minded *Mother Earth News.*

At the moment the best estimate of draft resisters and deserters still in exile is sixty to a hundred thousand; about ten thousand are in civil or military prisons, on probation, or facing court action; and another eighty thousand are "underground" in America. These exiles, abroad and at home, and their families are very much on our minds as we edit these letters, as the dedication above suggests, for the prison experiences and the exile years of Alexander Berkman and Emma Goldman speak directly over the decades to the like circumstances of a large number of courageous men and women. Those who take up this volume, along with other general readers, should find their own hard times eased a little. Those who seek to continue their resistance with deepened understanding, patience, and love will find sustenance here.

By the 1970s surface manifestations suggested that the original energy of the New Consciousness had been pretty well played out, although divisions within American society remained deep and it was still too early to tell whether the preceding decade was one of those turning points "at which history fails to turn," as Louis Namier said of the 1840s. If it does not come round, the fault will not all lie with the young and not so young in what once seemed truly "the movement." Only now as we write, in the wake of the Watergate disclosures, is it clear how serious a threat the counterculture has seemed to those who wield power. Even the most knowledgeable activist, keenly aware that the atmosphere of radical groups had been poisoned by snooping, suspicion, and official harassment, would never have suspected that electronic buggers and old-fashioned burglars were operating out of the White House to deny justice to radical defendants, discredit dissent, stifle the New Consciousness. Even less would anyone have thought that the late J. Edgar Hoover, who more than any other person was responsible for the deportation of Emma Goldman and Alexander Berkman, would have acted to restrain this high-level criminality by becoming a blackmailer for justice—and the FBI. Concerned with the vulnerability of his Bureau, Hoover, according to his one-time chief assistant, William Sullivan, threatened to reveal a file of illegal phone-tap records if his superiors in the Republican Administration persisted in ordering such flagrant "dirty tricks": "That fellow was a master blackmailer," declared Sullivan, "and did it with considerable finesse despite the deterioration of his mind" (London *Times,* May 16, 1973). So apparently was freedom fought for and partially preserved in our modern state.

But no small part of all this scum atop official waters would have surprised Emma Goldman and Alexander Berkman, which truth argues powerfully that, with these letters from exile, they have come home again none too soon.

RICHARD AND
ANNA MARIA DRINNON

S.S. Eurybates
North Atlantic
May–June 1973

To 1919:
Autobiographical
Fragment
and Chronology

OF primary importance in his own right, Alexander Berkman has long merited a full-scale biography. The lack of one leaves a big hole in our understanding of modern radicalism and contributes to the regrettable tendency to see him as a mere adjunct to his more ebullient comrade. His prison memoirs go a good way toward righting the imbalance, but they carry the reader only a little beyond 1906. Berkman figures prominently in Emma Goldman's autobiography and in biographies of her, of course, but in none of these works is he put at center stage.

In July 1930 Berkman had himself moved to meet the need in a prospectus of "a book I have in mind. Its title is to be: I HAD TO LEAVE. It will be autobiographical, perhaps held in a light and humorous vein, and will deal with the situations in my life when 'I had to leave.' Thus, as a mere youth, I had to leave Russia, because of a disagreement with my rich uncle and also to avoid forced military service. I had, later on, to leave on many occasions." That he did, from an imposing list of countries, but he did not sit down to detail the circumstances. By November 1932 he had only a seven-page "rough outline" of an autobiography for which he then proposed the ironic title *An Enemy of Society.* Unhappily this too remained unwritten.

His outline to 1919 appears here in belated recognition of the life that might have been and as a convenient way to give the reader a sense of the flow of people and events in it down to the American Deportations Delirium. It is followed by a very brief chronology of Emma Goldman's life during the same period, which order, for at least this once, gives Berkman top billing.

Autobiography of Alexander Berkman (Rough Outline)

Early Days: [b. November 21, 1870; Wilno.] Life at home and at school in St. Petersburg. My bourgeois father and aristocratic mother. Jews and Gentiles. I question my father about the Turkish prisoners of war begging alms in the streets.

Our Family Skeleton: Strange rumors about my mother and her brother Maxim.

Echoes of the Polish rebellion of 1863. I hear of the dreaded Nihilists and revolution.

A Terrified Household: A bomb explodes as I recite my lesson in school [March 1881]. The assassination of Czar Alexander II. Secret groups in our class. Police search our house. Uncle Maxim is arrested for conspiring against the Czar's life. The funeral of the dead Czar. A terrorized city.

Family Troubles: Rumors of my beloved Uncle Maxim's execution. My terrible grief. Death of my father [*ca.* 1882]. We lose the right of residing in the capital. Race prejudice and discrimination. Breaking up our business [the wholesale of "uppers"—the upper leather part of shoes] and home.

Provincial Russia: The Ghetto. Life in Wilno and Kovno. My sister Sonya and my two elder brothers. In school and university. My rich Uncle Nathan [Natansohn]—dictator of Kovno. His peculiar family.

The Troubles of Youth: Class distinctions in school and at home. I am forbidden to associate with menials. Our warring school gangs on the River Niemen. Boys and girls—the mysteries of sex. Visiting university students initiate me into Nihilism. Secret associations and forbidden books.

My First Rebellion: I defy my rich Uncle Nathan and defend a servant girl against my mother. Punished in school for my essay, "There Is No God," written when I was thirteen years old [1883]. Chumming with a factory boy and teaching him to read. I discover capitalism. I worship my martyred Uncle Maxim.

Planning an Escape: I learn that Uncle Maxim [Natansohn, his mother Yetta's brother, later head of the Executive Committee of the Social Revolutionist Party, and affectionately known on the Russian Left as "The Old Man"] is alive and has escaped from Siberia. My brother Max is refused admission to the universities, because he is a Jew. My violent indignation. More trouble at school. Max preparing to enter a German university. I conspire to accompany him. A narrow escape in stealing our way across the border. I go to Hamburg. Traveling steerage to America.

In Free America: [From February 1888.] Life on the East Side of New York. A new-fledged workingman at seventeen. The troubles of a greenhorn. I find friends and a sweetheart. Wealth and poverty. I meet Russian political exiles and frequent revolutionary groups in New York. I join the anarchists. Echoes of the Chicago Haymarket affair.

The World of Labor: Factories and machines. I work as cigarmaker and cloak-operator. Friends and enemies. East-Side cafés and meetings. The great proletariat. The troubles of an immigrant. Prominent revolutionaries.

Reality versus Idealism: Life and struggle. Devotion to my ideals. My intimate comrades and our first "commune colony." Planning to return to Russia for revolutionary work. John Most and the German anarchist movement in America. My friends Emma Goldman and Fedya [Modest Stein]. Love, friendship, and revolution.

The Homestead Strike: The steelworkers of Pennsylvania. Andrew Carnegie and Henry Clay Frick. The bloodbath on the Monongahela [1892]. Carnegie and his hired Pinkertons. The whole country shocked. I decide to go to Homestead. Carnegie escapes to his castle in Scotland. My attempt on the life of Frick. The travesty of my trial. I am sentenced to twenty-two years' prison.

In the Penitentiary: Life in prison [1892–1906]. Guards and convicts. I organize a strike for better food and treatment. Am sentenced to the dungeon. Prison torture. Attempting suicide and escape. I spend ten years in solitary confinement. The grist of the prison-mill. Types of prisoners. Stories of crimes. Robbing the stomach. Fake prison investigations. My prison chums. Love and sex in prison.

My Resurrection: Freedom after fourteen years in prison [May 18, 1906]. The shocks of reality. Great expectations and crushing disillusionment. How the world had changed. Old-time friends and new actualities. Afraid of meeting people. My first lecture tour. I am in Frick's stronghold again. A visit to Homestead. I disappear: [friends fear I am] either dead or kidnapped by Frick.

My New Lease on Life: Police brutality and the arrest of my comrades. I am roused to work and fight. The labor and new revolutionary movement. Russian political refugees: echoes of the Russian revolution of 1905. My new activities. I start a cooperative printing shop. The "Americanized" East Side. Labor leaders, socialists, IWW, bundists, and anarchists.

Some More Trouble: A mass meeting in Cooper Union. I object to a speaker's remarks and am railroaded to Blackwell's Island. I am editor of *Mother Earth*, Emma Goldman's anarchist publication [1908–15]. Trouble with [Anthony] Comstock. Illiberal American liberals and muddle-headed radicals. I organize the first Anarchist Federation in America. Trouble with the police. Free-speech fights.

Struggles of Labor: The beginning of American imperialism and my first anti-war work. The Industrial Workers of the World and the American Federation of Labor. Outstanding personalities. I help to found the Francisco Ferrer Association for libertarian education. My new role as radical Sunday-school teacher. I write my prison memoirs [1912]. The unemployed movement; taking possession of churches [winter 1913–14]. The Ludlow (Colorado) massacre; strikes and great labor trials. Big Bill Haywood, [Morris] Hillquit, Emma Goldman, Margaret Sanger, [Elizabeth] Gurley Flynn, [Carlo] Tresca, and other personalities. The Union Square tragedy. I defend the McNamara brothers [John J. & James B.]. The Los Angeles *Times* explosion [1911]. General [Harrison Grey] Otis. Mother Jones and martial law. Clarence Darrow gets acquitted and convicts the McNamara brothers, his clients. Golden-rule Lincoln Steffens is double-crossed at his own game. We fight it out with the police at Union Square. I lead the siege of Tarrytown, home of [John D.] Rockefeller. The inside story of some explosions. I am charged with inciting to riot and face prison again.

On the Coast: A lecture tour across the country [1915]. The Mexican revolutionists in California. I meet a descendant of the Aztecs. *The Blast,* my revolutionary labor paper in San Francisco [1916]. Persecution by the Catholic Church. The Mexican Revolution. *The Blast* editorial: "Wilson or Villa —which the greater bandit?" *The Blast* suppressed, but continues to circulate. The American war hysteria. The Preparedness Parade bomb explosion in San Francisco [July 22, 1916]. The arrest of Tom Mooney, [Warren] Billings, and other labor men. I organize their defense. The conspiracy against Mooney. Fremont Older and the labor leaders assure me Mooney is guilty. I tour the country in his behalf and work for Mooney in New York.

The War: America enters the War [April 1917]. Jingo Quakers and radicals. The No-War campaign and my fight against conscription. Exciting mass meetings. I break my leg and talk on crutches. Defying police and soldiers. The Revolution breaks out in Russia and I plan to go there. I am arrested for obstructing the draft [June 15, 1917]. In the Tombs. California demands my extradition in connection with the Mooney case. The Kronstadt (Russia) sailors threaten the life of the American Ambassador [David] Francis in case I am extradited to California. [Woodrow] Wilson sends a confidential messenger (Colonel [Edward M.] House) to the governor of New York. The governor refuses to extradite me. My trial for "conspiracy to obstruct the draft."

The Atlanta Penitentiary: Two years in the Georgia State [U.S.] prison [1917–19]. "Politicals worse than criminals." Conscientious objectors and Eugene V. Debs. Our chain-gang warden. I protest against an officer shooting a Negro convict in the back and killing him. Punished in the dungeon and solitary for the rest of my time. [Liberated, October 1, 1919.]

Emma Goldman Chronology

Birth, Kovno (Kaunas in modern Lithuania), *June 27, 1869.* Girlhood and adolescence, Kovno, Popelan, Königsberg, and St. Petersburg, *1869–85.* Migration to the United States, *1885.* Factory worker, Rochester and New Haven, *1886–89.* Marriage to Jacob Kersner, *1887.* Divorce, *1888.* Joined anarchists in New York City, *August 15, 1889.*

First speaking tour, *1890.* Complicity in Berkman's attempt to kill Frick, *1892.* Union Square speech and arrest for inciting to riot, *August 1893.* Prison on Blackwell's Island, *1893–August 1894.* Nurse's training, Vienna, *1895–96.* Official attempts to implicate her in the assassination of President McKinley, *1901.* Midwife and nurse on the East Side, *1901–05.* Publisher-editor of *Mother Earth,* *1906–17.* Delegate to the Amsterdam Anarchist Congress, *1907.* Chicago free-speech fight, *1908.* New York free-speech fight, *1909.* University of Wisconsin free-speech fight, *1910.* Published her *Anarchism and Other Essays, 1911.*

San Diego free-speech fight, *1912–15.* Wrote *The Social Significance of the Modern Drama,* 1914. Birth-control lectures, *1915–16.* Arrest in New York for her lecture "on a medical question," *February 1916.* Fifteen days in the Queens County Jail, *April–May 1916.* Mooney defense, *1916.* Organized the No-Conscription League, *May 1917.* Arrested with Berkman for "conspiracy to induce persons not to register," *June 15, 1917.* Trial, *June 27–July 9, 1917.* Missouri State Prison (Jefferson City), *1918.* Celebrated her fiftieth birthday in her cell, *June 27, 1919.* Liberated, *September 28, 1919.*

1

Cast Out

Deportation: First deportation of politicals from the United States [December 21, 1919]. The hell of Ellis Island and our kidnapping in the dead of night. The leaky boat "Buford" and its passengers. A near-mutiny. Sailors and soldiers offer to turn the ship over to me. The "sealed orders of the captain." We make demands and gain them. In danger of landing in the country of the Whites. Traveling in Finland under military convoy. Finnish soldiers steal our provisions. Crossing the border [into Russia, January 18, 1920].

Alexander Berkman, *An Enemy of Society*

IN his Flag Day Address of June 14, 1917, President Wilson pledged "woe to the man or group of men that seeks to stand in our way in this day of high resolution." Woe was already stalking the footsteps of Emma Goldman and Alexander Berkman for their refusal to share in this high moral resolution and for their taking the lead in opposing the draft. On the following day, June 15, they were arrested and on July 9, at the conclusion of their trial, they were sentenced to two years in prison and fined ten thousand dollars each. The prison letters that follow were written toward the tail end of their terms, well after the Armistice had been signed, and after the reaction had set in.

Berkman did hard time, in part because of his protest against a guard's wanton murder of a black convict. He survived an extended bread-and-water diet in the tomb-like Hole only to spend the last seven and a half months of his sentence in solitary and isolation. The brittle tone of his letters, their obscure allusions and cryptic references to individuals, some of whom remain unidentified, reflect his circumstances and his desire to thwart prison censorship. None of his letters to Emma or of hers to him survive from this period, for they were both involuntary guests of Uncle Sam and forbidden to write each other. M. Eleanor Fitzgerald, or Fitzie, Berkman's companion and their co-worker, did smuggle a note out of Atlanta for Emma, but it has disappeared. As you will see, however, Berkman was very much on Emma's mind: Her letters repeatedly voiced her concern over "our boy in the South."

By contrast Emma did good time, although she was experiencing the menopause, found the "task" in the prison sewing shop exhausting, and throughout was tormented by the helplessness and hopelessness of her sister inmates. Kate Richards O'Hare was a leading socialist, close associate of Eugene V. Debs, and war opponent also convicted of violating the Espionage Act. Her arrival and that of young Ella Antolini, another

"political," made time pass more quickly. Ellen Kennan was a former
Denver school teacher. Stella Cominsky was the daughter of Emma's
half-sister Lena, a favorite niece, and the companion of the Shakespearean
actor and painter, Teddy Ballantine, whom she later married.

Both emerged from prison with their spirits unbroken, although Berkman's health was shattered. It is worth noting that at his deportation
hearing in Atlanta and at Emma's later in New York, one of the officials in
attendance was J. Edgar Hoover, who was handling their cases for the
Department of Justice. Their individual statements on the hearings cut to
the heart of their quarrel with American officialdom. Finally, their open
letter ("Dear friends") on the eve of being cast out expressed their hopes
and fears: Their spunky, if not cocky, "we are of the glowing future," was
counterbalanced by the rather grim vow: "Our work will go on to the last
breath."

EG TO ELLEN KENNAN, July 24, 1919, JEFFERSON CITY

Ellen dearest,

. . . Thank you, dear, for your beautiful birthday letter. Yes, I think a
number of people thought of me that day. Quite a few sent letters,
telegrams, flowers, and many other gifts. I felt quite important on that day,
though I was really ill in my cell and had as my next cell-door neighbor a
sick lady. For a time Kate O'Hare was very ill, but she seems to have
recuperated and is now feeling as well as one can in prison. Among the
many things which came, though not as a birthday gift, and later, were two
large bunches of roses—all the way from Moscow. Not really the roses, but
the money for them. Bill Shatov [old friend and co-worker], of whom you
have undoubtedly heard, sent money to a friend in Paris and he in turn
gave it to Mary [Heaton Vorse] O'Brien who was there at the time. She
gave it to Stella and in that way the beautiful roses reached me. More
beautiful however is the spirit which prompted the gift. Think of it, our
friends in Russia who are in death's grip with the blackest reaction that has
ever conspired against the efforts of the people, yet they have time to think
of us here, and of our small vices among which my love for flowers is by no
means the least. Anyway, the three politicals in this institution, Kate, Ella
[Antolini], and myself, enjoyed the gift and the spirit. Kate still has some
of the ferns that came with the roses; they seem to symbolize the spirit of
Russia which cannot be daunted. The ferns, though in the stuffy cell for
nearly two weeks, are still fresh. They are just like the plant which Big Ben
[Reitman] sent me for Christmas, indestructible.

I have a bit of good news for you and all of our New York friends. Kate
was seen yesterday by a man from Washington who questioned her about

her stand, should she be granted a pardon. He was anxious to know whether she would make a demonstration in case a pardon was not extended to the other political prisoners. He wanted her to make other promises as to what she would do when she is released, which of course she refused, but she did say that she would make no demonstration. No doubt she feels that she can do that much better once she is out; in fact she said as much to the man, that she will never rest until all politicals are freed. From the foregoing you will see that Washington is very anxious to get rid of Kate and Debs—I understand RPS [Rose Paster Stokes?] is also included. Wouldn't that be wonderful! I shall now perhaps not need to worry about leaving Kate behind; it would have been terribly hard for me, as you can well imagine. Now we expect that she may go almost any day. I rejoice even though the rest of my time will be very dismal. You will possibly know as soon as we when the pardon is granted, as the papers will be sure to feature it.

I don't know whether you saw Fitzie lately and whether you know what a frightful time our boy in the South [AB] is having. The latest is that he will lose five days of his time. Can you imagine a greater cruelty? For months now he has been in solitary confinement, denied all privileges until very recently when he was granted them only partially. He is not allowed to go to the movie, get any kind of decent reading matter, or have sufficient exercise. You can imagine how heavily time must hang on his hands, and now he will have to remain in that hideous place an additional five days; it is exasperating. How weak and insecure must our mighty government feel, if it must stoop to such petty persecution. How futile its effect on a spirit like our boy's, even though his condition is so galling at the present time. The girls sent me copies of his letters; they are simply wonderful, more wonderful because they come from a man who has spent the best years of his life in prison. Yet his fire and faith are unquenchable. . . .

I think of you a great deal, Ellen dearest; coming into my life has been a great event. I am not in a position to make plans for the future, but if I remain in New York, I should love to take an apartment with you. How does this strike you? Of course I shall be with Stella at first, but I will have to have a place of my own. Having been used to a private room for nineteen months, it will not be easy for me to live where there are many people. But two such maiden ladies as you and I could manage harmoniously together, don't you think? No dear, I am not getting the *Call*. I don't know why; fortunately Kate is and it is all right as long as she is here. With a fond embrace and much love,

EG

P.S. Dearest, enclosed is a $1 bill for which you're to get me two crepe de chine ties; buy two ties. One in Alice blue or some other nice blue—not too light. The other in a rich yellow.

EG TO STELLA COMINSKY, August 30, 1919, JEFFERSON CITY

Dearest,

I began this letter last night but had to give it up. I worked dreadfully hard all day yesterday, so as not to have to go down this morning. Then, when I got to my cell, I was all in. I have not been feeling very well this week. I think it is the change of weather. It has turned cool suddenly and rained nearly all week. So my old bones are rattling again. As a matter of fact, I have been exceptionally well these last two months—better than at any time during my stay here. I ascribe it to my being able to stay out of the shop on Saturdays—and even more so to our weekly picnics. Four hours in the open each week with the chance of moving about a bit makes all the difference in the world. It is only this week that I have been aching all over but I kept at work. I don't want to go before the doctor again, if I can help it. Of course, I know that it never was Dr. McNearney who ordered us to the shop that time on threat of being put on punishment for forty-eight hours. But if I can manage without seeing him, I will be satisfied. In any event you need not worry; it is really nothing at all.

Well, dearest, I have already done four of my thirty days for kind Uncle Sam [in payment of the $10,000 fine]. If brother [Judge Julius] Mayer had not honored us—AB and I would now be free. But we ought to be grateful to that Prussian of Prussians for the honor bestowed upon us—he has demonstrated our value far beyond [what] my best friends could have done. Twenty-six days longer—really less than that because the days you will be here will hardly count. I am sure Mr. P. [Warden William R. Painter] will let you see me. I don't see why he would want to make exceptions when he has been so generous about visits all the time. I only wish more friends could have come. But it is well you wrote him. And about Addie [an inmate] too, you must let me know directly you hear from him.

Funny, it never occurred to me to let you know why Addie is here. For murder, dearest; I don't know the details of the case. I never asked. I wish I had Kate's capacity to ferret out things. She knows the history of every woman in this place. Not for the life of me can I ask anyone about the thing which brought her here. To me it is more than terrible that she is here. Then, too, I know that if she were not poor and friendless, she would most likely not be here. In all the nineteen months, not one woman of means was brought here. Yet I know that many have committed the offense and possibly graver ones than Addie or any other. But you will be amused at the conception of propriety on the part of my fellow comrades. When I told Addie that some of our friends wanted to know what she is here for, she said "I don't blame 'em, they might think I am here for

stealing or using dope." You see, from Addie's point of honor, murder is a higher crime than stealing or using dope. Yet the outside world thinks the so-called criminal without any conception of ethics. I am not able ever to see the difference between the outside and the inside world. They are both equally small and equally big according to the point of view. I don't believe Addie will be paroled to you. But at least the girl will know we have tried. I cannot make out the judgment used in paroling prisoners. This week three women have been paroled. Two have been here only half the time of Addie and have not worked as hard as she. The third one is about to become a mother, so there is sense in her parole. Of course, as far as I am concerned all the prisoners should be let go—it would be better for society and more beneficial to those who watch over them. More than ever I am convinced that, next to the outrage of locking people away where they are degraded to the condition of inanimate matter, is the outrage of condemning people to be their jailers and keepers. The best of them gradually grow hard and inhuman or they do not keep their jobs very long.

Yesterday I made out my application blank for discharge. The [U.S.] Commissioner will now have plenty of time to "look into the matter." As I wrote you last week, I will be expected to give proofs of my inability to pay the fine. I suppose when H[arry] W[einberger] gets back to town he will go after [Bolton] Hall, [Gilbert E.] Roe, and a few others for affidavits. I may have to swear to an affidavit myself which I am perfectly willing to do. Mr. P[ainter] will let me know in time. About AB's bond, I understood that [Charney] Vladek had made some arrangements last year when he was out to see the boy. I will write Harry Weinberger Sunday and Fitzie Tuesday to see about the matter at once. I should say the bond must be ready—it would be awful to let the boy [AB] be dragged off to the rotten jail after his terrible time in solitary. And, dearest, my bond too will have to be ready. The 27th is a Saturday—unless the bond is all prepared, I will be kept in jail over Sunday and you will have to stick around the two extra days. That can easily be avoided, if you come prepared. The trouble is, we will not know how much bond will be required. I wonder if Harry Weinberger could get a line on that. I will write him. And whom do you have in mind about bond? Would Jessie [Ashley's] sister go my bond? She has means of her own and must also have gotten all of Jessie's property. How strange all our wealthy radicals are—the most generous among them never leave anything for the work they so love during their lifetime. Perhaps I should not say that about Jessie—I don't know what provisions she has left. But all the others I have known never left a red cent to the work. Let me know whom you mean to approach about the bond. Anyway, dearest, you must come all ready. . . .

I have asked Miss S [Lilah Smith?], to see if she can get me a sailor or little soft felt traveling hat in town. She is going either today or Monday, so I will be able to let you know whether it will be necessary to get one in

Rochester. If Miss S can find the kind I want, she will have several sent out here for me to try them on. You know how hard it is to fit me in hats. My head may have been made for the block but it is not fit for a hat. Then the gloves, I would prefer to have them from Altman's or Constable's, at least they have some with stubby fingers like mine. I will ask Fitzie to get me a pair and send them out direct to me. I have decided to get black gloves, as the others soil too much in traveling. While you are in Rochester get me a nice soft roching [lawn linen] for the wrists of my black dress and have your mother sew it in. Bennie [Capes] is sending me some collars of which you get one. Dear Bennie, it was such a joy to see him again. He was so disappointed not to be able to see little Ella [Antolini]. But Mr. Painter would not let him see her. He wrote Bennie he could not see what interest he has in her. Of course, Mr. P does not know that community of ideas with us often means more than community of blood. I am going to speak with Mr. P before I leave to let Bennie see Ella when I am gone. He comes through here so often and the child has no one to see her and still will have five months. By the way, dearie, do not forget Ella's birthday—the flowers. I think you better have the florist send her a little plant with some red flowers. It will keep longer. And did you write Ellen K[ennan] to get me a red crepe kimono for her? Bennie will also send her something. At least the child will have a few tokens of love, even if she meets her twentieth birthday in prison. . . .

Devotedly,
EG

P.S. Kiss the kid [Ian] for me. Thank [Eugene] O'Neill for the volume of plays. Write Butler Davenport again. Received [the] large box of apples; all the girls enjoyed [them].

AB TO M. ELEANOR FITZGERALD, September 7, 1919, ATLANTA

Well, dear woman,

You see I'm back to my old letterhead. This means that hereafter I may write every week, though I remain in solitary, as before. It's three weeks, and three days—twenty-three days, not counting today which is already half gone: It is 1 P.M. Who said there are only twenty-four hours in a day—and night? That may be true of March and April and such months, but not of August and September. Of course, I have no work to do—that makes it worse, and I've had to cut out a good deal of my reading on account of my eyes. So that Old Father Time seems to me mightily slow of late—but it isn't long now, and I guess I'll have to be patient with the Old

Man. You all speak—Stella and Kal also—of a few weeks' vacation in that wonder spot on the [Cape] Cod, but it seems to me a daydream. Well, we'll see. I confess I'd enjoy it, though: these two years, and especially the last six months, have been hard. I'm afraid I'm not as young as I used to be—in Allegheny, for instance. I'll be thirty-three years in November, or forty-nine if you want to count the sixteen years I didn't *live*. The beautiful rose "kissed by Minnie [Fishman]" (no one else? safety first) came yesterday with your letter, dear. It was a kind of lifesaver—a needed change from the postal-card diet. That isn't quite fair, though, for I had four very good letters from you, besides six postals, counting since my last letter of August 24. Also good letters from Pol and Stella. I've been wondering what's become of Minna [Lowensohn] and all the others. And by the way, what about Dr. [Michael] Cohn's letter? I did not receive it. Her visit home did not do Gertrude [Nafe] much good. Upon her return she sent me a letter, signing herself "yours respectfully"! And Lilly Kisliuk addressed her postal to me at Jefferson City. You are back now in New York and I suppose already in full harness. I wish you could have stayed in P[rovincetown]. Pol says it's such a beautiful place; it's easy to be literary there. And I notice her own letters are assuming that character. . . . My little niece refers to that marriage of convenience as if I knew all about it. But I don't. Edwina hinted, but I didn't want to talk about it, at that time. Such marriages have often proved happy. I hope it isn't too late, though. Some remarks I made in a previous letter referred to a different phase of the matter. And dear LD [Lavina Dock?] thinks the radicals get it in the neck, etc. And that "the radical gesture is defeated almost always on the practical plane." We all—everything living—finally "get it in the neck." The ultimate goal is six feet of clay, but I'd rather die the victim of my faith then live the dupe of vain self-aggrandizement or ambition. It's all in the point of view. I do *not* think we get it in the neck, except as individuals; as idealists we always win; yes, on the practical plane. Huss dies to give birth to Luther and to triumph with him. And Sophia Perovskaya conquers in [Mme Alexandra] Kolontay. I hold that ultimately it's the ideal that conquers, and having conquered, it mounts to still higher and further visions. As to the individual—he is the stepping stone of man's progress, but remember there are times when the most elevated place in the world is a scaffold. Dear woman, have you profited by your vacation? It was too short. Are you about to send my things? It's nearly time. If you answer this promptly, I'd get your letter just before I write again. And now, so long, dear. It seems so near already, but who knows? Yet you may depend on it, I shall be equal to any emergency. Do you mean to meet me anywhere on the road? Dear Kal must be counting the minutes of our meeting. So am I. Where shall we twain meet again? If perchance in hades, I'll call a strike of the firemen and stokers. Much love,

                                                                        AB

STATEMENT BY ALEXANDER BERKMAN IN RE DEPORTATION

Made to the officials of the
U.S. Federal Immigration Service
at the
Federal Penitentiary, Atlanta, Georgia
September 18, 1919

The purpose of the present hearing is to determine my "attitude of mind." It does not, admittedly, concern itself with my actions, past or present. It is purely an inquiry into my views and opinions.

I deny the right of anyone—individually or collectively—to set up an inquisition of thought. Thought is, or should be, free. My social views and political opinions are my personal concern. I owe no one responsibility for them. Responsibility begins only with the effects of thought expressed in action. Not before. Free thought, necessarily involving freedom of speech and press, I may tersely define thus: no opinion a law—no opinion a crime. For the government to attempt to control thought, to prescribe certain opinions or proscribe others, is the height of despotism.

This proposed hearing is an invasion of my conscience. I therefore refuse, most emphatically, to participate in it.

                                              ALEXANDER BERKMAN

STATEMENT BY EMMA GOLDMAN AT THE FEDERAL HEARING IN RE DEPORTATION

New York, October 27, 1919

At the very outset of this hearing I wish to register my protest against these star-chamber proceedings, whose very spirit is nothing less than a revival of the ancient days of the Spanish Inquisition or the more recently defunct Third Degree system of Czarist Russia.

This star-chamber hearing is, furthermore, a denial of the insistent claim on the part of the government that in this country we have free speech and a free press, and that every offender against the law—even the lowliest of men—is entitled to his day in open court, and to be heard and judged by a jury of his peers.

If the present proceedings are for the purpose of proving some alleged offense committed by me, some evil or anti-social act, then I protest against the secrecy and third-degree methods of this so-called "trial." But if I am not charged with any specific offense or act, if—as I have reason to believe—this is purely an inquiry into my social and political opinions, then I protest still more vigorously against these proceedings, as utterly tyrannical and diametrically opposed to the fundamental guarantees of a true democracy.

Every human being is entitled to hold any opinion that appeals to her or him without making herself or himself liable to persecution. Ever since I have been in this country—and I have lived here practically all my life—it has been dinned into my ears that under the institutions of this alleged democracy one is entirely free to think and feel as he pleases. What becomes of this sacred guarantee of freedom of thought and conscience when persons are being persecuted and driven out for the very motives and purposes for which the pioneers who built up this country laid down their lives?

And what is the object of this star-chamber proceeding, that is admittedly based on the so-called anti-anarchist law [of 1903]? Is not the only purpose of this law, and of the deportations en masse, to suppress every symptom of popular discontent now manifesting itself through this country, as well as in all the European lands? It requires no great prophetic gift to foresee that this new governmental policy of deportation is but the first step toward the introduction into this country of the old Russian system of exile for the high treason of entertaining new ideas of social life and industrial reconstruction. Today so-called aliens are deported; tomorrow native Americans will be banished. Already some patrioteers are suggesting that native American sons, to whom democracy is not a sham but a sacred ideal, should be exiled. To be sure, America does not yet possess a suitable place like Siberia to which her exiled sons might be sent, but since she has begun to acquire colonial possessions, in contradiction of the principles she stood for for over a century, it will not be difficult to find an American Siberia once the precedent of banishment is established. . . .

Under the mask of the same anti-anarchist law every criticism of a corrupt administration, every attack on governmental abuse, every manifestation of sympathy with the struggle of another country in the pangs of a new birth—in short, every free expression of untrammeled thought may be suppressed utterly, without even the semblance of an unprejudiced hearing or a fair trial. It is for these reasons, chiefly, that I strenuously protest against this despotic law and its star-chamber methods of procedure. I protest against the whole spirit underlying it—the spirit of an irresponsible hysteria, the result of the terrible war, and of the evil tendencies of bigotry and persecution and violence which are the epilogue of five years of bloodshed. . . .

EMMA GOLDMAN

EG AND AB TO DEAR FRIENDS, December 19, 1919, ELLIS ISLAND

Dear, dear friends,

We have been told this afternoon that we must get ready as we may be shipped any moment. This, then, is our last chance to speak to you once more while still on American soil. Most of what we have to say about the black reaction now rampant in this land and the urgent need of concerted action to stem the tide, you will find in our last message to the American people—the pamphlet on deportation, written by us while here, and now in the hands of the printer. To you, dear, faithful friends, we want to send a parting word.

Do not be sad about our forced departure. Rather rejoice with us that our common enemies, prompted by fear and stupidity, have resorted to this mad act of driving political refugees out of the land. This act must ultimately lead to the undoing of the madmen themselves. For now the American people will see more clearly than our ardent work of thirty years could prove to them, that liberty in America has been sold into bondage, that justice has been outraged, and life made cheap and ugly.

We have great faith in the American people. We know that once the truth is borne in upon them what the masters have made [of] this once promising land, the people will rise to the situation. With Samson strength they will pull down the rotten structure of the capitalist regime. Confident in this, we leave with joy in our hearts. We go strengthened by our conviction that America will free herself not merely from the sham of paper guarantees, but in a fundamental sense, in her economic, social, and spiritual life.

Dear friends, it is an old truism which most of you have surely experienced: He who ascends to the greatest heights of faith is often hurled into the depths of doubt. We have known the ecstasy of the one and the torture of the other. If we have not despaired utterly, it is because of the boundless love and devotion of our friends. That has been our sustaining, our inspiring power. Few fighters in the struggle for human freedom have known such beautiful comradeship. If we have been among the most hated, reviled, and persecuted, we have also been the most beloved. What greater tribute to one's integrity can one wish?

As in the past, so now in this our last struggle on American soil, your love, your splendid devotion, your generous gifts, are our strength and encouragement. We feel too intensely to express our gratitude in words. We can only say that our physical separation can have no effect on our appreciation of your loyalty—it can only enhance it.

We do not know where the forces of reaction will land us. But wherever we shall be, our work will go on until our last breath. May you, too, continue your efforts. These are trying but wonderful times. Clear heads and brave hearts were never more needed. There is great work to do. May each one of you give the best that is in him to the great struggle, the last struggle between liberty and bondage, between well-being and poverty, between beauty and ugliness.

Be of good cheer, beloved comrades. Our enemies are fighting a losing battle. They are of the dying past. We are of the glowing future. Fraternally and joyously,

EMMA GOLDMAN
ALEXANDER BERKMAN

2

Communism
and the Intellectuals

In Russia we were met with open arms. . . . I kept on the most friendly terms with the communists, and was always treated with the greatest consideration by Lenin, Luna-charsky, Zinoviev, Chicherin, and all the other prominent bolsheviki. But my attitude was critical and I could not approve of many of their means and methods. I condemned the inequality practiced in economic and social matters, the political arbitrariness and brutality, and—above all—the sys-tem of terror and indiscriminate execution long after the "barricade period" of the Revolution had passed.

My break with the bolsheviki came with the Kronstadt events in March 1921. The Kronstadt sailors were, in the words of Lenin and Trotsky, the "pride and glory of the Revolution." But when the Kronstadt sailors demanded the right of choosing freely their representatives to the Kron-stadt soviet—as they had all right to demand—Lenin and Trotsky declared Kronstadt outlawed and trained guns on the city. The slaughter of ten thousand Kronstadt sailors, soldiers, and workers was the greatest crime committed by the soviet government against the Revolution and Russia. It symbolized the beginning of a new tyranny.

I broke with the bolsheviki and decided to leave the country. Which I did [with Emma Goldman and Alexander Shapiro, December 1921].

AB TO HUDSON HAWLEY, *June 12, 1932*, NICe

THE exiled pair were together in Russia and thus had no back-and-forth correspondence during those two years (1920–21). Their joint letter to M. Eleanor Fitzgerald came out of their first few weeks, when they were still suffering the initial shocks of deracination, "in utter darkness concerning happenings at home" and feeling "lonesome and forlorn here." Though we introduce no other letters to demonstrate this fact, they soon regained their stride and turned to useful work. Communists and their supporters later maintained otherwise, holding that their break with the regime stemmed from their disappointment over not being given "soft jobs," as Big Bill Haywood put it. But such vilification would not withstand close scrutiny. Angelica Balabanov, the first Secretary of the Third International and the then good friend of Lenin, pointed out in *My Life as a Rebel* (1938) that the two anarchists were in fact "happy to make any contribution to the 'Workers' Fatherland.'" Even after their disillusion mounted, she added, "they cheerfully went on working without complaints or recriminations."

The epigraph above on those months in revolutionary Russia thus provides a reliable foundation and context for the letters in this part. Berkman was appointed chairman of a special historical commission and Emma joined him in collecting materials for the Petrograd Museum of the Revolution. Had she been willing to yield unquestioning obedience to Lenin and his party, she might have had a choice of responsible positions, in education, nursing, or international propaganda. She was always less willing than Berkman, however, to be so obedient. Although he did not of course note this fact in his outline, he did so elsewhere. In a letter (February 13, 1933) to Harry Kelly, editor of the *Road to Freedom*, he noted that, "BEFORE Kronstadt I myself was still hopeful that the bolsheviki would change their policies and methods. EG was more against them than I then. It was Kronstadt that turned us BOTH completely and irrevocably against the bolsheviki." As you will see, especially in Part Three below, their letters contain echoes of the controversies of those days, when he charged her with being only a "parlor revolutionist" and she held him still "the old Adam," willing "to swallow everything as justification of the Revolution."

Once out of Russia, Berkman, Emma, and their friend Alexander Shapiro issued one of the first public appeals in behalf of the persecuted political prisoners (December 1921). After a few days in the Riga (Latvia) jail, they found refuge in Sweden, where they stayed until Berkman left sub rosa for Germany in March 1922 and Emma followed by more ortho- dox means the next month. Berkman remained in Berlin until December 1925, working against the terror as secretary-treasurer of the Political Prisoners Relief Committee (for Russia), editor of the *Bulletin of the Relief Fund* (sponsored by the International Working Men's Association), and as author of articles, pamphlets, and the important *Bolshevik Myth* (1925). As you will note in one of his letters to Michael Cohn (October 10, 1922), Berkman arranged to have a man inside Russia make the rounds of the various prisons and camps "to get little notes or letters from the prisoners and forward them to me." The result was a work for which he was mainly responsible, still a valuable source for early communist oppression, *Letters from Russian Prisons*, nominally edited by Roger Baldwin (1925). In late 1925 Berkman moved to Paris, where he continued to head up the Relief Committee work. In 1929, all this while a "stateless person," he moved to Nice.

While in Berlin Emma worked over her own experiences. When she received her author's copy, she was distressed to see that Doubleday and Page had changed her title, "My Two Years in Russia," to *My Disillu- sionment in Russia* (1923)—"a veritable misfit," she felt, for it implied her rejection of the Revolution as well as the bolshevik tyranny. Worse yet, the volume did not contain the final twelve chapters of her ms. After much to-do, the publishers issued the missing chapters under the still more egregious title *My Further Disillusionment in Russia* (1924). The entire, unmutilated text was published in England by C. W. Daniel as *My Disillusionment in Russia* (1925).

With the help of members of the Independent Labor Party, Emma was permitted to enter Britain in 1924. In 1925, to secure citizenship and a passport, she married James Colton, a longtime supporter and friend, collier and widower in his mid-sixties. Though she still had no place to lay her head, Colton's generosity and "sweet solidarity," as Emma put it, provided her with documents so that she could move more or less freely in England and on the Continent. Thereafter, while Berkman worked di- rectly to help the political prisoners, Emma sought to rouse English and American intellectuals against the Bolshevik Myth. From 1926 to 1928 she toured and lectured in Canada. In 1928 she retired to St. Tropez, France, to write her autobiography and from then until 1936 made her cottage there her "permanent" home. She toured Scandinavia and Germany in 1932. On a lecture tour in 1933, she was expelled from Holland. In early 1934 she was readmitted to the United States for a ninety-day visit. She re-entered Canada in 1934 and returned to France in 1935.

Since she was so constantly on the move and Berkman was relatively immobilized by his lack of papers, their correspondence during these years was rich and frequent. It was nothing for Emma, in particular, to write her "Old Scout" a five thousand-word letter and then return to their conversation within a day or two in another pamphlet-sized communication.

The "poison" that entered radical ranks back in the United States, the odds against their attempts to tell the truth about conditions in Russia, the moral myopia that led many radical intellectuals to apologize for communist oppression—all this and more emerged from these exchanges.

AB TO M. ELEANOR FITZGERALD, February 28, 1920, MOSCOW

My dearest Fitzie,

Rather peculiar that I should write you today, dear. Just a year ago, today, I was way down south—literally "way down"—without any word from you or other friends for three months. And now again two months have passed, and not a line from folks at home. Did I say two months, and is it really only two months? It is hard to believe. It feels more like two years—if I did not fear that you would think it a wild exaggeration, I should say twenty, not two, years. But that is how I really feel. And I know that Emma feels the same way. We have, since we left you, lived over so much, received so many and variegated new impressions, seen so much that is wonderful and terrible, that it seems quite impossible that so much can be lived through in only two months. What makes things so much harder for us is the fact that we are in utter darkness concerning happenings at home, or what has befallen those dearest to us, and our friends and comrades in the U.S. Till yesterday we had not seen an American paper, since December 21. By sheer good luck we got hold now of the New York *Call*, dated December 21, 22, and the 25th. We gather from it that you knew what happened to us on the night of December 20th. Also that you received the wireless sent you from the "Buford," about January 8th, saying that "all is well"—that is all we could wire. We also believe that you received the radiogram we sent you from Petrograd about our great reception on soviet soil. But whether you received anything else, we know not, but are very anxious to learn. We sent you a number of letters from the English Channel, then again when we reached the Kiel Canal. Some letters were also mailed to you, Stella, etc., from Antwerp, and some messages and letters you were to receive in person through a friend we made on the ship, known as Mac [the assistant steward]. We directed him to call on Stella, in case you should happen to be out of town—that is, we thought there was such a possibility. By this time all the mail and the man himself should have reached you or Stella. But how are we to know—that's the hell of a problem.

Anyhow, here we are, visiting Moscow, after a few weeks in Petrograd. This is sent you through the kindness of friends, and we hope that it will reach you. And even more important, to make an Irish bull, is that news from you in the way of a reply to this letter, according to instructions given here, should come to us—and as soon as possible. You know, we presume, that Russia has concluded peace with Estonia. Perhaps you could send a letter, with a personal note from you, to the American Consul in Reval, Estonia, requesting him to hand it to the Russian representative there, or to send it directly to the Commissar of Foreign Affairs in Moscow. Perhaps you will have to ask instructions about this matter in Washington. Let Stella address *all* mail to her uncle [AB], c/o S.B. Zorin, Hotel Astoria, Petrograd. . . .

There may be also other ways of reaching us with mail. See Rose, the sister of the dentist who fixed my teeth before I left (and, by the way, the tooth broke off again). She ought to be able to arrange communications with the old Professor Yitschok Isik—but perhaps, and most likely, you have already tried it. Another thing, if another group of deportees is being sent out, you might give mail for us to some responsible members of that group. We also need very badly five hundred dollars *in gold*—only gold, for many reasons. Also a number of very necessary things, a list of which you will find below—to be sent in trunks or strong boxes, marked S.B. Zorin. . . .

We both feel very lonesome and forlorn here. It is very difficult to acclimatize yourself in a country from which you were absent over thirty years, even under ordinary conditions. But the present conditions here are not ordinary, by any means; and things are therefore so much more difficult. The blockade is responsible for terrible hunger and suffering. Your ordinary idea of it does not even approach the real truth. It is the greatest crime in history, and I want to impress upon every progressive element the utmost necessity of working to lift the cursed blockade.

Most of the men of the first group sent out with us have departed for various destinations, to work or to visit relatives. Adolph Schnabel and [Peter] Bianki have gone with Bill Shatov to Siberia to help in upbuilding of the railroads. Porkus, Dora [Lipkin], and Ethel [Bernstein], [Morris] Becker, and others are in Petrograd. We are getting acquainted with people and things here, where we may probably return again soon after we have spent a few more weeks in Petrograd. (We shall go to Petrograd in a week or so, as we left all our things there.) We have met some friends we had known in the U.S., but of Sam [Lipman?], the friend of Polya, or of Louise [Berger], we have not heard so far. They are somewhere in the provinces, I suppose.

After a while we may get the time and opportunity to see a little more of this vast country, outside of Petrograd and Moscow. In the place where I am staying at present I met a young American woman, Mrs. Harrison, correspondent for the New York *Post*, a very clever and plucky woman. Think of it, alone and without knowledge of the language she somehow managed to make her way here, and by this time you have probably read her accounts in her paper. She has also been in Poland, and she tells of terrible conditions of disorganization, hunger, and disorder there, as well as of most unspeakable pogroms. . . .

The things we need: Farina, barley, rice, beans, peas, pancake flour, grapenuts, sugar, salt, dried fruit, condensed milk, condensed heat (without the pots); cigarettes, pipes and pipe tobacco, matches, a few good pocket lighters (to save matches; sold at United Cigar Stores), with stuff to fill them with; bacon; dozen cans each of salmon, sardines, kippered herring, preserves, jellies, meats, corned beef; plenty of soup cubes, *hard* crackers (made for soldiers—the dried bread Bessie [Kimmelman?] made was spoiled by the salt water), baking powder, yeast in cans, coffee, tea, cocoa, sweet chocolates in cakes, Fels Naptha soap, soapine, etc. *Most* necessary: medicines, especially for colds, coughs, stomach disorders, quinine, aspirin, codeine, dry mustard, couple thermometers, etc. Also necessary, a gross of black wire hairpins, safety and other pins, needles of various sizes and for darning, and thread, fine combs, BVDs for AB and an extra pair of spectacles for him (Optician Harris has the prescription— same as my last pair), summer socks, toothbrushes, and other toilet articles; fountain-pen ink, blades for auto-strap razor—all those things [are] impossible to get here. Also shoes, even old ones, rubber heels, insoles. Half-dozen outfits for infants (wife of Bill and some other friends expect babies soon). Send money first, by reliable person; the things, by deportees or some other way. Tell all deportees that without the very warmest underwear, clothing, high boots or overshoes, etc., it is unthinkable to spend a winter here. Now the winter is about to break. The spring is very slushy; the summer warm, even hot. . . .

I am afraid this letter will not reach you for your birthday, St. Pat's day, but I am thinking of it. I was in the south at your last birthday, am in the east from you now, and the devil only knows where I shall be next year this day. Things are very uncertain at this stage of the game. But I would give a good deal for a look at you, dear girl. I hope that you will soon be able to reach me, at least with a letter. . . .

I have repeated in this letter most of the things said in my previous letters to you, for I don't know whether any, or which, of them will reach you. There is much I should like to tell you, but I shall leave it for a later time. I am thinking of the Dolores days and wondering if the fates still have any of them left in store. They seem so far, far away, and at present beyond human reach.

Love to all our dear friends and comrades. Life seems a strange puzzle, and those who think they can solve it are happy mortals indeed. I was of their number, once upon a time, millions of years ago. My head is in chaos but the best thoughts of my heart go out to you across the hills and the waters and the valleys of human tears and suffering.

Much love,
Sasha

EG TO ELLEN KENNAN, April 9, 1922, STOCKHOLM

My dearest Ellen,

Now that Stella has gone, I have practically no one in New York who would keep in touch with me. Of course, I have dear Fitzie, but she is very busy and not much of a prolific correspondent. I have my brother and many friends and comrades. But I mean someone like you, a dear and devoted friend. You see, Ellen girl, I have never doubted your love and friendship, even though I never heard from you while in Russia, except for one little letter which came through Mrs. Hellgreen. It was funny too, that it should have come through her. She was such a rabid bolshevik. She looked me up when she and her husband first arrived. But as soon as she got to the foreign office she kept aloof, as if I were a dangerous person to associate with. I do not blame her, she must have been cautioned against us, though at the time we were ourselves in "good standing in the orthodox church." Your letter was brought to me by Agnes Smedley, who is a dear girl and a real personality. Mrs. Hellgreen did not even have the courage to take the letter to me. But this is all shoved behind me; it is not worth talking about.

Of course, I knew that you would have written often had you known how to reach me. I know your loyalty and devotion. I longed for both while in Russia so much: I would have given anything to see and be with you. One misses one's friends, when one is surrounded by automatons who move according to a program and a machine, people who consider friendship and emotions as so much "bourgeois sentimentality." I missed my friends, I can tell you, for no one is ever going to make me believe that one is the less a revolutionist because one does not consider revolution in terms of brutality and cold indifference to all human sorrow. But enough of that phase.

I have been out of Russia now five months, but my Russian experience will never leave me. The tragedy is too overwhelming to ever get away from me. I wish I could write about just how it impressed me. But I am not master enough of the pen, and what is more few would believe my story possible. It is always true that reality is much more vivid than fiction, yet people rarely believe reality and fact. However, it is not the events that took place during my two years in Russia which are so difficult to describe; it is much more the effect they have had upon my spirit and the scars they have left upon my soul which I will never, never be able to make known. Perhaps if you were near me and we could talk as we often have in the past, you would understand; yes, you of all my women friends would understand. But to write about it all is bitter hard. Yet I want to write, I want to try to bring home some of the tragic things, if only I were not at sea so much about a place to live.

You have probably heard, dear Ellen, that we are having quite a time in getting into some country where we would be allowed to breathe. We were admitted here only on condition that we do not remain long in Sweden; since then, we have tried everywhere, or rather our friends have, but in vain. With the exception of Czechoslovakia, we were either refused, or like Austria, were asked to sign a "pledge" that we would abstain from all political activities. We refused to sign, of course, so now Austria is out of the question. Germany refused us months ago. Then our friends worked hard hoping to have the refusal changed. They got permission from the Berlin chief of police for us to come to Berlin for four weeks. But the German foreign office here would not credit that permission. I then applied for a transit visa to Czechoslovakia; that was two weeks ago and no answer so far. I am in despair. Fortunately I have been assured that once I get to Prague there will be no further trouble, so I must get to Prague no matter how; revolutionists have found ways before. And I am still a revolutionist, though the good catholic communists will deny that. By the way, dear, see Fitzie and tell her what I wrote here about the visa and say that Sasha *has gone on a visit.* Let her write to him [at] Linder Gosslerstr. 15, Berlin O, 17. Let her use an inside envelope and merely put on the inside [or rather the *outside* envelope] for Fisher. I must now shift for myself, but it was no use for Sasha to postpone his visit.

I wonder, dear, how my articles in the [New York] *World* affected you? I can well imagine that I have been put in sackcloth and ashes by many of my former friends. But I somehow feel you will understand and not condemn me. You will know that nothing but my desire to shed light on the terrible calamity of Russia had induced me to appear in the *World.* Needless to say, I should have preferred another paper. I see the [New York] *Call* now hides behind the statement that my mss. were not submitted to it, but I am convinced the *Call* would never have brought [out] my articles. I was amused to learn that the *Call* in the past stood up for me. I wonder when that was. Well, it's all in one's life, to be misunderstood and repudiated by one's friends. It cannot be helped. I do wish sometimes I were as shallow as a Louise Bryant; everything would be so simple.

I am glad to hear that dear Gertrude [Nafe] is well and happy with her baby. Give her my fondest love and kiss the baby for me. Do you correspond with the Monroes [Lena and Frank]? Perhaps you will send them the *World* and my love. Do you remember the Zomers? I had several letters from them; they are in Holland. They are lovely people. They spoke of you in their letter with much affection.

Dearest Ellen, please write me often and tell me what is going on in New York. I see the *Call* pretty regularly, but one gets no idea of the things one is most interested in, [so] do write me. Do you ever see Roger Baldwin? I want to be remembered to him and to Leonard Abbott, if you should see him. Write me to the S. Linder address; in my case put E. on the inside envelope. I can imagine the manhunt that will begin when we will not be found, though I shall be in Prague legally, if I only get there.*

Much love to you, my dear, dear Ellen. I am glad you liked my little gift.

E

AB TO DR. MICHAEL COHN, *October 10, 1922, BERLIN*

My dearest friend,

Because you *are* my dearest friend, I am going to write to you without any preliminaries. Will it surprise you to hear me say that you are the *only* one to whom I can speak frankly of things that trouble me? Well, there is no one else. Fitzie and I have grown apart—it seems we are strangers now. Our correspondence has practically ceased—we live in different worlds, mentally and spiritually, and we have lost touch with each other. No one is to blame, of course. It is just a combination of circumstances over which a mortal has no control. That chapter is closed.

As to the local conditions, it is the same, though in a different way. You will understand, dear Mac, I can't write of it. Paper is treacherous. Enough to say that a house can be divided against itself: differences of temperament, of basic feeling and viewpoint, etc. In short, a lifelong and true friendship, yet always conscious of the sharp line of division which closes the springs of the inner life.

In short, there are a few things that trouble me deeply of late—so deeply that I can't do any work, and that fact itself aggravates the situation still more. And I have been feeling sometimes that I simply must cry out in desperation, and I have been longing to see you and to free myself by confiding in you. Too bad you will not come for some months yet. Yet I must tell you a few things now—it may lighten my heart.

* Instead, as we indicate in the introduction to this part, she got to Berlin "legally."

As a rule, I am not given to talking about my feelings or personal affairs. But now I must. A terrible thing is the human heart that threatens to burst unless it can share its joys, and still more its sorrows, with some other understanding and sympathetic heart. So far I have opened my heart and spoken my troubles only to one—to my diary, that is to me a vital necessity. (I always have one; my last I started after leaving Russia.) But for a good while past I have felt the need of talking to some living soul, and now I feel I simply must say a few things in this relation—to you, of course, dear, true friend.

I don't know how to begin. The fact is, I am disheartened, discouraged, almost desperate. It is mostly in reference to the movement, and specifically in regard to my own work. From Russia I get terrible reports. Hundreds of our people in the prisons; all of them in need, many suffering with the dreaded tsinga (scorbut [scurvy]), and needing special attention and selected foods. [Alexander] Shapiro [after his return] arrested, others sent to the worst solitudes of Archangel, and so on with the fearful story. I feel I ought to be there, to attend to things myself. But the work I want to do keeps me back: it could never be done there. Besides, I would hardly get a chance to do anything, I suppose. It would be another Shapiro case [i.e., arrest of a returnee]. Not that I am afraid of it—I am sick of everything, anyhow. But I am practical enough to see no purpose in going there now. I have sent to the people there a lot of money. (By and by I shall publish a full account of all receipts and expenditures—as soon as I get the report of our Moscow Society. They sent me one recently, but the government has evidently confiscated [it]. I am trying to get another.) I sent them money from Stockholm, several times. Then, per Shapiro, $500 (dollars) and 500 Swedish kronen (equal to $150). Now a friend is going there tomorrow, and I am sending by him over 2,000 Swedish kronen (about $600). All the money I sent so far, except $10, reached our people safely. Fortunately the money Shapiro carried also was turned over to our Society before he was arrested. The man who is going now is perfectly reliable, and not a comrade, and the sum I am giving him will reach them OK.

But all that money is like a drop in the ocean. For the present needs they will have enough, but how about the near future? We can't expect our comrades to be continuously contributing for the same purpose. There are other as important causes that demand aid. And as a matter of fact, our appeal for our Russian prisoners was generously answered by our comrades. But then of course the contributions began to fall off, and now the Stockholm *Brand* has informed me that almost nothing has been coming in of late. (Contributions for this purpose I directed in my appeal to be sent to the *Brand*.) And that was certainly to be expected.

I have arranged for our people in Russia to send a man to visit all the prisons, concentration camps, and exile places where our prisoners are detained, and to bring them food, clothing, etc. The winter must be terrible for them, as none of them have warm things (most of them have been taken to some distant part without a moment's notice and are therefore unprepared). So you can understand how quickly the money I sent them will be used up. The man who is to make the rounds of the different prisons is to send me regular reports; also, wherever possible, he is to get little notes or letters from the prisoners and forward them to me. We will thus (if everything goes well) get information about their conditions etc., and also be able to use it for our press.

For the present our people have enough funds, for as I have just said, a man is going there tomorrow and will bring them over 2,000 Swedish kronen. It is a big sum, and the Swedish krone stands high. The dollar, for instance, is now over eight million roubles. But the prices for things in Russia are equally high. I recently had a package of things sent to Petrograd. It is to be forwarded to Moscow, and now the boys in Petrograd informed me that it costs just nine million to send it there. Not a big package, either. That will give you an idea of the cost of living and other expenses.

While I am at this matter, I want to tell you that I have expended most of the $800 you sent for local needs. In fact, I have nothing left of it. Some other time I shall give you a detailed report—a confidential one, of course, for there are certain good reasons for it. Perhaps, if you are willing to wait for it, I shall do it in person when you are here. I hope to goodness that you will *surely* come in the spring, for there are many matters I must talk over with you in person, and besides, I must and want to see you on general principles. But for the present I will say this: $300 (out of the $800) was used as cash for the local people, to supply clothing for them. Then smaller sums for individual help in urgent cases. There is also a special item that involved a certain expense. It refers to something that I could tell you only in person. You remember when you were treasurer of a certain fund, to secure a certain "lawyer" for Rachmetov [i.e., AB himself] in the castle on the Ohio River [i.e., Western Pennsylvania Penitentiary]. Well, I have had a similar "lawyer" recently in my plans for a certain most important issue [probably bringing Nestor Makhno to Berlin; see below, p. 30]. Some of your money went on that, and I am sure that when you learn about the thing in detail, from myself personally, you will not only OK the matter, but it will give you great joy. However, so far there are no results on that question. It is a complex and difficult affair. It may even be that nothing will result from it, but it is something that is well worth trying, by all means. This is strictly confidential.

Some of your $800 fund I have also used to send little sums to Siberia —we have people there. I mentioned this in a previous letter.

By the way, do you know that several comrades escaped from prison in Petrograd? We are looking after them.

Speaking of money matters, I also want to tell you that of the $1,000 intended for publication of my pamphlets etc., I had to use several hundred to pay some of my debts that have accumulated since Stockholm days. That is my personal debts, for living expenses. The fact is, I have practically no source of income, and my expenses are considerable, especially owing to the constant "papers" etc. Unfortunately I have so far received almost nothing from the first pamphlet; as to the second one, it has only recently been sent out, so that returns cannot be expected so soon, if ever. I really do not believe that there will be any income from pamphlets. That would be all right, for I am mostly interested in their propaganda value. But the question is—where is my personal income to come from? The Holland comrades, for instance, had promised 70 gulden for my first pamphlet, which they issued in the Dutch language. They paid 10 gulden, and can't afford to pay more. The New York *Call* has also not paid at all for my article on the New Economic Policy, which they published (in two installments) long ago. And so it goes. It is a source of worry to me, because I hate to use up the money intended for publication of my pamphlets.

Well, to sum up: At present no money is needed for any of the various things in hand. The problem is only about the near future—say two or three months from now.

But, my dear friend, this is not really the main subject I meant to write to you about, and which I had in mind as I started this letter. What troubles me most is the writing and the publication of my diary and afterward the book on Russia. It is somewhat hard to explain myself on paper in this matter. I wish I could talk to you about it. I can merely hint at the thing here. The man who had made me an offer to take my diary has lately somewhat lost interest in the matter. That would not be the worst of it, if it were not for the fact of the *reasons* that have caused him to lose interest. You see, dear Mac, the man who made me that offer is the local representative of the publishing house that is to publish EG's book. You will understand my feeling of friendship and comradeship when I tell you that I have consented, willingly and cheerfully, that EG make use of all the data, material, documents, etc., which I had accumulated (and translated), for her book. Moreover, EG's forte is the platform, not the pen, as she herself knows very well. Therefore my days and weeks are now taken up, really entirely, as editor. It is not only that I get no time for my own work, but my diary and my book (if I ever get to it) must of necessity contain the very same things, data and documents, in exactly the same wording even, as EG's book, for the translations are all mine. As her book will be out first, what interest could my book (or even the diary) have on the very same subject, covering the same period, aspeking of the same events, of the same places, even, since we visited them together in our work for the Museum of Petrograd, and—worst of all—containing the very same documents, etc., etc.?

It is a tragic situation. Of course, my writing is different in style, and to some extent even in point of view, but the *meat* I have given away. And yet I could not do otherwise.

Dear boy, there is little use of speaking about it now. But I just felt I had to confide in you in this matter. It is much more serious than it looks on paper. Still, I will have to work out some solution of this terrible situation. For the present, however, I see no light. . . .*

This letter is not very cheerful, dear friend. But many things are oppressing me just now, so you will understand and bear with me. Maybe I can write you a better letter next time. I have filled it mostly with myself and my own troubles, but that does not mean that I am forgetful of others and their hard road in life. In fact, just now I am thinking that the weather is getting very cold, and our local people have no winter things. One of them—you know who—has a wife and five children. I am to see him tomorrow. The others are also no better off, even if they have less children. I am thinking of devoting what is left of those $800 to getting warm underwear, etc. for these people as far as the amount I have on hand will reach. . . . Greetings to you, Anne and family. As ever,

S

AB TO LILLIE SARNOV, *July* 22, 1924, BERLIN

Dear Comrade Sarnov:

Your letter of June 28 (written by you in the name of your group) and copies of the *Bulletin* #2 received. This reply is to you as well as to the comrades of the [Anarchist] Red Cross.

You know my position in regard to aid of the revolutionists imprisoned in Russia. As I said in the statement recently issued by myself and Mark Mratchny, I do NOT consider aid to imprisoned revolutionists in the light of political work. It is not necessary here to repeat all that I said in the statement, a copy of which I sent you.

To me, in this connection, supplying bread to a Maria Spiridonovna

---

* Years later, probably in 1939, when she went to Amsterdam to work with their correspondence in the International Institute of Social History, Emma read AB's carbon copy of this letter and revealed in an initialed marginal note that she still failed to comprehend why he felt it a "terrible situation": "Poor Old Sasha, your feeling was unnecessary. *Bolshevik Myth* great." It was, and it was true that in some ways it was superior to *My Disillusionment,* true that she helped him in no end of ways with his books, and true as well that she was grateful for all that he had done for her in this instance. As she wrote Ellen Kennan from Berlin on January 12, 1923, she hoped to travel and study in Germany "just as soon as Sasha's book is done. You know how our boy is when he is engaged in literary work. All trouble, disturbance, and unpleasantness have to be kept from him. And that is the least I can do in return for the help he has given me with my book." Nevertheless, Emma failed to see that her need to speak out of her grief had blinded her to the misery of her comrade and his need to express himself—and that not only later and with what was left over. In times past Emma had leaned on their friendship in ways that veered toward exploitation. On this occasion she did more than lean.

(who is a Left Social Revolutionist) is just as imperative as to aid Aaron Baron (who is an anarchist). It is not a question of the political views of the prisoners. It is enough for me that they are sincere revolutionists.

Concerning your remark that we cannot work with Left SR's, I may tell you that we—at least I—could also not work together with many of the ANARCHISTS who are in the prisons of the bolsheviki. Yet I am willing to help them, as prisoners. Among the anarchists in prison are many individualists, Stirnerians [i.e., followers of Max Stirner], universalists, Gordinists [i.e., followers of Abba Gordin] (who are worse than crazy), etc., etc. Some among them pure cranks who did us more harm than good in the Revolution. Yet even YOU send help to ALL anarchists, not asking what their particular views and opinions are. Some of those "anarchists" cannot even be considered as anarchists in OUR sense, yet we are willing to help ALL of them. I can assure you that as a revolutionist I felt nearer Spiridonovna, Kamkov, or Trutovsky (I knew them all personally and spent many days with them in Moscow), than to some of those individualists and Stirnerians whom you are willing—and justly—to regard as anarchists. In short, I would help Sophia Perovskaya and Zheliabov in prison, the same as I would help Baron or Meier-Rubinchik. (If you really wanted to carry your view out logically, you should aid ONLY anarchist-communists in prison, for the universalists, for instance, are as far from us as the Left SR's and perhaps even farther in point of ideas.)

As a matter of fact, the anarchists in the prisons of Russia SHARE the things they receive with the Left SR's, and the latter do the same. Among revolutionists in prison political distinctions are abolished so far as food etc. is concerned. You will therefore realize how stupid it is of that fellow in the New York *Izvestia* who asked me whether I would also "work with Denikin and Wrangel to aid their prisoners." We are speaking of revolutionists in prison, not of counter-revolutionists. To me the Left SR's ARE revolutionists, even if I disagree with their political views.

Well, you are at liberty to have your own opinion on the matter. That is why I call myself an anarchist, leaving others free to act and think as they believe best. But at the same time I claim the right for myself to act as I think proper under given circumstances. . . .

I personally am indifferent as to where and how people send help to Russia. I am only interested in seeing that our prisoners should receive aid. HOW and BY WHOM is just the same, just so that they get it.

This is about all there is to be said on the subject. I have explained my position to you, and I hope that you clearly understand it.

Fraternally,
AB

AB TO DR. MICHAEL COHN, *September 16, 1924, BERLIN*

My dear Mac,

I am writing this in a very urgent matter, in re Nestor Makhno. The man has for some time been in Danzig, together with his wife and child born in a prison in Poland. They had to get out of Poland, because M's life was not safe there. He was in constant danger both from the Whites and the Reds. So much so, that the Polish authorities permitted him to carry a revolver in self-defense.

In Danzig he was soon arrested, the police demanding that he leave the Free City of Danzig. It now appears that the arrest was due to the machinations of the bolsheviki. But M could not leave, as he had no visa to any place. We succeeded in securing permission from the Berlin police Presidium for M to come to Berlin—three times we did so—but some forces behind the scenes mysteriously prevented his coming here, every time. At last we found out that it was the Danzig German Consul who refused to sign his visa, in spite of the permission we had here from the Berlin police.

Meanwhile the police of Danzig arrested him again for not leaving—he and his wife, though the latter was soon released. We succeeded in releasing M again, by using every resource in money and influence we had here in Berlin. I even had to take in confidence some American friends here, journalists, in order to aid in the matter.

And thus it came about that we found out what the secret springs are which are operating in the case of Makhno. It appears that, in spite of the Presidium permitting M to live in Berlin, *some one* in the Foreign Ministry here had put his VETO on the visa. That some one proves to be Baron Malzan, the head of the Russian Department of the German Foreign Ministry. Malzan is entirely pro-bolshevik. No secret in Berlin that he is such—whether bought or otherwise, is not known. In short, Malzan has stopped M from coming to Germany. Even a Durchreise [transit visa] is refused. Of course, M has no visa anywhere for the present, though we are working for it.

Now we brought M's wife here, with baby. She is penniless, and so is M in Danzig. You can well imagine that the whole business has cost a lot of money and all our resources are now entirely exhausted. M is quite desperate over the helpless situation. If we had a good sum now, there is a chance of having him disappear from Danzig, of which the authorities of that city would be very glad. We could then have him live quietly here for a while, since the Berlin police, not friendly to the bolsheviki, would allow him to stay here. It is only the Foreign Office that does not issue a visa for M, but once here he would be OK.

But we are entirely stuck now, as there are no funds coming from anywhere, and we have all here (myself, [Vsevolod] Volin, etc.) used up what little of our own we had. We don't know what is going to happen in the near future. The bolsheviki are lying in wait to grab M, the first chance they get. It means a question of life and death for him, as you well know.

For the present we are keeping him in Danzig, but he can't remain there very long any more. We have to send a man there to get him out, in a manner in which Sasha [i.e., Berkman himself] came here from Sweden. We have talked the matter over with M's wife, Volin, etc. Our only hope now is in you. Can you cable through American Express in Berlin to Schmidt-Bergmann some help for M? I'll send this per Luft Post [air mail] to you. I am writing this in haste. Hope it will reach you in Brooklyn. I don't even know where you are, as I have had no reply to quite a number of my letters to you. I hope everything is well with you—I've been anxious about your long silence. Please write soon. Greetings to you, Anne, and family. As ever,

S

P.S. Just as I am writing this, Volin and M's wife come in. Situation urgent. They also brought a letter from M. Cherniak, used to be barber in Brooklyn, perhaps you remember him. With four others (one a woman) Cherniak is now arrested in Kowel, Poland, and faces serious charges. Call for help, of course. So it goes almost every day. It's just maddening.

EG TO AB, *December 20, 1924, LONDON*

My dearest Sash,

I just came back from Rebecca [West's] apartment, where I had lunch with her. She is *positively* going to write the introduction to your book [*Bolshevik Myth*]. She would have done it this week, but she must finish two articles for *Harper's*. She said to write you that you can depend on her doing the introduction right after Christmas. Indeed you can depend on any promise Rebecca makes. It is not because she gives a promise but because she is so carried away by your book and by the work on Russia we are doing. To prove to you how deeply interested the girl is, I want to tell you that she was going to turn your ms. over to Jonathan Cape, one of the younger publishers. She had spoken to him about your work before she knew that her agent had offered my book to the same publisher. If he turns mine down, which he may certainly do, we are going to send him your ms. Rebecca is so set on trying to find a publisher for your work on Russia. I wish now mine had not been offered to Jonathan Cape. However, we will try for another. Besides, Cape may not care to handle mine now that the book is so botched [see above, p. 18]. Meanwhile you must make sure whether Fitzie did not turn over the English rights to Liveright. She might have, you know. That would be even more stupid than my turning over *all* the rights to [Clinton P.] Brainard [of the McClure Syndicate]. But I had so little experience. Anyway, find out. There is no use starting with the publishers unless we know you still own the English rights. Get Fitzie to cable you. Then after Christmas, when Cape will have read my book, we will start on yours.

Yes, Rebecca read your [*Prison*] *Memoirs*. I wrote you that ages ago. Stella gave it to her. Rebecca thinks it a very great book. I talked to her today about finding a publisher. She seemed to think it might not be so easy as your work on Russia. I think just the reverse. After the holidays we will start with your *Memoirs*. Rebecca will be only too glad to write an introduction to that as well, or she may get [H.G.] Wells to do it. We will see. I should say you would want to meet her. She is the most perfect specimen of modern womanhood I have met. She has a brilliant mind, she has looks, and she is so beautifully feminine, just the kind you'd love. Well, maybe some day you will meet her.

I thought I had sent you her article in *Good Housekeeping*. Are you quite sure you did not get it? I must make a search in Doris [Zhook's] rooms; I may have given it to her to read. I am living in such a whirl, crowded with so many things and work, I do not know how the days go. I will see about the magazine before I close this letter.

Dearest own Sash, I think it is ridiculous for you to worry so much about what the civil liberty [American Civil Liberties Union] people will say. They'd have to be crazy to suspect you of not having done all you could. If [Roger] Baldwin did not cable in time, he has himself to blame. He must see that you had to go ahead without delay, since he wanted the work done in three months. Write him a determined letter and tell him you went ahead since he did not cable you and that now the expenses must be paid. By the way, he can see by the letter (a copy of which you sent me) and the account how you stand and that you have certainly not wasted any money. That is all the obligation you owe Baldwin or his group. But for you to worry yourself sick seems absurd, as if it matters what Baldwin thinks, or will say. Please dearie, do not worry so much.

Look at this rotten crooked letter, will you? [See Introduction, p. xviii.] Try as I may I can never get it quite straight. There must be something crooked in my make-up somewheres, don't you think?

To more serious things: You say you are worrying. What do you suppose I must do? My situation is really a desperate one. The tories have taken a stand against the communists, in France they are being hounded, the Pope comes out against them. And here I am doing the same. It is no wonder that everybody refuses to join me. It really means working hand in glove with the reactionaries. On the other hand I know I must go ahead and that our position is of a different nature. It is the old good luck of the damned gang in Moscow, something always happens to silence everybody. Now the report of the faker Purcelle and the rest [of the British Trade Union Delegation to Russia], that will scare away the few who promised to help. I am simply in despair, besides having a very bad taste in my mouth. Well, tomorrow will decide much. The [Harold] Laskis have invited thirty-five people. Rebecca is going to be there. Wells will evidently not. Rebecca told me he went to the country for the weekend. The English are great for that. I do not know who will come and how many we will get. But unless we will get a few to give the meeting moral backing, it will be no end of risk to have it at all. I doubt whether I alone without an organization will be able to fill a large hall. As Rebecca said, no one ever has a meeting or lecture unless arranged by some organization. You see my difficulties, don't you, dear?

And now comes another trouble; it seems Kingsway [Hall] too will want an insurance against damages. They are all afraid the communists will come and try to break up the meeting. Now if an insurance will be necessary for Kingsway, then Queen's Hall would be preferable because the standing of the place itself would secure us against trouble. Anyway, we have already been at halls five weeks and we are not a step nearer. I am expecting to hear from the chap who is looking after halls. If Kingsway insists on security, I will call a special meeting of the few comrades who make up the committee and see if they will not decide on Queen's Hall after all. The whole situation is anything but encouraging. In fact I have already worried so much, I am feeling rotten.

I do not know what the papers have written, but I see no reason for rejoicing with my "success." Fact is, I have had no success. People came to the dinner [the impressive welcoming dinner on November 12, 1924, attended by Rebecca West, Bertrand Russell, *et al.*], because they must have thought I have come to champion Russia. They have dropped off one by one since they found out my actual purpose in coming to England. The only things have been the four articles, which have had wide publicity. And the lecture before the American students [at Oxford]. By the way, Professor [Samuel Eliot] Morison wrote me I might put him on the committee. I think it is very brave of him, much more so than the stand of Mrs. Cobden Sanderson, who wrote me she could not take a public stand against Russia, as she is afraid of the reactionaries. I wish you were here, dear Dush, it would not feel so difficult to go ahead against so many odds.

Speaking of the American students, two of them are expecting to be in Berlin, Barker and Ted McLean Switz [see below, p. 43]. I gave Switz your address and I told him to write you for a rendezvous. You must take time to see the boys; they are tremendously worthwhile, awfully good material not only because of Russia, but for our ideas. Please see them. I also want Rudolf [Rocker] and [Augustine] Souchy to see them; they are interested in syndicalism. I have written both a long letter but forgot to mention the boys to Rudolf and Souchy. I will have to write them cards to let them know.

If only [John] Turner could be prevailed upon to make some kind of a declaration at the meeting, that would absolutely secure success and importance. But I dare not hope. These trade unionists are like thieves, they hang together. My only hope is that since John is out of the trade unions as an official, he may speak out. The [Labor] Mission was to arrive today; if it did, John must have gone to Brighton, where his family lives. I will no doubt hear from him Monday. Another thing, I see that the Moscow agents are banking on the report which the Mission is to give before the trade unions at a special conference; it may well be that John will not want to make any statement whatever until his colleagues have given their report. In that case I may even be in favor of postponing my meeting. I will be able to judge when I see John, possibly Monday. Perhaps he has stopped off in Berlin on his way; then Rudolf has surely seen him. I hope you too.

Yes, dear, Moscow gets everybody, it even got your young admirer Vera. I had a letter from Manya Semenev, she heard . . . Vera has joined the Communist Party. How do you like that? As I did not expect much from Vera (I knew while I was in Russia that whatever ideas she had were largely because of being carried away with you, just hero worship, nothing deeper), I am not disappointed. But I suppose you will be. Well, do not let it worry you. Only it goes to prove what a hold the regime has on everybody. If it can break such a man as Savinkov, why not a child like Vera? . . .

I am glad to get a copy of the medical report, I need that and all other material for the people I meet, Laski, [Henry W.] Nevinson, etc. Send the stuff the mensheviks are getting out to meet the whitewash of Purcelle; I will need it. I have just this minute had a letter from [Colonel Josiah] Wedgwood that he will preside at my meeting, but that he could get no one else so far to join a committee. Can you beat it? He is off for the holidays, so he will not be at Laskis'. I am inclined to think that Wedgwood and Rebecca West will be the only ones who will back my meeting. Professor Morison will, but he is not known in labor circles here. How Moscow has poisoned the world, and what a task we have before us. . . .

Yes, darling boy, I must get a better typist. Where? that is the question. I could get any number, if I could employ them by the week. No one wants to come for just a few half-days in the week and I cannot afford to have them by the week. I could get one of two typists, very good but unable to take dictation; one is [Varlaam] Cherkezov's niece who has just lost her position, and the other is a friend of Doris [Zhook], but both are Russian and used to ordinary office work. What am I to do with them? I think after the holidays I will go to the Corona or Underwood people and have them send me a good stenographer and typist. I have already gotten rid of the one who could not read her own notes.

I have no material whatever about Izmailovich [Left SR]. Can you go after Steinberg to send me some? I may get an article placed about the Heroic Women of the Revolution. But even if I do not, I am now working on something else. I am trying to interest some of the numerous woman societies to get up a meeting about the women in Russian prisons, [Maria] Spridonovna as the outstanding figure and the rest around her. Through Rebecca I have met several very vital women; one [is] Lady Rhonndda, a very radical person and a burning feminist; she is getting up a group of women to meet me right after the holidays. Through them we hope to launch a big meeting to arouse interest in our Russian women. I will therefore need material about Izmailovich; I have the others. This will show you that I have ever so many irons in the fire, if only I can forge them. I go ahead but I am not very optimistic about my success. The Gods know it will not be my fault, if I fail. . . .

I must get this into the post office tonight or you will not get it Monday. Besides I have written you about everything. I may write again tomorrow giving an account about the Laski gathering. O yes, Rebecca wants to know how many words she is to write, let me know. I embrace you, dearest Sash. Devotedly,

E

P.S. Enclosed dollar is for some flowers for Milly [Rocker]; I sent her son a dollar and Rudolf my book. Also sent Therese one dollar. I can do so little this year.
P.S.S. I haven't even time to look this letter over. Do be charitable, dearie.

EG TO AB, *December 22, 1924, LONDON*

Dearest S,

I am rushed sick but I must write you a short letter. I am in utter despair over the contemptible whitewash of the Purcelle gang. I am waiting anxiously to hear from Turner, have no idea whether he is already here. If he does not give out some kind of a dissenting report, or consents to speak at the proposed meeting, all my efforts of the last three months will be in vain. The damnable report of Purcelle has already born its rotten fruit. Yesterday at Laski's, of thirty people not one would go on a committee, if I should use the proposed meeting for a presentation of facts about the bolshevik regime. Some of them are willing to go on a Defense Committee of the Politicals, if I will speak [only] about the conditions of the politicals. In other words, if we have our meeting for which we will have to do the work and stand all the responsibilities, my address will have to confine itself to the politicals—that is, if I want any kind of committee. How do you like that?

In a measure I cannot blame the people I met last night, among whom were Professor Graham Wallace, Nevinson, and other important men and women. Of course, Shaw was not there. Wells also was not because he had not yet gotten back. They are all members of the Independent Labor Party. By the way anybody at all worthwhile here of the younger men and women are in the ILP. There is no other labor movement except the trade unions. All these people are aspiring members of Parliament. Now I would not bother about them; the trouble is that no one goes to meetings in England unless it is arranged by some organization or party. As Rebecca said, "I never heard of meetings by individuals." That means that we will run a terrible risk unless we can announce the meetings as backed by some kind of an organization. If only we had people of our own. That is the bitter thing to me; we have absolutely no one, not among the English people, and the Jews are unknown. It is heartbreaking. I must therefore have some committee and I will not get it for what I had intended to do—present the facts about Russia and my conclusions. God damn that fake Purcelle.

Well, I had in mind a protest meeting about the politicals—I think I even wrote you that some time ago. But it seemed to be starting from the tail end before going into the whole question of the Revolution and the bolsheviki. But better than give up the idea of a meeting at all, it will have to be a protest meeting. Laski seems to think that a lot of people can be gotten for that. Well, I am not even sure about that, but I will give Laski the benefit of the doubt. He has undertaken to organize the committee. I hope he succeeds. Meanwhile there is more trouble. We cannot get Kingsway Hall; they are afraid of trouble from the communists. We will therefore have to take Queen's Hall, after all. For this reason I had to call a special meeting of the few comrades for tomorrow evening; perhaps they will be willing to contribute a little more. I have about 45 pounds collected and the meeting will cost 160. Even if I put every penny of my own into it, we will still be short, and the worry will make me crazy. As it is I am a wreck from lack of sleep and feel ill all over. It is mainly the realization of the terrific power of the bolshevik lie which so depresses me. . . .

Dearest own, I must close, I am in such a hurry. Short as this letter is, it is still double your letters. But I forgive you, dearest, I know how hard worked you are. Only you have results and I have not; I am sick of talking, talking, talking about Russia and yet not [able] to move any one of these politicians. Rebecca is arranging for me to meet Wells; maybe I can have some effect on him. I am beginning to doubt my persuasive powers. My Christmas will probably not be very cheerful. I may make a dinner for Minna [Loy?] and invite a few old fogies who are as lonely as I am. . . . If only I had success for our people in Russia, I would not feel so dejected. I came home sick last night after Laski's.

A pleasant Christmas to you, my dearest, so glad you will be with dear Rudolf and Milly. I will be with you all in thoughts. I embrace and kiss you tenderly,

E

EG TO HAROLD J. LASKI, January 9, 1925, LONDON

Dear Prof. Laski:

I tried to get you on the phone twice today but once received no reply at all and in the evening, Mrs. [Doris] Zhook, who spoke for me, was told that you were out. I am very anxious to get the document which is the signed statement of the physicians who examined the bodies of the unfortunate victims at Solovetski. I wonder whether you could let me have it by tomorrow evening? If you have sent it to Mr. Henry Nevinson, or Bertrand Russell, perhaps you would call them up and ask them to return it to me by express post. The matter is rather urgent, because I am writing an article for a London paper about the politicals and I must have the document to quote from.

Your letter of December 29th reached me safely. I should have replied to it ere this, but I have been very busy with articles for America and an ever-increasing correspondence in this country. As you see, I am not easily daunted. I feel I must go ahead on behalf of Russia, even though you and your friends do not feel inclined to help.

I confess, I was not particularly disappointed in what you had to say in your letter. Already at your house on December 21st I had formed a definite feeling that most of the people present are entirely too aloof and too remote from the woes of Russia to make a stand against the forces which continue to crush the country and its people. I am, however, disappointed in Mr. Bertrand Russell and yourself. Since I began to read Mr. Russell's works and when I met him in Russia, I believed that he held the principles of political freedom to be above any other consideration. In fact, at the dinner, he was [so] much more outspoken against the curtailment of liberty in whatever form that I was sure he would be among the first to want the evils of the present regime in Russia discussed and that he would come to the assistance of the men and women who are languishing in Russian prisons for opinion's sake.* The argument advanced by Mr. Russell, that, since there is no other political group of an advanced nature to take the place of the bolshevik government, he does not believe in the effectiveness of my work, seems to me to be out of keeping with the

---

* A letter from Emma, written while she was still in Berlin, concludes the Russia section of Bertrand Russell's autobiography. Perhaps its inclusion at that strategic point is sufficient comment in itself on the political battles of the time, but his explanatory note, while it recaptures succinctly the mood of the British left and the enormous odds against any attempt to make the Russian terror known, is noteworthy primarily for what it does not say about his own changing views over the decades. Russell limited himself to the observation that "Emma Goldman did at last acquire permission to come to England. A dinner was given in her honour at which I was present. When she rose to speak, she was welcomed enthusiastically; but when she sat down, there was dead silence. This was because almost the whole of her speech was against the Bolsheviks" (*Autobiography* [Boston: Little, Brown, 1967-69], II, 173-74).

scholarly mind of a man like Mr. Russell. What possible bearing can that have on the stand on behalf of some justice to the political victims of the government? I have said on the occasion of your gathering that as long as every political opinion is dead, the organization broken up, and their adherents wasting their lives in Russian prisons and concentration camps, it is difficult to say what political group is likely to be superior to the present on the *throne* of Russia. But, granted that Mr. Russell's contention is logical—does that mean that all liberty-loving men and women outside of Russia must supinely sit by while the bolsheviki are getting away with murder? Frankly, I see neither logic nor justice in the argument advanced by Mr. Russell.

In connection with this, it may not be amiss to state that efforts on behalf of the Russian politicals or a frank and fearless exposé of the actual conditions in the country have no relation whatever with any attempt or desire to overthrow the bolshevik government. These efforts would, however, tend to have a modifying effect upon the bolshevik government—would certainly help to ameliorate the present appalling conditions of the politicals and possibly also induce the present regime to establish at least a limited amount of freedom of press, speech, and assembly.

I wonder whether Mr. Russell would have hesitated to lend his name or use his pen and voice on behalf of the politicals under Czardom? What, then, is the impelling reason for a man of his fine qualities to refuse assistance to the victims who are crying for help under the present regime? Is it not perhaps because he, like Mr. Clifford Allen and many other good people in the labor and socialist movements, believe that the "bolsheviki are engaged in an experiment which is going in the right direction." I am inclined to think that it is this delusion more than any other reason which has such a tremendous sway over the advanced section of the various movements. I have found the same delusion at work in the United States and here, too, it is at work. No doubt, that is the most impelling force which is deciding the unwillingness of the Independent Labor Party to take a stand. Or, is it that as a Party already having tasted power and determined to take hold of power again, that it cannot afford to quarrel with colleagues in the Russian government?

The labor movement, who, as you say, would rather not oppose things in Russia, because they feel that the mensheviki would probably not have been better, seem to have forgotten the old proverb: "two wrongs do not make one right." I readily concede that the mensheviki may not have been better: in fact, I have pointed out in the closing chapter of my book that every political group which stresses dictatorship and holds to the Jesuitical formula that "the end justifies any means" would have been driven to do exactly as the bolsheviki are doing unto this day. But, that cannot excuse the extermination of the mensheviki by the present regime any more than the extermination of the bolsheviki would have been excused had the mensheviki been in power. The question, as I understand it, is the Dictatorship and the Terror, such [as] a dictatorship must make use of, [and] not the name of the particular group at the back of it. This seems to me to be the dominant issue confronting various men and women of revolutionary leanings and not *who* is being persecuted or by *whom*. I hold, therefore, that the argument of your trade union friends is very lame, to say the least.

The suggestion that the Trade Union Delegation should first be talked to privately, before any public work ought to be started, would be in order, if the delegation had been in Russia long enough to go beneath the surface—not as guests of the government and not officially conducted. But, with only five weeks in the country, depending largely upon biased interpreters and listening only to the glowing accounts received from those in whose interest it is to proclaim that there is "Peace in Warsaw"—such testimony can have no weight with people who know the country and its language. The other night I had an opportunity to convince myself of the utter falsity which must have been conveyed to the delegates by one of their interpreters. I was present at Miss Booth's when Mr. Young had the effrontery to state "that the Cheka is abolished and that the GPU has no more power than Scotland Yard." That, in the face of the overwhelming facts of the arbitrary power of the GPU recorded in the entire bolshevik press in Russia (mind, I do not mean to impugn the sincerity of the Trade Delegation, but I do mean to charge them with lack of political grasp of the Russian situation, ignorance as to the terrible conditions of the masses, above all excessive partiality to the ruling regime—all of which makes the opinions of the delegation utterly worthless to fair-minded men and women). I therefore do not see the contribution they could make, if they were consulted, as was suggested by some of your friends.

You and your friends have stressed the point that anything that might be done for the politicals must not be done under anti-bolshevik auspices "such as yours" (i.e., mine). I confess I do not understand what is meant by that, unless it is my position as an anarchist which so frightens your friends. I am sure this cannot be the motive in Mr. Russell's objection. Nor do I believe that this has anything to do with yours. If I am not mistaken, Mr. Russell is pretty much of an anarchist himself. Certainly his attack on *all governments* at the dinner was anarchistic enough even to suit me. On the other hand, you, dear professor, were willing to concede on the evening when I first called on you that "the ideas of Bakunin and Kropotkin have been quite vindicated by the Russian experiment." (I should say, by the bankruptcy of the state everywhere.) And, if it is not my anarchism, what is it that your friends mean when they say: "anti-bolshevik auspices such as yours"?

However, it is not a question of what I will or will not do. The cause of the politicals is sufficiently urgent to be taken up by you and others of your friends, if you are really interested in helping them. I shall, of course, go ahead in my own way, which does not mean that I am unwilling to render whatever assistance I can in furnishing you with authentic material or in any other way possible. In connection with this I am enclosing copies of a letter from my friend, Henry Alsberg, and an appeal signed by a committee of men and women whose names, I am sure, are familiar to you. Could you not undertake to start a similar organization here? I am sure I have no desire to be in the forefront or having my name broadcast: my fervent desire is chiefly to bring some encouragement and relief to the thousands who are languishing in bolshevik prisons, concentration camps, and places of exile. By the way, it took Henry Alsberg nearly a year to wake the American labor and radical elements to the crimes that are daily occurrences in Russia. Perhaps I ought not to be discouraged that I have accomplished so little in three months. In the end the truth will out, though I often think that the power of a lie is more persevering than the truth. Yet, for those of us who will make no peace with a lie, there is no other course but to go on determinedly and unafraid. If I can even in the least expose the Bolshevik Myth, arouse people to its danger, and help the politicals, I shall not mind the difficulties confronting me in this country.

Yes, my book is episodical. It was not intended to be anything else. Your contention that the closing chapter of the second volume should have been enlarged is correct. The subject it treats would need a whole volume, but as I was limited by space, I had to confine myself to the concentrated form. I thank you very much for the names of the publishers you have suggested [John Murray and Thornton Butterworth]. One of them has read the ms. and refused; the other one will be seen, if Jonathan Cape, who is now reading it, refuses to handle it.

Sincerely yours,
Emma Goldman

ERIC B. MORTON TO EG, February 23, 1925, SAN FRANCISCO

[At the top of Morton's first page Emma penned a note, no doubt to Berkman: "Send back. This letter was certainly a great surprise." Later, probably when she was going through their correspondence in Amsterdam, she added the explanation: "Eric Morton helped with tunnel for AB." In the late 1890s Berkman had planned an escape from the Western Pennsylvania Penitentiary. The desperate venture was frustrated when the tunnel terminated in the prison yard under a pile of bricks and stone which had just been dumped there for a building project nearby. A confederate was responsible for this fiasco—Morton had wanted to follow Berkman's diagram, which called for the tunnel to terminate in an unused outhouse. As Emma described him, the Norwegian Morton was "a veritable viking, in spirit and physique, a man of intelligence, daring, and will-power." His letter here, twenty-five years later, shows he remained a man of wit and considerable charm. (see also p. 72.)]

My dear cub,

Hallo! How are you? And where are you bound for? I understand you haven't been deported for several weeks now. Is business dull or are there no more places to deport you to? Mary was here yesterday and showed me some letters and clippings that were very interesting and she gave me your address, which I hope will prove sufficiently permanent for this letter to reach you. Like a good patriotic, 125 per cent American I am celebrating Washington's birthday today. Of course I can't go out like Washington did with my cocked hat full of whiskey and invite everybody to drink to the success of my political party under penalty of a smack in the snoot, but inside of four walls there is no difficulty in getting celebration chemicals provided one has lots of lucre and a copperlined stomach. Doctors who prescribe for thirsty patients, preachers and rabbis who dispense wine for sacramental purposes, bootleggers who are as thick as flies around a manure pile in summer time and now pay fines instead of licenses, lawyers who defend them, and prohibition agents who retire after six months service to live off their accumulated wealth—all these cooperate beautifully and find prohibition a grand success. It is here to stay. But while a glass of beer is unconstitutional, the various legislatures have just defeated a constitutional amendment to abolish child labor. Those who introduced this amendment never intended it to carry anyway, for they worded it so a farm boy of seventeen might be forbidden to help his father pitch hay.

The war ended whatever liberty still was left in the U.S. The Ku Klux Klan is the most flourishing organization. I am so thoroughly disgusted that, were I younger, I would wrap my slippers in my handkerchief, take my spectacles' case, and visit you in London.

Having met you in Chicago, New York, Pittsburgh, Paris, Los Angeles, and San Francisco, we might as well add that English village to the list. I have an idea that I would find it hard to adjust myself to the standard of living of London workmen and I have reached the age where bosses don't hire me on appearance. I have got to confine myself to good work where acquired skill and workmanship count more than speed. For the last seven years I have worked for the S. G. Guny Co. making artistic furniture, but lately they got a British manager, who was so patriotic he could only tolerate countrymen, so I got out, but being the secretary of the union I have the advantage that I generally learn where there is a job open.

Well, Emma, the Russian Revolution made an awful pessimist out of me. Not alone because I was disappointed in the communist regime, but the way it affected the radical movement here.

Old time comrades sank into mere hero worshipers. No, "hero" is not the right word; it was rather a belief in the infallibility of popes simply because they had red banners. It was the fetish of the flag all over again. They never realized, as Byron says, that, "Man, the feeble tenant of an hour/Debased by slavery and corrupt by pow'r," never created a government that had not for its main purpose the perpetuation of its own power. I can't understand how a fellow like Jay can get into his head that men who exercise tyranny every day, ostensibly to prevent counter-revolution, will by some hocus pocus turn libertarians in the future. [William Z.] Foster's propaganda never was convincing to me. It was carried on systematically and intelligently, but to me it seemed cold. While I do not actually know, I always had a feeling that it was subsidized from Russia. And when Bob [Minor] was here he gave me a very interesting private talk lasting four hours on his experiences and [on] conditions in Russia. It was marvelously descriptive, but I could not draw the same conclusions as Bob from it. I am told that Bob is a real religious communist now and is developing considerable religious intolerance, referring to those who differ from his sacred doctrines as *fake* revolutionists. When my daughter Anita, who was entertainment director of the Young Workers League (that is, the communist Sunday-school), heard it, she resigned and she now asks me to tell you that she is cured of communism. So much for the daddy-complex. She will soon be sixteen now and sends her best regards to you. Though she cannot remember you, she has heard so much bad about you, she is sure there is something good about you. Good religious communists use you as a sort of bogey-man.

I read the *Bulletin [of the Relief Fund]* from Berlin relative to politicals in Russia. I note that they have at least a spokesman and a chance to dicker about being treated as criminals. There is no such chance here. There are about ninety politicals in San Quentin who on the average spend more time in the dungeons than criminals do. If anyone attempts to act as a spokesman, in the hole he goes. Then the others strike and in the hole *they* go. As to food, they cannot get any whatever from the outside. Beans every meal except 4th of July, Thanksgiving, and Christmas. Every job in jail is judged good or bad according to the chance it offers for better food. J. B. [McNamara] has one of the best jobs. He waits on the prisoners on hangman's row. They get most anything they want in the line of food and, being well fed up, they make a prettier picture when they march to the scaffold in front of the photographers. Schmitty [Matthew Schmidt] and Tom Mooney also have good food jobs. The International Workers Aid Society, a communist offspring, is appealing for funds for political prisoners and gives statistics on the number in various countries, but conveniently forgets Russia. Since so many states passed criminal syndicalism laws, defense leagues have sprung up most everywhere. Insofar as they create publicity, their work is all right, but actual relief they cannot accomplish—beyond feeding hungry lawyers.

It is a damned shame and I hate to confess it, but I do not visit my friends in San Quentin but very seldom. I am not cheerful enough to cheer them up and I get myself into a frame of mind, a sort of downcast, ineffective desperation that lasts a long time. . . .

Give my best regards to Sasha and tell him his leaflet has done good work in that it has enabled some of us who were unfamiliar with Russian conditions to meet the communist brethren with facts. Sasha's way of quoting dates and documents carries conviction. I am sorry I can't see my way clear to do anything to assist him in his work financially, but when my day's labor is done I retire to my rocking chair and between reading, resting, and rheumatism, there is not much energy left.

This week's *Nation* has a pretty fair review of your book and some months ago I read a comparison in the *American Mercury* between your book and that of Anna Louise Strong, I think it was. I haven't read either book, but I feel a sort of proprietary interest in you. Therefore, I always enjoy sticking articles like that under some communistic nose in order that they may get a faint smell of truth.

Well, dear little cub, be as good as you can without too much effort. There was a time when I used to write you forty-page letters, but facts and fancies rolled off the pen easier in those days. I wish you could come back here. It would not be difficult to do so, but you are too damned irrepressible to remain incognito.

In the memory of auld lang syne with love & kisses,

Your old Bear

EG TO TED McLEAN SWITZ, *March 10, 1930, PARIS*

Dear, dear Ted,

It was great to get your letter and such an interesting one. First of all, let me congratulate you, my dear, in having reached such a value to our present industrial system. I am sure no one would pay you such a high salary, if you were not worth at least double as much, if not more. Very few of us ever can boast of such an achievement. It shows that you know your subject and that you are of importance as a chemist.

Dearest boy, I feel very happy indeed to have done as much for you as you would like me to believe. Certainly any person can be proud of the credit you give me and of having done for any human being all that is implied in your letter. But you see, my dear, I have lived too long in the world and I know human possibilities a little bit. I am certain that all we could do, even the greatest of us, is to bring out what is inherent in our fellows. We can never put anything into them. So if it is true that I have helped you, that I have shown you the world of revolutionary thought, of literature, poetry, and other things, it is only because you had the tendency for all that. I have merely given it the [occasion? push?] and you rolled on.

You are mistaken, my dear, if you think it hurts me to learn about your political views. I am neither hurt nor surprised. I think it perfectly logical for you to have turned Marxian. The particular science you have chosen depends on matter-of-fact, and so does the Marx theory. I should have been surprised if you had become an anarchist, although personally you are that more than you imagine. As you know, I believe so implicitly in the right of everyone to his own opinions that I could not possibly feel hurt if they tell me the truth. My impatience is only with the charlatans, with the many loudmouthed people in the communist ranks, who shout their communism and gain nothing at all by it. Not only am I not hurt with the real people, but I respect them no matter how little I agree with their ideas.

Certainly I know that what is going on in Russia is not "the product of Russo-Asiatic barbarism." When did you ever hear me say that it is? Far from believing that, I have always maintained that the Russian tragedy is that it is saddled with a theory for which the Russian people are by their very psychology utterly unfitted. . . . Of course you may tell me that the Russian people are accepting this theory. Dear Ted. Let's have no fake business between you and me. You know as well as I that the people in Russia accept because they are being forced at the point of a gun to acquiesce and not because they have come to see that Marxism is the solution for all their ills.

My objection to bolshevism is nothing more or less than what my objection to Marxism has always been. Indeed, I have maintained even while I was in Russia that the bolsheviki are merely working out what all social democrats, whatever their nationality, have propagated and would impose were they in power. The bolsheviki and the mensheviki are not even stepsisters and -brothers, since they are from one father. (You see, among the Jews children of the same father by different wives are not considered stepsisters and -brothers. They are, if they are from the same mother, but different fathers.) Therefore I have always maintained that all the socialists, whether mensheviki, bolsheviki, or essers [Socialist Revolutionaries?] are of the same father, think and feel the same, and would force everybody else to do so if they had power, precisely because I see in Marxism a machine which grinds every innate quality into dust, which destroys real values, and which establishes a level that can only be sustained by means of the Chekah and Terror. That I have fought all my life.

You say you cannot understand how it is that I can overlook "the tremendous achievements that are being attained (which even the bourgeoisie admit)." Dearest Teddy. It is precisely because the bourgeoisie not only admits but gloats over these achievements that I cannot enthuse in them. No greater commentary is necessary on the failure of the Revolution in Russia than the lavish praise which the bourgeoisie all over the world is now bestowing on the party and the government which you admire.

No dear boy, it is not because, as you so generously suggest, that "I am kind and good and not enough of a realist" that I will never make peace with the soviet government. It is not because I am kind and good and not enough of a realist that I persevere in my stand against the present Russia. It is because I see the Revolution destroyed. I see acts of terror committed in the name of revolution which has nothing to do with it, which is the inevitable offspring of Marxism.

Thank you for classing the anarchists with the kulaks, the priests, and the rest. But granted that they deserve no more human treatment than the other reactionary elements, your argument that the anarchists, mensheviks, essers, kulaks, etc. are getting in Russia no more than what the communists are receiving in Italy, Germany, and the other fascist countries does not hold water. None of these countries makes any claim of being a socialist republic or having had a social revolution, or of representing the proletariat. Aside from the fact that no two evils make one good, we are not supposed to expect humanity and justice in capitalistic countries. But we have all the right in the world to expect something different from a country that makes such high pretenses as soviet Russia. To me, the Russian Revolution was fought in order to establish the value of human life and not to destroy every value. It was fought to establish some semblance of freedom and not for the purpose of trampling everything under foot. So you see, my dear, that your argument, as you will yourself admit, is too stale. It does not deserve repetition.

It is hardly necessary for me to tell you that my premise of criticism of the bolsheviki is not the premise of the "Pope, the Archbishop of Canterbury, and Arthur Henderson, as well as our own AF of L." You know that without my telling you. You ask these gentlemen whether they would accept Emma Goldman any more than they would Trotsky or Stalin, and you will find out how quickly they will repudiate me. Indeed, much quicker than they will Stalin, because he represents organized force, which is only to be reckoned with, and that terrible destructive institution, the Chekah. EG only represents an ideal which today may seem removed from reality but which time will prove to be the most real thing in any sane society.

How childish it is to put me among the black forces fighting Russia is best proven by the fact that I am still considered a personum non gratis with all governments, including the French. Only last week, I was given a test of it in the form of an order issued in 1901 [by Waldeck Rousseau, the then Minister of the Interior, who had been dead for twenty years] ordering me out of France. It was stopped temporarily by [Henri] Torrés [the attorney], whom I engaged to look after my case. He has been assured that it will be wiped off the slate within the near future. *I am telling you this not for publication* but merely to show you that with all the frantic efforts of your comrades to discredit my revolutionary zeal, I have the honor of still being considered very dangerous by every government. It merely shows that governments see clearer who their enemies are.

But enough, my dear. I think you are wonderful in having mastered the Russian language. I should love to talk it with you. If you sail in June for Germany, you will find me there. I expect to be in Berlin at the time. I would love to see you, as you can well imagine, before you go and after your return from Russia.

I too hear nothing from Tommy [Wright Thomas], but I had Barker [also a former American scholar at Oxford] on a visit here and his wife. He is fine as ever.

I will always be glad to hear from you.

Affectionately,
[EG]

AB TO EG, *November 14, 1931, ST. TROPEZ*

Well, dear,

The rain stopped this morning, yet it looks gray. But it is only 8 A.M., so it may clear up. If it does not pour, I'll go to mail this.

Yesterday was really fierce here, not even the neighbor's dog or cat came around—it poured so. I hope it is not the same weather in Nice and Paris.

Have found a very peculiar book in your room. *Solitaria* by V. V. Rozanov, a writer who died in 1919, in Russia. In English, though the translation is very faulty. Wonder where you got it—maybe Boni and Liveright sent it to you—they published it. Have you read it? Very strange fellow, that Rozanov. Wrote in the most reactionary papers, advocated the pogroms on Jews, said they used Christian blood etc., but in his private notes he does not believe even in the existence of Christ, attacks Christianity, likes the Jews, shows their religion more sensible than the Christian etc. It was partly need of money that made him write such stuff, and partly because he was of the Katkov Slavophile gang etc. But a very peculiar man, of some genius even. Has deep thoughts and slightly resembles Nietzsche in certain ways, and also as mystical as Dostoyevsky. Strange combination. Believed in the phallic cult, hardly believed in a god at all. It is a notebook—very frank, in places even what the censor called indecent.

As it rains here all the time, the only thing to do is to read. . . . So I am also finishing Steffens, and incidentally finishing the *Sons and Lovers* that I once started to read in New York. Lawrence is given to too much nature description. Neither the girl nor Paul can take a single turn in the garden or anywhere without Lawrence describing this and that flower etc., for half a page, on every page. Gets tedious. I noticed it also in his other books. A great nature lover, no doubt, but too much of it for the reader. Also, he drags things out too long. A great psychologist, though he is given to putting too much "mysterious" impulses in his heroines.

Lincoln Steffens's book [*Autobiography*, 1931] is very entertaining. Damned well written, and he is clever as hell and full of humor. But when you sum the whole thing up, what he really has to say is terribly BANAL and gets on my nerves. All his life he spent in finding out rottenness in this city and in that, and it took years to convince him what an intelligent police-court reporter should learn in two weeks—the brutality of the police, the injustice of the courts, the corruption of politics and business. He had to investigate a dozen cities, then a number of states, then Washington and the federal government to learn what he should have seen in a month. He took a lifetime and his own book stamps him, for all his cleverness, a cretin and a moron. It takes him eight hundred pages to prove that it is economic conditions that corrupt men—rich and poor alike, politicians and businessmen, from policeman to president. It took his whole life to find that axiom out and even now he does not know what to do about it. Weak himself, he admires "strong" men, the dictators, Lenin, Mussolini. He has actually come to believe in dictatorship, in peace and in revolution—the strong method is now the thing to him, no matter what it does. He calls his life a spiral, but it is a spiral spring that always shoots back to its original place and gets nowhere. Yet he ends by saying that he lived his life and it was worth living, that he learned—what? That Russia and the U.S. are both coming to the better future. Russia by the direct way, the U.S. by a roundabout way! In short, it will all come right some day, and meanwhile he goes again to Los Angeles to see the *Times* and beg them to keep their old Golden Rule contract and release [J.B.] McNamara and Schmidty [Matthew Schmidt]—and they promise!!

The God-damned idiot, that's all one can say. A dangerous idiot, at that. . . .

Do you intend to stay in England for some time, and how are the engagements for lectures?

Stella's letters I am returning to you, as well as the others. Stella seems greatly worried about financial things. No wonder, with two kids it is no joke. Of course it was perfectly OK for her to marry Teddy [Ballantine]. As a matter of fact I always thought they were married. His family would sure cut her off and mainly the children from whatever they may have left when Teddy's mother dies.

It all seems so insignificant these days. It is good to retire from one's habitual life, environment, and interests back to nature a bit, even if it pours. The world goes right on in its idiotic life and books like those of

Steffens's make it feel that everything will come out all right, of itself really, and that there is nothing very much wrong with things, except as Steffens says, "our thinking about them." One wonders what all this so-called progress, free-speech fights, propaganda, etc. are worth. In the conclusion of his book and life Steffens actually says that all his former belief in democracy, liberty, free speech, etc. was all childish, lack of real understanding. What can you expect of the average man then? And [Alexander] Shapiro complains to you that we don't "do" anything for Spain! I have to laugh. Tell him in my name that nothing can "be done for Spain" or for any other country. They'd have to do it for themselves. And if they don't know what or how, so much the worse for them. Nobody can help them.

Well, enough of that. I am getting disgusted with things. There really seems no such thing as progress. There are changes, not always for the best, either. But as to real progress, where is it, and what has all the work of radicals, revolutionists, anarchists, etc. accomplished? Say, in the U.S., for instance. Or in any other country, for that matter. Here is France, where the revolutionary spirit, syndicalism, etc. used to be high at one time. And now? There is really nothing of it left. And if it will always depend on a few individuals whether there should be a revolutionary spirit and progress, then it is useless. For these few either die or grab power, as Lenin, for instance, and then the old vicious circle is repeated again. Shapiro does not seem to have learned that yet. And syndicalism? I fear me much it would be a greater tyranny and dictatorship than Leninism.

But enough of that. Speaking of Stella and marriage, I am thinking myself of marrying some day. Before I die I want to realize for Emmy [Eckstein, his young companion], her highest ideal—which is to be married. It may be foolish to us, and so it is, but to her it means life itself. Her great misery is that she is only a mistress, and she knows she will have to go back to her family after I die and get whatever is her share of her mother's property. She will not be recognized by her family unless she returns as a married woman. Well, the securing of the marriage certificate has ceased to mean anything to me, and so some day I want to make her happy with it. She certainly deserves it—she has devoted her whole life to me, as far as her ability and power goes.

And speaking of Emmy—she is a striking example of the power of instinct, of heredity, and early environment and education. I have always believed strongly in heredity, as you know, and I am more than convinced now that the rebellious spirit is inborn. I have spent with her months and months in discussing capitalism, authority, punishment, etc., etc. She has typed my books and articles, etc., and she sufficiently understands with her MIND what it is all about and how terrible the effects of capitalism are etc. But her INSTINCT is for conservation, for the need of authority, of law, etc. Nothing, no argument, can change that in her. Things are wrong, she admits it, yet they cannot be otherwise, and without authority and law there would be worse chaos. Things should be changed, yes, but not by abolishing authority. In short, it is the conservative, reformer mind, and the world is full of it. That can only be changed by either killing off all those of such a mind, as the bolsheviki have tried, or letting them die off somehow, and training the new generation in bolshevism or anarchism. But that would be substituting another dogma and new preconceptions and prejudices for the old, as indeed the bolsheviki are doing. And as the anarchists would also inevitably do had they the power, even if only the educational power under economic conditions where the individual would be dependent for his living on a certain mental attitude, as under syndicalism, for instance. So, where is the solution? I really see none, except perhaps through the millions of years that are coming.

Well, dear, it is because of the rain here that I am imposing all this stuff upon you. But you must have other things to do, which I have not—at least here. So I had better quit. Enough and too much for today.

Love,
S

P.S. No mail today.

EG TO AB, *November 18, 1931, PARIS*

Dear,

I wrote you a long letter Sunday and mailed it Monday. Yesterday I sent off the parcels for you and Emmy and a postcard. Today I want to answer your most interesting letters of Friday and Saturday. It is so seldom now that we get a chance for a heart-to-heart talk. Or that you take the time to write me of the things you are thinking about or have at heart. You will probably not know ever how much I miss this from you. Not because talk counts. But because one wants to come close to the human being who has been so long in one's life as you have. And that has unfortunately not been possible, at least not often. I am therefore glad you were in "Bon Esprit" [the St. Tropez cottage] where you had the time and the thought to let yourself go a bit. . . .

Misery seeks companionship. So I was delighted to find that your attitude to the world situation is as mine. I too have come to the conclusion, bitter as it is, that hardly anything has come of our years of effort. And that the mass is really hopeless as far as real progress and freedom are concerned. The trouble is the recognition of a fact does not make it easier to reconcile oneself to it. For instance, I have come to see that nothing I can do in the way of bringing our ideas before the people will leave much trace or make a lasting impression. Yet I never was in greater revolt against my being gagged as I am now. What sense is there to continue living when

I have no outlet of any sort? Even if I had material security, which of course I have not, nor do I expect to get it from *Living My Life,* it would still be inane to go on merely eating, drinking, and having a roof over my head. I can't stand the thought of it. So you see, my dear, though "Du hast mir aus dem Herzen gesprochen" [you have spoken my deepest belief] as regards the masses, the inherent love of power to dominate others whoever wields that power, anarchists and syndicalists included, the still voice in me will not be silenced, the voice which wants to cry out against the wretchedness and injustice in the world. I can compare my state with that of a being suffering from an incurable disease. He knows there is no remedy. Yet he goes on trying every doctor, and every kind of quack. I know there is no place where I can or will gain a footing and once more throw in my lot with our people who continue in the struggle of liberation. Yet I cling to the silly hope as a drowning man does to a straw.

Fact is, dear heart, you do the same. You say in yours of the 15th that if you have to get out of here, you'll go to Spain. You know as well as I that you could do nothing there. Yet you want to go because you want to be close to the activities of our comrades and if possible make yourself felt among them. It is no use, Sash, you and I have been in battle too long to content ourselves with a humdrum existence. And yet we both know how little we have achieved in the past and how little we will leave behind when we go. . . .

Before I forget it, Sonia Shapiro told me Sanya [Alexander] is feeling bad that you did not send him a copy of your *Now and After.* I explained that you simply must have forgotten. If you have a copy, send it to him. Sylvia Beach had three copies of your *Prison Memoirs;* she sold two and is to give me the money for them. I am leaving the third with her in case there should be a demand.

To come back to your letters, I have read both volumes of Lincoln Steffens. You are right: the second is more interesting. And like you I was furious at his inanities. He has learned nothing from his vast experience except quiescence. Ours is the best of worlds and what is bad will adjust itself. It is a very comfortable philosophy. It is after all the escape of people too weak to overcome difficulties, people who are afraid to be hurt or get into trouble. I quite agree with you that Lincoln's adoration for the strong arm springs from his own weak and ineffectual nature. And I am inclined to think that is also the motivation of the worship of Shaw at the shrine of dictatorship. Such people are almost a greater menace than the dictators. To fight them is like whipping a new-born infant. It is nothing at all to pit one's strength or ability against the Mussolinis.

Yes, I have read Rozanov. I sent for it . . . when I saw it reviewed. I was interested in him because I knew that [Jean Richard] Bloch and Andrei Bielli were his pupils. In fact, Rozanov was the father of mysticism, or symbolism, in writing. I fear though I am too much part of the earth to enjoy Rozanov's philosophy. Still the man could write. When I get back I will reread him. Perhaps I did so too hastily last time. . . .

[EG]

EG TO AB, December 1, 1932, ST. TROPEZ

Dear Sash,

. . . What do you say to our friend Trotsky? Some irony that he had to accept the invitation of the social predateli.* And the protection of the capitalist police. It must have been a sight for the gods to see the array of police in the hall in Copenhagen, protecting Trotsky against his former comrades. By the way, it was the same hall where I spoke. The communists made noise enough, but there was no police at my meeting, you bet. And capitalist money also does not smell, it seems. History does play tricks with the mighty. Doesn't it, dear? But yesteryear the butcher of Kronstadt, today humble and subdued. It were funny, if it were not so sad.

I wonder if you read the account in the *Posledni* of a gathering of newspaper men in London who had been in Russia. One of them was Hamilton Fyfe. Evidently he is no longer so enthusiastic about Russia. He together with George Lansbury were wild over my criticism of Russia in '24. He would not take a letter I wrote to the *Daily Herald* asking why never a word in his paper against the persecution of politicals in Russia? It takes time, longer than one has the patience to endure. But the truth will out, even about that fake Russia. I should say things are worse than in 1924. . . .

Good night, dear,

[EG]

AB TO EG, December 3, 1932, NICE

Dear Em,

. . . Trotsky? Well, he shows he is an awful coward. Afraid of his precious life. But he did not have much consideration for the lives of others when he used to order wholesale executions, not to speak of the razed villages, and of Kronstadt, etc. Would serve him right if some one shoots him. He is afraid to see reporters even. Might be a Russian among them, you know, whose father or brother had been killed by Trotsky. But he'll make money all right. . . .

Affectionately,

S

* Russian for traitors—Trotsky and other communists customarily referred to social democrats as "social traitors."

AB TO EG, July 27, 1934, NICE

Dear,

I am sorry you worried so much over my silence. It was just indisposition to write. Today received your letter of the 16th. I know what a tremendous correspondence you keep up, but you must not think I have the same energy. Never had it and less even now. . . .

I know you must be in debt and hard up. So never mind about sending me money just now. No, I did not get any money from Stella for May [Schneider]; nor have I heard from Chicago or from anywhere else about money. Not so far, anyhow.

Is not George Soule one of the men who used to write for Margaret Anderson's magazine [*Little Review*]? A rather slender, blond fellow. If it is the same man, then I met him at Margaret's in Chicago. But maybe it is not the same man. Anyhow, there seems a definite trend in the U.S., as in other countries, toward communism. Particularly among the liberals and intellectuals. The same here in France. It does not surprise me about Harold Laski. I read some of his articles recently, before he went to Russia, and I could see he was inclining to bolshevism. He does not seem to believe any too much in government, probably is something of a Spencerian, but the bolsheviki get them all. He will be another one to say that bolshevism is good for Russia, though not for England, or at least in a different form for England.

To me it seems that there is no stemming the tide just now. There is coming a fight, everywhere, between communism and fascism. Who will win is hard to tell, but I think that in the long run it will be the bolsheviki. Then people will see that we were right, but I fear that THEN there will be no chance to propagate our ideas, for the communists will crush us as they did in Russia. To combine either with the socialists or communists is suicide for anarchism. . . .

The letter of Joe Goldman to you and your reply to Ben Capes received in your letter today. Very good, I am of the same opinion. It is a great pity that our people are always taken in by the APPARENT needs of the hour. Yes, you are right, it was the same thing in the case of [John Peter] Altgeld and [William Jennings] Bryan. They [i.e., the comrades] never learn. It is time to understand that bolshevism and anarchism are at OPPOSITE POLES. But it shows the desperation of our people and the desire to "do something," no matter how and what.

This is enough for today, dear. Max Nettlau wrote he is on his way home from Spain. Says he is OK at home, and the letter was received just a day before [Engelbert] Dollfuss was killed. This thing may yet prove the beginning of international complications, and maybe of war. Who can tell? But I think that a war there will be, maybe in a year or two, and I am afraid the damned masses will again go to the slaughter.

Nettlau writes that on the 19th of August Federico Urales will be seventy years old and he indirectly suggests that it would be fine if you and also I would each send a greeting to Urales, one that "could also be published." I may send him a line. He gives Urales' address as 37, Calle Escornalbou (Guinardó), Barcelona.

The news of Erich Muehsam's death [in Germany] is a great shock. I think they must have killed him. In any case they drove him to death. And many others also. The world has become callous to such things. People used to be outraged, even into action, when such things happened in Czarist Russia. Now it has become a daily thing. And communists are beheaded almost every day in Germany, also in other countries. Everywhere the same story. Nor do I see any hope just now in Spain. Seems to me there is a good deal of bluff there. Our people claim so much power, and they can hardly manage to issue the *Bulletin* [*of the Relief Fund*]. Now they had to move from Madrid to Barcelona, and things do not seem promising there, either. There is a lot of revolutionary spirit in Spain, maybe even anarchist spirit, but it is scattered and unorganized, and to a great extent without definite purpose.

Well, enough, dear. We do not live in a cheerful time. But we must hope that things will brighten up. At least I can only hope, while you may still be active in that direction. That too should give you at least some satisfaction. I embrace you affectionately,

S

EG TO FREDA KIRCHWEY, August 2, 1934, TORONTO

Dear Freda Kirchwey:

Thanks for your letter. I wondered why you did not write sooner. I concluded that you may have gone away on your holiday. I asked my niece Ruth Commins to get in touch with you by telephone. Meanwhile your letter came. I am delighted to know that you and your confrères like my article. It is all right about the cuts you have made. I feel sure you have not deleted the important parts. About the proofs: Please send them to my nephew Saxe Commins, 1361 Madison Avenue. I have already written him to get in touch with you. I should like a set sent here. I want to see how the article ["The Tragedy of the Political Exiles," *Nation*, October 10, 1934] reads after the deletions.

Dear Freda Kirchwey, it would take too long to argue our differences regarding Russia. I understand your point of view and that of the *Nation* only too well. As liberals you are naturally satisfied with small favors you see in the Russian experiment. Being a revolutionist, I cannot content myself with the real or imaginary (mostly imaginary) achievement of the soviet government. You say "the soviet government has abolished the GPU and has relaxed its control over various cultural expressions; the schools, too, are being liberalized." I agree that these "changes" have been made—on paper. But I am just as certain as I can be that in their application everything will remain the same in Russia as before.

To cite one instance: When the Cheka was turned into the GPU you and all other apologists of soviet Russia proclaimed the glad tidings to the whole world. Because I refused to believe in the change I was denounced as a counter-revolutionist and charged with having sold myself to the capitalistic class. Nevertheless we who had insisted that terror goes merrily on have been vindicated by many subsequent events. And now the soviet press itself admits that the GPU had "overstepped" its power, had sent innumerable people to concentration camps and to Siberia without a hearing or trial by the old Czarist administrative methods. To be sure the soviet satraps will not admit the tortures employed by the GPU and the barbarous treatment meted out to tens of thousands of unfortunate victims. No, not only of political opponents, but masses of workers and peasants, not to mention the Trotsky adherents.

No doubt the next change Stalin will make, the world will learn that the department that had replaced the GPU had been using the same terrors as its forebears. I do not have to wait till then. I know there is no change and there can be no change as long as the dictatorship exists. The very fact that Yagoda has remained the commissar of the new political department is proof for my contention.

The trouble with you, my dear, and all others who are carried away by the soviet experiment is that you fail to realize that the methods employed by the communist state are inherent in the dictatorship. It doesn't matter by whatever name the methods go. They are essential to the dictatorship and can be nothing else but terror.*

The liberals and radicals have denied the existence of the famine in '32–'33, as they also deny the fact that the peasantry is being terrorized into the collectives, or exiled by the thousands. Yet, it remains true nevertheless. This has been proven by students and observers of conditions in Russia—by people who have lived there for years, have traveled the length and breadth of the country—incidentally, people who are favorable to the soviet government. Naturally the interests of enthusiastic visitors à la Bernard Shaw and others swallow everything given to them by their

---

* Worthy of passing note is the fact that these sentences might have served four decades later as an appropriate epigraph for Alexander Solzhenitsyn's indictment of the horrors of the Gulag Archipelago. Unhappily that empire of police and prison terror was indeed flourishing in the 1930s and, as Emma foresaw, grew to even more monstrous dimensions in the succeeding decades.

official guides. Not so people who live in Russia for years as correspondents, keen students, and observers. . . .

I cannot share enthusiasm for the "collective society" the soviet government is attempting to create. I hardly need to emphasize my stand on private capitalism. I have fought it all my life. But collective slavery is nothing to be excited about or any improvement on the slavery created by the capitalistic class. It is merely a change of masters. With this distinction—that one may sometimes hope to find among capitalist masters one more humane than another. But, the state capitalist machine in operation in Russia has no humanity whatever. It crushes all alike. I for one cannot accept it. Nor do I understand how liberals and radicals can accept a complete state of monopoly of every breath of life and action which is the very nature and expression of the dictatorship.

The fact that the bourgeois press has in the past and does now misrepresent Russia should not have bearing on those who all their lives have fought for libertarian ideas. After all, the most important phase of a critical attitude to Russia is the premise from which one starts. I do not criticize Russia because Stalin is too revolutionary, but because he is not revolutionary at all. You will agree that that is not the position of the capitalist papers. It seems to me that liberals cannot consistently smooth over every outrage committed in the name of socialism, at the same time objecting to the suppression of liberal ideas at home. Yet they have maintained a conspiracy of silence about everything in Russia, although they are fighting similar evils in other countries.

As regards the "many fundamental economic, social and political changes brought about by the Russian Revolution." You are the first to credit these changes to the Revolution. All other admirers and apologists of the dictatorship have lost sight of the Revolution altogether and have credited everything to the soviet government. It happens that the Russian Revolution and the communist state are as far apart as the poles. I cheerfully admit that the Russian Revolution has struck deeply into the minds and hearts of the Russian people; that it has created a new human type. But what bearing has that on the state machine that has crushed the Revolution? I could cite innumerable examples to prove my point, but one will suffice. It is the eagerness of the great powers to take Stalin's regime to their bosom. Yes, even such ultra-revolutionary governments as Mussolini's and Hitler's. Russia wants to make peace with Germany. This, after the bloodbath of June 30th, after the strangulation of a man like Muehsam and thousands of other victims done to death by Hitler's henchmen. But I fear that the adherents of the wonders in Stalin's dominion are worse than the blind. They have eyes, but they refuse to see.

Certainly, we anarchists realize that "all governments maintain themselves by force and that the measure of repression varies almost directly with the degree of stability and security achieved by any given group in power." But there is this much to be considered. Other governments do not pretend to be the advance guard of the masses. They do not claim to work for socialism or communism. Nor can other governments boast of three revolutions in twelve years. We therefore have the right to demand more from such a government than any other. I expect nothing from the bourgeoisie. In fact I marvel that there are still a few liberties left in capitalist countries. But I do demand more from a revolutionary government. Yet far from living up to its pretense it denies its principles every day. In point of truth there is less socialism or communism in Russia now than in the most difficult years when the Revolution was surrounded on many fronts.

No one would be happier than I if I could have given credit to the soviet regime for some "modifications of their repressive tactics." But the many underground letters we receive from our unfortunate comrades in Stalin's Polit-Isolators and remote parts of Siberia speak too eloquently against the so-called modifications.

You see, my dear, my understanding of revolution is not a continued extermination of political dissenters. I was told once by Robert Minor that individual human life does not matter after all. I consider that an outrage of revolutionary ethics. Individual life is important and should not be cheapened and degraded into mere automaton. That is my main quarrel with the communist state.

Sincerely yours,

[EG]

AB TO EG, November 4, 1934, NICE

Dearest Em,

I am in Nice. When I came in I found here already a call from my "man." I went at once to see him. He is on a vacation, but another man looked up the matter. I got six months all right, so that part of it is OK. I'll get the new [permission] paper in about a week or so. . . .

I see what a difficult situation you have there with the new craze of our people about making a common front with the communists. To think of them wanting to make common cause with them and even believing they could accomplish anything! It is worse than stupid. It is just downright idiotic. They have evidently learned nothing. It is the same as Zenzl [Muehsam] thinking she can "exploit" the communists for her purposes! I wrote her about it and Mollie [Steimer] also did. But in such matters advice is useless. It is a CONSTITUTIONAL weakness in our people even to conceive such an idea. They will be swallowed, that's all. It is really the same, in essence, as the Mussolini idea of the corporative state: bringing labor and capital "together." The result is the same as bringing the wolf and sheep together. Peace is established by the wolf making a meal of the sheep. That will be the fate of our people in the common front with the communists.

But what is the use eating your heart out about it, dear? To FORCE our people, even morally, into the right path, is entirely useless as well as a hopeless thing. For you may convince them against the common front—for a while. I feel that AT HEART they are NOT anarchists, however they may mouth about it. For it shows absolute lack of understanding of the anarchist spirit and meaning, and also lack of understanding what the communist tactics, aims, and purposes REALLY are. And if such understanding is lacking, it is useless to persuade our people against their intended step. For such persuasion CANNOT be of lasting effect. The moment your influence is lost, in your absence, they will NATURALLY act again according to their INNER feeling. And it is that inner feeling that is the trouble in the whole matter. They feel, see, judge, and act wrong, and that is not to be changed with that bunch. The only hope is in a NEW generation of anarchists that will really FEEL their anarchism. And that will take time, much time. I am afraid the world is bound to go through dictatorship before it will come to its senses. Dictatorship of such as the Mussolinis and Hitlers, and later on the communist dictatorship. From what we know of history and from our own experience in Russia etc., that really seems inevitable. Very tragic, but I am afraid it is so. I embrace you, dear little fighter and faithful soul.

Yours ever,
S

EG TO AB, January 5, 1935, MONTREAL

Dearest Sash,

. . . I enclose a clipping about the resignation of Horace Kallen, Clifton Fadiman, Carl Van Doren, and Suzanne La Follette from the International Labor Defense League. It had to be wholesale murder before they would budge from their infatuation of the communist gang. Like [Oswald Garrison] Villard, who finally protested against the Russian "purge." It is sickening to see how callous everybody has become. No one is interested any longer in human suffering and in incessant butchery. Yes, they kick when it is in Germany or their own countries. But Russia can and does get away with murder. As you so well said in your letter to Stella, Hitler is beginning to be praised. Sure, nothing succeeds like success. Fact is, dearest, we are fools. We cling to an ideal no one wants or cares about. I am the greater fool of the two of us. I go on eating out my heart and poisoning every moment of my life in the attempt to rouse people's sensibilities. At least if I could do it with closed eyes. The irony is I see the futility of my efforts and yet I can't let go. Just clear meshugeh [crazy], that's what I am. . . . I embrace you with love,

Em

EG TO AB, January 24, 1935, MONTREAL

My dearest,

. . . John Haynes Holmes lectured here. I had him for tea Monday. Lucky people who can see crowds all day, eat, and enjoy their lives on the day of lectures. The older I get the greater the purgatory. Holmes is a good sort personally, but a terrible demagogue on the platform. Mixing everything together, for instance that Lenin immediately after the Revolution set to work to rebuild Russia and such other perfectly idiotic statements delivered in the most sensational Barnum and Bailey manner. I hate to say such unkind things about him. For did he not put me among the "ten greatest women in modern times"? And did he not give the most laudatory review of *Living My Life?* I am an ingrate. But I can't bear demagoguery. He may not even be aware of it. I think he is like most Americans, naive and childish in social and political affairs. Like Roger Baldwin. You will see the idiotic statement he made about Russia in the last *Nation* I sent you. I can't believe that he is not actually of the opinion he advances. Yet it seems incredible for an intelligent man to believe that the workers in Russia are economically free. But then Roger is by no means alone. I can't begin to tell you what a fad and a superstition Russia has become among adherents as well as opponents. Just think, Scott Nearing was here for three lectures. He packed a large hall every evening. Tuesday John Strachey spoke; 1,200 people paid 75 cents and $1 admission. There is some reason for hearing Strachey, he is an ex-MP, belongs to one of the most distinguished British families of writers. He himself is the only brilliant exponent of bolshevism outside of Russia. I read his work *The Coming Struggle for Power*. It is really brilliant and if one did not know the crookedness of Marxism and Leninism, most convincing. In fact I would have gone to hear him myself, if I had not bought tickets to Eva Le Galliene's performance of *L'Aiglon*, a stupid play, though she is a supreme artist. Anyway, everyone who comes here singing the praises of Russia draws mobs. This merely goes to prove the sweep of the dreadful fake and how it has caught the imagination of most people. What wonder that I have such a frightful task? Well, it has to be faced: no one wants what we have to give. Not now and not for many years to come.

And yet it is interesting to hear Holmes say, "Well, EG, you and Berkman are coming into your own. You were the first to disclose the butcheries in Russia. Now we all know and have to admit it." You see it required the "purge" to rouse the Holmes, Villards, and a few others. The rest have remained indifferent or continue to justify the murder. Dush, dearest own dush, I am a fool to keep pegging away at windmills. . . .

Em

EG TO ROGER BALDWIN, June 19, 1935, ST. TROPEZ

Dear Roger,

If I remember rightly, you were to come abroad. I hope this is still the case and that you will also pay us a visit. The plunge from seventeen months' intensive activities to the isolation and routine of St. Tropez makes me feel the need of my friends on the American continent more than when I myself was nearer to them. Well, whether this will find you in New York or not, I am sure it will be forwarded. You see, I don't want you to think I had forgotten you. It is only that I came back so completely fagged out mentally, I had not the energy to keep up my correspondence. Perhaps it is not mental exhaustion so much as the realization the ninety days in America [February–April 1934] gave me. To wit that I had failed to acclimatize myself during all these years to any place in Europe. For a revolutionist and internationalist it is indeed disgraceful to be so rooted to the soil of one country. Perhaps one cannot adjust oneself easily in later years as one does in one's youth. Whatever the reason, I have to admit defeat. The ninety days of my return dispelled whatever doubts I had on that score. I know now that I will remain an alien abroad for the rest of my life. Not a happy feeling. But it will have to be endured. It is only for the present when the old wound has begun to bleed again that I feel futile to myself and my comrades.

You will understand that such a mood is not conducive to writing. Besides, the response to the appeal has shown very little interest in another book from me. Not that I blame anyone. Times are hard and in the present world uncertainty and madness people have other things to think about than literary effusions about personalities in my life. After all, one must be honest with oneself. *Living My Life* has also not set the world on fire. Yes, the reviews were marvelous, yours among the most understanding and sympathetic. But reviews do not sell books. Advertising does that. And Mr. Alfred A. Knopf believes in advertising only best sellers. That and the high price for the two volumes just killed my chances. This is ancient history. I merely refer to it to give you my reaction about the proposed second work by me. I may feel differently later on. Just now I have no inner urge to write, and those who have been approached also have not shown need of reading what I might have to say.

Another factor which would make it impossible to begin writing is my old pal AB. While he looks much better than I had expected from the reports I got all last year, he is far from being strong. He tires easily from writing. Yet he must keep at the [Rocker] translation he has undertaken. To continue with that he needs inspiration and care. I prefer he should get that than write myself. Well, I take comfort in the certainty that the social revolution will come whether or not I give the world another "master" piece. I wish I had the same certainty that it will be more successful than the social revolution in Russia.

How do you find my dear Ann Lord? I was delighted to learn that she is connected with the American Civil Liberties Union, if only in an indirect way. She is such a genuine and lovely spirit. I feel sure you find it pleasant to work with her. She was a great comfort to me the few months we were together.

Dear Roger, in your letter under date of April 16th you say apropos of the rotten use of my article by Hearst [in the New York *American*, April 7, 1935]: "One of the great difficulties about any criticism of the Soviet Union from the left is the misuse to which the reactionaries put it." You then go on to say that you had often considered it more important to keep silent rather than permit the reactionaries to misuse your criticism. I am not quoting you in this part. I merely give the gist. Well, I can't agree with that attitude. It seems to me that one's first consideration in any critical attitude must be whether the wrong thus criticized rests on facts. The gravity of the issue alone should decide one's criticism. For, if one is first going to consider the use reactionaries are going to make, one will always have to remain silent. And by silence one becomes a party to the wrong. What is more to the point, one thereby betrays one's faith with the masses, indeed with one's highest ideals. True, you do not believe that the bolsheviki are bartering away the Revolution, that they have betrayed the trust of the Russian masses, indeed, the trust of the international prole- tariat. That somewhat mitigates your silence when speaking out is so necessary. But I do believe it. Every day more proof comes from Moscow how brazenly the regime has denied the Revolution. How then, can I keep silent, or be concerned first of all to what use the reactionaries will put my criticism? Compared with the crime of Moscow against the spirit of the Revolution and its aims, the misuse of my article by Hearst is insignificant altogether. You might as well expect silence on my part in the face of the daily proofs for the Judas treachery of Stalin and his aides. Never since the selling of Christ for thirty pieces of silver has such a heinous crime been committed by men who dare speak in the name of the Revolution.

No, it was not my concern with the misuse Hearst made of my article. All I was concerned about was that the liberal element in the States should know that I had nothing whatever to do with the Hearst rotten deal. Now that my statement has appeared in the *Nation* and in the New York *Evening Post*, as well as the anarchist press, I no longer care about Hearst or anything the communists say about me. I do not even care about the effect the gang had on the appeal.

I wonder how you feel about the latest stunt of Stalin re his love match with French militarism? Do you believe in silence in this too? You remember when we met in Niagara Falls what I told you about the united front with the communists in the work against war and fascism. I told you there is no reliance whatever in the Jesuits, that they will go back on their anti-war stand when Moscow gives the order. That is exactly what the French communists will now do, stop their passionate campaign against French militarism. I would not be surprised if they also stopped their anti-fascist attacks when it will suit the designs of Stalin to make common cause with Hitler and Mussolini.* In what way are the French fascists and militarists better? Yet here is the virgin pure communist leader Stalin shamelessly going to bed with the bourgeois harlot, France, and everybody finds it suite comme il faut [quite proper]. It is enough to make the gods laugh. Well, you and the other intellectuals in Europe and America may keep silent. Never will I do it. In the last analysis one must not do what Ibsen has Stockman say, "spit in one's own face."

This is our old bone of contention. Isn't it, dear Roger? Thank goodness, Stalin has no power over our freedom to disagree or our desire to remain friends. So you must come along. I will be delighted to have you.

Please give my kind greetings to Miss Doty [Baldwin's secretary?]. I am so glad one of my sex proves more consistent than you, dear Roger, and other males who think as you in re Russia. But then, it is your charm that makes one forget your illogicality and inconsistency.

Affectionately,

[EG]

EG TO AB, November 26, 1935, LONDON

Dearest Sash,

Today is the first day since I wrote your birthday letter that I can permit myself the luxury of writing you. You have no idea how I had to drudge since my arrival, all the time being in awful pain in my leg. I guess I must have been bitten by a bug because the cold I got in the crossing was over in forty-eight hours. But my leg is still pretty sore, though no longer as inflamed and swollen as it was. Neither is the pain so unbearable. Imagine then preparing a difficult lecture like Mussolini, Hitler, and Stalin and delivering it under such a handicap. Yes, I found it extremely difficult to

* As you will observe, Emma all but supplied the date of the Hitler–Stalin Pact (August 23, 1939).

compress such a vast subject in one lecture. I found an awful lot of material in [Armando] Borghi's book on *Mussolini, Red and Black,* and in Don [Levine's] *Stalin.* Besides considerable material on Hitler. Dealing with such a subject, it is absolutely essential to be able to document every statement. As it was I had the devil's own time last night with the communists. It was of course unpardonable on the part of the comrades to saddle me with a new subject, when I had sent them a list of twenty. And it was a crazy idea to have the subject announced in the Jewish district. Well, the communists came out in full force. They did everything except break up the meeting. But that was only due to my presence of mind, and my self-control on the platform. But I came away with frightful pain in my lungs and chest. And today I feel as if I had been gone over with a steam roller. I have not met with such a wild, ignorant, and fanatical group of people in a long while. They are terrible, really as terrible as the nazis or fascists. Well, it's over. Only I wanted you to know why I have permitted more than a week to pass by without writing you, except postcards.

I speak again Thursday on Fallacies of Political Action. I am not so worried about that as I was about yesterday's lecture. By the way, the hall was jammed to suffocation. But it is not very large, holds about 250 people. I don't know what Thursday will bring. Sunday I go to Leeds for one lecture. The 7th to Plymouth for a week. They have already arranged four lectures and the comrades expect to have more. So it is not likely that I will have much time for rest. . . .

Devotedly,
E

AB TO EG, *January 9, 1936, NICE*

Dear girl,

. . . Well, dear, your energy and vitality are to me a source of constant wonder and admiration. The things you manage to do, the numbers of people to see, parties to attend, and at the same time read and prepare lectures, and—not to forget, to write long letters! It is simply astounding. . . .

About Mollie [Steimer] and the statement you want to write to the New York *Times* re the Russian persecuted. Well, I don't think an appeal in the *Times* would do any good, but a statement regarding the persecution of anarchists, seeing that the socialist statement completely ignored it, is in place. The time is past when Russia was to be treated differently than Italy or Germany. I would expose Stalin in the New York *Times* the same as I should expose Hitler, if they would give me a chance.

As to Mollie saying that our comrades in exile etc. in Russia would object to a statement in their behalf in a capitalist paper—that is very likely. But our work cannot be controlled by the attitude of comrades in Russia, for the latter are not in a position to judge. They are too much torn away from the world and events to be able to judge the situation.

As to the so-called lefts—that is, the liberal elements—I have no use for that brand in the U.S., where I know them. They are a very dangerous element: they will go with the crowd that is liable to succeed. Now they are bolshevizing, but most of them would not want America to become bolshevik—if they know what is going on in Russia. In any case, they'd be the first to be put to the wall by the triumphant bolsheviki, in the U.S. as in Russia.

As to the liberals in England—I don't know much about them, but I am inclined to believe they are of the same brand as their American brethren.

Well, dear, it is clear that you have not a very easy field to hoe in England. But it will be in England as in the U.S. Unless a mass movement—revolutionary anarchist—can be created, we shall only have a few followers here and there. We have failed to create a mass movement in the U.S.—it was only fellow travelers, as they call it in Russia now, sympathizers more or less—because a mass movement must have an immediate, constant, daily active interest in the work of the movement [i.e., people]. That we lack, and that we will have to create, if we mean to play any role in the social life, on a vital scale. How that is to be done, that's another question, and a very difficult one. . . .

Affectionately,

S

If you like something

DIFFERENT

READ

Revolutionary Labor Paper

Forbidden in the U. S. Mails

Published every 1st and 15th of the month
by ALEXANDER BERKMAN

569 Dolores Street

San Francisco

$1.00 the year   Send for free sample copy

196   (OVER)

American (still) radicals at work

EMMA GOLDMAN

will deliver three farewell lectures in Chicago
before going to Jefferson Prison for 2 years

Friday Evening January 11, 8 P. M.

Douglas Park Auditorium
Ogden and Kedzie Aves.

SUBJECT

America and The Russian Revolution

Saturday Evening, January 12, 8 P. M.

at East End Hall
North Clark and Erie

SUBJECT

Women Martyrs of Russia

FINAL LECTURE

Sunday Afternoon January 13, 3 P. M.

at West Side Auditorium
Taylor St. and Racine Ave.

SUBJECT

The Spiritual Awakening

OF RUSSIA
WHEN WILL AMERICA AWAKEN?

ADMISSION 25 CENTS
QUESTIONS AND DISCUSSIONS

**UNDER THE AUSPICES OF THE NON-PARTISAN
RADICAL LEAGUE**   358

MOTHER EARTH

Vol. X.   January, 1916   No. 11

CONTENTS

EMMA GOLDMAN, - - **Publisher and Editor**

Office: 20 East 125th Street, New York City

Telephone, Harlem 6194

Price, 10 Cents per Copy   One Dollar per Year

AB in Moscow, 1920
IISH

EG in Moscow, 1921
NEW YORK PUBLIC LIBRARY

Perpetual exile commences, Stockholm, 1922   IISH

Brief reunion: AB and "Fritzie" (M. Eleanor Fitzgerald), Berlin, ca. 1925

FLECHINE/IISH

Edited by Alexander Berkman   Labor Papers : Please reprint

BULLETIN OF THE RELIEF FUND

of the International Working Men's Association

for Anarchists and Anarcho-Syndicalists Imprisoned or Exiled in Russia

| No. 4 | PARIS-BERLIN | November, 1927 |

A DECADE OF BOLSHEVISM

The Communist dictatorship in Russia has completed its first decade. It may therefore be interesting and instructive to sum up the achievements of the Bolsheviki during that time, to visualise the results of their rule.

But "results" are a relative matter. One can form an estimate of them only by comparing them with the things that were to be achieved, with the objects sought.

What were the objects of the Russian Revolution? What have the Bolsheviki achieved?

The Romanov regime was an absolutism ; Russia under the Tsars was the most enslaved country in Europe. The people hungered for liberty.

The February-March Revolution, 1917, abolished that absolutism. The people became free.

But that freedom was only negative. The people were free from the chains that had held them bound for centuries. Now their liberated arms and spirit longed to apply themselves, sought the opportunity to do, to act. But THAT freedom had not yet been achieved. The people were free FROM some things, but not TO do the things they wanted.

They wanted positive freedom. The workers wanted the opportunity to use the tools and machinery they had themselves made ; they wanted to use them to create more wealth and to enjoy that wealth. The peasant wanted free access to the land and a chance to cultivate it without being robbed of the products of his hard toil. The people at large wanted to apply their new-won freedom to the pursuit of life and happiness.

The negative liberty of the February-March Revolution was therefore quite unsatisfactory, unconvincing and inadequate. That is why the people soon began to continue the revolution, to deepen it into a social transformation. To make the social revolution, in short. The soldiers dropped their guns and left the fronts en masse. They knew they had nothing to fight for in foreign countries. They returned to their fathers and brothers, the peasants, and together they drove the landlords away and went to work on their own mother-land. The industrial proletariat at the same time expropriated the lords of industry and possessed themselves of the mills, mines and factories. Thus the laboring masses of Russia came into their own, for the first time in the history of the world.

As always during revolution, this activity of the Russian masses proceeded outside the sphere of governmental influence. The struggle against oppression — whether political, economic or social — against the exploitation of man by man, is always at the same time also a struggle against government itself, against government as such.

The Russian Revolution, like every revolution, faced this alternative : to build freely, independently of government and even despite it ; or to choose government with all the limitation and stagnation that it involves. The path of the Russian Revolution lay in the constructive self-reliance of the masses, in the direction of no-government, of Anarchism.

Between February and October, 1917, the Revolution instinctively followed that path. It destroyed the old State mechanism and proclaimed the principle of the federation of Soviets. It used the method of direct expropriation to abolish private capitalistic ownership. In the field of economic reconstruction it employed the principle of the federation of shop and factory committees for the management of production. Proletarian and peasant organisations attended to distribution and exchange. House committees looked after the proper assignment of living quarters. Street and district committees secured public safety.

This was the course of the October-November revolution. In that spirit it kept growing and developing.

But this development of the Revolution was not in consonance with the philosophy of Marx and the purpose of the Communist Party. The latter sought to gain control of the movement of the masses, and gradually succeeding, it gave an entirely different turn to the work of social reconstruction.

Under cover of the motto, "the dictatorship of the proletariat", it began to build a centralised, bureaucratic State. In the name of the "defence of the Revolution" it abolished popular liberties and instituted a system of new oppression and terror.

The Bolshevik idea was, in effect, that the Social Revolution must be directed by a special staff, vested with dictatorial powers. The fundamental characteristic of that idea was a deep distrust of the masses. According to the Bolsheviki, the masses must be made free by force. "Proletarian compulsion in all its forms", wrote Bukharin, the foremost Communist theoretician, "beginning with summary execution and ending with compulsory labor, is a method of reworking the human material of the capitalistic epoch into Communist humanity".

The Communist Party proceeded "reworking" the human material. Compulsion and terrorism became the main means toward it. Freedom of thought, of the press, of public assembly, self-determination of the worker and of his unions, the initiative and freedom of labor — all this was declared old rubbish, "bourgeois prejudices". The "dictatorship of the proletariat" became the absolutism of a handful of Bolsheviki in the Kremlin.

Practically the Communist dictatorship worked out as follows : free exchange of opinion was suppressed ; the initiative of the individual as well as of the collectivity, so vital in life, and particularly in revolutionary times, was eliminated ; voluntary co-operation and organised free efforts were wiped out ; every revolutionary element, not Bolshevik, was exterminated or imprisoned. The people's Soviets were transformed into sections of the ruling political party ; the labor organisations found themselves deprived of all power and activity, serving only as the official mouthpiece of the Party orders. Each and every citizen became the servant of the Bolshevik State, its obedient functionary, unquestioningly executing the will of his master, the all-powerful Kremlin dictators.

The inevitable results did not fail soon to manifest themselves. The Bolshevik policies corrupted and disintegrated the Revolution, slayed its soul and destroyed its moral and spiritual significance. By its bloody despotism, by its tyrannous paternalism, both petty and stupid, by the perfidy which replaced its former revolutionary idealism, by its deadening formalism and criminal indifference to the interests and aspirations of the laboring

AB's "voice in the wilderness"   IISH

EG, St. Tropez, 1929

AB presented this photograph to EG, along with a note on the back
to his "dearest Em" signed with his customary "S" for Sasha

May be you can recognise
a "few things here
dearest Em

Back of the your "Dance"
is your set of
"Mother Earth" over the
fireplace.
And above it. ???

affectionately

Ever S.

St. Cloud
Sept. 5, 1927.

3

Anarchism and
Violence

From Pillar to Post: Arrested in Latvia: the revenge of a Chekist. Spending Christmas [1921] in prison with Emma Goldman and another friend [Alexander Shapiro]. Liberated with apologies and "advised" to leave the country. Chasing for visas. Danger and fun. Invited to Sweden by Prime Minister Branting. I write an article for a Stockholm paper in behalf of the persecuted politicals in Russia. Result: the bourgeois press attacks Prime Minister Branting for offering the hospitality of Sweden to "dangerous anarchists." We are requested to leave. Refused a visa by several countries. I stowaway on a tramp steamer during a great snowstorm. I manage to get to Hamburg and lose no time reaching Berlin [March 1922]. Life in Germany during the inflation [1922–25]. . . . I rechristen myself "Dr. Schmidt" and try to explain where and why I was born. The adventures of living without "documents." Discovery in Bavaria and my timely escape.

ALEXANDER BERKMAN, *An Enemy of Society*

"NO doubt our faith has been shaken by the fiasco in Russia," Emma observed, "and yet I do not think it is so much our faith in anarchism as an ultimate ideal of society as it is the revolutionary part in it." The experience of bolshevism up close had indeed strengthened their distrust of the state and deepened their commitment to freedom. By Kronstadt, and for Emma before, both had had the lesson driven home that revolutionary means must be welded unbreakably to revolutionary ends. They knew all along that the dissolution of power, not its acquisition, was primary among the goals of real revolution, but Russia put this insight into focus: How is the insurrectionary thrust toward freedom to be protected against betrayal by the centralizers? Emma Goldman and Alexander Berkman had, in short, identified in their pain and sorrow a central problem of anarchist thought, or of what Milton Kotler has called "the central dilemma of revolution," that is, "how democracy of local control can withstand nationalist re-establishment of central power" (*Neighborhood Government*, 1969).

The letters that follow are in a sense the obverse or positive counterpart of those in the preceding section: there Alexander Berkman and Emma Goldman drew up their indictment of compulsory communism; here they made their case for libertarian or anarchist communism. On the run, nearly crushed by what they had witnessed, always insecure, they somehow found the strength to rework their ideas so anarchist thought could better cope with the dilemma of revolution and in particular with violence as the well-worn shortcut to central power and its concomitant armies, secret police, prisons, concentration camps, and other instruments of terror.

Emma energetically set about working out a theory of revolution as essentially "a process of reconstruction, destroying as little as possible," came round to the belief that acts of violence had proved useless, and

chided her comrade for not having outgrown the old revolutionary traditions and beliefs in which he had been "steeped." Berkman rejected her
views as too sentimental and womanish and found historical precedents
and justifications for acts of terror. For Emma, such appeals to history had
become the new superstition, like the will of God. And so they went at it,
with each other and others, honestly, sometimes with insight, and always
with impressive credentials as expert witnesses, since they had lived close to
violence all their lives. At stake was their faith in anarchism or, as Emma
put it, faith in an ideal "which to me contains all the beauty and wonder
there is in life."

How anarchism might meet the challenge of violence as a topic was
touched off by the Russian Revolution, the reaction, the rise of fascism,
the threat of a new war. It involved the role of the beleaguered individual,
the elevation of demagogues, the acquiesence of the masses. It was
channeled and shaped by their writings during this period, which included
their books on Russia, Berkman's simply stated *Now and After: The ABC
of Communist Anarchism*, which was published by Vanguard in 1929,
Emma's *Living My Life*, published by Knopf in 1931, and in various
articles and pamphlets, including Emma's "Was My Life Worth Living?"
Harper's, CLXX (December 1934), 52–58; "There Is No Communism in
Russia," *American Mercury*, XXXIV (April 1935), 393–401; and the
posthumous *The Place of the Individual in Society* (Chicago: Free Society
Forum, 1940 [?]). Although their arguments are in their publications, the
personal experiences and the events out of which they emerged are in these
letters. Here you can see how they encouraged each other during times of
despair, how they worked together in agreement and disagreement—how,
as Berkman put it, "we have always shared joy and misery alike."

EG TO HAVELOCK ELLIS, November 8, 1925, BRISTOL

Dear Mr. Ellis:
Your kind letter of October 24th was forwarded to me in this city,
where I have been since the 16th of October, delivering a series of lectures
on the Russian drama. I will repeat the same series in London at Keats
House, Hampstead, beginning November 12th. I dare not hope that you
will have the inclination or the time to attend some of the lectures of
interest to you. But if you could, I should be very happy indeed.

Thank you so much for the kind appraisement of *My Disillusionment
in Russia*. Your kind words mean very much to me, but why do you think I
will not agree with your point of view regarding the possibilities of revolution to produce real anarchism? Indeed I do agree. I have never, as far as
I can remember, believed that revolutions will usher in a social structure

which will rest upon individual liberty and voluntary social cooperation. I DID believe that the present system will not go without some violent upheaval. Not because I am in favor of violence, but because old institutions have a tremendous tenacity to hang on. However, I have not thought in the past and it certainly does not occur to me now that a violent change of institutions would be sufficient to usher in a new era.

It is true that my Russian experience has made me see what I did not see before, namely the imperative necessity of intensive educational work which would help to emancipate people from their deep-rooted fetishes and superstitions. With many revolutionists I foolishly believed that the principal thing is to get people to rise against the oppressive institutions and that everything else will take care of itself. I have learned since the fallacy of this on the part of Bakunin—much as I continue to revere him in other respects—that the " 'Spirit of Destruction' also contains the element of construction."

Certainly the Russian experiment failed to demonstrate this idea. The people who so heroically made the Revolution were so easily whipped into line and so easily became submissive to the communist state because they were taught that it is sufficient to make a revolution and the rest will follow. Two years in Russia compelled me to transvalue my values. I assure you it was not an easy task. I found that the most difficult thing is not to bear what other people think of you, but what you think of yourself. Equally difficult is the realization that one was mistaken. Well, there was no choice left except to face facts, which I think I have done.

I repeat, I still believe that great social changes have not and cannot take place without some clash. After all, revolutions are nothing else but the breaking point of accumulated evolutionary forces. Such a breaking point is inherent in nature and expresses itself through violent storms. Equally so are the forces inherent in life. Every change from the old to something new creates violent upheavals in our being. So too, such upheavals take place in the social and economic life of the world. But I have come to the conclusion that the amount of violence in any revolution will depend entirely upon the amount of preparation on the part of the conflicting forces—the amount of INNER preparation.

By preparation I mean the growth out of old habits and ideas. I know that that is a difficult process, and yet people will have to realize the process and will have to be willing to go through it, if revolutions are not to end, as they have in the past, in a new despotism which out-tyrannizes the old. I realize that we can neither make nor prevent revolutions. They are as inevitable as hurricanes. But at least we can prevent endless repetition of the mistakes and cruelties of the past. In my critical work against the present regime in Russia I am constantly confronted with the suggestion that after all the bolsheviki are merely repeating the methods of the jacobins and that they could not do otherwise. That seems an absurd position to take, especially on the part of people who proclaim their faith in progress. I am never able to understand what they mean by progress, if they approve of methods employed in the past. To me progress means a change not only in ideas but also in method. Here we are, 140 years after the French Revolution, with advancements in every domain of human thought and social affairs, and yet we have developed nothing better than photographic repetition of the methods of the French Revolution. In fact we have, to use an American expression, "gone the French Revolution one better." Even at the very height of the jacobins they did not succeed in so completely suppressing every thought and every breath of life as the bolsheviki have. I feel, therefore, that the attitude of a great many people toward Russia and Russian reality merely demonstrates a great confusion of mind and unwillingness or inability to face the facts.

Take for instance the attitude of the socialist and trade-union elements in this country. They are straining every nerve to dam the onrushing tide of reaction, and justly so. Yet these very same people will have nothing to do with the least criticism of the terrible reaction in Russia. All the good people like Mr. [Bernard] Shaw, Col. [Josiah] Wedgwood, [H. G.] Wells, Mr. [George] Lansbury, and the rest, rushed to the defense of the communists, which is very commendable of course. Yet they keep silent on the cruel fact that in Russia today political opponents of the regime have not even the right of asking to be released on surety or to defend themselves. Frankly, I have no patience with such inconsistencies. I certainly do not approve of the persecution of communists. But to protest against this and to keep silent on a wrong equally great, if not greater, since things done in Russia are in the name of socialism, to me is rank hypocrisy.

Well, I could go on and on, but I do not wish to burden you with a long epistle. I do, however, want you to know that I am not foolish enough to believe that revolutions at best will usher in anarchism. They may pave the way, but there will still be no end of groundwork to be done, before anarchism will become the basis of individual and social life. Of one thing I am certain, however, that no other theory has the inherent quality to establish individual freedom and social harmony.

Kind greetings,
[Emma Goldman]

EG TO BEN CAPES, *February 16, 1927, PARIS*

Dearest Bennie boy,

As you see, I am still in Paris. I am leaving the 27th of this month for London, so it will be best if you write me to my old address there. I will not live at Titchfield Terrace any more, but the woman who has the house is an old comrade [Doris Zhook] and will look after my mail, so you are safe in writing there all the time. . . .

The wave of nationalism of the Jews is nothing new as far as I can see. It was the same after the Kishenev pogroms and every other massacre. I know that men like Zhitlovsky and others are sincere in their nationalistic feeling and strivings. To me, however, there is nothing more reactionary than just that feeling. I spoke on the subject years ago. And more than ever the last years have convinced me that there is no hope for mankind so long as they are divided through boundaries and blinded by their nationalistic viewpoints. You will find that Rudolf [Rocker] maintains the same position. I am so glad he will be able to prevent the error into which our comrades and many other well-meaning radicals fall into when they look to nationalism as the solution of the pressing problems.

As to the contentions of [Ludwig] Lewisohn that the striving of Jews has been and is away from the state: That is undoubtedly true, but that is largely because, as Ibsen said, "The Jewish [people], not being handicapped by a state, were able to contribute to the highest culture of the world." It is certain that the moment the Jews will have their own state, they will become as reactionary and centralistic as all other nations. However, I cannot discuss the subject before I read *Israel*. I hope you will send it soon.

I am so glad you will make it your business to get to Chicago for Rudolf's visit. Aside from the tremendous good the man will do, his personality is sure to inspire all who come in contact with him. He is wonderful, one of the truly big men in our movement, and the finest human being in public life today. What a pity he does not lecture in English. I am sure it would have tremendous success, besides awakening the living dead in the various movements. And you will like Milly; she is such a lovable creature and such a true comrade. I wish I could be with you and Rudolf and Milly. But that is a thing which will never be realized, at least not in America.

I should say the individual can have and does have tremendous influence. It is only the individual who can arouse and inspire, never the mass. If only there were more worthwhile individuals. The Rockers are rare, very rare.

I am glad to know that [your daughter] Florence is beginning to realize the emptiness of college life and how little it has to do with real education. I hope she will go on developing and growing. It is always best to let young people come to see things for themselves; they gain more by it and have deeper respect and regard for the ideas of their parents if they are not interfered with. I am glad too that you both have remained great chums. May it always be that way. Give her my love, and also to [your wife] Ida and the boy.

I wonder has anyone written you that Eric B. Morton lost his daughter Anita. She died of cancer, poor soul, after a prolonged illness. Almost at the last moment Morton wrote me to get after an English authority on cancer, Blair Bell, a Liverpool man. Which of course I did at once. Alas, the girl died within three days after the letter was written to me. And Bell could do nothing anyway; he said he'd have to see the patient first. EB is broken up not a little. He wrote me with great pride last year that Anita, who had belonged to a circle of the Young Communist League, left the organization because the idiotic communists called him a counter-revolutionist. She was evidently a clever girl. It is all so sad. But EB has remained the same genuine human being, with a lot of quality of character and an independent mind.

Well, dear, I hope I have made up by the length of my letter for the time I kept you waiting. Write when the spirit moves you. I am always so glad to hear from you, my dear.

Affectionately,
EG

AB TO EG, *June 24, 1927, PARIS*

Dearest Em,

In a few days is your birthday. Seldom before did I long so to be together with you on this date as now. Because somehow you seem awfully far away. And your plans are so uncertain that I find myself always thinking about this: are you coming or are you staying there [in Canada] for this year? Because you wrote that Peggy [Guggenheim] has signed $500 for your autobiography and also some other people, so that there already must be a good sum for the fund. In that case, do you still think of remaining there? Of course, I realize that you have probably pledged yourself for lectures and meetings and maybe it is too late to change things.

I should like very much to have you here this summer—if you decide to begin your book and to return. But of course you know what the summer is in Paris. It seems to me that THIS summer is the worst I ever saw. Here it is the end of June. We have had a few very hot days in April even. Then the rains started, and there has not been a day that was free from rain or the threat of rain. And it is chilly, even cold. It is 10 A.M. and I sit here in my room dressed and with my morning gown on, and still I am cold. No sunshine at all. I have not become warmed up since winter yet.

Well, you know how I love the sun, and this weather has a very bad effect on me. I must tell you frankly, dear: since I wrote the short introduction to the book [*ABC of Communist Anarchism*], which I sent to you, I have not written a single page, though I have been at my desk every morning from 8 o'clock till 1 P.M., and then again from 3 to 5 or 6.

I have gotten in such a condition that I can't think straight and can't write. Well, you know what it means. You know how some parts of your book [or rather the ms. "Foremost Russian Dramatists"] worried you in St. Tropez. But at least it was chiefly at the END of your work. But here I am at the very beginning and I am just stuck. Over and over again I have tried to start the second chapter and every word I write makes me dissatisfied and I change it and the next day I don't like it again and change [it] and then I tear up the whole thing. I begin again, and with the same result.

The thing has gotten terribly on my nerves. Well, I don't have to explain to YOU this condition. You know from your own experience, and you also know how I feel when I can't write what I want to. You know how I feel before a lecture. Well, this is a thousand times worse.

I can't explain to myself the reason. I have dropped the work for several days, then I feel that the thing is not hard to write at all and I seem to have it all clear in my mind. But the moment I get back to it, it begins all over again. Maybe it is also the weather—it depresses me. Anyhow, I have now gotten to the point where I don't feel that I can write it at all. Neither the ABC, nor the way I meant to write before. The whole matter oppresses me terribly. I am almost in the state in which I was [when] reading proof on my [Prison] Memoirs. You remember. I can't tell any more a good sentence from a bad one. My head is just in a whirl.

Now, dear, I don't want to make you feel bad about it, but I want your opinion. I feel like giving up the work, but I hate to do it, and yet I have lost faith in being able to write it. I know how terribly the comrades will be disappointed and what a Blamage [disgrace] it will be. But what can be done? The book is supposed to be ready for October or November. But it can never be, even if I should be able to write it after a while. Of course, it is not important, if it will be ready later, but I don't feel that I can work on it at all. I feel entirely arbeitsunfahig [incapable of working].

In every other way so—it is even an effort for me to write a letter. But I think that is because I feel very oppressed by the book—deprimiert, as Emmy says.

Speaking of her, she tries to help in every way. Walks on tiptoe all day and is kind and nice in spite of my crankiness. The house is clean and quiet, the meals are good, and everything is all right, and absolutely no reason why I should not be able to write. There is nothing to worry me—and yet I can't write. It is the fact that I *have* to write this book that worries me.

It was a big mistake that I accepted it. Maybe I could write it, if I did not have the feeling that it has been ordered from me, that people are waiting for it, and so on. Anyhow, I have now decided to take a week entirely off. To go out, see people, forget about the book entirely. Then to begin again.

If I can't write then either, then I must give it up. Of course, I will have to return the $150 that Minna [Lowensohn] (the [Anarchist] Federation) sent to me. I've used more than a hundred of it already, but somehow I shall have to make it good. Of course, I'll have to find then something to do that will bring in a little—Emmy can borrow a little money, though not much. (In case of necessity I could write Mac [Cohn] about it. He stopped sending [money] when I wrote him that I accepted the book and that the Federation sent me $150. I told him then that it relieves him.)

Well, I hate to write you all this, for I know it will make you miserable. But we have always shared joy and misery alike, and I feel better by telling you about all this.

Perhaps I should postpone writing it till next year? What do you think? Because you would then be here, won't you, and I think then—when you work on your book [the autobiography], and I on mine [the ABC]—I should be able to work better. But I am not even sure of that, dear. Some other work, I am sure, I could write better when you are about, when I can consult you, and so on. But *this* work—I don't know, dear. Maybe I can't write it because we have lost our former enthusiasm about it—I am afraid to think of it, for if *that* is the real reason, then there is no hope for it. It means that I could not write this book *at all*.

So you see how it stands, dear. It is rotten. I am terribly worried about it, and that also makes me unable to write.

I want your advice. Better cable me. But as I write this, I ask myself *what* advice you could cable, and if advice by cable could help me any. Still, I want your advice, dear. But I don't want you to act hastily, to drop everything there and to come here. No, dear, that is not necessary and, who knows, it may not even help me, perhaps. Because I really think it is the weather that oppresses me, mostly. I even thought of going south, but I don't want to risk it, because of the expense, since I have to pay rent till October here, anyway. But chiefly because I have a feeling in me that I wouldn't be able to write in the south either. The weather etc. all may have some oppressing effect on me. But the *chief reason*, I think, is some feeling in myself, way deep down, that I won't write it to my satisfaction. And that feeling makes it impossible for me to write at all.

So it is my own condition of mind, and not any external cause, that prevents my writing. Of course, if you plan to return in connection with your book, then I should be very happy. But I don't want you to do it specially. It may serve no purpose perhaps. For somehow I feel a disgust about writing the book and something repellent in me about it, and so even your presence will not help.

Well, I am going to take off a week, or even two maybe, and then I'll see. Maybe it is all just a *temporary* feeling. I hope it will pass. I'll let you know. I can't write of other things today. Nor is there anything important. [Henry] Alsberg was to have arrived. . . . He has not shown up. He had asked me to write him to the American Express about meeting me. I wrote, long ago. No word from him, though he has also my St. Cloud address.

Senya [Flechine] started to work at a photographer's. I hope it will be at last a trade for him. Mollie [Steimer] got the money you sent.

Everything else is as of old. I embrace you, dearest heart,

[S]

EG TO AB, July 4, 1927, TORONTO

My dearest,

Your letter of June 24th reached me today, just within ten days. That is quick sailing. It found me with a crowd of people in my place, my sister Lena [Cominsky], her husband, brother Herman, his wife and child—a Mishpocheh [family] I really have nothing in common with. They motored over from Rochester Saturday and are leaving tomorrow. I should not have minded my sister and brother, but the wife of Herman is simply fierce, she is so loud and so impossible. Well, fortunately the visit is not for long. Now they have gone to their room and Lena has gone to bed so I am writing this in my kitchen where it is quiet and I do not have to disturb anybody.

Sash, my dearest, the first impulse when I read your letter was to cable you that I will book passage on the first steamer out. Your letter made me see how miserable you must feel, not being one who complains easily. You may believe me when I tell you that I would give much, if I could follow my impulse. But even if I set aside the consideration of the people I have organized and who are so eager for me to remain, I could still not sail now because I have no money. The gifts of people for my birthday would barely pay for my passage back to France. And then what? I think I already wrote you that all the money which has come in for the fund of the autobiography are seven hundred dollars. What am I to do with that? How long would it last me, if I were to return and start to draw on it? I could not even find the excuse that I would immediately begin writing. I could not, if I tried, as I would need months to gather my material, possibly to go over to England to work in the British Museum for a few months. That would swallow up a lot of money. And what after that? . . .

However, I do want to help you overcome what is already forming into an obsession with you, the idée fixe that you must have the book ready by October, or any definite time. I know it is this which makes you feel so terrible [about] not being able to write. Now, there is no reason on earth to feel that way. I have written you in my long letter a week ago yesterday that a book [such] as you have in mind cannot be shaken out of one's sleeves. It must be done carefully and easily and not in a rushed way. Besides, neither you nor I can write to order. It is therefore necessary first of all that you set your mind at ease. That you realize you have not sold your soul to the Federation; you are not bound to masturbate mentally until you will be ill and then bring forth a Wasserkopf [waterhead, i.e., person suffering from hydrocephalus]. Now listen, dearest, if you think it will help you to get rid of your feeling of obligation, write the Federation as follows, "I have begun to write the book but I have discovered that it is not a work of four months, or any specific time. It is an undertaking which requires much thought, reflection, and contemplation. That you must have unlimited time." I am sure the Federation will understand. Once this is done, I would suggest another thing. Go away to the seashore for a few weeks. The only expense you will have is extra rent for the time and travel; it will cost no more for food, or very little extra. You certainly need sunshine. I know how dull rainy weather affects us both, but I know that lack of sunshine affects you even more than it does me. It is therefore of the utmost importance that you should get away for a few weeks, perhaps to St. Tropez. . . . The question is, how do you stand for money? Has the Federation sent more than $150? Has Fitzie sent you some money? I know that Howard Young collected $50 for your book and that Ben Capes has collected $35, which he sent Fitzie. Now these $85 would be enough for a few weeks in the south. I am writing Fitzie to send that money, as she may not be in a hurry, thinking you do not need it. You simply must get away for a few weeks or for a month. Dismiss the book from your mind altogether and bake in the sun, bathe, swim, play ball. Really, dearest, you must do it. As to your house, lock and board it up; nobody will steal it, or the contents. . . .

You may ask, "what about the book when I return?" You will continue as you have started, which, as I have both cabled and written you, is a splendid style and will turn out to be the most valuable ABC work on anarchism in existence and so badly needed. At any rate you could continue in the style you began until you come to the part when you will have to deal with anarchism during revolution. Then you will either change the style, or if you find it too difficult, I suggest that you will then ask the collaboration of Rudolf Rocker. It is a most common thing for two or even three people to collaborate on a work. Saxe [Cominsky or Commins, her nephew] wrote his work [*Psychology: A Simplification* (1927)] with his friend [Lloyd Ring] Coleman. Professor [Charles] Beard just had a work on America published with his wife [Mary]. And there are any number of such cooperations. I feel that Rudolf is the one and the only man who is close to us not only temperamentally but also in ideas. He could work out the difficult part with you together, or you with him. Of course, you will share with him whatever you will get from the Federation according to the time he will need for his part. Another thing is that once you get into writing and I am back you may be able to do the whole book yourself. I feel that the thing which has sort of paralyzed you is the consciousness that you must have the book done by October, which is sheer nonsense. Whoever heard of writing an important work in a few months? Anyway, Dush, think over my suggestions and if you agree, lose no time in getting the load off your mind.

No doubt our faith has been shattered considerably by the fiasco in Russia. And yet I do not think it is so much our faith in anarchism as an ultimate ideal of society as it is the revolutionary part in it. Naturally, this lack of faith has much to do with your inability to write. But more than anything else it is the consciousness of being bound to time and the Federation. Get rid of both, [but] not by returning the money. That is impossible, dearest, because it is no longer a question of the $150 you received. The sale booklets are in circulation and money is being raised in a number of places. It would be ridiculous to stop it all. Of course, if after you have had a few weeks' sunshine and you come to the conclusion that writing is impossible, you will probably have to give it up and write the Federation quite frankly how you feel. But I do not think you should do it now. See how it feels when you free yourself from the *whip* which now drives you, time, obligation to have the book ready to the minute. And also after you have had some sunshine. There will be time enough then to come out frankly. . . .

Dearest, I am sure that Emmy is doing her utmost to make it easy and comfortable for you and I am most happy that this is the case. Naturally she cannot help you with the writing, you have to be near people who have gone through the events in our movement in the world. Not that I feel my presence will enable you to write, unless you feel the urge to do so; still we have done things together and as you say in your letter, it might help you when I too will be writing. There is no doubt that one needs a literary atmosphere to be able to work. But again I say, let us see how it will *be when you have relieved your mind of having to write, or having to send the ms. within a few months.* Perhaps your bent is literary and not theoretical; you are at your best in descriptive things, I know that. You have really never tried socio-theoretic writing on a large scale. That may well be your difficulty, and of course our change of attitude toward the whole social question. I know how I feel, I find it most difficult to discuss theories. Well, Dush, if you will find after you have thrown off the burden of being coerced, and of a definite time when you must be ready that it is impossible to write, you will give it up. Never mind the "Blamage." Frankness is always the most important thing, frankness and honesty with oneself, never mind what the comrades will say. . . .

Well, my dearest own pal, it is 12:30 A.M. I must close. I will add a few lines in the morning before I seal the letter; maybe there will be something from you telling me you feel better. I would gladly send you a cable, but one can say nothing in a regular cable and the weekend letter cannot be sent until Saturday; by that time I may have an answer from you in reply to the cable I sent you the 25th.

My dear Sash, please do throw off the thought and feeling that you must force yourself to write because you promised, and all such nonsense. You will feel better then. Affectionate greetings to Emmy. I embrace you tenderly. Devoted love,

E

AB TO EG, *December 7, 1927, ST. CLOUD*

Dearest Em,

Your long letter of November 18 and the next of November 25 both came together, today. Also enclosures, clippings, and papers.

I see your letters are no more cheerful than before. You ask for a frank reply. Well, I think I have always been frank with you. The difference between some people is that one may say an unpleasant thing in an unpleasant manner, while the other says the same thing in a less offensive way. The latter is my mode.

First, about your "field." You know what I said in St. Tropez. I did not much believe you would find such a field in Canada, or anywhere. I was, though, in favor of your TRYING Canada, mainly because I knew you would never be convinced unless you tried the matter out yourself. I am sure that if you had given it up as a result of [Dr. Michael] Cohn's advice, you would have kept on thinking that you missed a chance. It is always that way in life. We think we "miss" something in not doing a certain thing, and then we must convince ourselves.

Well, I don't think you have to regret going to Canada. There is nothing to regret. But I suppose you are convinced that our movement is dead, was in fact never much alive, and that there is no field for you in Canada. I personally do not even believe that there is a field for you in the U.S. or anywhere else. In the U.S., for instance, you would have crowds for a while, then the novelty would wear off, and you would find that reaction is triumphant everywhere. Times are worse now even than before the war.

It is tragic, and I realize what it all means to you, personally. Yet you are too individualistic. In your letters to me, as well as to other people, I find much more emphasis on the tragic aspect of the case, so far as you personally are concerned, than upon the tragedy of the thing so far as anarchism and the anarchist ideas and propaganda are concerned. I know how great your tragedy in this matter is. But the other tragedy is still greater, very much greater. It seems to me there is no field in the world for the propaganda of anarchistic ideas; at least not just now. That there is no opportunity is merely the consequence of the fact that there is no need for it, no field for it. Yet I am fully convinced that the world does need our work and that some day it will count. But the present reaction simply excludes all chances of work for us—temporarily, anyhow. I mean, any effective work.

It is therefore that I declined, some time ago, your plan of a weekly paper in Canada—I knew then as I know now that there is no field for it. The same applies to Mexico, and to other places. One can *artificially* create some temporary interest, some excitement, and then the thing dies out. I have come to the conclusion that work in the unions offers much greater chance of real propaganda and education than just lectures for outside and chance audiences. But that is another subject.

I want to say by all that that there is either something wrong with our ideas (maybe they don't fit life) or with our mode of propaganda for the last forty years. In any case, if you have no large meetings etc. there, it is not YOUR fault. The fault is much deeper.

From that I conclude that there is no use at all [in] your remaining there. Why continue work that serves really no purpose? It does not even secure your mere living.

I am therefore very much in favor of your returning as soon as you can.

Now, you condition, to some extent, your return upon my life here. I don't see why you do so. We are old friends and what difference does it make who is in my life as my sweetheart? You always remain for me what you always were in my life. I really don't see why you stress the point so much.

As to my work, you know how much your opinion helps me. I have often wished you would be somewhere where I could at least reach you within a day or two days, even by mail, so as to consult you on various points. Canada is too far away for that. As it is, I have been looking forward anxiously and impatiently for your opinion of the eight chapters I sent you. It is true that we often have entirely different views on many matters; we come to the same conclusions, very often, by entirely different routes, sometimes even by opposite routes. But we have always helped each other in our work, in spite of all that.

In the last analysis, of course, each must do his own thinking and his own writing. I could no more write your book than you could mine. But each can help the other with advice, suggestion, etc. Yet I would not want you to return simply for that reason, because I am sure that you will be miserable with life in Paris.

That may surprise you, but I am sure of it. One can live in Paris and enjoy it *with money.* You will find Paris very much dearer than it was when you left. Money goes like hell every time I visit Paris even for a few hours. Imagine that we two spend over a hundred dollars a month, and neither of us has bought hardly anything to wear. We seldom go to the theater or a concert, unless I get free tickets. And we invite almost no one here; we live very modestly and economically. Emmy is a good cook and careful with

money, and yet we spend more than $100 a month, because she occasion-
ally gets gifts of money, small sums, from her people, yet all of it goes
without one noticing where to. Because life in France has become very
dear. If you will have to economize every penny in Paris, you will not find it
much to your liking. Besides, I know you need company, people, you will
have many visitors, and all that means special expense. That means that
life in Paris for you would be quite expensive and that you will not be able
to work here, either. One must live away from friends in order to do serious
work.

That means the south, then. It is cheaper there. . . .

That brings me to help with the book again. The point is this: once I
started the book as I did, I must continue on the same plan. It cannot be
changed any more; I mean the plan cannot. I can alter the simple language
a bit into more complex, but that also is not particularly necessary. Now,
that means that I cannot go into any deep theories of anarchism, particularly not of the past. Because if the book is written for the AVERAGE reader,
for the working man, then he is not interested in anarchist theories, either
past or present. I must keep the book logical. And logically I should treat
the WHOLE book from the standpoint of COMMON SENSE, as I have treated
all the other questions so far.

If that is so, then I cannot write theory. I must write definite PLANS and
SUGGESTIONS as to 1) how to bring about the revolution; 2) how to carry the
revolution on; 3) how to develop out of the revolution anarchist conditions.

Of course, I can mention the theories, but only insofar as they will serve
the purpose of my book. But to detail especially the theories (Proudhon,
Bakunin, or Kropotkin)—it seems to me that it will be entirely out of place
in my book—the way it is written so far.

On this I particularly want your opinion and advice. You see, dear, if
you were here right now, I mean in Paris, I would simply take the train and
consult you on all that bothers me. But it would be too selfish of me to
want you to come back here just for the sole purpose of having you near to
consult. As I say—if there is nothing to hold you there, come back and let's
have some time together.

You fear that it might hurt Emmy. You mean, I suppose, if I spend all
my time away from here? But I could not afford to do that, anyhow, as I am
so far behind with my work. My progress is damned slow. I'm afraid I won't
be ready even by March. Not one half of the book is done yet, and even
that needs much changing. I only have about three chapters written, after
those eight that I sent you. And these three I have to rework a great deal.
By the way, did you not get yet those eight chapters?

Anyhow, my book often gets on my nerves, and people too, I must
say—of late. I have gotten to hate Paris and the fearful crowds there.
During the last two weeks I have been in Paris only twice and I was just

made sick by the masses on the street, the crazy rush, and stupidity of it all. I have gotten used to the quiet here, and I have no desire to see people. . . .

In conclusion, dear, I hope you will come [by the] end of January or as soon as you can. I embrace you as of old,

S

EG TO AB, *December 17, 1927, TORONTO*

Dearest,

Only yesterday did I get your ms. It took all this time to wrench it out from the teeth of the damned customs here. I read it last night and today I sent you a cable of the following contents: MANUSCRIPT SPLENDID MERRY CHRISTMAS JOYOUS NEW YEAR LOVE. The cable was sent from the main office of the Canadian Pacific; in case it does not reach you I will be able to trace it. Yes, dear heart, I could not resist the temptation to cable you. What is $1.53, if I can convey my impression of your work and send you a holiday greeting?

I realize that it must have been hell to write, but I think it was worth the effort. Without flattery or any attempt to kid you, I seriously feel that the chapters you sent me are splendid for the kind of book you have set yourself to do. It is so simple, a child should be able to understand it. If only you can proceed in this style and method you will really have made a great contribution toward the simplification of our literature. And inasmuch as you will bring it up to date, the book will also be most timely. Really, dear, you should not eat your heart out so much. You keep on worrying about the time it takes to write the book. What on earth does it matter, if it will take a year before the book is done? Nobody has written anything worthwhile in a rush and hurry. Why then do you let time weigh so heavily on your mind? The main thing is whether you are on the way of giving something worthwhile. I am positive you are. There might be one or a few changes necessary in the final revision. For instance, in your preface, which is short and to the point, I should not refer to Kropotkin or anyone else not having done a book accessible to the man on the street. It is unnecessary. Fact is, [Errico] Malatesta's "Talk Between Two Workers" on anarchism is as simply written as yours, the difference being that you are going to have a whole book in that plain style and that your work will deal with the subject in the light of modern events. Therein will be its great value. And you are on the right track and have so far written in truly direct and splendid speech. I realize this method is hardest, but you are doing it, dear, so why worry so much? Just go on and leave the rest to the time of revision. I am sure you will find it much easier to revise, leave out or add what you will find necessary once the whole book is written, than doing it bit by bit. You are losing the connection now and only eating yourself up.

More and more I am convinced that we must have a new literature. I have recently gone over some of Peter's [i.e., Kropotkin's] works, *Conquest of Bread*, his pamphlets, and *Fields and Factories*. In some things the old man was remarkably clairvoyant and prophetic. For instance, in his prediction of what the authoritarian socialists will do on the day after the revolution. Every word uttered twenty-five years ago or even longer has come true. They sound almost as if written in Russia in 1917. Or when he wrote, also in *Conquest of Bread*, that "The Social Democrats will hang the Anarchists, the Fabians will hang the Social Democrats, and the Reactionaries will in the end hang the Fabians." That too is gradually coming true. In other words the old man saw many years in advance. But more important is his remarkable keenness as to the advance of science, chemistry for instance, which will revolutionize agriculture, will make it possible to produce intensively on a small area by artificial light and heat enough to feed tens of thousands. The same regarding modern invention as to the tremendous increase in production. Really, it is uncanny how well he knew the future. In this respect Peter's works are really up to date. But I will grant you that he was very romantic when it comes to his prophecy [of] how the masses will act on the day after the revolution. It's in this line that he was mistaken, of course, and that something new based on the experience in Russia must be given. The entire old school, Kropotkin, Bakunin, and the rest, had a childish faith in what Peter calls "the creative spirit of the people." I'll be damned if I can see it. If the people could really create out of themselves, could a thousand Lenins or the rest have put the noose back on the throat of the Russian masses? I don't think so. I honestly believe it is necessary to stress the fact that the masses, while creating the wealth of the world under duress, have not yet learned to create it voluntarily for their own needs and that of their fellows. And unless they learn it, every revolution will and must fail.

Now, dearest Sash, your book, while giving a searching analysis of the causes of capitalism, the wage system, etc., etc., will also have to strike a new note along the lines I have indicated above. Hold the mirror of slavish acquiesence and willingness to follow any charlatan who can hoodwink the workers up before your readers, to stress the urgent necessity for the masses to learn how to construct, to rebuild, to do independent work for themselves and the community without the feel of the master's whip. You will come to that part later, I know. I am only suggesting it now while it is on my mind. Meanwhile, you should feel encouraged that what you have written so far is certainly very much worthwhile and that you should go ahead in the same strain. . . .

Kind greetings to Emmy. Goodby, dearest Dush. Lots of love,

[EG]

AB TO EG, June 25, 1928, PARIS

Dearest Em,

It is early in the morning and the first thing I want to do is to send you a greeting to the 27th.

But I have a feeling that you will not enjoy your birthday very much, because your book weighs on your mind. So does mine. Yet I think we are both wrong. We take things too seriously. But of course that is in our natures and we can't help it. But we take our *work* also entirely too seriously and that embitters many an hour for us.

At times we realize how little it all matters. How little life itself matters and how empty it is. But enough—this is no mood for a birthday. But I think a little of this is necessary when worrying about one's work—it may help to get over the hard places. . . .

I don't know why you have such difficulty in starting your work. Maybe you can't concentrate because of too many distractions and visitors. We had talked the first part over and came to the conclusion that you begin with your childhood. In any case, you have a lot to write about your childhood and it should be done in a full, reminiscent way.

Or you begin with Rochester and your coming to New York and then review your early impressions as a strong influence in your development.

I want to hear how matters are going.

At this side, I have come to problems that cannot be solved satisfactorily. For instance:

(1) Has the revolution a right to defend itself? Then what is to be done to active enemies and counter-revolutionists? It leads logically to prison or [concentration] camp.

(2) If there is some trouble somewhere—a murderer or raper, etc., has been caught by the crowd—will you let the mob spirit prevail? Or is it not better to create opportunity for a hearing for the accused? That means tribunes and courts and police. And what should the courts do? It is no use having them if they cannot restrain the further activities of the guilty man. It means again prison.

(3) Given an example—what is likely to happen: People starting to make a pogrom in Russia; or whites trying to lynch a Negro in America (this during the revolutionary epoch)—shall we let it go at that? Is not active interference necessary? By whom? By "the people"? But suppose those present are afraid to interfere. It means again that armed force is necessary in such cases, even against the mob. And the leaders of the mob who persist in exciting race or other hatred—should they be permitted to go on?

I fear there is *no* answer to these questions, except the organization of house and street guards etc.—in fact, of police, under whatever name they might be known. But that again brings us to courts and prisons, for you can't allow the police to settle matters. If anyone is arrested, he must have a chance of a hearing. But if there is a court, when and what are its powers? Can it restrain the offender and how? It comes to prison again.

But once we begin with prisons, there is no end to it.

Yet how avoid it? If I write the second part of my book *logically*, as it should be written, then it won't square with anarchistic views. To avoid these questions is impossible. That means then a *transitory period* with punishments, prisons, etc., which is sure to develop the bolshevik ways and methods.

Da ist der "trouble." Everyone avoids these problems. But then what is the use of writing my second part? I have been thinking hard about these matters; there are moments when I feel that the revolution cannot work on anarchist principles. But once the old methods are followed, they'll never lead to anarchism. That is the choice we have to make.

Let me know what you think about this. . . .

I'll take a quiet drink alone Wednesday in memory of the 27th.

Affectionately,
S

EG TO EVELYN SCOTT, *June 26, 1928, ST. TROPEZ*

Dearest Evelyn,

. . . My dear, it is very kind of you to have such faith in my book. If I had half the belief in it which you and the few other gracious friends [have], writing would be a pleasure instead of a curse. To me one of the great delusions is the notion that writing is joy. (It may be to some, as interjected by my impetuous secretary—damn her—but it is not to most.) In fact, some of the greatest writers have suffered agony of spirit during the process. I may not have greatness in common with them but, by Jesus, I've got the agony.

Apropos of my secretary Demie [Emily Holmes Coleman]—she is really no good as an ordinary typist (lie)—she not only thinks while I dictate, but she corrects me every time I say anything she doesn't agree with. You can see she follows my train of thought—in fact, so much so that she calls me a god-damned liar and yet we have been together only three weeks. But she is such an ass that I don't mind what she says in the least.

I am glad, my dear, that you understand my feeling in respect to the relation between social and historic events and one's own life. People who will have it that human beings rise out of their background, never having had their roots in the past, simply don't know what they are talking about. It is true that in order to survive one's traditions or background one must have considerable will power and determination. But it is also true that some of the most sensitive and subtle beings—by the very virtue of their sensitiveness—have been crushed by the circumstances. I am not sure that they have not given greater things to the world than some of us who have overcome every difficulty. We still have very little knowledge of human values—of the things men and women could do were they given a chance. Why then feel that those who have succeeded (I do not mean in a material sense) are more worthwhile than those who have not? For myself, I have always believed that the deepest failures have very often been the greatest successes. Emil Ludwig can certainly write. It is this capacity which makes his Napoleon so plausible. I am sure it is that, much more than Napoleon. And it is his childlike faith in him which helped Ludwig create so vivid and glowing a personality.

But I am much more inclined to agree with Tolstoy that Napoleon was great because of the smallness of the people surrounding him—the cowardice which took possession of the world after the French Revolution—the cringing fear of its own skin which saw in Napoleon a savior. All that merely proves in my estimation the eternal truism that those who raise an individual to a pedestal are usually the first to tear him down. Nothing in life is so blind and so cruel as adulation which arises from ignorance and fear and not from understanding. . . .

I want very much to have the memoirs done by June 1929. That year will have deep meaning to me. In the first place I will have rounded out sixty years—certainly the largest part of one's life. And I will have given forty years to my ideas. I realize that most of them were spent in chasing windmills, in trying to present to the world an ideal which to me contains all the beauty and wonder there is in life—the only raison d'être for my existence, and the world less than ever wants to know anything about it. You can imagine that I would despair utterly if I did not believe in the ultimate triumph of my ideal. And even more so if it had not been—and will continue to be so the rest of my life—the one dominating motive. You can see why I should like to finish my memoirs by next June. But of course I do not intend to rush or do slipshod work. I certainly need to take my time about it. . . .

Lovingly,
[EG]

EG TO AB, June 29, 1928, ST. TROPEZ

My dearest,

Although I worked until one last night and read until two, I woke up very early this morning. I was awakened by the sound of hay cutting. A friend of Mussiers' came about five to cut his wine [or vines] and flowers, the faded ones of course. It was a peculiar sensation to hear the scythe go on monotonously; it made one drowsy, yet unable to sleep. Anyhow I got up, had my coffee, cut flowers for the day. And now I want to talk to you.

Since I began writing at 9 P.M. Tuesday, I have written six thousand words. I have no idea whether the damned thing is good or rotten, whether it hangs together, sounds plausible, or whether it is chaotic or unreal. I will be able to judge better when the stuff is typewritten. This afternoon we begin with the job. I will dictate to Demie [Emily Holmes Coleman] on the machine. You know how difficult my writing is, especially when written in haste and excitement. Besides I can go on correcting and changing as I dictate. It will probably take us two afternoons to do the job, as I must go slow with Demie. . . .

I have made up my mind not to let you see a line until you have finished your book. I simply won't let anything take much of your time or interfere with your writing. There is really no need. Sufficient unto the day for you to tell me the stuff is no good. . . .

A little break in my work won't do any harm. Anyway I hope to hear from Fitzie and you today when she is starting. Funny life is, here we have been worrying who should meet Fitzie, then that crazy Djuna [Barnes] kidnaps her. Damned fool. Why did she not let you know she is going to Havre, or take you along? Really, the Lesbians are a crazy lot. Their antagonism to the male is almost a disease with them. I simply can't bear such narrowness.

What looked to be a dreary and lonesome birthday turned out to be a gay affair. All thanks to my thoughtful secretary. She had quite a conspiracy, invited the Gershoys, Saxe [Commins'] friends, bought three bottles of champagne and some delicious cakes, and marched everything up to our terrace, ice and all. I had suspected that Demie is up to something; she is a poor conspirator. But I did not expect champagne. Well, we drank until eleven and then went down to the village to dance. We came back at two in the morning. I got up a bit tired yesterday, but I wrote all afternoon. So you see the champagne must have been good, it had no after effects. I enjoyed the party immensely but even more so Demie's fine spirit, her thoughtfulness. . . .

Now to your letter of the 25th. You are certainly right when you say we take our work too seriously. But we would not be ourselves, if we approached our work in any other way. After all, it is not whether what we do matters to others but how much it matters to ourselves. To do our work lightly, or to be haunted by the thought that it does not matter because life itself does not matter, would mean that we could do no work at all, writing or otherwise. And without the work we care about, life itself would be impossible. It certainly would to me and I am inclined [to think] it would be the same with you.

Your problems are of course tremendous. If they were not, there would have been no object in writing your book. It is because you want to give something new, answer some of the problems in a new way, that your book is important. But on the other hand you are trying to do the impossible, you are trying to solve all problems in one work. Not only is this impossible but no one human being can solve all problems, nor are they solvable in a theoretic way. The most anyone can do is to solve fundamental problems from which to build further. The rest must be solved by the need of the hour or moment—in fact, by life itself.

However, a few of the questions puzzling you I think could and should be answered. First, "Has the revolution a right to defend itself?" Certainly, if you believe that no fundamental change can take place without a revolution, you must also believe in its right of defense. It is only Tolstoy's or Gandhi's position which would make it inconsistent to take up arms in defense of the revolution. I wish I could take their position. Emotionally I really do. I feel violence in whatever form never has and probably never will bring constructive results. But my mind and my knowledge of life tell me that changes will always be violent. At least I want to eliminate as much as possible the need for violence. I want the revolution to be understood as a process of reconstruction rather than what we believed it to be until now, a process of destruction. But no matter how much we will try, the change is bound to be violent and [we] will need to be ready for defense. The question is, defense against what and of what? This brings me to your second question, "active enemies?" What do you mean by "active": opposition by means of opinion, theoretic activities, writing, speaking? If you mean that, then I insist that you must come out unreservedly for the unlimited right of free speech, press, and assembly. Anything else will create all the evils you want the revolution to fight. Surely we have learned enough of the effect of suppression in America, then in Russia, to continue to believe for one moment that the revolution can ever gain anything by gagging people. All it succeeds in doing is to drive thought into secret channels which means the utmost danger to the revolution. Fact is, very few people who can express themselves through the word make good conspirators. I know that from myself. And if you will look up the lives of nearly every one of the terrorists of the past, you will find invariably that they either never had a chance to speak out, or that they were not ready [or capable] of expression by means of the word. After all the dominant motive of any act or word is the need to express oneself and what one feels deepest. I say, therefore, that unlimited free speech even in the revolutionary period is a thousand times less harmful than thoughts driven to secrecy. If however you mean by active opposition, armed attack on the revolution, then I say the defense must be armed. Naturally if you are attacked by a robber and you have a weapon, you will use it. I see no inconsistency in that at all. But while armed defense is inevitable and justifiable, prisons are not, whatever the offense. Granted that rape or robbery may happen, they are after all isolated cases. I do not think they need to happen even in the most critical period of the revolution, so long as everyone is given a chance to participate in the rebuilding of society, so long as each can be made to feel a personal interest in the process of building. Why should there be robbery? Why should the meaning even be used? If a man holds up someone now, it is considered robbery—how can it be that when no one has more wealth than another, when he receives out of the common stock as much as anyone else, or rather as much as there is to go around? You can't begin to solve problems that have changed their very nature and meaning. . . . That seems ridiculous.

Rape is another matter, I grant you, that may happen since sexual hunger or aberrations will continue for all times. But because of an occasional rape, should society set aside special places and a special class, a complete and expensive machinery to restrain an occasional rapist, when we know from centuries of experience that prisons do not restrain, or even lynchings, or capital punishment of any sort? I therefore say that you must set your face sternly against the very idea of prisons: the whole revolution would be utterly futile, if such terrible institutions as prisons, institutions which have proven a failure in the system we want to get rid of, are again established.

"Mob treatment": No certainly not. Anyone caught in a violent act against his fellow should be given all the chances to be heard in his own defense. He should have the feeling that he is not being tried, [but] that he is being heard to get at the cause or motive of his act. That if he cannot explain it himself, he should be studied by eminent men to whom the human soul is not a means to wealth, station, and prestige, but a terribly vital and interesting phenomenon that needs careful treatment and care. I can only say what I have so often said in reply to the very question you find difficult to answer. What we need is to revalue our conception of human acts. For instance, no one suggests that we should lock up a tubercular person; why then should he be locked up for something conditioned in his being for which he is even less responsible than tuberculosis? I think the sympathetic treatment of such an offender in a sane society would act as a better cure, stronger deterrent, than prison or punishment of any sort.

Pogroms, lynchings, any mob action is of the same nature as armed attack on the revolution: one has the right to fight it back with arms, to defend oneself or the person attacked. But one cannot. . . .

> [Here the letter breaks off, with the remainder missing or destroyed. Luckily Emma returned immediately to the discussion in the letter which follows.]

EG TO AB, July 3, 1928, ST. TROPEZ

My dearest,

. . . When I wrote you I had solved some questions while in Canada I did not mean that I had given thought to every breath of a community during a revolutionary period. I had in mind a few fundamental issues from which all else springs. Now I insist that a transvaluation of the very nature and function of revolution is bound to have a profound effect on some of the questions now troubling you and for which I am certain there is no solution separate and distinct from the nature of revolution itself. I repeat what I have told you in the first talks we had and have written in my last long letter, unless we set our face against the old attitude to revolution as a violent eruption destroying everything of what had been built up over centuries of painful and painstaking effort, not by the bourgeoisie as we used to maintain, but by the combined effort of humanity, we must become bolsheviks, accept terror and all it implies, or become Tolstoyans. There is no other way.

On the other hand, if we agree that revolution must essentially be a process of reconstruction, destroying as little as possible—nothing at all in fact except such industries that make for war and disease—if we can realize and boldly declare that the only purpose of revolution must be transformation, then terror must go with the rest and prisons and other evil things of today must go with the rest. I will grant you that it is not enough to declare that revolution must become a process of transformation. But how is it to become that? This brings me to the second conclusion I have come to while in Canada and which we discussed so many times. Namely the nature of expropriation. In the past we believed and many of our comrades still do that the purpose of the revolution is to expropriate everybody, whether large or small owner of his place of work, that they must be divested of everything and that it must become the property of the workers; in other words, everything must be taken away from one class and given to another. The layers are to be changed [but] the thing which holds it [i.e., the class structure] in its place remains. Now we have seen in Russia that this has been fatal. The expropriation of handicrafts without an industry that can produce the needs of the country has led to the chaos from which the Moscow regime is now desperately trying to extricate itself. . . . Once we transvalue the value of indiscriminate expropriation to the expropriation of powerful combines [and] of large land holding and once we declare that the expropriated wealth is not merely to change hands from one class to another, but from the few for the common use of the entire community . . . 99% of the evils which necessitated the terror in Russia will die a natural death. Where then does theft come in, or robbery? Or even much counter-revolution? You know as well as I that most of the supposed revolutionary plots were concocted in the Cheka. And that after the old nature and application of revolution [i.e., after application of old theories of revolution]. The new conception leaves very little cause for counter-revolution. Should it occur nevertheless and should it assert itself in an armed attack, the community which now has a share in the revolution because of the interest given has the right to defend the revolution against such attack. But I am inclined to think that where most of the community is involved, armed attack is sure to be reduced to the utmost minimum and for such a minimum you cannot continue the very thing revolution aims to undermine, prisons, police, Cheka. This holds good as regards rape, which is rare enough even under our present regime. It used to be punished by death in the past. Man has progressed somewhat, since rape is no longer considered on a par with murder. In fact, if you were acquainted with the vast amount of works on modern criminology (I read about ten while in Canada), you'd see that even today rape is being studied as part of other sexual manifestations and not as crime; you would also find that quite a different kind of treatment is being suggested by psychologists (who do not even claim radicalism) than prison. In short, it seems to me that instead of concentrating on fundamentals, you have wandered off to detailed manifestations inherent in fundamentals. You have run into a Sackgasse [blind alley], Sasha dear. If you continue, you will never finish your book. For there is no end to the intricacies of life which may arise as a result of abnormal conditions.

There is one passage in your letter on page five which made me jump. It is the third paragraph and gives your conclusion after the various doubts you express as to what revolution can or should do, prisons, punishment, etc. And it reads "in other words: can a revolution solve this problem? I am beginning to think that it cannot." My dearest Sasha, when in the first days of our Russian life, still believing in the old form of revolution, I once said—I remember the wording very distinctly: "If revolution cannot solve the need of violence and terror, then . . . . I am against revolution." You flew at me in rage, said I had never been a real revolutionist and a lot more. Well, you now seem to come to the same conclusion, our difference now being that you are loath to let go the thought of revolution in terms of destruction and terror. And that I am done with for all times. I insist if we can undergo changes in every other method of dealing with social issues, we will also learn to change in the methods of revolution. I think it can be done. If not, I shall relinquish my belief in revolution. That not only because of so much waste of human lives, but also because it is all so futile, an endless repetition of the same old refrain, "The French Revolution Was That Way. All Revolutions Must Be That Way." History dictates the course. History has become the new superstition like the will of god. I for one no longer believe in that, dear Sash.

It's of course difficult to discuss these questions on paper. But I merely want to throw out a few hints as matters now appear to me. For the rest, I know as well as you, old man, that no one can solve the problems of another. . . .

I hope you are getting on with your book, dear heart. And that your teeth will soon be in order. Greet Emmy for me. Much love,

[EG]

EVELYN SCOTT TO EG, July 31, 1928, WOODSTOCK, NEW YORK

Dearest Emma,

. . . Well, as to the agony, I don't really believe anybody, making an effort to say honestly, with that exactitude which an aesthetic sense demands, really enjoys writing. (With apologies for contradicting the optimistic interjections of the nice secretary.) Rhetoric may pour from the typewriter in a deluge, but I ain't got much faith in the ease, to anybody, of more fastidious utterance. There is a thrill (to me anyhow) in conception, in the prevision of a book; but the materialization of the psychic essence I find about as slow and painful to the flesh as bringing a young child through the teething process. The myth of "inspiration" must have discouraged many, don't you think? I believe the myth has a basis in the instant of conception; but I'm afraid the ingenuous fail to perceive the actuality of time in any creative process. They miss the fact that every work, to be alive, has to be lived through, as if pages were a day, in the very flesh and blood of the person writing. But since you are attacking the problem with no illusions at all, maybe your almost over-preparedness will permit you an élan in proportion at the unexpected moment of full-fledged accomplishment.

There is a satisfaction in the completeness of a finished work—it being, apparently, about the only thing in life that ever is finished—with the relief it gives one to lay down the burden of an obligation to attempt perfection. I don't know why it is we are in such a hurry to accept new slavery after new slavery. But there it is anyhow. That's the "curse." And may I say, apropos the agony you speak of, that as far as a test in observation can take me, I can almost "prove" the agony and greatness the double aspects of the same condition. And so, lady, please let's dispense with inappropriate modesty from you.

The discussion of greatness reminds me of one of those imbecile questionnaire affairs which I read yesterday in the [New York] World, when an opinion as to the six greatest men in history was asked of many. I could detect in the replies of most of our important public characters a complete confusion between success and greatness, and even success and bravery and other qualities apparently obvious. The most diagrammatic illustration of this confusion was the mention of [Charles] Lindbergh as an isolated example of bravery in flying. Of course he did go alone; but that did not appear to be the point. The idea intent in the popular mind was not that he went but that he got there; and the confusion of the issue as to bravery did not appear apparent to anybody.

I feel much as you do, I imagine. Where a personality leaves its imprint coercively, through the effects of utilizing fear in others, its importance in the times is less proof of its greatness than of the insignificance of those surrounding it. A personality that succeeds through material power succeeds indirectly, as a consequence of its qualities (shrewdness, ruthlessness, contempt of sympathy, disregard of imagination as applied to humans), true enough; yet it is not those qualities, regarded immediately, which are illumining the era. Maybe we violently disagree here; but I believe in a metaphysical background to the parables of Christianity. As I see it, greatness can make no real contribution to the life about. Hence the martyrs. Of course it has to be an inevitable, not a pious martyrdom. Masochists don't get into my heaven any more than sadists. But I do believe that true greatness cannot measure and calculate the worldly profits. Every extension of human vision seems to me to come to men with as little deliberation as is in their physical growth; and if they are martyrs in consequence of exceeding the times, they are martyrs according to a sort of reversed natural selection which seems to say that the great must suffer. When a great man is hated and his enemies seek to destroy him, it is to destroy that which he inevitably is. He cannot prevent destruction as he is attacked from without, except by a more torturing and futile effort to destroy himself as he is within. Of course Napoleon, in the end, did die a martyr of a sort. As long as he deceived men into seeing him, not as he was, but in disguise, as the symbol of their own desires, he succeeded. But when the veil fell away from his personality they hated him for what he was, just as they would always have hated him if his shrewdness had not taken care that they were to see him as something particular for them. So, in a way, he was a peculiarly unsuccessful man. . . .

Well, the eyes are warning me against comments too ponderous for the length of the letter. You can qualify for martyrdom, Emma, but I hope and believe that there are times in which the resentment of a personality which has remained true to itself does not culminate logically. As I always said, the insidious menace of the printed word, and especially the creative word, is not always appreciated by those who ought to fear the living (those struggling to suppress life fearing those struggling to enlarge our consciousness of it).

I wish I had a secretary who, besides giving provocative hints of her own interesting self, could teach me how to spell. Very much love and good luck and godspeeds to the work and you,

                                                      Evelyn

AB TO EG, November 19, 1928, ST. CLOUD

Dear,

... As to your previous letter, it is no use disturbing you with discussions. It is very hard to understand human nature, all the psychologists and novelists notwithstanding. And I think that the best of friends also never understand each other, though they may THINK they do. I only want to refer to those two historic mistakes in my book that you speak of. I looked the matter up; I find no mistakes there. You will remember that when in prison I took a different view of the [Leon] Czolgosz act [i.e., assassination of McKinley] than you. You must remember our correspondence about it. I held then that POLITICAL acts of violence are not in place in the U.S., but that only ECONOMIC acts could be understood and justified etc. And that view I developed in the book from the actual prison letters I had in Ossining. There is neither any mistake nor discrepancy there. As to what you say about my "awe" before the comrades, you confuse it with my attitude as to the value of personal example, and I still hold that personal example is one of the strongest mediums to influence people in favor or against certain ideas.

As to the other alleged mistake, it is due to your misconception again. Of course you visited me BEFORE the McKinley affair. I never thought differently, because I well remember that in prison it was said later that you came to talk the "plan" [i.e., the escape attempt] over with me. And in my book the letter about the matter is DATED when the letter was WRITTEN, December 20 [1901], but the letter deals with things that happened long before. The previous letters on the foregoing page explain that I was in hospital, then that I had a visit from Harry Gordon, etc. Then on December 20 I first speak of your visit and I mention that the sub rosa route was interrupted so that I could not write before. Then I speak of the Buffalo matter [i.e., McKinley's assassination] etc. So from the letter it is plain that your visit had taken place long before those events.

Well, I hope that your getting back to work tonight has helped. I hope you continue well with 1900 and 1901. You really must bear in mind that you need not worry about how much you write up to a given day, because I think you have done extremely well. In a few months you have written more than half of your autobiography. It is from that standpoint that you must look at the matter. . . .

As ever, affectionately,

S

EG TO AB, *November 23, 1928, ST.* TROPEZ

Dear Sash,

It is 4 P.M. now. Have just made a break in my writing to prepare our dinner and write you in between. After dinner I go back to my book. After days of agony trying to get into the swing, I finally have succeeded, so I mean to continue tonight. If I do not grow too tired, I may work through all night to finish with 1900. Then I would only have one year more to do; not even the whole year, only until after the death of the unfortunate boy on October 29 [1901, when Leon Czolgosz was executed]. Don't think I am rushing too much. I am anxious to get through with the closing chapter of the first part of my life. But I know it is no use racing. . . .

Demie has been very restless. She is wild about seeing her boy and I rather think there is something else, Henry [Alsberg]. Nothing on his side though and the other I prefer not to discuss. Demie got me a substitute as she wouldn't leave me alone, although I told her it would be good for me to get the practice. In another few years people will run from me as they always do from old age. I will have to be alone then. But Demie is a devoted soul; she simply would not budge until Henry said he would stay with me. Poor Henry, he is being victimized. However, he likes my cooking and I think he also likes me. He knows I have no design on his maidenhead. On the 8th he may go back with me to Paris. He's got a new bug—Palestine. The poor boy is forever trying to run away from himself. He did a little writing he tells me, so that is something. . . .

That is a very good statement about that dirty business of Makhno [i.e., Makhno's charges against Vsevolod Volin and other comrades]. Indeed I want to sign it, not that I think it will do much good. The poison is in the revolutionary ranks everywhere [and] in ours evidently more. Did Rudolf write you that Oestreich has sued him for libel? Rudolf writes he will refuse to defend himself in a capitalist court on such a charge and that he will refuse to pay a fine. . . . Can you imagine anything more terrible? You say in the statement that the war and other causes are responsible for such poison. My dear, thirty years ago Lucy Parsons [wife of Albert R. Parsons, the anarchist and Haymarket victim] dragged a man she had been living with into court over a couple of pieces of furniture. It's in people; the movement or lack of it has nothing to do with such things. The fault is all ours because we were in a romantic Dusel [daze] about what a theory or a movement can do in changing people.

You are right, my dear, it is very hard to understand human nature and certainly you are doubly right when you say it is hard to find understanding between friends. But since everything is relative in life, one does get at the soul of a friend, if one is observant and has the capacity for love. I don't mean the physical love, I mean a great devotion strong enough to stand the test of time. Such capacity gives one a sixth sense and makes one see things in the friend which he either doesn't see himself or seeing has not the strength to admit.

How can I forget your stand on Czolgosz's act? It was a greater blow to me than anything that happened during that terrible period. It effected me more than [Johann] Most's stand on your act. After all, Most had only talked about violence. You had used it and went to prison for it. You had known the agony of repudiation, condemnation, and isolation. That you could sit down and cold-bloodedly analyze an act of violence nine years after your own, actually implying that your act was more important, was the most terrible thing I had yet experienced. It merely showed me that you had not changed one inch, that you had remained the blind fanatic who could see only one angle of life and one angle of human action. That's why I said the other day that the letter dated December as it appears in the book [*Prison Memoirs of an Anarchist*] is historically not correct. You were not capable at the time, 1901, to philosophize as you did in the letter of December 1901, especially the thoughts expressed on page 415. You did not even reason that way when you came out in 1906. I don't mean that you were not intellectually capable, of course not. But you were still so steeped in the old revolutionary traditions and beliefs that you could not possibly have reasoned that way in 1901. And what is more, dear Saṣh, deep down in your soul you are still the old Adam. Didn't I see it in Russia, where you fought me tooth and nail because I would not swallow everything as justification of the Revolution? How many times did you throw it into my teeth that I had only been a parlor revolutionist? That the end justifies the means, that the individual is of no account, etc., etc.? Believe me, dearest, I do not say this in anger; I am beyond that now, I hope; it is merely to get your reactions in their proper time and place, that's all. As to your stand on Czolgosz, I find it just as absurd now as I did then. Acts of violence, except as demonstrations of a sensitive human soul, have proven utterly useless. From that point of view Czolgosz's act was as futile as yours. It neither left the slightest effect; the price you have paid and that poor boy to me are far beyond the sin. But to say that a political act is less valuable was nonsense to me then and still is. In the McKinley case it is doubly so, because his policy of annexation marked the beginning of American imperialism and all the subsequent reaction. Of course Czolgosz could not forsee all of that. But in 1901 there were already great signs of imperialism, inaugurated by McKinley's regime. You will say he was only a tool. Yes, and so was Frick. He was the mouthpiece of Carnegie; he represented his interest as much as McKinley represented Wall Street. You will say McKinley was an elected person, or at least that is the superstition. True, but then Czolgosz's act was particularly valuable as a means to destroy the myth. But why argue now, dear heart? In the light of our experience we know that acts of violence are inevitable. But as to removing anything, or even showing up an evil, they are pathetically inadequate. Your act was noble and still more so your fortitude in prison, just as many other such acts and brave souls—let's not take away from their luster by ridiculous utilitarian hairsplitting as to which is more important. It is as futile as the argument about mind and matter, at least to me.

Yes, it was my mistake about your date of my second visit. I first thought you wrote I had been to see you again after the act of Czolgosz.

"Personal example." Whoever denied that? But what value can it have, when one does things utterly false to oneself, even if approved by comrades? Fess up kid, how much of your private life or acts would our comrades approve, if they knew about them? Or of mine? Yet I can honestly say that I have never committed anything which was false to my ideas, though heaven knows I cannot say that I have not been false to myself. Like you I once thought the cause everything and the comrades capable of appreciating example. I think, if you will search your heart, you will find that you have simply not entirely outgrown your old beliefs. Neither have I, for that matter, only that you cling to them more. Since the action of our comrades in your case, even more so in the case of Czolgosz, and since the petty cruel recriminations against the few, myself included, I no longer consider comrades capable of learning by good example. The choice few are all to me; their opinion everything; their respect and friendship my greatest support. For the rest, I have grown indifferent. The process isn't since yesterday: it began with the attitude of many comrades to your act, made terrific strides in 1901, gained impetus during my work with Ben Reitman, and reached the climax since I came out of Russia.

Never mind about Michael [Cohn]. He evidently does not want to have anything to do with my book. I wrote him from Toronto and at my request you wrote him last spring. He has not answered. It is not important. I know that before I left for Europe [in 1895] I approached [S.] Yanofsky [editor of the *Freie Arbeiter Stimme*] to raise money for the tunnel [for AB's attempt to escape from prison]. I am not certain whether I told him the purpose or not. I am going to write him; he may remember. I am only sure that I had approached him and that he had promised to do his utmost. I remember how surprised I was then because Yanofsky was a fanatical Mostianer [i.e., follower of Johann Most] and had treated me shabbily when we first met. Later, when more money was needed, you wrote direct to Yanofsky. I was already in Europe then. I don't know whether he ever told you that Eric B. Morton's expenses and [Anthony] Kincella's to come to Pittsburgh and their first months [there working on the tunnel] were paid with $200 Carl Schmidt [Carl Stone in *Living My Life*, p. 268] had given me toward my European trip. I wrote about the whole thing this week. You can imagine how surprised that Philistine will be when he reads that. He was only interested in EG the woman, he wrote me in Paris, not her ideas or her lovers. . . .

Devotedly,

E

AB TO EG, Monday [late November 1928], ST. CLOUD

Dear,

Am glad to get your long letter. I cannot say that I agree with some of your points, but what is the use of discussing them? Each will remain with his old opinion, anyhow. I have come to think that views, opinions, etc. are less a matter of thinking than of temperament. So the more useless is discussion.

I hold, however, that what I wrote in the *Memoirs* is entirely correct in every particular, historically and psychologically. As to Leon, I know very well that in my prison letter I told you that I understood the reasons that compelled him to the act, but that the usefulness, socially, of the act is quite another matter. I hold the same opinion now. That is why we do not condemn any such acts, because we understand the reasons. But that does not mean that we cannot form our opinion about its social effects and usefulness. Of course no one can really foresee "usefulness," but that is already a philosophic consideration, not to the point here. And again, I still hold the opinion, as I did formerly, that a terroristic act should take in consideration the effect on the public mind—not on comrades, as you say. (The same refers to my remark [about the effectiveness] of [personal] example.) There were in Russia those "bezmotivniki," who believed in terror "without motives," on general principles. I never had any sympathy with such an attitude, though even that I could not condemn. So I think that my act, not because it was mine, but because it was one easy to understand by most people, was more useful than Leon's. I still hold that in the U.S., especially, economic acts could be understood by the masses better than political ones. Though I am in general now not in favor of terroristic tactics, except under very exceptional conditions.

You say my opinion was a terrible blow to you. That's too sentimental for me. It merely means to say that one should not analyze things, not think over them, and have no critical opinion. You'd hardly admit it in this formulation. Yet it is the same. Just what you say in your letter: "That you could sit down and cold-bloodedly analyze such an act nine years after your own." Nine years is certainly time to think such things over, and prison, away from the impressions of the moment, the best place. That you THEN felt shocked, I can understand. But that even now you are shocked, that is too much.

In Russia? The same thing. Your opposition to the bolsheviks seemed to me too sentimental and womanish. I needed more convincing proofs, and until I had them I could not honestly change my attitude. After all, I think that is the difference of the male and female mentality. Of course you will no doubt deny that there is any such difference; at least you used to deny it, as you denied the effect of heredity and as you now even minimize the influence of environment. But these are all points on which we never agreed in the past and I do not expect that we will in the future. Each must follow the logic of his own mind and temperament.

That acts of violence accomplish nothing, I do not agree at all. The terrorism of the Russian revolutionists aroused the whole world to the despotism of the Czars. [George] Kennan's book [*Siberia and the Exile System* (1891)] merely culminated the matter. Kennan [the American journalist] could not have written about them had they not committed their acts, been sent to Siberia, etc. As to what you say of comrades and their approval, that is indifferent to me. My attitude always was and still is that anyone preaching an idea, particularly a high ideal, must try to live, so far at least as possible, in consonance with it, for his own sake as well as for the furtherance of his ideal in the minds of those to whom he is preaching it. That is, the people at large. Voltairine [De Cleyre] was right in this, except that she went to extremes. The life, works, and death of certain persons have always exerted a much greater effect than their preaching. That is historic.

Not that I mean to say that my own life has always been in consonance with this. Of course not. I am speaking of what I believe in this matter. For the rest, one makes mistakes, of course. But the question here is of the right attitude.

The question of whether the comrades can "appreciate" is neither here nor there. One should act and live according to his OWN attitude in the matter. But what his attitude is, that is important.

By the way, the *Freie Arbeiter Stimme* has been publishing excerpts from Yanofsky's memoirs. In the last two issues, November 16 and the preceeding one, there is the story of the tunnel and Yan's part of it. When he first published a notice in the first number of the *FAS*, which he then began to edit, he says, he "saved my life," because I had despaired then. I can't say that I remember it. He says he received a letter then from me. Further he speaks of meeting Tony [Kincella], who impressed him favorably, and his visits to Pittsburgh, etc. I'll keep the numbers for you.

I am glad you are doing well with your writing. And maybe Alsberg being with you will be an inspiration. I hope so. Well, enough for today.

Affectionately,

S

EG TO HENRY ALSBERG, March 24, 1931, NICE

Dear Hank,

I have your two letters. You certainly did splurge yourself, Henry, my boy, in your long interesting epistle, a rare treat from you, both in length and quality. . . .

Now about the Gandhi method. I confess that before Russia I might not have been able to see its efficacy as a means of combat. But the horrors of the soviet regime have forced me to revalue my values about active resistance. I can see now as I could not before the possibility of making an impression by the means practiced in India. The trouble is that such methods are not merely the result of education, but to a much larger extent a question of temperament. The people of India have practiced passive resistance before; therefore it comes to them naturally. I do not believe it would be so natural a manifestation on the part of Western humanity—a humanity fed for centuries on the Jewish and Christian religions, both of which stand for violence, notwithstanding the theory of the other cheek. To eradicate ideas of violence would be the problem. I do not think education could or would do it. Of course that is no reason why we should not propagate it. You are quite right that Gandhi is very much of a go-getter and obsessed by nationalism, which is only another term for all the evils [of] the state. I cannot get very enthusiastic over the events in India for I know that they aim to replace one state by another. It may be true that Gandhi hopes that after his people have achieved independence they will be able to develop to anti-stateism and individual freedom. If he should, I will find myself as mistaken as others have, for it is power which is the crux of the matter, whoever wields it.

I quite agree with you about what you say about beauty. I cannot imagine a free society without beauty, for of what use liberty, if not to strive for beauty? Not the kind of beauty the art for art's sake exponents clamor for, but beauty of personality, human relationship, and the finer things in nature or in life. All these things are essential to a new form of life, and because I think so, I have always been opposed to sectarianism or shall I say, asceticism, or the idea that through the suppression of our senses we will achieve saintliness. I am afraid that Gandhi seems to think that, but perhaps I ought not to say so, as I do not know Gandhi's ideas except as interpreted by others. In any event India is worth watching, and if I had money I would go there and see things for myself. I am sure, dear Henry, you will always be in opposition to the majority. I have always maintained that the majority under anarchism will no doubt be on a higher level, but even so the individual will always be in advance of it. It is inevitable. Affectionately,

[EG]

EG TO MAX NETTLAU, January 24, 1932, PARIS

My dear good comrade,

Thank you for all the nice things you say about *Living My Life* in your letter of December 23rd. I value your opinion of the work very highly. . . .

I think you overrate my influence on Johann Most. True, he cared a great deal about me, and I about him, but he was already too set in his views and habits, and I was a mere slip of a girl, without experience, without the necessary ways to influence anyone of his caliber. No, I could not have changed him. Except, perhaps, if I had been willing to lose myself in him and his needs. Frankly, I was not. My own passionate ideal was more to me then, and at all times, than anything I could allow to stand in its way. The price was high, I admit, but I am sure I would do it all over again, if I had to. One must follow one's bent, if one wants to remain true to oneself.

You will pardon me when I tell you I was amused to find you would have justified my horsewhipping Most for personal reasons, because he had slandered me, and not for his denial of AB and his act. Well, if it will ease your mind, I will say he did slander me to a most scandalous degree. But that was not what impelled my action. I had so little personal life then that nothing anyone had done against me really mattered. But AB and his act mattered everything to me. You forget that Most's stand rent our ranks, the majority going with him, and only a few willing to stand by AB. In view of the fact that Most had always proclaimed acts of violence from the housetops, his attitude toward AB was too great a shock for me to reason about. You forget that I was only twenty-three, then, with no other aim or purpose in life except the ideal. One does not reason at that age, and that fervent stage, as one does in maturer years; I admit that nothing Most, or anyone else might have done, since 1892, would induce me to horsewhip them. Indeed, I have often regretted to have attacked the man who was my teacher, and whom I idolized for many years. But it was impelling to do so then.

Of course, Berkman's life was more important to me than Frick's death. But we were of the generation and period that believed implicitly in the notion of the end justifying the means. I was willing to give my own life for an act, and though it was bitterly hard, I was also willing that Berkman should give his. I admit that when the news came of Frick's recovery I was exceedingly glad, for it meant also the saving of AB's life. Anyhow, if you have read further in the book, you will have found that AB's act and his subsequent Calvary, have been my cross, and still are. That never again had I anything directly to do with an act of violence, though I have always taken my stand on the side of those who did. I have fought shy, all my life, from joining the cry of "Crucify!" Even if I did not agree with the acts, I understood the impelling motives of them. I have described that in my essay on "The Psychology of Violence" and also in *Living My Life.* . . .

Thanks very much, dear comrade, for your compliment, that I am among the few women who can think, without having lost anything of my femininity. Some of the reviewers have denied me the capacity of that, even the best of them, written by a woman [the *Nation* review (December 2, 1931) by Freda Kirchwey], and most penetratingly, has stated that EG did not think. I am enclosing some new reviews. Please send them back.

By the time this letter is transcribed I will probably know where you can address me next.

Affectionately,

[EG]

AB TO EG, *February 9, 1932,* NICE

Dear,

Just received yours of the 8th. Your mail reaches sooner here than mine reaches you.

Four [typewriter] ribbons also just arrived, this morning. Thanks. Two I shall keep for you.

Well, I am glad you liked the second synopsis better than the first. No, I don't think the first was strained. At least it did not seem so to me. And as a matter of fact I like making synopses. Only, of course, the house was in chaos and I did not even have a desk. The large desk takes up so much space I had to put it into the cellar. It took three big men an hour to do it. So I am now using my old St. Cloud writing desk. The rooms are a bit bigger here and quite nice and cost less.

By this time you must have received also my typed script of your suggested synopsis. I think it is OK. I suggest you send my second synopsis and the last to Saxe. "Woman without a Country" is also all right to send there.

I made the synopses, the first two, personal for the very reason that I think that a magazine is the more likely to take it the more personal it is. My idea was that you begin with the reason why the radical is disenchanted and end by showing that history still proves the revolutionary correct and that his disenchantment is, after all, only temporary, for there is still hope for the world; in fact, the only hope and that the very one that the radical has always preached: liberty.

I do not at all agree with you; that is, I could not say, as you do, "my state of black pessimism and despair." I don't feel that way at all. And if you really feel that way (unless only at certain moments), I don't think you'd have the energy or will to go on a lecture tour. You could not lecture, if you really were in such pessimism.

Of course we are disappointed in Russia. But, then, revolutions have never in history gone the way the revolutionists had expected them to go. The French Revolution brought Napoleon and dictatorship and wars. Still, in the course of time the main principles of the French Revolution—equality before the law, popular political democracy—have fought their way through and become established. Of course they have given nothing to the people, but that is another matter.

The Russian Revolution was fought for economic democracy and that has not been achieved, but the germs of it ARE to be found in the Russian mind today, and though it may take a hundred years, that economic democracy will be achieved. It may be poor consolation to us individually, but a revolution must be judged, in the last analysis, from a non-personal view. At any rate, the views of anarchists in re breaking down capitalism and the inevitable failure of all state machinery including socialism have been PROVEN by events since the war. Bolshevism and fascism also PROVE that there is NO OTHER salvation except a society based on economic equality without any political invasion or control. THAT MUCH our ideas have been justified by recent history, and it is for THIS reason that I see no justification in black despair.

As to the realization of our ideals, well, if ONE revolution has failed to materialize them, that is nothing against them. It took several revolutions to realize the ideals of former epochs.

It is true that the present world tendency is not encouraging. But after all these things change; after war and revolution there usually comes reaction. But that reaction is always followed by further progress along lines of common sense and greater liberty.

It is THIS thought that I had in mind for developing in an article on the "Disenchanted Radical." He is not really disenchanted, and that is why I said that I prefer the term disillusioned. That refers, of course, to the radical IN GENERAL, especially those who believed that a POLITICAL party revolution can really change things fundamentally. Disillusioned in the methods etc. used by political revolutionists. We are not disenchanted in our ideals, but only disillusioned in the achievements of the Russian Revolution.

Etc. on these lines.

That about Copenhagen [i.e., the mix-up over lectures there] is just terrible. I think you ought to give the whole thing up and go direct to Hamburg. It's hell to be kept in such uncertainty as you have been all this time. But if you have to speak to the conservative bunch on dictatorship, you could speak on OTHER dictatorships, together also with Russia, showing that the PRINCIPLE of dictatorship must work out alike everywhere, no matter what the phrases [i.e., rhetoric], and no matter even what the possible intentions. . . . I embrace you, dear, and wish you a little cheer,

S

AB TO MOLLIE STEIMER, August 16, 1933, NICE

My dear Mollie,

. . . You need not try to convince me that we must do something in the matter of the situation in Germany. I referred to it in detail—as to what we can and cannot do—in my long letter [of July 14, 1933]. Now you seem to agree that we cannot appeal in behalf of ONE person. But you still ask why we appealed in behalf of Mooney—one person. (As a matter of fact, I never appealed for Mooney without also appealing for Billings.) But the Mooney case cannot be compared with Muehsam's case. It is ridiculous to make such a comparison. In Germany there is a dictatorship, and Muehsam is but one of the many victims. There was no dictatorship in California in 1916-17 and Mooney, Billings, etc. were just picked out from the great body of labor as the special victims of the California capitalist class. But if I have to explain this to you, time is too short for it.

The situation in Germany is PAST appeals. I have made plenty of appeals in my life—when there was at least the smallest shadow of a chance that such appeals will do the least good, even among our own people. But the time for appeals in re German persecution has passed. ACTION is needed. Unfortunately we have no people for such action. Let us realize that. It is very sad, but it is the fact.

As to the committee that you mention (about which it was decided, as you write, when Rudolf was with you), I have never heard of it. I doubt even that EG knows that she is on that committee [in behalf of the German politicals]. Has she been notified or asked about it? She never mentioned it to me. And what is the use when you name a committee that can't do anything? You say yourself that Orobon [Fernandez], [Mark] Mratchny, and [Albert] de Jong are too busy, and [Helmut] Ruediger must keep quiet. So who remains of your committee? It is dead before it is born. And what could Emma do in this matter? Ony write to a few people to interest them in this—but all the people we have already written to have remained either indifferent or said that they could do nothing.

This idea of "assigning a few comrades" to do a certain thing is just a way of doing nothing. Nor can you organize any fund these days for anything. There is not a single person that even answered my letters re Germany and Muehsam that I have written months ago, mostly to America. What's the use fooling ourselves, I ask you seriously, Mollie.

Moreover, the persecutions in Germany are now an OLD STORY and no one cares about it any more. Too much time has been lost about it.

I am sorry I cannot tell you anything encouraging, but we must face facts. Fascism is growing. It is coming to Austria, England, and even Ireland. It is everywhere already, even if in some places still underground. And do not forget that this fascism, whether in black shirts, brown shirts, blue or red shirts, is supported by the masses. Else it could not exist. We are in the same situation the Socialist Revolutionist Party was in Russia at the end of the last century. They were compelled to resort to terrorism as the only method left them. We cannot even do that, because we have neither the people nor the means for it. The Socialist Revolutionists of Russia had those things, and thus they made themselves heard. Moreover, I doubt whether at the present stage of the world the tactics of the old-time Russian Social Revolutionists would have the same effect as then. Because then, in Russia, it was mere apathy on the part of the people that supported the existing regime; apathy, indifference, and ignorance. Today it is different in Europe. It is the masses themselves who consciously support Mussolini, Hitler, etc. I meet a good many people here in Nice —Italians, Germans, and even some French and Americans—who admire Mussolini and Hitler. So there you are.

There is a wave of reaction all through the world. That wave will have to pass, but we are too powerless to stem against it. Maybe it will soon bring another war. And against that we are also powerless. The truth is, our movement has accomplished nothing, anywhere.

That does not mean that we should not try to enlighten the people. But at the same time I cannot fool myself with any belief that we can do something for our people in the prisons of Germany. No more than we could free our people from the Russian prisons. But for the latter we could at least arouse some little sympathy and get some financial help. But NOW for German prisoners we cannot even do this. I have tried it, so I know.

To sum up, the only suggestion I can make that seems to me to hold some little promise of effectual action: the same I spoke of in my last, in connection with some decisive action by our comrades in Spain.* That, if carried out in a real manner, would do more good than all appeals. Only I fear that we have not the men even in Spain to accomplish that.

---

* On July 8, 1933, Mollie Steimer had written Berkman asking him to head up the appeal for their victimized comrades in Germany. His long reply, dated July 14th and later filed in AB package number IV at the International Institute of Social History, has unfortunately been misplaced. It contained the decisive action he spoke of in his "last": He proposed something more effective "than mere protests on paper." Under the present conditions in Germany, he believed in drastic measures: "I have grown older since 1892, and I have gained experience. But neither my character nor my views have changed in any fundamental manner. Nor my temperament and revolutionary logic. I believe today, as I believed in 1892, in the justification and *necessity* (under certain circumstances) of revolutionary action, collective as well as individual. I believe that assassinations and taking hostages would be the

There is no news here.

Things are rotten in every way. Greetings to you and Senya from us both here.

As ever,

S

AB TO EG, March 4, 1934, NICE

Dear,

I can well imagine that you are busy these days. Stella and Dr. Cohn have written me about those receptions etc. you had in New York. And then I had a lot of clippings, so I was informed.

I don't know, however, what has happened since then. There is nothing in the New York *Herald* (Paris edition) and I have not yet heard from anyone about your lecture tour. I hope things are going well, though. I am only a bit uneasy about the rotten communists. I have read about their breaking up that Madison Square Garden meeting in re Austria. They are capable of doing anything. In the U.S. especially they seem to have become the worst kind of gangsters.

Of course I know you could handle them, if they resort only to the usual disturbance. But it is different when they begin roughhouse. I hope that will not be the case though. . . .

It would be very fine if you get orders from magazines for articles. And you wrote that *Harper's* means to give you an order for later on. I wish it were some publication like the *Saturday Evening Post*, for they pay much better. However, I realize that NOW you cannot bother with articles. You hardly get time to go to Tante [Meyer—i.e., the toilet]—fortunately you do not spend as much time there as I, else you would have no time even for lectures. . . .

As I say, I have more time now, and I could make some notes for you. But the subject you speak of—on individualism and the individual—I have tried to make some notes on it. But they are no good.

It is a most difficult subject, especially for me, my dear. I have almost lost all faith in the "free individual as the basis of a free society." The more I see how this "free individual" acts in times of stress, in times when the

---

most effective and ethical methods just now in reference to the Hitler regime. I also believe, very strongly, that an international boycott of Germany, economic and social, would be the most desirable thing. Never mind that some innocent people would suffer. . . . There ARE NO INNOCENT people in the world today, for everyone is responsible for the hell we live in. . . . And even if there were some innocent people to suffer as a result of a boycott of Germany, that would have no weight with me whatever: they deserve to suffer for their abject submission to the Hitler regime and its unspeakable, worse-than-feudal barbarities." He thus proposed the boycott and the taking of high dignitaries, especially ambassadors, hostage. He pledged his participation and asked her to destroy the letter.

"free individual" SHOULD express himself, the less faith I have in him.

Events in the world all go to prove that the individual is nothing but a sheep. He will follow where the majority runs, or where some strong man will order him to go. Maybe there is really no such thing that we call the "free individual," except for a few exceptions. But these exceptions are too few to build social life on. The "free individual" is usually a dictator, in one way or another. In a social and political way, if he gets the chance. Otherwise a dictator in his own personal and family life. I mean that the "free individual" is the strong personality, the strong man or woman. And the strong one is most generally a dictator, both by psychology and circumstances. By circumstances, because he has to deal with sheep.

Of course there are now and then some "free individuals" in the real, in the anarchist sense. But maybe one in ten thousand. What hope is there then to ever build a free society with so rare birds?

However, this may be neither here nor there. It is just my feeling on the matter. But that feeling is the reason that I cannot make any notes on this subject that could be of any value to you or of any help. . . .

Well, there is no news here, dear. The Austrian tragedy at least showed that some of the workers in that country have the right spirit. But their leaders left them in the hole of course. . . . France is gradually going the same way. It means fascism everywhere in Europe. And it gains in England, too.

Wish I could write a more cheerful letter. But enough for today. I hope, dear, things are going well with you. I embrace you affectionately,

S

EG TO AB, March 23, 1934, CHICAGO

Dearest Sash,

. . . I am a little surprised over what you said about the individual. I thought that we have always agreed on the point, especially of late years, that the mass unfortunately cannot be depended upon, that it will always fall under the influence of some unscrupulous spellbinders. It is the individual who at all times, in whatever walk of life or whatever human endeavor, who has stood out against the mob. Provided, of course, he or she also dared enough to do so. True that some individuals have used their personalities to ensnare, [to] enslave the masses and rule them with an iron rod, but it is equally true that individuals at all times have been the prophets, seers, and creative forces for good. If the former have succeeded, it is mostly because the mass followed them gladly. At any rate, this is the subject that *Harper's* wants. Their idea is an exposé of the place of the individual freed from ruthless individualism on one side and the modern herd idea of dictatorship on the other. It seems to me much can be said on that. As I said, perhaps the article by [Theodore] Dreiser which seems very nebulous and idiotic might suggest something to you.

Thanks for the enclosure of the Russian article on the individual. I haven't yet read it but I will. If I can lay my hands on the letter from the editor of *Harper's*, I will enclose it. It will, I am sure, give you an idea of what they want. . . .

There are many more things, my dear, I would like to write you, but it is impossible now. Perhaps before the letter is mailed I will add a few lines by hand. Give my love to Emmy. Give my affectionate greetings to Aunty [Mrs. Gordon Crotch] and greet any of the friends who may have returned to Nice. Keep on writing me to [or c/o] Stella. She will forward my letters wherever I will be. I hope you are telling me the truth when you say you are keeping well. I will trust you with my life but I don't trust you about telling me about your own physical condition. Better remind Emmy that she promised to tell me truthfully how you are. Devoted love,

Emma

AB TO EG, April 7, 1934, NICE

Dearest Em,

You are probably wondering why I am not writing. Well, for ten days now I have been hoping every day to write to you and send you at the same time at least one of the articles. But nothing is ready, so I decided to send you a line anyhow, so you should not be anxious about me.

As I wrote you before, that I would put the [Harry and Lucy] Lang work aside before the end of March, so I did. On March 28th I started on the articles. First on the individual. It did not go at all, so I decided to start on that comparison between bolshevik communism and anarchist communism. I thought this would be easier, but it wasn't.

Well, I used to write an article in a day or two, when I really used to settle down to my machine. But it is different now. It is already the 7th of April, and I have been at those two articles every day and all day long since the 28th of March. On the first article (individual) I just have a few insignificant notes. The other I am still working on. I hope that in about two or three days the communist article may be ready. Whether it will really be good, I doubt me very much.

I'll send the article as soon as it is typed clean. Then I'll get back again to the individual. But somehow I feel I can't do a decent article on it. I'll try, though. I felt from the very beginning that I can't do it. I know what is wanted, but that does not help me much. Well, anyhow, I'll do what I can and then send it to you.

Well, dear, I received your letters and I also heard from Stella. I am happy to know that the Chicago meetings were successful. Yes, I got your cable from Chicago about the meetings and also about the Rocker book. As I already wrote you some time ago, I DID GET the Rocker ms. from Spain. I got it in two packages, the whole of it. I say this again because in your last letter (of March 23, dictated to Cecil [Cohen]) you wonder whether I will get it from Spain. Maybe you then did not yet have my letter in which I told you I had it already. . . .

Hope things will come out better now, I mean the meetings, and that you will get renewal of time. I embrace you, affectionately,

Sasha

EG TO AB, June 16, 1934, TORONTO

My dearest,

I wanted so much to get out a letter to you yesterday in time to catch the "Empress Britain" that left today from Montreal, a five-day boat. But it was impossible. I was still in labor pains with the communist article. Now this won't go until Wednesday. Of course it will leave Toronto Monday. But it will not sail until Wednesday. There is a German boat the 19th. But of course I never use the damned nazi ships. . . .

Now as to my articles, I am enclosing a copy of "My Impressions in America." I hope you will like it in spite of its gushiness. I feel sure you will not find that I have in any way trimmed my ideas. Nor have I exaggerated my impressions. It is only that I had to make it more than usually personal and sentimental. It is too bad I was unable to do so in the article for the *Ladies Home Journal.* I am sure it would have been accepted. Well, we would be as poor as we are now, since we are not like the Sandstroms [neighbors in St. Tropez], we cannot hoard money. As to whether *Redbook* or any other such magazine will take the article about my impressions, that's another question. I will let you know when I hear from the editor of *Redbook.* If he returns it, Ann [Lord] will try her luck. She has connections with quite a few commercial magazines. She may succeed.

When I cabled you that the additional pages of the communism article were splendid I had in mind the first ms. as well. My objection was that you used up twenty-four pages on a critical analysis of the bolshevik sort of communism. And only one page about anarchist communism. Well, when I came to work on both mss. I discovered much to my distress that the second part would take the entire sails out of the ms. about the individual. For it is almost the identical reasoning about the state and authority that you have in the second part of the communist ms. Of course, if I had not undertaken to give *Harper's* an article on the place of the individual, the second part of communism would have come in handy. As it was I could not use it, except the last two or three pages. Believe it or not, dearest Sash,

I found it almost as difficult to make the combination as if I were writing a new article altogether. It took me almost as long as my impressions. Well, it's done. I finished it yesterday. Next week the final typing will be made.

You will find some changes in your ms. Not very many though. For instance, where you speak of Russia's youth. I had to put in a few lines to show that there were young people in Russia who, though communists, did not swallow the whole hog. It would have been a gross exaggeration to deny that. The escape of some komsoltzi and those who are in prisons and camps prove that the entire young generation isn't poisoned. Another thing is the new decree against every adult member of [the family of] anyone guilty of so-called treason and counter-revolution. You must have seen it in the *Posledni*. The *Times* had a long quotation and comment. It is really beyond belief. So I used it in the article. I had also written at length about Kropotkin's interpretation of anarchist communism. But in the end I did not use it. First it would make our article too long. Secondly it would also hamper the article about the individual. I may use it for that. I can't say I am satisfied with the positive side of our article. It is entirely out of proportion to the critical part. I tried to cut the last, but found it impossible because everything you have written is necessary and essential to the proper understanding of compulsory communism. But more needed to be said about the libertarian side. With the first part so long it was impossible to make the defense of our idea of communism as it should have been done. I am supposed to write only about five thousand words. The article as I have arranged it has eight thousand words. I hope the *Mercury* will not find it too long. I will write [Charles] Angov, the managing editor who ordered the article, that if any cutting is to be done he should do it in the critical part. I should hate to have anything taken away from our own ideas because, as I have already said, the presentation is not very profound.

Monday I will begin on the individual. I feel it will be the hardest thing to do. I know it would be different, if we could have a good long talk about it, an exchange of our thoughts as in the past. I am glad you agree this is very necessary. For myself I can say that being removed from people who think and with whom one can exchange one's thoughts is sheer agony. This town is deadly dull. I don't know a single being whose thoughts are worth anything. Our own comrades are mentally mediocre. In short there is no inspiration of any kind. It is fortunate that I am busy with writing. Else I should wither inside of me. It was the same when I was here before. If I had any doubts about the need of intellectual stimuli, my return to America would have cured me. As I have already written you before, I felt twenty years off my shoulders because everywhere I met wide awake people who were really intensely interested in ideas. What I mean to say is that I miss your companionship more than I can tell you. Especially while writing. . . .

To come back to the ms. about the individual. I find that you have done what you complain about Rudolf. You have concentrated on the state as the sole and only enemy of the individual. And you repeat the same thought on every page. To be sure, the state is the main offender. But by no means the only one. Society at large, at least as it exists today, is no less an enemy of the individual. It hates nothing so much as anything unlike itself, any digression from the "normal" or the routine of life, whether in habits, ideas, or even clothes. Habit and traditions are the archenemies of the individual, as are the home, the family, the school, and of course the church and state. So while taking your treatment of the subject as a starter, I will have to bring out the other points myself. It will mean sweating blood of course. But it has to be done: $300 is no small matter.

I am glad you agree about [Horace] Kallen. I should like to quote some of his lucid parts. But I am afraid *Harper's* may not like it so much as anything I myself have to say. But Kallen is so clear and so profound in his analysis of the individual and the forces that hamper his growth and development. I really know no other work like it [*Individualism: An American Way of Life* (1933)]. It is anarchism presented in a very clear and beautiful manner and style. I reread his *Free Society* [1934]. It is also a great work, except that he sees in cooperation the solution of the social problem. Cooperative societies for consumption and production he insists would bring about a new way of life. I don't know whether he had ever read anything about Die Gennossenschafts Gesellschaft as it was organized more than thirty years ago. [Gustav] Landauer and others were the originators of the idea and there was quite a library on the subject. At any rate Kallen's *Free Society* is exactly along the same lines. But whereas Landauer shows in Die Gennossenschaften merely a means to an end, Kallen believes it to be the End. His reasoning is absolutely anarchistic. But I see where he declares that he does not believe in the possibility of a free society without some form of constituted organization. He does not call it government. That would stand against his being an anarchist. Also [there is] the fact that he never once refers to anarchism. Well, when I get through with my articles, I will write Kallen. I want him to tell me how he can write so exaltedly about the individual and his place in a free society without being an anarchist. . . .

Darlin' of my heart, who should know you so well as your old sailor. Of course you need a fighting atmosphere. You have had it all your life. In prison perhaps even more than outside. Yes, I know we are getting old. But the lack of something we have had all our lives makes us older. I know that about myself. And I am certain you would be rejuvenated, if you were not torn from all your moorings. And not only do you need a militant atmosphere. You need also intellectual kinship. Well, it is too tragic that you should be denied the forces that would revive your fire and your inspiration.

My dear, my dear, thank you for your wishes of luck with Frank Heiner.

There is no chance. Not only his blindness is against any consummation of what in his imagination is so marvelous and what I long for. There are many other reasons why it should not be. Even if I should again enter America it will not be to be for long near Frank Heiner. It will be for a few months, after which I will be separated from him by three thousand miles for a number of years perhaps. And there is his wife. She seems a very beautiful soul. I had several letters from her that express true greatness, and a large, free, and brave spirit. Her life is evidently a martyrdom. She carries almost the entire brunt of the support of the family and she has been confronted with his amours on more than one occasion. As she is his eyes, she also reads the letters he receives and probably also the letters he writes (he uses a braille machine). It would therefore mean to stand before her with my insides turned out. Not only could I not bear this, but I could not let her see my feelings for her own sake. After all, she is no saint. No matter how big she is, it would torture her to read my reaction to Frank, whom she evidently adores. So you see die Geschichte klappt nicht [it wouldn't do]. Besides, I could never get over the feeling that Heiner loves and wants me because he cannot see the difference between sixty-five and thirty, or even forty.* He is very moving in his plea that some of the greatest men have loved women double their age. He sent me a list of names even I had not known. Well, life is meshugeh [absurd]—to come upon something very beautiful and tender and yet, not to be able to partake of it.

Genug [enough] for today, dearest Sash. I will add something Monday. The next on the list for a letter is clever little Emmy. . . .

Love,
E

---

* Heiner, whom Emma had met in Chicago during her recent lecture tour, was thirty-six, a graduate of the Chicago College of Osteopathy, and presently one of Ernest W. Burgess's graduate students in sociology at the University of Chicago. He pursued his desire for a more intimate relationship and, after Emma finally put aside her misgivings, visited her in Toronto for two weeks in August 1934. After he left, Emma finally finished the article on individualism. As she wrote Berkman, "Between you and me and the lamp post, it was Frank's inspiration that made the writing of the article possible at all. I would have to be a Keats to describe what his visit, alas so painfully brief, has done to me. My lingo is too poor. I could not write while he was still with me. Knowing that the dream and intoxication will soon be over, I dared not give a moment to anything else, leastwise to writing articles. It all seemed inadequate and piffling. But when he left I immediately set to work for fear the spell would be broken and I would be thrown back into the emptiness of my Toronto life and the mediocrity of my surroundings. So you see, my own precious old chum, I wrote the article and whatever is good in it to 'my boy' friend. To his exaltation about life, to his passionate faith in our ideal." (These paragraphs and this note might more properly appear in Part Four, "Women and Men," which fact reminds us again that correspondents do not write with the needs of editors in mind.)

AB TO EG, June 21, 1934, ST. TROPEZ

Dearest Em,

Not that I have anything special to write; but I see that there is a boat going to Montreal on the 23rd, so I want to send you a few lines.

The place is beautiful here and I certainly enjoy it. I have systematized my work. Usually get up at 5 A.M. At 6 A.M. at my desk. Take a raw egg about 10 A.M. and maybe also a glass of milk or fruit, and work till noon. When things go well, I am then through for the day and can rest or monkey about the yard. This is OK, then.

I had a letter from Joe Goldman, Chicago. Says he may soon send some more money and asks the best way. He paid $6.25 for sending the money last time. Robbery, of course. I told him just to send me an American Express check, or a certified check of any good bank on the American Express, Nice. That would not cost so much and I would have no trouble collecting.

He also asks how the work is going. Told him, OK. I have already over 250 pages translated [of Rudolf Rocker's ms.]. Rough, of course. When I have about half the book done, I start revision, and then comes the final typing, and then I shall send the stuff to Chicago. But that will probably not be before a good while yet, and it depends also how the revision will progress. As I get into the work more, it goes easier.

Here nothing new. A big mistral started yesterday, the first real one this year. Is blowing hard as hell. . . .

Besides the twelve-page letter and that of June 7th, I also received your eight-page letter, not dated.* It would take too much time to argue out the question of the individual. You say you believe in him as the only social factor, and that the masses are too easily swayed. Well, my dear, that is just what I believe, too. But that means that we have no faith any more in the realization of our ideas. Or at least damned little. For if the masses cannot be relied on since they are so easily swayed by demagogues, then who is going to do it? The few exceptional individuals? They can't bring about a *social* change. Unless they do it as it has been done till now—by violence, political activity, by the state, in short.

---

* In her undated letter (of *ca.* late May or early June 1934), which we failed to relocate in Amsterdam, she had written that his article on the individual showed too clearly that he had "labored desperately hard": it lacked spirit and was thus "not convincing." She cited a play, *Yellowjack*, as one of the daily proofs she had of the importance of the individual. Directly anticipating Ralph Gabriel's discussion of Walter Reed in *The Course of American Democratic Thought* (1940), Emma cited the play's hero as a case in point, for when he discovered that the mosquito transmitted yellow fever, he persevered, even though he was jeered at and ridiculed by superior officers, and thereby helped deliver mankind from the disease. It is a pity the letter has disappeared, for it was an effective rebuttal of some of AB's points.

Well, it is too big a subject for discussion in a letter. I merely wanted to point out to you that THAT is just the reason why our movement makes little progress—in fact, practically none at all, as a movement. Exceptional individuals like Frank Heiner there have always been and always will be, but that is not a popular movement for a great social ideal. And without it the ideal cannot be materialized. Unless social conditions, by the pressure of necessity, and only very little influenced by the few individuals, will in the course of time "get there." That means about fifty thousand years, as [William Marion] Reedy once wrote in his "Daughter of a Dream." Maybe he was not so far from the truth, either.*

You argue about the power of the individual will. That's granted. But it has too little bearing on social changes. The individual will can make no great revolutions, though it may influence others to do so. But since these others are also influenced in the opposite way, what becomes of the social revolution? Even if it takes place, there are always those ready to influence the masses in favor of a new dictatorship, as in Russia, Italy, Germany.

I cannot go into deeper argumentation, but it simply means (if we build only on the individual) that anarchism must come in the course of social evolution and NOT by social revolution.

But you seem to misunderstand my position entirely. I do not doubt the "prime importance of the individual," as you put it. But these important individuals are too few in any age to bring about any fundamental social changes. Their ideas HELP in influencing others, just as the ideas of similar important individuals of reactionary ideas ALSO influence the masses. The struggle then is between those different ideas and it takes centuries for the "truth" to conquer; and then there comes a Hitler and all those great ideas are stifled.

You may say, not for good. Sure not: But it is again a question and a struggle of centuries, as it will probably be in Russia. In a word, IF the masses are really not to be depended on, then revolution has no sense; for *after* the "strong individual" comes again, and usually he is reactionary, seeks power, etc.

Well, dear, this is not really the place for such discussion. When you come back we'll talk it all over. It is getting late and I want to send this letter out so it can catch the boat on time. . . . I embrace you and hope, dear, that you did not have to work too hard on those damned articles.

Affectionately,

[AB]

---

* AB was a bit far from the truth here, if Reedy was not. The latter, editor of the St. Louis *Mirror*, had in fact written on November 5, 1908: "There is nothing wrong with Miss Goldman's gospel that I can see, except this: She is about eight thousand years ahead of her age." Berkman's fifty thousand measured rather directly his loss of faith in the "free individual as the basis of a free society." Still, while recognizing this, Emma could properly protest his addition of tens of thousands of years to Reedy's figure.

AB TO EG, November 25, 1934, NICE

Dearest Em,

At last the first five chapters of the Rudolf Rocker ms. have been sent to Joe Goldman, Chicago! It is terrible how long it took me to get the damned thing in final shape. I had to rework and again rework it. I simply could not give it out of my hand before it read sensibly. I left out small passages here and there, and then it was hell to make connections. . . .

In one of those chapters I sent you, you will find Rudolf's argument about the "will to power" being more potent that economic conditions. I think he considerably exaggerated the point. As you know, I have always considered economics the MOST important factor in individual as well as social life, though NOT the ONLY factor. I think Rudolf has greatly minimized the force of economics in his treatment of the subject. In his succeeding chapters he shows that economic conditions and aspirations were responsible for most wars, but he again refers to politics as the factor often behind them. But I think that politics itself is only a reflex of economics. Take for instance all the politics of our own day. There is absolutely nothing back of them except the desire for new markets, for raw materials or new territory, which is all economic, of course. That the people are often misled by pretenses of ideal consideration is true. But the people do not make war. The people are misled, but the fact remains that they are misled ALSO for economic reasons—and all those "reasons of state" that Rudolf speaks so much about are ALSO masked economic reasons of the privileged classes. In short, I think his argument on that point is weak.

Enough for today, dear. Must write Joe Goldman. I hope you are feeling well, and try to be as cheerful as possible in this rotten world. I embrace you, dear,

S

EG TO AB, February 12, 1935, MONTREAL

Sash, my dear,

. . . You will be interested in the enclosed article, [Charney] Vladek's interview about the condition of the Jews. He is right, of course, the main cause of anti-Jewish feeling is economic, and that no doubt would be eliminated in a sane economic society. But there is so much more to anti-Semitism, tradition of centuries, ingrained antipathies, and what not. I don't see how that is going to be done away with even in a free society. Witness Russia. One thing is certain, Palestine won't. There is already as much disagreement and antagonism in Palestine among the Jews as outside of it. Sabotinsky spoke here Sunday. I did not hear him. But I understand he sailed into the Zionists. I don't know whether you know that he plays the part of Mussolini among the Jews. He is for dictatorship, and a strong military power, and what not. Anyway, for the present the situation of Jews all over the world is not enviable. I can see the anti-Jewish feeling here and the discrimination. It's sad. . . .

The "Berengaria" sails from New York Friday. So I will mail this tomorrow. Perhaps there will be a letter from you. Love to Emmy and loads of it to you, dearest, own Sash,

Emma

AB TO PAULINE TURKEL, *March 21, 1935, NICE*

My dear Pauline,

I am sorry I could not reply to your last (of February 11th) before this. Life is one damned thing after another, and there is little time for correspondence. However, I really meant to write you before, for there are some things in your letter that need attention. . . .

You say that you have "a sneaky suspicion" that I "have doubted anarchism once in a while." I don't know, my dear Pauline, what has given you such an impression. No, I have never doubted it. I mean, I have never doubted that there is no way out for mankind except anarchism. I am as sure today as I ever was that neither war nor capitalism will ever be abolished, nor any of the evils that those things represent, until society will become sensible enough to introduce international cooperation and individual liberty on the basis of a free communism.

That, in my estimation, is the ONLY solution to our troubles. The human mind has so far not thought out a better way. And I am just as convinced today as I ever was that neither socialism nor bolshevism will bring relief to man.

But maybe you referred to the TIME when anarchism will become a reality. Well, in that regard the present trend of events is certainly not encouraging. There was a time, in the youth of the revolutionary movement in the U.S., when we all thought that the social revolution was not very far off, and revolution then meant to us practically anarchism. Now we know that the social revolution is not in the offing yet, and even when it comes it will only by the first step on the road *toward* anarchist communism. Yes, that may take a long time, and maybe mankind will destroy itself before then. But when I say that I have no doubts about anarchism as an ideal, I mean that IF mankind continues to live—as I think it will in spite of everything—then the progress of mechanics and science on the one hand, the growing unbearableness of conditions on the other, plus the idealism that I consider inherent in human nature—will necessarily lead to anarchism, or to some social system resembling it in its essential features.

Maybe you are surprised that I say idealism is inherent in human nature. It may sound rather strange in the face of present tendencies. And yet what I say is true. The people are indeed deluded by all kinds of fakes, and yet beneath it all is the hunger of the people for an ideal. Look at Russia, or even at Germany. The LEADERS seek power and glory and personal emoluments. But the great MASSES actually believe they are working for an ideal. They have been MADE to believe it, and their ideal is counterfeit, but that does not alter the fact that they BELIEVE they are struggling for an ideal.

It is in THIS that I find hope for mankind. And it has been the same all through human history. Did not the American MASSES believe during the last war that they were fighting to abolish war and to make "the world safe for democracy?" And if you go back to older days, it was the same. Do you think that those millions that gave their lives in the Crusades did so for any other reason than that they were moved by a great FAITH? They wanted to save the Holy Sepulchre from the barbarians. You probably remember from your history that there were even entire armies consisting exclusively of children of tender age. Millions of them were slaughtered in the Crusades. Did those youngsters fight for anything but the faith that was in them?

The communists in Russia—not the leaders but the rank and file—have been going hungry and suffering and working hard in the enthusiasm of their great ideal. And the millions of nazis in Germany who believe in Hitler—by what are they motivated? By the ideal of a regenerated Germany!

The tragedy is that those ideals are false, but yet it all proves that men DO long and fight for ideals. And in THAT is the great hope of humanity. Some day people will find the REAL ideal—and they will fight for it and realize it.

In closing—for I must get back to my work—one must not limit his view of such BIG questions to the momentary situation. That is why I never turn pessimist. You say "we cannot stop fascism." Well, suppose we cannot; what of it? The world has often gone through mass aberrations. History is replete with such examples—there have been the Crusades, you know, which were similar aberrations that lasted *several centuries*. And the Hundred Years' War, and the Thirty Years' War, etc., etc. But out of all that mankind came out ALIVE, and progress continued for all that and all that. And though mankind is still very much deluded by false ideas and still very stupid, yet the average man today is FAR above the type of the Middle Ages and even of the man of fifty years ago. Whoever believed that war should be abolished fifty years ago? Today every government talks of it. Pretense, you say. All right, but they are FORCED to MAKE that pretense and why? Because the POPULAR SENTIMENT has changed.

So, in spite of all pessimists, there HAS BEEN a change in the attitude of men. And that change goes on all the time, even if it is so slow that some people do not see it. And so it will go on, and neither fascism, Hitler, Mussolini, nor the Popes and other gods can change that inherent fact of human nature. Fascism and nationalism are nothing new. Under different names they existed in old Rome and Greece and in the feudal times. They PASSED and so will the modern fascism pass—and that is why I do not doubt my anarchism.

Well, enough of it. So, cheer up, dear girl. The skies are black just now, but the sun always breaks out again. I may not see much of it in my time, but idealism to me does not mean the hope of realizing one's dream in one's own lifetime. Idealism means, at least to me, FAITH in one's ideal. And that I have.

Things here pretty low. We see only Nellie [Harris] occasionally. No one else we know in the city. By the way, we are giving up our apartment the end of this month. Write me to St. Tropez. EG expects to be back the first week of May. Love to you, dear girl, from Emmy and

[AB]

EG TO C. V. COOK, September 29, 1935, ST. TROPEZ

Dear C. V.:

. . . your lengthy dissertation on the nature of revolution is to my mind very much confused. I certainly never visualized revolution as a sudden cloudburst. I have always maintained that revolution is the culminating point of all the preceding evolutionary forces. In this sense revolution is as inevitable as the clash of the forces in nature that have reached their breaking point. To say that you will have none of revolution is as illogical as if you would say you will have none of a thunderstorm. It will come whether you so wish it or not. And that is the kind of revolution that happened in Russia. That also explains the extraordinary lack of violence during the actual overthrow of the old regime. Violence, terror, and the coercions came only with the advent of the bolshevik state. You are unfortunately making the same mistake as so many others. You confuse the soviet ascendency to power with the Revolution. Nothing is further removed from the historic facts. The first Revolution in Russia took place because the whole system had disintegrated and had come to a head as a poisonous growth that bursts at the first pinprick. The second and main Revolution was the result of a century of evolutionary social ideas to the effect that the peasant had a right to the land and the worker to the means of production. The peasantry and the workers in the period between March and October simply carried out what they had been taught and prepared for. They took the land and the factories. That was the ACTUAL REVOLUTION and not the seal put to it by Lenin. With every fibre I was then and am now for such a revolution. Of course you are right when you say social progress is slow. That is to say we think it is slow because we cannot perceive it with our naked eye. We see the progress only when the social forces break loose in a revolutionary manifestation. In conclusion I wish to say that it is with the social forces as with the human body. We go about for years in the best of health. A sudden breakdown throws us on our back and makes us aware of the poisonous elements in our system we never imagined to be there. In a sense our collapse is nature's warning and our illness a means of rebuilding our physical forces. Naturally, revolution, being the articulation of the social changes preceding it, must needs be all-inclusive and far-reaching. I cannot see, therefore, how any clear mind can be opposed to revolution. True, revolutions have been misused and prostituted. But that had nothing to do with the thing itself. Whether you will agree with me or not I can only tell you that my Russian experience, far from weakening my belief in revolution, has strengthened it. More than ever am I convinced that fundamental changes will never come except through revolution. And that revolution can be constructive, if its intrinsic meaning and value have been grasped. . . .

[Now] my dear, what makes you think Berkman and I did not know the cost when we went into the anti-war work? We foresaw the consequences only too clearly. But we felt that to stop anti-war work just because America had entered the war, when we had been opposed to it all our conscious years, was to go back on everything we had ever held high. We left such a betrayal to the pacifists and anti-militarists. We could not do it, if our lives had depended on it. But what had that to do with my becoming an alien? I might have been much more of an alien and a traitor to boot if I had refrained from anti-war work. This way even our bitterest enemies cannot charge us with having denied our ideas. In point of fact, it was no less a conservative paper than the *Times* that wrote, "Whatever may be said against Berkman and Goldman, no one can charge them with cowardice. They have always stood their ground and they have bravely paid the price." Not that I care about the *Times*. But I merely want to point out that though I have lost my right to America, I have not forfeited the prestige I had built up in America. More important still is the fact that tens of thousands, to take only a small figure, have come to see that our anti-war position was right and to respect us for it. I would not change that for any safety and security America could give me. I assure you I would do it all over again, as indeed I intend to go ahead against the new war when I come to England. Believe me it will not be because I want to "break" into the penitentiary. Rather will it be because I have never been able to understand how people can stand for an ideal in time of peace and deny it in time of danger. At least I never could. I don't want you to follow my example. Naturally, everyone must decide such things for himself.

[Finally] . . . about your stand in re the [American] Civil Liberties

Union and Roger Baldwin: I am absolutely at variance with him on Russia. But as far as his efforts for the communists are concerned, not you but he is right. And so is the CLU. So long as the communists are being robbed of their freedom of speech and are being hounded from pillar to post, it is the business of an organization like the CLU to defend them. That does not mean that it must be silent on the abuses of power of the communists and on the fact that they are doing the same in Russia and would [do] in America as they are being done [to] by the reactionaries in other countries. After all, free speech does not mean that people may say what is pleasant to us. It also means that they may have the right to criticize us. Or it is not free speech. It is in fact the kind of freedom [Herbert or J. Edgar?] Hoover believes in. That is just the trouble: so few people understand the meaning of freedom. You will forgive me, my dear, but I think you are most inconsistent, if you refuse to support an organization like the CLU because it aids the communists. I think it is the most vital organization in America. And it is doing splendid work. . . .

Well, my dear, this is a long yarn, and you will have to take a day off to read it, but you've wished it on yourself.

Affectionately,

[EG]

AB TO EG, December 9, 1935, NICE

Dearest Em,

Have cleaned out my machine and put in a new ribbon, so I hope it will write a bit better. . . .

All your letters received, dear. I know what a hard struggle you are having, and I wish I could be of some help to you. But that is out of the question, of course. But I do hope your meetings are improving. You are now in Plymouth, and I wonder how the lectures have been going there. England has certainly been the most thankless place for radical ideas, even throughout the centuries. Yet at the same time it has been the home of liberalism; that is, of a comparatively liberal attitude in general. Tradition is very strong in England, and they are given to holding on to the existing, and changes there have always been very slow in coming through. But once imbued with a new idea they have usually stood by it, those strange Anglo-Saxons. Besides, they are a headstrong and "practical" people; they want to see where they are going to land before they jump. They want things "proved" to them first, and that is also the reason why their philosophy has always been of the "practical" kind rather than of the speculative, like the German philosophy, for instance. Of course that has some great advantages: they have avoided the pitfalls of philosophic speculation and have never developed such metaphysics as the Germans did. But on the other hand this attitude makes them less apt to embrace a philosophy like anarchism, for new views of life cannot be "proved" like mathematical problems. One must feel their truth intuitively and have the courage to try them out in life.

Well, I guess you are too busy now to worry over these matters. But I say this only with the hope that you will not eat your heart out over the coldness of your audiences and of the public in general toward our ideas. Maybe I say this because Nettlau has urged me to write a book (irrespective of whether it will ever be published, he said) on the necessity of making our appeal for anarchism to the more intelligent classes rather than to the masses. Well, I am not thinking of writing any such book, of course, but I entirely disagree with his idea. We may interest here and there a handful of the "intelligent," but that will be a passing and superficial interest without any results of value. I think that the only chance of anarchism is in winning the masses for our ideas; or at least the intelligent and active part of those masses, no matter if they are a minority. Nor can we ever do even that unless we in some way combine our anarchist preaching with the actual facts of life and make our ideas applicable, even to some extent, to the actual problems and realities of existence.

Literature, art, and philosophy have from time immemorial reflected the spirit of liberty and even expressed anarchist ideas, even beginning with the Stoics. But it had no effect and can have no effect unless those aspirations actually mirror the needs and demands of the people at large. That is why revolutions have always fallen short of their original aims: the people were satisfied with much less than the ideal purposes of the revolution, and politicians and demagogues are always at hand to exploit the situation for their own objects. . . .

I hope you will not be so cold there again. Though it is reported that a cold spell is passing over the entire of Europe. Even here it has been unusually cold and still is. I hope the spell will soon pass.

Well, dear heart, I guess this is enough for today. I don't write often because there is nothing to write about, really. We are both well, and that is about all I can say. Machine beginning to bother again, letters are all worn out. Still, I think you will have no trouble reading this. Love to you. My next letter will be to London,

S

4

Women and Men

I do not believe that middle-aged women lose their sexual attraction or "usefulness," as you call it. That is only one
of the many prejudices in regard to women. I know scores of
women who are wonderfully youthful, vivacious, and interesting who are past middle age. It is only the idiotic discrimination society makes between the man and woman of the
same age. Thus any man, no matter how decrepit, can and
does attract young girls. Why should it not be the same in
the case of the woman? In point of fact, it is. I could give you
some examples of men of thirty-five having fallen in love
with women of sixty. Why not, if the women are attractive,
have a young spirit, have a fine and alert mind, and are
emotionally strong. It is this which makes relationship
between two people where the woman is older so difficult
and often very tragic. . . . Today the outside world will not
forgive such beauty and harmony. It will drag it through the
mire and make both the man and the woman so conscious of
their different ages it must needs end in misery and unhappiness.

EG TO BEN TAYLOR, *June 11, 1936*, ST. TROPEZ

LIKE the nineteenth-century exile Margaret Fuller, Emma Goldman had one of the best minds around and she was just as readily dismissed by arrogant males as an emotional woman. In her review of *Living My Life* (*Nation*, December 2, 1931) Freda Kirchwey accepted the masculine consensus in her verdict, which Emma reported to Berkman in exasperation, that "EG never acted as a result of having thought out her action. She acted by impulse." Even Evelyn Scott, though she granted Emma common sense or, as she put it in her precise way, "the kind of mentality usually called masculine," still seemed to join the critics in her insistence that "your element is passion."

In the correspondence of the two comrades, this issue repeatedly surfaced and her arguments, as on the Russian terror, were rejected by Berkman as too sentimental and womanish. He maintained that man and woman are so different, not only biologically but also mentally, that their understanding of certain questions, such as sex and violence, political action, and revolution, is bound to be different. The gulf between the sexes remains on the level of understanding personal relationships, he asserted: "You and I represent ALL the differences that there are between man and woman as a sex. So where can there ever be any agreement on such matters between us?" But, as you would by now expect, discuss such matters they did and with characteristic intensity: the plight of modern woman, social prejudices against unions in which one of the partners is much older, children of radicals, the phenomena then known as flappers, homosexuality, the like.

Readers of her letters to Harold Laski, Havelock Ellis, Roger Baldwin, *et al.* in the preceding parts, and with Frank Harris, Max Nettlau, *et al.* in this, may be a bit more hesitant about accepting the judgment that Emma Goldman could not think straight. Maybe, we suggest in passing, at her best Emma, again like Margaret Fuller, so fused thought and emotion that she went beyond the conventional sexual categories to clear *and* passionate human thought. At all events, she would have been the last to assert she thought unemotionally: "If you do not feel a thing," she was fond of saying, "you will never guess its meaning." Her participation in the dialogue meant that they would directly relate abstract arguments to specific cases: their dear friends Fitzie, Angelica Balabanov, and Agnes Smedley, his former loves, her former companion Ben Reitman, the son of Nicola Sacco, others. Their correspondence on this theme was especially rich, for Emma, in writing her autobiography, brought old controversies to the surface during this period, opened old wounds—in a sense she had to go through the painful process of re-*Living My Life* before the finished ms. could be sent off to the publisher.

Their letters also pivoted, of course, around their current experiences. After their deportation, by grace of one of history's wry ironies, the "High Priestess of Free Love," as some thought of Emma in the United States, found herself, through no fault of her own, leading virtually a celibate life. After Russia she was briefly involved with a young Swede, Arthur Swenson, in Stockholm and Berlin. And after her return to the United States in 1934, she had a profoundly moving two-week idyl with Frank Heiner, a blind sociologist she had met in Chicago.

In Berlin Berkman had met the young woman who became his companion for the next decade and more. Emmy Eckstein was thirty years younger than he, babyish, neurotic, possessed of all the petty bourgeois prejudices both he and Emma normally despised, but she was also capable of cheerful and lasting devotion to her aging companion. Under the best of circumstances she would have found the close ties of the two older people trying. The circumstances were not good and her neurasthenia and jealousy of Berkman's friends, especially of Emma, did not help. But it was Berkman's infatuation for a person so foreign to his and Emma's experience, ideas, and values that threw them all together to act out what became pretty pathetic scenes. And, as he pointed out, Emma had her own responsibility for the tensions. Never an easy person to live with, she had become more irascible over the years and no doubt unintentionally hurt Emmy on numerous occasions. In fairness we should add that Berkman, caught between two fires, never fully acknowledged to Emma the pathological sweep of Emmy's jealousies. One of his characteristic diary entries (for August 7, 1932), one not involving Emma, read:

> I went with Eve and Emmy to Café Paris [in Nice]. When Eve arrived she acted as if *not* to kiss me as is her wont. I got up from the table, pulled her up, and kissed her. I wanted her to feel that she can be with me in the presence of Emmy the same as always. There have been before remarks about Emmy's jealousy. Well, Emmy got wild and made scene—"don't talk to me." That night was terrible.

But, with this little help, their letters to and about Emmy, along with those that related to Arthur Swenson and Frank Heiner, these and the others should speak for themselves. All of them, whether by and about man or woman, echoed the haunting question posed by a great feminist: "The modern woman cannot be the wife and mother in the old sense, and the new medium has not yet been devised, I mean the way of being wife, mother, friend and yet retain one's complete freedom. Will it ever?"

FRANK HARRIS TO EG, *January 23, 1925, NICE*

My dear Emma,

Your letter with its enclosures didn't surprise me: the English Labor Party is the most timid and cowardly I know anything about, and they have to boot a contempt for truth that goes with their lack of knowledge. You will yet be forced, I think, to come here and write you life. I'm just about to publish the second volume of *My Life [and Loves]*. If I can get 10,000 or 15,000 dollars out of it, I shall be on my feet again and I've paid to learn the ropes and you can profit by my knowledge. Furthermore, we want a woman's view of life and freedom in sex matters, want it badly: your life and mine will be the first chapters in the Bible of Humanity. Tell me about Rebecca West; she interests me; they say she was [H.G.] Wells's mistress: Was she? Has she brains? She wrote about me as God might write about a cockroach; but that only shows she doesn't understand or hadn't read enough. . . .

Wife sings tomorrow in a concert: doggie has a cold; otherwise we are all well and full of good wishes for you. Ever yours affectionately,

Frank Harris

ISADORA DUNCAN TO AB, *April 8, 1925, NICE*

Dearest Sasha,

Do not imagine because I don't write that I do not constantly think of you. You are woven in all my feelings and musings. I don't write because it is too difficult for me to take a pen, dip it in ink, and try to trace on paper my thoughts of you. You know you have the habit of a *writer*, whereas I am used to expressing myself in gesture—and art.

The present to find I am for the first time in my life quite without action—it is chiefly on account of our friend Isaac Don Levine, who promised me more things from Earth and Heaven than one mortal could perform—but I being very credulous have always believed in "Miracles," so I waited for this—Miracle—but he has suddenly disappeared completely and no word of him. I have been waiting all this time to write with him this book which was to bring money to continue my school [of the dance]. They write me that they are without food or fuel in Moscow. Do you know *where* has disappeared this "Miracle"? Or I am beginning to think I should rechristen him *Will O' The Wisp.*

Dear Sasha, how I wish you could come here [from Berlin]. I have taken a studio by the sea and could always give you a divan where you could recline and I would dance for you. Can't you come? If there is trouble with [a] passport, it might be arranged. . . .

You see, I am always ready to believe in a new "Myth," since the bolshevik one didn't turn out.

Dearest Sasha, I kiss you a thousand times and wish with all my heart you could come here. We could walk by the sea or perhaps we could go out in a little boat and sail toward the rising sun.* With all my love,

Isadora

EG TO AB, *May 28, 1925, LONDON*

Dearest,

I ought not to write you today; I feel in a rotten mood. I could not close my eyes all night because of the damned contract [for *My Disillusionment in Russia*]. I don't understand what has become of it. Certainly if you sent it to me, I should have it. . . .

The contract is not the only thing that put me into a desperate mood, it is the impenetrable icy crust of the people in this country. Even the best of them paralyze me. They are so indifferent, so God damned self-centered, nothing touches them. It's like Professor [Samuel Eliot] Morison wrote me, "I have been trying to get English students to learn something of American history with the same result as you. If only one could make the English angry. The only man who could do it was Samuel Adams when he

---

* Although Berkman's letters to Isadora Duncan have evidently not survived, we do know he joined her for that walk by the sea, if not for the sail in the little boat. After her bizarre death in an auto accident, he did no more than record the fact in his diary on September 16, 1927. But a few months later he was himself in Nice, after a bitter quarrel with Emmy Eckstein, and was moved to write out his reflections about the dead woman. In his entry of January 17, 1928, he noted that he had promised her three weeks' help with her book and she had taken an apartment on the Boardwalk where they were to work together. Yet auto trips to Monte Carlo and other diversions intervened, time passed and nothing was on paper, whereupon Berkman lost patience with her and "one afternoon I just left." Though she sent after him, he was sore and refused to return. Now it all seemed so long ago: "Can't even frequent the places I did then—too expensive for my means. And Isadora is gone, poor soul. She's better off now. It was time. But she was a big woman, a great and noble character, outside of her art." Depressed by his memories and the same Boardwalk sights, Berkman put down the other side of the romantic rising-sun imagery, the sad, lonely side: "The waves sullenly dash against the rocks . . . the stupidity and senselessness of it all came strong upon me as I sat there this afternoon. Even fleeting thoughts of [self-]destruction. Yes, loneliness is a bad thing."

threw tea in the Boston harbor. And then there was a revolution." Certainly nothing makes the English snob angry, or ruffles him except the destruction of property. We sent out our appeal; we got so far one pound; there is no interest in the politicals, or in anything else.

I went to see Havelock Ellis today, fine old gentleman with a tremendously vivid mind, but as cold as a cucumber. The whole hour I sat in his house I felt as if something were clutching at my throat; I never met among any [other] people men and women so detached from human interest in their personal approach to people as I have met here. Ellis is one. Yet he is not that at all in his writings. In fact, he shows so much understanding and interest. But whether it is a reserve practiced for centuries, or hell knows what, the moment you come into contact with an Englishman you feel a cold breeze which holds you at a distance for miles. Or is it that I am so hungry for some human response or interest? Is it my fault? Oh, I don't know, I only know I feel rotten here not to have found one human being in eight months who cares a damn for anything outside of his own interests. I am not now thinking of the few comrades I have met in Norwich or Bristol, especially Bristol where the few really care for things outside of their own. But here in London there is positively not a soul. How is one to build up anything or feel inspired to do anything?

I also went to visit Edward Carpenter. He is of a different type, but so old in body, and even mind, he is eighty-two years old, he could not concentrate on anything for more than five minutes. There I found a situation which is interesting as a study, even if it is funny. Carpenter *lives* with a man whom he picked up from the gutter thirty-five years ago, Goe is his name. Everybody knows Goe. Well, the effect of Carpenter's relation to this Goe is identical to the relation of an old husband to a younger wife. Carpenter looks positively shabby in his clothes, but you should see Goe. He is dressed in the latest-fashion suit, with a fine shirt, ring on his finger, and full of his own importance. Poor Carpenter could not get a word in edgeways; Goe keeps up the conversation and keeps everybody and everything away from him. I was somewhat puzzled by Goe's talk at the station while we were waiting for Carpenter, who had gone to a nearby town to visit a niece of his. Goe told us of how many calls for money and other favors poor Ed has, and how poor Ed must be looked after. When I got to the house I realized what Goe was driving at; he evidently thought I came for something. Well, there is one thing to be said for Goe: he takes good care of Ed; the house is spotlessly clean and neat. There is another man outside of Goe, the cook. And, Edward treats Goe every bit as a man treats his younger wife. It really was funny.

But the main pathos, though screamingly comic, is the fact that the cook seems to be the lover of Goe, or at least the younger friend to compensate him for the old age of EC. Really dear, life is a circus if only one has enough sense of humor, which I do not have today.

Both Carpenter and Goe asked very interested questions about you
and when you are coming to England. They have your [Prison] Memoirs
and they told me how impressed they were and how they would like to
meet you. Are you as wonderful as the book leads one to believe? That I
denied, of course. I am sure their interest is mainly because of the homosexual part in your book. EC was always interested in that part of life. Have
you ever read his Intermediate Sex? By the way, I understand EC has
written a book on Shelley, making out, I suppose, that he was intermediate. And the fun is that the work appeared under the signature of Goe
as well. You should hear Goe talk. It is "Me Pachali." Well, as along as EC
has a pleasant and comfortable [old] age, what is the difference? Dear, send
Carpenter your [Bolshevik] Myth with some inscription. . . .

Dear old Sash, you and I will yet end up life agreeing on most issues we
fought so valiantly when we were young, or was it because we were together? Anyway, what you say in regard to Agnes Smedley, though it has
not much bearing on her, is yet true. We all need love and affection and
understanding, and woman needs a damn sight more of that when she
grows older. I am sure that is the main cause of my misery since I left
America. For since then I have had no one, or met anyone who gave a fig
for what I do and what becomes of me. Of course, you dear, I am not
speaking of our friendship; that is a thing apart. But I mean exactly what
you mean, someone intimate, someone personal who would take some
interest, show affection, and really care. I think in the case of one who gave
out so much in her life, it is doubly tragic not to have anyone, to really be
quite alone. Oh, I know, I have the kids [Stella and her family, Saxe, et al.]
at home and a few dear comrades in America and Rudolf and Milly etc.
But it is not that, it is not that. I am consumed by longing for love and
affection for some human being of my own. I know the agony of loneliness
and yearning. I therefore agree fully with you that both men and women
need some person who really cares. The woman needs it more and finds it
impossible to meet anyone when she has reached a certain age. That is her
tragedy.

However, I do not see how this applies to the condition of Agnes. In
the first place, she has a number of men who care violently about her,
Chatto [Virendranath Chattopadhyaya], Mirza, and others [i.e., Indian
revolutionaries]. She has outgrown Chatto, but she seems to be very much
in love with the other. It can therefore not be the lack of male
companionship or love. I don't know what it is; she certainly is a nervous
wreck. And I myself am too miserable most of the time to be of any
comfort to others. Still, I will have to write her soon. . . .

I must close now, dearest. Sorry my letter is so gloomy.

Love,
E

EG TO FRANK HARRIS, August 7, 1925, LONDON

My dear Frank,

On my return from Bristol, I found such a lot of work that I had to plunge into it in mad style. That explains the delay in answering your dear letters. . . .

Now, to your second volume [of *My Life and Loves*]: I have already written you that I found it fascinating. Now I want to add something more. Aside from your wonderful portrait of Maupassant and story about Randolph Churchill, which alone would merit you a niche among the greatest, I was deeply moved by your preface and concluding chapter. More than anything else, they show the real Frank Harris—the sweet, generous, beautiful spirit, a spirit so few have ever seen or know how to appreciate. I am so glad you have written in such a mellow, tender, and self-analyzing manner. I am so anxious that people should know you as I know you. I am sure the preface and concluding chapter will help them to see you in a true light.

There are two thoughts expressed in the preface and the last chapter which strengthened my impression when I read the first volume of your *Life* and also the fourth volume of *Contemporary Portraits.* I said nothing at the time, because I feared that you would not understand me and I am too fond of you to want to hurt you. But now I feel I can speak out. First, in your preface you say that you have come to realize that it is impossible to tell the full truth in regard to intimate relations. I am not quoting because I have not the volume at hand; I merely give the gist. Well, Frank dear, when I read your first volume, I realized at once how utterly impossible it is to be perfectly frank about sex experiences and to do so in an artistic and convincing manner. Believe me, it is not because I have any puritanic feeling or that I care in the least for the condemnation of people. My reasons for the impression regarding the facts of sex are that I do not consider the mere physical fact sufficient to convey the tremendous effect it has upon human emotions and sensations. Perhaps it is because to woman sex has a far greater effect than to man. It creates a greater storm in her being and lingers on when the man is satisfied and at ease. At any rate, I feel that the effect of the sexual relation is psychological and cannot be described in mere physical terms. I mean, of course, sex between two harmonious people, both equally intense. In your description of the physical aspect you have made it vivid enough and yet depth is lacking. Not because you have not the great gift of portraying depth, but because you have concentrated too much on the mere physical description of the various forms of sexual relation. I do not say that you should not have done so, I only mean that for me, at any rate, it will be utterly impossible to describe the physical side which is, after all, very limited, while the psychological is rich and varied. I hope you will not misunderstand, dear Frank.

Secondly, I am very glad indeed that you have come to see that your fourth volume of *Portraits* is not of such a high standard as your first and second. I think the third is like the fourth and does not compare with the first two; they are real masterpieces, works that will live and make your name outstanding among letters. The third and fourth seem to me to have been written in great haste. Please do not think that I am critical of the fourth volume, because of the portrait of myself. Heaven forbid! I appreciate what you have written about me so much that I could not express [it] in so many words, but I know how beautifully you can write. I was sorry that your fourth volume should not come up to your usual stature: that you should say so yourself shows how very honest and unyielding you are with yourself. Very few artists are capable of that. . . .

I had a sweet letter from Nellie, and immediately wrote her to Biarritz. How does it feel to be a "straw-widower?" Dear Frank, you are not angry with me for my criticism, are you? Surely, you know how fond I am of you and how very highly I think of you as the artist and great friend.

Affectionately,
[EG]

EG TO AB, *September 4, 1925, LONDON*

My dearest,

I wrote you a few lines yesterday when I returned from Plymouth. I was in such a wretched state I could hardly see what I was writing. My head ached so and my joints were so sore every step was agony. Then I was so terribly depressed. The strain and anxiety about Fitz, the bitter disappointment of her visit, all put together made me too miserable to write. I took a bath and some aspirin and went to bed at 7 o'clock; you can imagine how miserable I must have felt, if I do such a thing. Well, I slept with only one awakening until seven this morning. My head is better, but I still feel very achy and so heavy-hearted. Nevertheless, I dressed and went to the British Museum, only to find that they were having their annual cleaning, and that is has been closed for four days and will not be opened until tomorrow. So here I am in my room at the typewriter.

I cannot say that I am in fit condition to explain our dear Fitzie to you. First because I am convinced that it is not given us to explain our own conflicts going on in our being, much less the conflict and contradictions going on in others. No matter how much we know them, or love them, I am certain we do not ever [really] know them, man or woman. However, as far as it is possible to know a human being, I think I do know Fitzie, she has talked to me much freer than to most of her friends when she was here two years ago, and this time. Unfortunately, Fitz had only two bright days while here, the first day of her arrival and her last day here. She then tried to pour out her aching heart. Will I be able to convey to you what she said? I fear not. If you were here and I could talk to you, perhaps. But writing things down on paper [makes them] appear so cold and you might misunderstand. I am worried about that. It would be too awful, if I failed to show you the real tragedy of Fitzie, and to make you realize how much you have meant in her life. Well, I will try.

Fitzie's main tragedy which is pulling at her heart is really the tragedy of all of us modern women. It is a fact that we are removed only by a very short period from our traditions, the traditions of being loved, cared for, protected, secured, and above all, the time when women could look forward to an old age of children, a home and someone to brighten their lives. Being away from all that by a mere fraction of time, most modern women, especially when they see age growing upon them, and if they have given out of themselves so abundantly, begin to feel the utter emptiness of their existence, the lack of the *man*, whom they love and who loves them, the comradeship and companionship that grows out of such a relation, the home, a child. And above all the economic security either through the man or their own definite independent efforts. Nearly every modern woman I have known and have read about has come to the condition of Fitzie. All have felt and feel that their lives are empty and that they have nothing to look forward to.

Now in Fitzie's case there is something more, no not Jimmy [Light?] by a long shot, but you. You were her grand passion and your work filled her life and gave it meaning. As Fitzie kindly said, "Sasha and you have made me and have filled my life with all that was worth struggling for. Then when you both went to prison and everything else was destroyed, I went to the Provincetown theater hoping I might be able to express what you and Sasha stood for by means of the theater, at any rate until you would both be released from prison. Then when you were deported and the last hope of our work together [was] completely crushed, I clung to the theater as the only means of expression." I am giving you Fitzie's words as nearly as I can. This helped me to realize that Fitzie while we were in prison clung to the hope that when you came out she would be able to take up life and work again with you, for in you she found the man she loved, the idealist, and the child as well. Her episode while you were in prison was nothing at all. Had you remained in America Fitzie would have left the theater and whoever was temporarily in her life and would have gone with you, especially if you had understood her better and had not pulled at her vitals so much as you did at the time. But then Fitzie understood that you were ill and in a shattered condition when you came out of Atlanta—she would have soon gotten over that part.

Well, we were deported, we were away, and there was no hope of our return and [resumption of] Fitzie's life and work with you. During that time she attached herself to the theater not merely as a means of livelihood, but because she hoped she could continue advanced ideas by means of the drama and that she could make her life count for something, for something that would fill the gap your loss had created in her soul. When Fitzie came back two years ago she was too ill physically to feel anything in the way of sex, but her love for you had not changed. Had you been in an English-speaking country with some means to secure you both, I do not think Fitzie would have gone back. Then too she found you entangled with two affairs. Not that she minded it, but she was afraid that there would be too many complications. And Fitzie was tired to death from such complications. She had gone through hell itself with [Harry] Weinberger. To her he was a passing attraction, largely because of his devotion to us during our trouble and her utter loneliness when she was robbed of everything. To him it was a question of life and death. He held on to Fitzie like one possessed and when he saw that she did not feel quite the same for him as he did for her, he became cruel, unreasonable, positively brutal, as most men do when they see the woman slip away. He tore Fitzie to pieces, waylaid her, threatened to shoot himself, made public scenes. In short [he] did everything to repel her and left her wounded and broken. And this brings me to another cause of Fitzie's unhappiness, which is also the cause of unhappiness of many other advanced women. It is this, the woman wants affection, devotion, tenderness more than sex. Very few modern men realize that. I do not mean that Fitzie has lost her sexual passion, not at all, but she has been so torn and pulled about by it, she has been so wounded and hurt by nearly every one of her sex experiences that she almost dreads it now. But she does long for affection, for tenderness, for understanding. You did not give her that two years ago, Sasha dear, so Fitzie went back to take up the threads of her New York life again, holding on to the hope that at least if she could help to bring out young talent, young native talent, her life would have some meaning. Well, she failed again.

Now comes the climax, the theater gave her little else but responsibility, worry, everybody's trouble. She spent her time and substance in separating feuds, in explaining everybody's pettiness and jealousies. Until finally she became a nervous wreck. She felt she had to get away. She told me she felt as if some unknown force pulled her to Europe, to you, to Djuna [Barnes], of whom she seems very fond, and to me. And when she came to you she realized that she had chased phantoms while all the while she wanted the meaning of life contained in you and what your work has given her. Mark you, Fitzie did not say it in so many words. In fact she never spoke of you alone, but always of "you, Emma and Sasha." But I understood her only too well. It was not even so much you the man, or I the woman, but our part in her life, the real friends she had and who had enriched her life. She realized that all she had done the last six years, all she had hoped for, and the people who were in her life, had left her stranded, empty, useless, and without anything to look forward to. It was a terrific upheaval in her brain while she was with you, though she was not aware of it so much at the time. And perhaps she would not have become aware of it until her return to her New York life. But when she met the Provincetown people [over here], they simply brought her back to the last six years and brought out more poignantly the conflict in her. The conflict between what you and perhaps I have meant to her, or rather the work and dreams with us and the emptiness that Provincetown stands for—hence the breakdown. I am sure that was the cause of it all. I mean the last straw which broke her reserve and her control, though that was not the *Particular Thing*, as you call it. The *Particular Thing* is the tragedy of all emancipated women, myself included. We are still rooted in the old soil, though our visions are of the future and our desire is to be free and independent. In the case of women who like Fitzie have no creative abilities, the tragedy is deeper, because they, even more than the others, can express themselves only in love and devotion for the man and the child, or for both in the man.

I have tried, dear, just to give you an inkling of the thing which is making Fitzie so unhappy. I fear I have not succeeded. I hope though you will try to understand that it is deeper than this or that man, or whatever sex experience Fitzie might have had. It is a longing for fulfillment which very few modern women find because most modern men too are rooted in the old traditions. They too want the woman as wife and mother more than as lover and friend. The modern woman cannot be the wife and mother in the old sense, and the new medium has not yet been devised, I mean the way of being wife, mother, friend and yet retain one's complete freedom. Will it ever? . . .

I was terribly affected by Fitzie's going back to the land that has shut me out. I felt it especially when I got on board the "France." I would have given years of my life if I could have gone along with her. Ah, well. Life is one huge failure to most of us. The only way to endure it is to keep a stiff upper lip and drink to the next experience. . . .

Well, dear Sash, I have written myself dry, I must stop. How I do such long letters? Well, I do damned little else. If I could write sketches or articles as easy as letters, I would probably be able to earn a lot of money. But my letters mean nothing now except to those who receive them. After my death they may fetch some money. . . .

Goodby, dear, I still have a lot to write, today being Friday, Stella, Harry Weinberger, etc. I embrace you tenderly,

E

P.S. The very letter I wanted to be perfect looks like a battlefield. I am hopeless, I know.

EG TO AB, *September 10, 1925, LONDON*

Dearest,

There is certainly a community of moods and feelings between us.* I too have been terribly depressed since Fitzie's departure and I have not been able to get back to work. It is always bad to break in on work when one is in the midst of it. . . .

What you say in regard to the deeper cause of our tragedies is correct, if only we knew what this complicated, baffling, elusive thing human nature is. I confess the older I get, the less I know about it. Of course the price we modern women and men too pay for our own development and growth is very great and painful, but one must go ahead or remain in the dull state of the cow. For it is not only the modern woman, but all civilized people who pay a certain price for their awakening. Another thing is that even the ordinary woman is not sure that she will have her children, her man, her home in her old age. Nothing is certain in our time, or perhaps never was at any time, for those who must struggle for their existence. In what way, then, is the ordinary woman better off than we are? I rather think she is worse off. For while the modern woman, if more exacting and has greater and deeper needs, so too she has considerable richness out of her finer sensibilities and deeper understanding. There is nothing without a price and we must be ready to pay it. Fact is, we have no choice. There is a terrific urge toward freedom, toward the struggle for higher ideals which no one can resist. What then is to be done?

In the case of women like Fitzie the situation is aggravated by their inability to do independent work which would fill their lives. Of course, no work fills one's life, one needs love and comradeship at all times. But while some of us can forget themselves a little in the work we are doing, or want to do, Fitzie and others like her find little comfort in the work they are doing—especially when they see nothing really worthwhile come out of their efforts. In our case the misery has been increased by the collapse of our faith through Russia. I can honestly say that I never felt the terrible loneliness and such defeat while I was in America and still fervently believed in the social revolution, which I no longer do. And that at bottom is also the case with you dearest. Perhaps with all sensitive, earnest people. Look at Angelica [Balabanov]. She wrote me a card en tour that she is crossing Europe with heavy head and heart. I am sure she never before was conscious of heaviness, for she is the type who lived almost entirely for her ideal. Or such women as Babushka [Catherine Breshkovskaya]. But all their hopes and ideals have been shattered and not having personal interests they must be wretched and in despair. It is worse with those of us who

---

* Unfortunately we have been unable to locate AB's side of this particular exchange.

have versatile natures, those who love beauty, art, music, those who need companionship. Ah, well, it is as it is. . . .

Tonight is the opening of [Eugene O'Neill's] *Emperor Jones.* I wish you could go with me. I am taking a little English woman who is helping with the course of lectures here. I was terribly excited about tonight, but I feel so depressed today. Harry Ballantine dashed in last night; he will also be at the theater and so will the Healeys; I suppose many Americans will. I'd love to have you here, my own precious chum. Yes, dearest, we must meet in Paris, I am awfully hungry for the sight of you and for your companionship. I'd feel in a better mood to work, if I could have a little time with you. I am arranging to be free from the 20th of December to the end of January. I simply must manage to get away from here and meet you somewhere. I embrace you tenderly,

E

AGNES SMEDLEY TO EG, Sunday, BERLIN

My dear Emma,

Now I shall at last reply to your long letter of April 23rd. I am better. But were I to follow my real feelings, my letter would be a document unfit for human eyes.

Your life appears to me to be filled with many interesting things—activity and then more activity. Why you are not content I do not know. I don't believe you are a person who could be content, even if you had the world by the tail and were twisting it to suit yourself. Still you would say that you were doing nothing and were failing in your work! Objectively you do enough and more than enough. But you seem to be like me, content only when you have so much to do that you can do nothing. That is subjective discontent. . . .

And yet, why can I not find the person in whom I feel perfect rest and contentment—complete understanding? People are interesting, Emma, but I never find the person with whom I feel spiritually intimate. . . .

You may laugh. You are a person who mingles with people easily—you and Chatto. Clap! And they are drawn to you like flies to a fly-paper. And they serve you and worship you. Perhaps it does not matter to you, if they are far from you spiritually. You take what there is to be had and *schluss* [that's the end of it]. You are wise and sane. But I am lonely and insane. I have found but two people in life to whom I stand as intimately (spiritually speaking) as human beings can ever stand to each other, and one was Bakar. But it is in the nature of things that he should have been the very person who *should* have stood on the other side of the gulf. . . .

I am not writing at all. My drama has been locked up in the drawer of my desk. My articles likewise. The article on Käthe Kollwitz exists only in my imagination and will perhaps continue to do so. My mind is simply incapable of writing, and I, in order to drag on living, have taken to teaching. I hate it. But my mind is so deeply disturbed at all times, so unspeakably unhappy, that it is absolutely impossible for me to write. I cannot tell you the depths into which I have sunk mentally. I simply cannot rise out of it. I haven't enough hope and desire in me to write a line. I just exist, hoping that maybe something will happen on the morrow which will give me back the illusion that life is worthwhile and that writing is worthwhile. In the meantime I drag on from day to day, a rag—nothing but a rag.

Chatto will be better eventually. He is now in Saxony. He is in the city a few days during the week only and the rest of the time is collecting advertisements for his magazine and in order to make money. He is under treatment only twice a week, and that is too little. He is looking very tired and old. My heart is filled with pity. I could erase that look and give him back much strength, if I would return and live with him, or even tell him that I intend to do so. But I cannot. Often I think that he is of far more value than I am; everybody knows that—all of you anarchists and revolutionaries, all of the Indians, everybody who knows us both. But I still cannot force myself back. Sometimes I am on the verge of doing it. He is so deeply miserable and worn down much of the time. Still I know that if I return to him, I shall kill myself within a month. And I often wonder if I shall not do it eventually anyway, even if I do not return. My mind concerns itself with such things when I lie awake for hours at night. Yet it seems so useless for his life to be wasted all for the sake of a woman. It is only that, for I cannot give him the help he needs half as much as another woman could. He is laboring under illusion, only. I tell you I am in a mess, mentally. I know what you say—go away—as you have said. That is the intelligent viewpoint. I am not dealing with a man who regards me intelligently, but only emotionally. Had he had an intelligent view, he would have left me three years ago, when I wanted to go. Life does not exist only by intelligence. During the summer I shall be in Denmark and in Czechoslovakia and I hope that in this manner the chains will be broken, for he will know that I am still in Europe, and yet he will be separated from me and will be forced to find new friends and associates—and I hope other women. . . .

You ask about Bakar's brother. He is in very fine health now, and I have no more trouble. You are right about mothering boys. This was hardly such a case. You mention Arthur [Swenson] in that connection. And you are wrong in thinking that I misunderstood anything at all. I did not and I do not. I took it for granted that you were caring for a young man, just as your house was always a roosting place for all sorts of birds of passage. Nothing else ever entered my mind and it was Stella, who, in Bad Liebenstein, told me I was naive, and insisted upon saying that your relationship to Arthur was of another sort. Even then I let it drop. It did not matter to me and even so I did not see anything one way or the other to talk about. And, with all due respect for your love of Stella, I did not always pay special attention to Stella's opinions. . . . But now that you mention it, I can only say that this mother love which lies in us women is a hell of a thing to deal with, and I suppose it causes more sting than anything else. I suppose there is no pain to equal that of an older woman for a younger man. I think that even if I knew a woman who was an enemy of mine, I would still try and spare her that pain. For it leaves scars which never quite heal.

Of course, all this has nothing to do with Bakar's brother here. I brought it up merely because you mention it. There was nothing of that kind between us. I do everything I can for the boy, and it is true that he became rather dependent upon me emotionally. But then I tried to put him on his feet, and when he refused to stand, I put him under psychoanalytic treatment like my own. And within one week he was on his own feet, resuming his regular work and turning his attention to his landlady's daughter! The next lady in sight! And now I think it is his doctor—who is a young woman—to whom his heart belongs! And in six months it will be someone else! He is in the age where he will do such things until his sex life is regulated. It wasn't *me* as me. It was me because I was a woman and mended his clothes and helped him when he needed it. What really broke me in the whole thing was Chatto's attitude toward me and the situation. He acted as if I were a criminal. He merely used it as a club over my head, and when I put the boy under treatment, he was bitter and hostile against me. He had nothing to suggest himself to meet the situation. He only accused me of all sorts of things. And now that the boy is again on his feet and hasn't even the interest to see me often, still Chatto is angry because I was right and proved to him that I was right.

Men are damned fools. I mean, *husbands* are damned fools. I'll never have one again, so help me God. Never again will I put my life under the influence of any man who lives. And if I ever love one, I'll see to it that a good safe distance is kept between us. I have been hurt quite enough for not only one life, but for a thousand. It reminds me of that ancient Chinese couplet:

> Man reaches scarce a hundred; yet his tears
> Would fill a lifetime of a thousand years.

Well, enough wailing. I should perhaps follow the advice of old Captain Shotover in Shaw's play, *Heartbreak House*, in which he exclaims with disgust when the millionaire is sniffling because a woman has broken his heart: "Silence! Let the heart break in silence!"

I disagree with you about love and sadism etc., but I won't write more today. This is enough to occupy your time for once. My love to you, dearest Emma,

Agnes

EVELYN SCOTT TO EG, *October 6, 1926, LISBON*

Dearest Emma,

    ... All of us enjoyed the "Voltairine De Cleyre" and "John Most" particularly. In spite of the abstract nature of idealism and your own fine and intense devotion to it, I think your profound warmth of feeling for these individuals much more moving—needs must be more moving—than the more measured though certainly interesting discussion on the "General Strike" and "America by Comparison." And of the two—maybe through the accident of personal appeal, for the Most one is very excellent—the Voltairine appeals to me the most. You certainly have shown the most beautiful comprehension of the strong and weak points in a temperament too forceful to be called pathetic, and yet in which there is an innocence of belief, if I may use the phrase, that, only by virtue (or fault, as you like) of its harshness takes on the consciousness of tragedy. I honestly never read a critical biography in brief which gave me a finer—and very few as fine—or more rounded sense of the unique human entity that is the subject.

    There are two kinds of writing that I most enjoy. In one type, which is really less personal than your own however abstractly motivated kind, there is a passionate meticulousness of observation which concerns itself, with a morally indiscriminate ardor, with the details of sense impressions, with the eternal and—logically considered—irrelevant sequence of minutia—a kind of super Flaubertism. And there is another kind, more sensitive to suffering or the spectacle of suffering, which has a characteristic impatience so fierce that its moral eclecticism tends to simplify its materials. The last kind makes, through its ardent identity with the sufferer, an instinctive selection of those aspects of human nature which constitute what the religious-minded call revelation. This kind knows, with an immediate understanding, the condition of the psyche at those moments in which feeling is most agonizingly intense—and it knows these high points through its own experience and more fully than the less moral writer ever can—for it seems to me that moral theories or ideal enunciations of theories are the inevitable reaction to suffering felt or witnessed by a sensitive imagination. To be absolutely frank, as you asked, I don't think the writer of this last type can convey an equal sense of actuality to the less poignant but, perhaps, as I look at it, anyhow, equally real sequence of more extrovert moments. Pain and pleasure, in their overlapping, are, both, in the nature of intoxicants when they are partaken of in their full strength, and those who have suffered exceedingly (or been happy exceedingly, which is much the same) I do believe, having partaken of this super-vivid consciousness, begin to depend on this knowledge of the real as exceeding all others. If their philosophy is idealism, logic supports it. Anyhow, I think they do depend on it. Consequently, in writing, it is this supreme moment in which they are instinctively (or deliberately) most interested, and it is in revealing that aspect of subjectivity that they excel. I think you are that kind of a person, and the more poignant your theme the surer your instinct for interpreting it. I know you would be commonly placed in the intellectual category—but the excellence of your mind does not seem to me the essential factor in describing you. And the same of Voltairine De Cleyre, whom you have understood so well, [and] with John Most, too, I should think. I don't care how well your mind functions, your element is passion and it is where your common sense acts only to measure taste and appropriateness, and your feeling is dominant that your expression is most revealing. I can see you are capable of much tolerance, and your pragmatic (common sense) view of things runs parallel with your other view at will, and I realize that said common sense—the kind of mentality usually called masculine—has given you all kinds of capabilities for practical leadership you wouldn't have had otherwise. Just the same, where I take off my hat to Emma Goldman with the most sincere respect to the human and the artist is to her underlying spirit which says common sense and the restraint of the purely mental, or the mentally controlled, outlook be damned. In these articles, it is the sympathy with the passionate temperament which makes your interpretation so complete. And—if I am not wearing you out with airing of opinions on you, about which subject I maybe ought to keep my mouth shut—I would guess, in all your writing—that done, which I have not read, and that which you will do—it is the capacity to let go which does and will point the greatness. I know your mental awareness is such that you demand the fine motive, the rational motive, before you take the plunge—but the plunge is into your own psyche, and the mental impatience (which you may deny since you control it so much) seems to me beautifully and entirely justified. Some people are born artists, but they are seldom, therefore, great artists because they are not great people. Most geniuses have an imperfect sense of art because their quick sensibilities allow life to impinge so overwhelmingly that they must struggle to survive the deluge. What they express in defiance of this struggle has the elements of something more profound, and becomes great art in spite of itself. I know numbers of people who are aesthetically sensitive who lack the will to coordinate the results of their impressionableness. A strong will always finds itself at bay and it develops through battles with other than aesthetic problems. When it turns to art to articulate the result is an imperfection which is above price. And now—again—that's why I think the autobiography and many other things must be written. . . .

Good luck from all of us to the Canadian tour—may it add ducats to fame. Please let me hear from you when you have time. . . .

Love from,
Evelyn

EG TO EVELYN SCOTT, November 21, 1927, TORONTO

Dearest Evelyn,

I have your short scrib which was not dated, and your interesting letter of the 3rd. As usual, your letter is full of color and meaning. What a wise girl you are, and how unerring your judgment in a great many things. I know, my dearest, that you do not want to feed me on the "Pollyanna" optimism. You are too deep yourself, and know the tragedy of life [too well] to be satisfied with things, and you have looked too much in my soul to think for a moment that any of the New Thought stuff can have an effect on me. Quite a number of people have tried to buoy me up by the shallow optimism pawned off by the New Thoughters. I had a funny experience with a woman who swears by hypnotism and new thought. It was while I was laid up with the pain in my spine, and could not sleep for a number of nights. She assured me solemnly that she could put me to sleep, and what do you suppose she did? She dangled her locket before my eyes for a few moments, murmured something, and kept on saying, "Sleep, Sleep." I kept my face straight for a while and finally asked her whether she thought such methods could have any effect on my brain. But this poor fool must have dealt with a lot of hysterical women with whom she no doubt had success. . . .

I don't think the large audiences at the Bernard Shaw lectures are an indication of the interest people in this city have in Shaw. It is much more due to the fact that it has become a vogue. By the way, did you read the article by [H.G.] Wells in last Sunday's *Times?* It is the most scathing arraignment of George Bernard Shaw I have ever read, and what is more important, no one has so caught the whole character of Shaw with all its superficialities, contradictions, and poses. I have never particularly cared for Wells's writings, but in his appraisement of Shaw he really spoke out of my own heart. Time and again I was considered a heathen because I insisted that Shaw is not an artist. He is clever and witty, to be sure, but he has no depth, neither have his characters, with perhaps one or two exceptions like Marchbanks, Dubdaad, and Guineviere. On the whole, though, his characters are puppets to do the bidding of Mr. Shaw, express his ideas, but otherwise without life or passion. But then Shaw is a puritan through and through, much as he might rave against puritanism. That is why he is rigid in some respects and ridiculously contradictory in others. His defense of fascism and Mussolini proved how utterly confused Shaw is in great social and political questions. He has played up to the gallery so long that it is not surprising he should have made the recent plunge. But then he succeeded and now he is considered the Wise Man of Western Europe.

To come back to the optimistic attitude toward life, Walt Whitman had an overdose of that. Sometimes his optimism appeals to me and other times it seems so childish. Whitman too was a considerable contradiction. In going over the material for my lecture I reread nearly everything that was written about him, and everything he wrote himself, and I found this extraordinary disparity between his brutal frankness in treating the question of sex, for instance, and his absolute reticence regarding his own sex experiences. In fact, old Walt began his career by flinging the red rag in the face of the Puritan Bull, and then spent the rest of his life in trying to explain what he meant by some of his ideas on sex and love. His Calamus poems are as homosexual as anything ever written. Aside of that, I came across the extraordinary phenomenon that Walt Whitman, while being a champion of women's independence, never cared for women; in fact his letters to all his women friends are dry and cold and empty. Not so the letters to the men who were in his life. Besides that he associated from his earliest youth with men, the toughest and roughest kind of men, and his years of friendship with Peter Doyle too, to whom he wrote endless love letters, all go to prove that Walt had a very strong homosexual streak. Yet he absolutely denied it, and even advanced the story, whether true or not has never been proven, that he was the father of six children. I cannot understand this contradiction, except by the imperative necessity in order to retain what few friendships he had in interpreting his love for men in the cosmic sense. I am inclined to think that even his most devoted friends, with the exception of Horace Traubel, would have dropped him like a shot if he had openly owned up to his leanings. This is best seen by the constant apologies that nearly all of his American and English biographers and commentators are making. The fools do not seem to realize that Walt Whitman's greatness as a rebel and poet may have been conditioned in his sexual differentiation, and that he could not be otherwise than what he was.

I dwelt on Walt Whitman largely because I feel that it will be extremely difficult to write a frank autobiography, not so much because I do not believe in frankness, but because one's life is too much interwoven with the lives of others, and while I am glad to say that very few people in my life were purists, still there are certain intimacies which they may not want to give to the public. No, I am not pathologically modest. I am quite willing to openly discuss anything that pertains to my own self, but it is another thing to take liberties with the motives and actions of people who have been in your life, so I am not looking to a very easy job, but I will try to do the best I can. Don't think it is a question of not wanting to hurt people. I hope that the people who had any bearing on my life are big enough not to feel hurt, but it is just a certain reluctance in prying open their innermost thoughts and feelings. Well, we will see—I am still far away from it. . . .

Don't forget, dear girl, to come to Toronto when you get as far as

Montreal, and to let me know in advance when to expect you. Devoted love,

[EG]

EG TO BEN REITMAN, *December 17, 1927, TORONTO*

Dear Ben,

Your letter reached me amid the preparation of my last lecture. I therefore could not write sooner. Besides what is there to write that you will take in the right spirit and with understanding? Since your last childish outbreak [discussed below], evidently intended to hurt me, I have come to think that you are no more responsible for whatever you say good or bad than the man who is color blind when he denies that there is such a thing as radiant sunsets, or a riot of color in the rainbow. Of course he cannot be blamed; neither can you. For whether you will ever know, old man, or not, you are often spiritually color blind. You absolutely lack the sight into the complexities of the human soul. Or is it that you are so terribly self-centered, so bent on always getting what you want the moment you want it, that you simply cannot consider whether one can or cannot respond to your needs? You fail to realize that it is not so much "harshness or cruelty or a desire to hurt" you that one cannot respond. Rather it is something which is not in one's power to do at that particular moment.

If this reaches you in one of your kindly moods, I hope you will take five minutes off your busy life and reflect on the following. For eight years, between the dreadful years of 1917 and 1925, you took yourself out of my life, as if you had never been there. As far as you were concerned I did not exist, nor any of the troubles, hardships, or suffering that were in my life. All right. Then you came to London, ostensibly to see me. I am not going to dwell on that terrible visit, since you yourself have given it the names it deserved. All right. Then I came to Canada and we began to get somewhat close to each other. Not that I ever could blot out the last ten years from my soul to begin anew the relationship which you yourself broke into bits in 1917. Still, we were on the way to some kind of a friendship rescued from the avalanche which killed our love. As weeks and months went on, though it never occurred to you to ask how I was getting along in a strange unyielding country, our correspondence helped to ease the pain of the past. When you wrote me of your illness my heart went out to you with all the affection and friendliness of real concern and devotion. I would have done anything in my power to get you back to health. I was glad for your visit. I was sick with pain when I saw you so ill and worn and dead. It was to me like seeing a beautiful strong tree broken and dying. But even on that visit, you had to show your impatience and violence at the last minute. But that did not matter. You were ill and nothing else mattered to me. I was

terribly anxious and when I finally learned that you were on the way to
recovery I felt exceedingly glad. All right.

Then you continued writing in a tone I had almost forgotten, it is so
long ago since I heard it. You announced your coming. You wrote me to let
you know whether it was convenient for me to see you at that particular
time. Naturally, I took it for granted that you really meant for me to be
frank. It was in the very beginning of my lectures, at a time when I had to
prepare my stuff, organize and manage every detail of the meetings, and I
knew that your visit would and could not satisfy either one of us. I wrote
you frankly as it stood with me at that time. But more than that I did not
want you to come here under false expectations. I wanted you to know that
while I was glad to have you come and while I hoped we could meet as real
friends, two people who have had much in common, had struggled,
dreamed and hoped together for so many years, two people who had lost
the one precious thing in their lives, their love, but at least who were able
to retain their friendship. I wrote in this spirit. But you understood nothing of it, you were color blind to the beauty of friendship. You could not
endure the idea that I should not be ready to receive you as my lover, as if
there had been no terrible ten years between the time when you left me to
the storm which swept over me and destroyed all I had built in pain and
tears for twenty-eight years, ten of which I had shared with you. No, you
could not understand; you never have understood.

The amusing part, amusing if it were not really so pathetic, is that you
thought you could hurt me by comparing the dog Schuettler [Captain of
the Chicago Police] to AB. Ridiculous. I was only bitterly sorry for you, old
Ben, that you could find no better friend in your life than a man-hunter, a
creature whose every breath of life was drawn from the suffering and sorrow
of his fellow man, whose whole life meant graft, lying, torture, and ag-
grandizement of his fellow man. Now really, did you think this comparison
would hurt me? Nonsense. It only did one thing, it taught me again that
you are never able to keep your personal relationship free from third
parties. What on earth has AB or anybody to do with you and me? Why
must you always, even after AB is completely out of your life, drag him in
when there is no occasion for it? I could understand it while we were all too
closely thrown together, when your feeling of antagonism to AB was called
out by my friendship for him because you loved me then, or you thought
you did. But why do you keep that up all these years? What can it now
matter to you how I feel about AB? You have deliberately taken yourself
out of our lives, our work, our ideas. What is worrying you, Ben, that you
must always harp back to AB? But what does it all matter, you are color
blind. You cannot distinguish between one [and] another. All right. . . .

If I had still a vestige of hope that you could meet me in friendship,
without demanding more than I can give, just meeting me in kindness and
understanding, I would certainly ask you to come before I leave Toronto or

Canada altogether. But you have taken even the last ray of hope from me, so what would be the use of our meeting again? . . .

I am sure you will have a pleasant Christmas; I hope the new year will fulfill your aims and plans. I mainly wish you health on this your birthday. I really do not remember whether it is the forty-eighth or forty-ninth.

[EG]

EG TO AB, *February 20, 1929, ST. TROPEZ*

Dear, old Sash,

You'd laugh your head off if you could see me as property owner. I never felt more ignorant and helpless unless it be during the time when you tried to make me swim. I know I ought to do something to help the work along and get rid of the confusion but all I do is to stand like a fool, not knowing whether to laugh or weep. I give you my word I never saw anything more exasperating than to see French workingmen on their job. I admire their sense for not doing more than they must for the pittance they are most likely being paid. But poor me, who's worried about a silly book, finds it damned hard to practice patience. The men came at 7:30 this morning. I worked until nearly two, so you can imagine how easy it was for me to get up at such an unearthly hour. But I consoled myself with the certainty that the men would start right in and have finished by noon. Like hell, they went off for their material and did not return until nearly ten o'clock. They went off at noon; it is almost two and they have not yet returned. One of them announced he could not finish the work today. I nearly had a fit. I told him I would give him a substantial pourboire [tip] but for the love of Jesus he must finish today. That fetched him. Still I would not swear he will be done. He just arrived and if you please he brought an assistant for a piece of work a German or American working-man would do in two hours without effort. Imagine what the French workers will do after a revolution. I am sure they'll beat the Russians in slowness and sabotage.

There is one consolation, the sun, blessed sun, it is coming down in full force as if it meant to make up for the dreadful weather we have had. I am sitting out on the terrace writing to you. By evening I hope to have my two stoves in order and the house warm. I feel like a dog complaining about cold when I think how you must have suffered. And still more the poor people in France and other countries. Yes, I know about the Rockers freezing; I heard from Milly. But even her description of the conditions seem rosy [in contrast] with the letter I got from Nettlau about the suffering of the people in Vienna. All routes cut off so that neither coal or eatables could be brought in. I can only hope that by this time the weather has improved. The unfortunate Austrians seem to have been accursed more than anybody else during the war and since the cruel peace. I cannot blame our dear Max Nettlau, if he is growing more nationalistic every day and more sensitive in regard to the abuses of the Austrian people.

Apropos of Nettlau, you should read his eulogy of the old-fashioned mothers with their brood of children. This was called out by my letter about the Spanish woman who seems to be nothing else but a breeding machine. It hurt poor Max terribly. Do I prefer the flapper, or the movie girls? The race must be replenished and the women who do it are performing great functions. Really, I rubbed my eyes. I could not believe an anarchist would still hold to the most antiquated ideas. But then Nettlau is German, more German since the war than he ever was. And I have met only two Germans in all my life who are free, our own Max [Baginsky] and Rudolf. The rest remain stationary on all points except economics. Especially as regards women, they are really antediluvian. . . .

It goes without saying that I should like to have you help me with the final revision, but since you announced that you cannot be away too long from Emmy, and I certainly have no desire to induce you to, I don't see how you can help me. I confess if matters were reversed, no man could stop me from coming to your help, if the separation would mean for the rest of my life. But that is neither here nor there. One thing is certain: I will not let my ms. out of my hands or presence; whoever will help me will have to be near me or I near her or him. That is how I feel about the matter, dear. And you know yourself that arguments are of little value where one feels with every fiber. The writing of my book has proven the hardest and most painful task I have ever undertaken or gone through. Not even when I thought I would have to go the way of Czolgosz did I feel such agony as I have since last June. It is not only the writing, it is living through what now lies in ashes and being made aware that I have nothing left in the way of personal relations from all who have been in my life and have torn my heart. You have failed to realize the deeper current of my misery since I started and there is another year to go through with it. How then can anyone expect me to let others revise this child of sorrow? Don't think I say all this in the sense of complaint or lament. I should have known that it will be torture to revive the past. I am now paying for it. I am not holding anyone responsible. I am trying to explain why I was grieved at your suggestion. . . . I will let you read the ms. when it is written; you can then tell me your views and give me your suggestions. I have always been delighted with some you gave me in the past. . . .

Of course, dear heart, I do mean to cut out only casual love affairs, although nearly all my experiences were so wrapped up with my work that it is difficult to separate them. I do not think there have been a half-dozen cases where the men were not either anarchists active in the movement or sympathetic to our ideas. Certainly Oerter was. Even Arthur was not antagonistic; he was a very ardent IWW—I mean the young Swedish flame

of mine [Arthur Swenson of Stockholm, who was thirty years old in 1922].
However, I intend giving only such cases, whether of love or other events in
my life, that really went deep, or were of wide scope. It is for this reason
that I left out Bernstein and now Oerter and that I have left out quite a
number of episodes. . . .

Dear, old Sash, this time I made no mistake in spelling. I had the word
Atiology [aetiology!] written before me by a man who certainly could not
make a mistake. True, the word is written in German ätiologische. The
writer is a friend of Henry [Alsberg's], a certain [Ernst?] Bloch, an educated
fellow. Henry wrote him in my behalf to find out the year when Freud
began his lectures; I was not sure whether it was 1895 or 1896. He replied it
was '96 and that Freud's subjects were "Die Ätiologische Rolle der Sexual-
ität bei den Neurosen." My recollection of these lectures is that he spoke
on inversion; in fact it was Freud who gave me my first understanding of
homosexuality. I had known of its existence in prisons through [Edward]
Brady and my own imprisonment and I had read the veiled references to
Oscar Wilde, but I knew nothing about its inverted phase until I heard
Freud in Vienna. Still I would like to know the exact meaning of the word
ätiologische. Perhaps you can find it in a Latin or medical dictionary.

Bless your heart, your wonderful sense of humor never leaves you. I
laughed heartily over your description of S. Yanofsky. Imagine a handsome
actress offering herself to him. If only you had been the critic [of his
memoirs], what a chance. Does Yanofsky also say whether he took her, or
did he decline? . . . Good night, dear heart,

[EG]

P.S. My new stove is going, but the work is not finished; it will take all of
tomorrow. Perhaps then I will have peace for a while and be able to resume
writing. So far I have been doing it on the installment plan, which is very
bad.

AB TO EG, May 11, 1929, ST. CLOUD

Yes, dear,

That is a regular Megillah [hodgepodge*] that I just received from you.
But it was an interesting letter. Now, point by point.

Weather was rotten here, rainy and gray most of the time, though not
cold. But yesterday it was sunny and today also nice. Even very warm. That
is, outside. In the house it is still chilly, but certainly the spring is here, and
it is even more than spring: the beginning of summer, and you know that I

---

* This translation, as many of the others, is free but we trust true to the spirit of the
original. Megillah means in Yiddish a scroll or the Book of Esther, by implication a galli-
maufry, and, in slang, the whole works, everything but the kitchen sink.

like the sun. But with you there, it must be quite warm and beautiful. The rain does not last long there at this time. . . .

You mentioned in a recent letter that you would refer in your book about the different attitude of people regarding an older woman who lives with a younger man, as compared with the attitudes to an older man living with a younger woman. There is LESS difference in that attitude than you imagine, as I know from experience. Even the "radicals" and our own comrades suffer from the same attitude, as I also know from experience. As to the conservative world, well, it is simply outrageous. You can imagine that we are here the talk of the whole village, because I am so much older and known as an anarchist, or "communist," as some call it. Not that I care for the talk. We have nothing to do with any of the local people. But one has to deal with the grocer, the butcher, etc., and these French people, whom I hate, know how to make insinuating remarks of a kind that don't give you a chance to smash their face. Even the gas man, the police officer, and the detective from Versailles (who keeps an eye on me) have repeatedly watched for my absence in the city to come into the house on some pretext of filling out papers etc. and then made advances to Emmy—in the French manner, you know. Even in the police bureau they told her openly that she ought to be ashamed to live with such an old man, and once in the subway a woman neighbor, a regular Hexe [witch], shouted all over the car that she is living with an anarchist, a man who can be her grandfather, etc. Well, enough of this. I merely mention this to show you that in general people's attitude in these matters is about the same, whether the older one is the man or the woman. And while I am on this subject I want to add that even our own friends are consciously and subconsciously of the same attitude, though they mask it with pretending that it is because she is "not in the movement," not intellectual, and similar stuff. And in this respect almost everyone of our people has behaved in the same manner, not excluding Alsberg, Saxe, etc. I inwardly smile at it, of course, but it is pretty rotten. And it was the same in St. Tropez, and that is why I could never go there with her again.

You might say it was also my attitude to Ben [Reitman]. I know that is your feeling. But it is not so at all. As a matter of fact I had the friendliest feelings to Ben, personally. My only objection was his MANNER of activity in the movement and his uncomradely treatment of comrades, his sensationalism, etc. But all that referred ONLY to the movement. I held that he never belonged to the movement, and I am still of that opinion, and I think events proved it. His psychology did not belong there, even if he did some useful work. Were he with you and INACTIVE in the movement, then I should have felt differently altogether.

Well, enough of this. You will not agree anyhow, and I know that you yourself have always been prejudiced against Emmy. . . .

Enough now. Must be off.

Affectionately,

S

EG TO AB, May 14, 1929, ST. TROPEZ

Dearest Sash,

Thank you for your letter and the sweet confidence it contains. It has always been a source of great grief to me that you had such little need to speak openly to me about things which oppress your mind or heart. It seemed awful that two people whose lives have been linked for forty years and who have known the torture of the damned should not be able to be frank and honest with each other. I can say for myself that as far as my own experiences are concerned, there hardly ever was anything I could not and would not gladly have confided in you. But whether it is conditioned in your nature, or created by years of hiding and seeking, you always have no end of conspiracies, not always easily concealed, at least not to my eye. I am glad that at least once you have spoken out. But you are right, of course, I cannot agree with most of what you wrote. I think you are utterly and woefully wrong in your contention that the difference in age of the man and the woman in relation to young loves is the same. And you are equally wrong in the motives you give to our friends for their attitude to Emmy. . . .

First about Ben, dear, old Sash, where did you ever get the idea that I suspected you of being jealous of Ben in any sexual sense, or in any other as far as jealousy is concerned? I could not ever suspect you of that because I had known long before Ben came into my life that whatever physical appeal I had for you before you went to prison was dead when you came out. I know we kept up our relation for a time, but I knew too much about such things to be deceived. I simply clung to the hope that I may be able to awaken the same feeling in you but when I came back from Amsterdam [in 1908] and saw your relation with Beckie [Edelson], I knew the end had come. I therefore never did suspect you of jealousy. What I did suspect—more than that what I knew—was that you are a prig who constantly worries that the comrades will say and how it will affect the movement when you yourself lived your life to suit yourself. I mean as far as women are concerned. It was painful to me, at the time, as it has been on many other occasions, to see you fly the movement in the face a hundred times and then condemn me for doing the same.

Just think of it, dear, to this day you keep on saying Ben did not belong to the movement. Granted this was true, which I do not agree (I will tell you why later), how can you say that with all the impossible people who were in the movement through you. Marie Ganz, for instance, [Charles]

Plunkett, Sullivan, and dozens of others who did a world of harm and then recanted all they had pretended to be. These people might have given you some physical satisfaction, I mean the many females, but certainly they did nothing to help in the work. Whereas Ben during ten years dedicated [himself] to me and my work as no other man ever had, making it possible for me to do the best and most extensive work I had done up to my meeting him. Not only that but it was Ben's help which had kept *Mother Earth* alive, as well as our publishing work; without him I would never have been able to publish my two books, Voltairine [De Cleyre's], and, yes, your [*Prison*] *Memoirs*. Let us be fair, dear Sash, it was Ben who helped me raise thousands of dollars which kept up a houseful of people and enabled me as well as yourself to do what we have done between 1908 and 1917.

Do I mean to deny Ben's faults? Of course not, my dear. I knew them too well and suffered from them too terribly to gainsay your criticism, now or any other time. You see, Sash my dear, my misfortune has been that I was never able to love with closed eyes. For that I would have had to have your beautiful naiveté which swears by everything the women in your life have and are palming off on you. My men could never do it because I have too much intuition and I could see through them in a very short time. That was my tragedy, and also my joy because I think it requires deeper love and more exalted experiences to love those in our life in spite of their faults. That's why I will continue to love you to my last breath, see, old scout.

I knew Ben inside and out two weeks after we went on tour; I not only knew but loathed his sensational ways, his bombast, his braggadocio, and his promiscuity, which lacked the least sense of selection. But over and above that there was something large, primitive, unpremeditated, and simple about Ben which had terrific charm. Had you and the other friends concerned in my salvation recognized this, had you shown Ben some faith, instead of writing to the university to find out about his medical degree (which the boy never could forget), in short had you shown as much understanding for his exotic being as you did so often when you saw such types as Ben in books, Ben would not have become a renegade. The trouble with you was, dear heart, as with all our comrades, you are a puritan at heart, you all talk about how one must help the outcast and the criminal, but when you are confronted with such a creature you turn from him in disgust, do not trust him, and deliberately drive him back to the depths he sprang from. I have been too long in the movement not to know how narrow and moral it is, how unforgiving and lacking in understanding toward everyone different from them. I was disappointed when I saw the same trait in you, dear. I had hoped that the purgatory you had gone through would have raised you far above the others in your appraisement of the human spirit; I expected it from you because I saw that in your own life, I mean in your amours, you were anything but consistent. Naturally it hurt me to the quick.

You will repeat your objections to Ben were because, as you say, "he did not belong in our ranks." All right, but what were your objections to Arthur [Swenson]? He never was in our ranks. Why did you treat him like a dog after he came to Berlin? Why did you fail to understand the terrific turmoil the boy created in my being? Let us not go on knocking about the bush, dear, look into yourself and you will find that you simply lack understanding and feeling for such experiences in others, while you try to explain and excuse similar experiences in yourself. . . .

Of course it is nonsense to say that the attitude to men and women in their love to younger people is the same in the world. It is nothing of the kind; the proof for that is in the pudding. Hundreds and hundreds of men marry women much younger than themselves; they have circles of friends; they are accepted by the world. This does not happen to women, not one in a million has a love affair for any length of time with a man younger than herself. If she has, she is the butt of her nearest and dearest friends and gradually becomes that in her own eyes. To say that our comrades and friends discriminate against Emmy because she is younger than you is so utterly nonsensical I don't see how this idea ever came to your mind. If that were the reason, how would you account for the affection, esteem and love everybody has for Nellie Harris? She is nearly thirty-two years younger than Frank. Yet all Frank's friends love and adore her in fact more than him. Don't you think this has something to do with Nellie's personality, with her charm and grace and above all her freedom from envy and jealousy of everybody who comes in Frank's life, whether man, woman or child? I think it has. . . .

Great heavens, I know any number of couples of different ages; nobody objects to them on that ground. The objection is due to something in the personality of the younger person, woman or man. It is different when the matter is reversed. Everybody objects, resents, in fact dislikes a woman who lives with a younger man; they think her a god-damned fool; no doubt she is that, but it is not the business or concern of friends to make her look and feel like a fool.

Now about the attitude of our people to Emmy. I will grant you that the comrades may object to her on the old fanatical grounds that she is not an "anarchist and not intellectual," all of which is rot of course, but I am as certain as I can be that no one among the comrades objects to her because she is younger than you. As to Henry and Saxe, Sasha my dear, how can such an idea enter your head? Really it is ludicrous. I know why they object because they have told me and I give you my word that your version is hopelessly far off the mark. As to what their reasons are, I wish I could speak frankly to you but I know what a wunder Punt [sore point] Emmy is to you and I do not wish to hurt you more than I feel certain you feel yourself.

The same about your idea that I am prejudiced. You have a kurzen zekoren [*sic*—short memory], you do not remember that it was I who constantly pleaded in Emmy's behalf in Berlin, and that it was I who talked with her for time on end over the phone trying hard to soothe and comfort her and explain your actions of which she complained. I returned from Canada with the best feelings toward the girl, but I was the one to help and suggest about her coming here. Would I have done all that, if I had been prejudiced? Certainly not. But I could, if I wished, tell you what has created my "prejudice." But what would be the use, it would only make you unhappy and I do not want that. In any event I am not against Emmy because she is younger, is not an anarchist, or is not intellectual; there are other phases about her that are against my grain and would be against yours, if you were not in love and always blind to the faults of those you love. So let's agree to disagree on that. I want you always to have your life in your own way. I cannot say I am always happy about certain things in your life, but it is your life and I do not want to intrude upon it, or change it, even if I could.

About the neighbors and their attitude. I am as sure as I can be that if Emmy had not poured out her heart to them, as she did to Mme Sandstrom and everybody else she meets, they would not have known whether she is married or single or anything else. And if they had known it anyhow, their objections too would not be on the ground of her being younger but on the ground of you being considered an anarchist or bolshevik. As if the French are so particular about marriage—there is hardly a Frenchman who has not a younger person than his wife as his mistress. It is absurd to think they object to Emmy on that score. She gave them the right to enter her life and now they are taking advantage of it. That is all.

As to men coming to make advances, great heavens, what novelty is that for Frenchmen? They make advances to women no matter what their age, married or single or widow, anybody with a skirt from the cradle to the age ninety. I would not let this worry me. But of course it is not fair that you should leave Emmy much alone in St. Cloud. I have told you that long ago—I have told you that here when you left her alone at the Sandstroms —I consider it a god-damned shame that you should be so tied, but as long as you care for the girl, you should not leave her always alone.

As to your stay here, dear, you shall act as you think best. I will not bind you. I admit I would enjoy having you here as long as possible but I don't want it at the expense of pain to Emmy or anybody. The older I get the less I want to cause pain. Life itself is painful enough. If only Emmy were not so terribly middle class, if only she would learn to understand that your friends are too deep in your life to eradicate them from your system. If only she knew that love consists in being large and understanding and not in a marriage ring or license. Then her life with you would be so much more harmonious and fine. But I suppose no one can get out of one's skin, and I am not in a position to judge or condemn. . . .

[EG]

AB TO EG, May 20, 1929, ST. CLOUD

Dearest Em,

Of course I know what the 18th [the anniversary of AB's release from prison] means to both of us and that it cannot mean the same to anyone else. And in the thought of it I spent a quiet day. I had invited Senya [Flechine] for dinner that day, but he got the pneumatique too late, so that he came out yesterday for lunch. Otherwise the day was very quiet, and the weather rather sunless and gray.

Now as to the contents of your long letter. You must always feel that you can speak freely and frankly with me. You can't offend me with whatever you say, for I know your heart is good and you mean everything for the best.

Why I don't speak often about such matters? You say it is secretiveness, even "conspiracies," as you put it, and of the kind that you know anyhow, even if you are not supposed to know. Well, that is using words very loosely. I know of no conspiracies, nor of anything that you must not know. Nor am I secretive in any real sense of the word. A secretive man is one who makes secrets of things. I make no secrets, at least not from you. But I simply do not talk about things. NOT because I mean to keep them secret, but because I am not a Schwatzer [babbler], and mainly BECAUSE I KNOW HOW USELESS it is to talk of them. Yes, even to one's best friends. And mostly even more than useless, positively harmful, because such talks and confidences merely ball things up worse, cause new misunderstandings, and clear up nothing. . . .

That is just as a general remark. Because I don't want you to think that I have "conspiracies" from you or that I am "secretive" because of any particular reason to be secretive. The dictionary will tell you that secretive means a tendency to conceal. Well, I may be somewhat secretive both by nature and experience. But not AS CONCERNS YOU. I have nothing to conceal from you. You know my life, don't you? But I am not talkative about these matters even to you, BECAUSE I am convinced it is *useless*. People live according to their feelings, not with their reason, generally speaking. And even those who try to harmonize feeling and reason can seldom understand each other, and least of all, if they belong to different sexes. You and I are too old to change our attitudes. And you and I represent ALL the differences that there are between man and woman as a sex. So where can there ever be any agreement on such matters between us? Even in other matters, political and social views, in which we sometimes agree, our agreement comes from entirely DIFFERENT standpoints and considerations. I suppose you have noticed this. And not only from different standpoints and considerations, but even sometimes from OPPOSITE ones. We may come to the same conclusion sometimes, but it has happened often that the basis from which I judged was actually opposed to your basis. That is because people are different in general, and man and woman particularly so. I know, of course, that all I say here is opposed to your feelings, and that only proves what I say. In short, I think man and woman are not only biologically but also mentally and psychically so different that understanding IN CERTAIN MATTERS is out of the question.

But that does not mean that they cannot be the best of friends and understand each other in matters that do not involve inherent differences of feeling and reason.

Well, it would serve no purpose to go into your arguments about Ben. We think differently on this matter, and neither will convince the other. I never mentioned in my previous letter the matter of "jealousy" in regard to Ben. Certainly not in the sense in which you argue. Maybe I was careless in the use of some word. Yes, of course, Ben did a lot to help in a financial sense. But I can only repeat that morally he was harmful.

I have often said that I had nothing whatever against Ben as a person. In fact, [I] even rather liked him for certain qualities. But when I say he was in the wrong place, it is a different consideration. You say others also proved in the course of time that they did not belong in our movement. Sure. But it took time to find out that those others did not belong, while anyone could tell *from the first moment* that neither by his psychology nor spirit did Ben belong to the movement.

You mentioned "facts" that are entirely new to me; that is to say, baseless. You say Marie Ganz, Plunkett, and Sullivan "came into the movement" through me. I don't know how you can make such wild statements. The New York [circles] were full of Marie Ganz [in 1914] and her talks to the unemployed long before I had ever seen her. And in fact I met her the first time at a street meeting which I had visited only as a spectator and where she spoke. Plunkett I never met until the day of his trial in Tarrytown. No doubt he must have been in the crowd that went over with me the first time to Tarrytown, but that was a big crowd and I did not know all the people in it. Sullivan was also of that crowd and I met him personally much later. But even if all those people had come into the movement through me, as you say, it would not sustain your argument about Ben. Ben was a Christian at heart all the time and psychologically, sometimes even unconsciously, antagonistic to the very spirit of our movement.

As to my inquiry of the university, I still hold that it was perfectly justified. He came as a stranger whom no one knew except yourself. From the very first his behavior and talk was NOT that of a man who had gone through any college. I even talked to him on medical matters and I could not see that it was a college man who talked to me. Maybe it was also due to his entire inability to express himself in words, especially in those early days. You know he could not combine two sentences in a logical and consecutive manner. Anyhow, I was justified in trying to find out at least whether he really was in the university. . . .

You ask me why I was bitter against Arthur in Berlin. Well, I see you realize that I was not bitter against him in Sweden. In fact, I liked him at first. But in Berlin I turned against him because I realized that he THEN did not care for you any more and that he was only exploiting you. This realization came to me before we left Sweden and I hoped that he would not come any more. It is not necessary to go into details for my reasons. I had enough of them.

I don't know why I should take up your time with all these matters, except that they were referred to in your last long letter. As to Emmy, it is also equally useless to speak of the matter. No, my dear, do not indulge yourself in the foolish and childish idea that I am blind and, as you say, always have been blind in these things. Maybe I am not so blind. Emmy is no angel, as none of us is. She has good points and bad points, as is usual with people. But I am sure that she longed to have your motherly affection when you came to Paris, and that your attitude prevented it. And more than prevented it. In Canada already you showed to me your attitude. When I wrote to you that she had left her people and that they are all down on her etc., etc., and that she is very devoted to me, etc., your only appreciation of the situation was expressed in these words: "Why shouldn't she love you!" Why, indeed, shouldn't a girl of twenty-four, as she was then, not love a man almost thirty years her senior; and one, at that, who is neither rich nor good-looking, and not one who will either marry her (which is important to her), nor secure her even to the least extent when he dies and when she will be scorned by her people as well as by mine. All that taken in consideration, "why shouldn't she love you!"

When you came to Paris, Emmy came to you with the best feelings and brought you flowers etc. Well, you know that you have a very sharp and biting way in certain situations, and at the very first meeting in Paris you struck her deeply by remarking, casually, that Sasha is ausgebummelt [played out] and that you are still young and full of life. Well, I leave you to decide whether it was the thing for you to talk that way to an over-sensitive girl, who is really a child in these matters, for Emmy never had any affairs with men, and I am the first man she loved, an ideal to her for whom she gave up home and parents and her chances of marriage etc. These things, my dear, may mean nothing to us, to you and me, but Emmy is of the middle class, German by upbringing, etc. and they mean a great deal to her. Your manner of course antagonized her and the manner of others was no better.

And so it went on. Not necessary to detail. The St. Tropez experience was a nightmare to her, naturally. Was stupid of me to bring her there. The more stupid to have her live and eat in one place and I in another. The first she heard there was that it was a "menage à trois" and so on and so forth. And all the remarks that you made to [Buck] Yawshavksy and his girl and to Demie and everyone else were naturally repeated, in an exaggerated form no doubt, to her. Of course I knew nothing about it then or I would not have kept her staying there, for she wanted to leave the first week already. But what is the use talking of all this? I cannot say that she has been treated right, either by you or by the other of my friends. You no doubt are firmly convinced that you treated her wonderfully, and I know you cannot be convinced otherwise. So, what is the use talking? You say she talked to people. No doubt she has. Your attitude particularly filled her with resentment. She had expected a different attitude in our ranks. She could not talk to me about it, as I would not permit such discussions. And as she has not a single friend in France, so she had to pour out her heart, I suppose, to such as Irma, Molly, or Elizabeth. And things no doubt came to you in exaggerated form, the same as your remarks to people came to her.

Well, you say Saxe, Dorothy, etc. "have reasons" for disliking Emmy. I suppose they have. But Dorothy NEVER saw Emmy till two days before Dorothy left for America, and that only to say hello. And Saxe saw her only once when he first came to my place and he had no occasion to speak to her. So that what "reasons they have" come only from the gossip of others.

I think Fitzie is right and she is the only one who has a real intuition in these matters. Fitzie says that when first meeting my friends Emmy feels self-conscious, knowing she is not of our circle and fearful of making a bad break etc., so that she seems to hold herself aloof, as if she does not want to be friendly. And that is exactly the case. I merely want to illustrate the "reasons" of Saxe and Dorothy by this: not ONCE during their whole stay in Paris did Saxe or Dorothy ask after Emmy, whether she is alive or dead or sick. Not once. And I have also noticed that Saxe is much prejudiced against your brother Moishe's wife [Babsie, who was about twenty years younger than Morris Goldman].

But what is the use of all this talk? Such is life and such are the people, even the best of them. Things are as they are and nothing can change, least of all talk about it. So let it be ended. . . .

Affectionately,

S

EG TO AB, May 24, 1929, ST. TROPEZ

Dearest Sash,

. . . You are right a thousand times, dearest Sash, that people, even the most devoted friends, know and understand little of each other. And that talk does not help to bring them to a better understanding. There is more truth than fiction in the German saying, "Wenn Du es nicht fuhlst, wirst Du es nie errathen." [If you do not feel a thing, you will never guess its meaning.] The trouble is, my dear, that you are not very chutko [knowing] in some things, certainly not in relation to the women who have been in your life. And without that you have never really understood any one of them, nor have you been able to know what is real about them and what fictitious. But this is as it is and it can't be tisser [otherwise].

I must correct you on Dorothy Commins. I am sorry if I gave you the impression that she ever spoke to me about Emmy. Never once did she mention her name. I did not mean her, though I may have written it really having Saxe in mind. Please believe me, I hate to have you think Dorothy had talked when she never did.

Yes, you are right, Fitzie has fine intuition, but please remember that Fitzie never saw Emmy in the presence of your other friends. If she did, I am just as sure as I can be that she would have the same impression as all of us have. And what is this impression, do you think? It is not so much that Emmy feels embarrassed and nervous in our presence—that is true to some extent of course—but that we feel embarrassed and nervous in hers. We don't know what to say or how to approach her. This is because we know how middle class she is and how truly pathological in her jealousy of everyone, and even more so because of you. We feel as if we were walking on glass. That is the whole crux of the situation.

Now I am not going to tell you how well I have treated Emmy. I don't see how I could be free with her, and without being that, it is impossible to be kind to anyone. But if everything she tells you is as true as the account of her visit to me, I can see why you have such a distorted idea of the attitude of your friends to Emmy. . . . As to my having said that you are "ausgebummelt," my dear old Sash, how can you believe such rot? Even if I had thought that you looked that way, would I ever tell her that, or anyone you live with? Fact is I have always spoken of your youth, your vigor, your remarkable spirit. How can I say such ridiculous things? The term itself would never come to me in a hundred years. Nor would I boast of my looks. Great scot, how can you believe such nonsense about one who has been in your life forty years and has served you as no woman ever has or will?

Please do not think I mean to suggest that Emmy has lied deliberately: no, but she seems to be like many women obsessed by her sense of possessions and making herself believe that it is necessary to belittle all other women in order to hold her man. She imagines a million things that are not there, uncertainty and fear always create that, dear Sash, in men and women, but especially the latter. Now please bear in mind that I never said what Emmy reported to you. But granted I had, I tried in ever so many ways to come near her while she was here, but it was useless, she simply would not unbend, sat watching every look and every gesture any woman at the table made to you, and simply paralyzed me so that I could not find the word that would make her see that, if for no other reason, it is for your sake that I want terribly to be friendly with her.

As to her expecting much of me because I am an anarchist, you have [so] queered the anarchists by your childish action with her and the other Berlin woman that nothing anyone of us might do would change Emmy's attitude toward our ideas. Even without that she would never see anything in them; she is too conservative in her every instinct for that. But you have added your sauce; now, no matter what I or anyone else might do, [it] would not change matters.

And so I have committed a terrible sin when I wrote you "why shouldn't she love you?" Well, dear heart, I repeat the same thing now, not from an anarchist point of view, which takes it for granted that one should do everything for the one we love. I insist on my question from the general human attitude toward love. You make it appear that Emmy is an exception in having gone with you, though you are thirty years older, have no means of support, and you did not marry her. Of course this is a lot for a middle-class German girl, but it is far from out of the ordinary. Thousands of young girls, far more beautiful than Emmy, from aristocratic homes, or extreme middle-class wealth, have gone with the man they love, no matter his age and station, with scavengers, or street sweepers, or even low-type men in the social scale. And they were not married either. Babsie, who comes from a puritan, Presbyterian, middle-class family, lived with Moe for years right under the nose of the hospital authorities in Lake View without being married. In fact it was that which lost Moe his position. They married only when Babsie was with child, but I am convinced that if she had been put up before the alternative of giving up Moe or marriage, she would have given up the latter. After Moe lost his position he was unable to earn a cent for years. Babsie was the main supporter, working on day and night cases for several years so Moe could Kvetch the bank with exams.* True, Moe is only twenty-two years older than Babsie; still it is not very far from yours, my dear. And Babsie is one in thousands.

Nellie has endured hell with Frank for years, having to put up with hundreds of women he brought into the house or talked about and boasted

---

* The Yiddish verb *kvetch* means "put pressure on." How her brother put pressure on the bank with "exams" is unknown.

of his relations. For years now Nellie never knows where she is going to get
the rent or pay the butcher; she carries all the burdens for a man of
seventy-three, an egoist of the worst description, centered on himself at the
exclusion of everybody else. Of course Nellie is married, that is about the
only difference. But on the other hand, Emmy does not have to be
confronted with hundreds of girls and women you bring to her, or write
about and have it published so everybody can know about it. If I took the
trouble, I could give you any number of examples to prove that it is
nothing out of the ordinary what Emmy has done.

However, I am afraid she makes you think so. In fact I am sure of it. I
still remember how utterly shocked I was when Fitzie told me that you had
told her how Emmy, in meeting some cripple, said she'd want you to have
some such a thing so she could show you her love. Well, you may take that
as a sign of love. I don't. I take it as a sign of the sense of possession gone
sadistic and pathological. Like the love of many parents who torture their
children with what they do for them and thereby poison their lives. Great
God, how can you take that as love, or tell me it is wonderful or
praiseworthy? It is nothing of the kind. But I shall never again approach
this subject. I hope you will forgive me this time. I wish I could get near
Emmy and cure her of her silly ways that she has lost her virtue and has
sacrificed and the devil only knows what. But I fear she will never accept
me: probably you are to blame by constantly telling her what EG can do, or
having my picture or books around. With anyone so morbid as she is about
her man, you should not have done it; it is bad tact. But in any event, I
know that she hates me with a deadly hate and so what can I do? I certainly
don't hate her. I'd give anything, if I could make her realize that—I would
like to make her realize that her love for you is enslaving and torturing and
is therefore not great. But then you probably enjoy such love, so I am glad
you have it in your life.

As to Ben, no, there is no use continuing about him any more than it is
to continue about Emmy. Your argument, however, that Ben did not
belong to the movement because he was a Christian is too funny for words.
Since when have we objected to Tolstoyans, for instance, in our ranks? I
don't say that Ben is a Tolstoyan, he is nothing now but a God-damned
fool. But he had much in him which might have been developed had not
my friends knocked him on the head from the first moment he came to
us. . . .

As to Arthur, did you think I did not know that he no longer cared for
me? Besides, Arthur was very frank about it: he told me himself that I no
longer attracted him physically. If he remained, it was because I fought a
silly losing fight in trying to win him back. Exploitation, dear, own Sash,
Beckie [Edelson] did that for eight years, yet you found nothing wrong in
that, far from it, you upbraided me time on end because I was not always
gracious about it. No, dear, in neither Ben's nor Arthur's case had it

anything so much to do with what they did to me as with your dislike. They did things which you naturally condemned. The trouble with you is that you then proceeded doing similar or sometimes stranger things which you justify to me or Fitzie or those you care about, though you are too intelligent not to admit yourself how inconsistent your acts are. But as you rightly say, Ben and Arthur are ages away, except that in writing about them [in *Living My Life*] I had to infuse life into the dead past. That is painful for me and has nothing to do with you.

I am sorry if I credited you with Ganz, Plunkett, and the rest. You see they were not in the movement or anywhere near us when I left in April of 1914. They flocked like bees to honey to our place while I was away, they were with you day and night, the debts I was confronted with on my return were proofs for the crowds who were fed and slept in the house, but without that I knew the whole thing from Fitzie. And even if she had said nothing, I had the stupid ravings of these kids in the July *Mother Earth* which made us both appear like damned fools. Not one of those who shouted violence and dynamite in that number has remained in our ranks. I am not blaming you, dear heart, naturally you believed in them and you wanted to help them. I only gave them as examples that one can never know in advance who does and who does not belong in a movement. . . .

I want to work this afternoon so I will close; I have already written too much I fear. Forgive me if I have said anything painful to you. I care for you too much and wish for your peace and happiness too much to say or do anything to hurt. But whether we understand each other or no, let's at least be frank and not misunderstand, or impugn unkind motives.

[EG]

AB TO EG, May 26, 1929, ST. CLOUD

My dear,

Never think that what you discuss or write to me can hurt me. I always want you to speak freely and frankly on any subject to me. I know how well you mean it and I prize your opinion, even if I don't always agree. As a matter of fact, I am glad that you expressed yourself on these subjects in the last letters.

Well, I know that there is a good deal of truth in what you say, though in some things I disagree with you. But it does not matter. People cannot agree in everything, and why should they always agree? As to Emmy, no, she does not hate you, though it is true that her love is very possessive. She has some of the bad traits you speak of, but she also has some good ones, which of course those that are strange to her cannot see. I find now, as I always did, that hereditary tendencies are a mighty force in one's character. Yet environment is also a great power, and so one must let conditions and special circumstances do their work. I think Emmy has changed considerably for the better in the last year. She is rather peculiar; very emotional and impulsive. But she is truthful and exceedingly frank when she feels at home with people, and in a quiet manner one can easily reason with her. As a matter of fact, she herself admits the stupidity of certain of her tendencies; but realizing that a thing is wrong does not always make us act right. The spirit may be willing, but the flesh is weak, as the Bible says. And in that relation I think one can grow. Therefore I do not believe that it is tactless that I have your books and pictures about. On the contrary, I think it is educative; it has had the effect of causing adaptation to certain conditions; conditions that are self-evident to us, of course, but seem strange to an outsider.

All in all, I have a sense of humor and I am not given to taking things too tragically. Not for long, anyhow. In life things usually adjust themselves, one way or another, and so Emmy is learning to adjust herself, even if the process is sometimes painful. . . .

Thanks for the beautiful roses and the cherries out of your own garden. I wonder on what date you mailed the box, for it reached here only yesterday afternoon. I suppose mails are slow, especially packages. The cherries came in fine condition, splendid taste. The roses unfortunately were not so lucky—or I was not so lucky with the roses, rather—I could save only two of them by cutting them a bit and putting them at once into fresh water with some salt in it. They are on my desk now and they fill the whole room with their perfume. . . .

Well, there is no more news and this is already a Megillah [hodgepodge]. I need not tell you that I fully realize what you are going through with your book, my dear sailor girl. Even more, no doubt, than I did with my *ABC.* Do you know that I went through much worse sensations with the *ABC* than with my *Memoirs?* The latter was bad enough, but the writing of the *ABC,* the days when I simply could not continue and so on, gave me serious thoughts of suicide, of destroying the ms., and other such pleasant reflections. But your autobiography is far, far more heart-rending, of course. So I know what it means to you, even if I seldom speak of it. But I want you to know that I would do anything to help you in this matter, if there were any way to do it. But I am afraid there is not (except of course mere suggestions or revision), for such things everyone must do entirely in his own way and with his own blood. So do not think, please, that it is sympathy or understanding that is lacking. Our psychological reactions are so different that even my suggestions would be of little aid to you. But if there were any way I could help, I hope you know I'd be only too happy to do it. I am glad to know you got out of the blind alley you are speaking of and that you are going forward. You have been so long at it that it must be terribly on your nerves. Perhaps it would be better to skip some things, as much as possible, and treat only of the most important events. I think, for instance, that the experience with Arthur, though important to you at the time, could very well be left out. For it would only repeat things you have already said in the book. This is only a faint suggestion of leaving out even vital things, if they represent, ESSENTIALLY, only a *repetition* of former experiences, even if different in form. And this should apply to various experiences, personal as well as social. Well, we'll talk it over soon. I have a lot to clean out here before I can leave, but I think I will go [to Nice] on the 3rd in the evening. Latest on the 4th.

I embrace you and may your work become easier and less torturing as you approach the finish.

Affectionately,

S

AB TO EG, Tuesday [ca. *Summer 1929*], NICE

Dear,

. . . As to M [Miriam Lerner?], yes, I noticed long ago that she is even worse than Demie. No selection whatever. This thing has almost become a disease with the so-called "modern" girl, espeically the American girl, and M is a more than typical case of it. It is a great pity. They have become "emancipated" from the old inhibitions, but they have not replaced them by any really earnest idea or deeper feeling. It is just a kind of superficial sexuality without rhyme or reason. More sensuality than anything else. At the bottom of it is an inner emptiness, sexual and otherwise. They hunger for a real affection, which they really do not get; they only get sex. And one of the reasons they do not get it, is because the thing has become both cause and effect. Need of affection is the cause of their behavior, and their behavior becomes the cause why they cannot get real affection, nor feel it after a while. And I saw the attitude of Max, and of other men in this relation. They look upon these types of girls very lightly, even scornfully, except that they want to use them. Max of course is a ninny and a fool, but most of the other men who invite such women "to stay with them a while" feel the same way, and they cannot really grow into a deeper affection for them, for there is a hidden lack of respect and understanding. They consider them light and just good enough to spend a little time with. Well, it is sad and the future of such girls is very tragic. In the course of the years, I suppose, this "new" woman will, I suppose, become more normal. But it may take a whole generation.

The unreliability and flightiness in changing their plans is also a part of the whole situation. I am sure M wants a room in the village just to be "freer." She could very well write at your place, and I do not believe that her present frame of mind will permit her to write. Well, it is her affair.

It is rotten, though, that all this should cause you worry about your book. I hope the matter has been settled by this time, so that you should know what is what. But do not worry about it, dear, you'll find someone to do your typing. . . .

Hope you are getting along better now with the writing. Remember me to the folks there. Am trying to get a credential for Mollie [Steimer].

Affectionately,

S

EG TO HENRY ALSBERG, June 27, 1930, BAD EILSEN, GERMANY

Dear Hank,

Your nice letter and check for fifty reached me yesterday. It was forwarded from Paris and took an age to get to me. Had it come today I would have taken the fifty to mean a birthday gift from some kind fairy. I am sixty-one years giddy and irresponsible today. It was a lonely birthday, far away from those I love and cherish. That's the penalty of getting old, in years at least. Und wer fragt nach mehr? [And who could ask for more?] . . .

I don't know [Dr. Michael] Cohn's reasons for the measly way he has come to Sasha's aid [when he was expelled from France in May]. No doubt he must have had money troubles, though why a man of his means should want to gamble [on the stock market] I do not understand. It was really not the money; it was the indifferent tone of the letter which hurt poor Sasha so. Cohn did not show the slightest interest whether Sasha can get back or not. But what the hell does it matter?

I am certain Sasha did not have such a hard time of it [i.e., his expulsion] as we did, Emmy and I. For one thing he has the wonderful gift of adjustment to almost every situation. How else would he have survived the hideous years? Then, as you say, every city has a Potsdamer Platz. In Antwerp his interest was in diamond dealers, Dutch Jews. One of them [M. Polak] brought him back. Savez? [Get me?] Of course it would have been of no use, if we had not secured permission from the Sureté for his return. But as it would have taken another month to get it through the foreign office, it was a godsend for Sasha to know people who deal in diamonds. God knows, Sasha has cost me more worry and tears in his short life than any amount of diamonds are worth. Speaking of Emmy, I know you do not like her. Nor did I. But then I knew nothing about her except reports and Sasha's childish ways of keeping us apart. But during the trouble, I had Emmy in the studio with me for three weeks and I learned to care for her a great deal. She is as reactionary as they make them and middle class to boot. But with that she has many really fine qualities. She is genuine, for one thing; there is no guile whatever in her; she is very kind. And her devotion to Sasha is simply extraordinary. Some luck that lobster has, to be always so loved by the women in his life. Another thing is Emmy is no fool, she has very considerable judgment of people, and what I like most, einen gesunden Mutterwitz [sound common sense]. Altogether she is quite the reverse from what I thought her to be. I could live in one house [with her] for years, I am sure of that. But how it will be to have Sasha and her I don't know. I shall have to act as the peacemaker, not the first time in my life in the relation between men I loved who have had other women. It seems to be my fate to prepare my lovers for other women and then act as confidante of the women. The irony, eh? . . .

You better write more of yourself, old scout. Have you done any writing at all? I wish I could sit you down next winter, when I myself won't have to write, and make you do it. I promise to give you all the gefilte Fisch and Blintzes you want or any other damned thing, if that will induce you to give what I am certain you have in you to give out, if you were not solch ein Faulenzer [such a lazybones].

Goodby, my dear.

Affectionately,
[EG]

EG TO EMMY ECKSTEIN, June 10, 1931, ST. TROPEZ

My dear Emmy,

I am sure it would be less painful for me and you, if I were to answer your letter in the same brief and categorical manner Sasha answered [Modest] Stein's letter which he sent him [i.e., AB] to his sixtieth birthday. I do not quite remember the text but I do recollect it was to the effect that after such a violent outbreak of accumulated bitterness, there was no need of further correspondence between him and Modska. I feel this should be my reply to your letter. However, my trouble has always been that I could never break off friendships and relationships quite so easily with just one stroke of the pen. I confess Sasha was always the wiser of us two. He understood that once people begin with recriminations, with bitter charges and condemnations, there is no hope of coming closer or to a better grasp of the motives which make human beings do things, or say them, which in their sane and quiet moments they could not possibly justify. But as I said, Sasha was always wiser and more categorical than I, and so I will try to answer your letter in the kindest possible spirit. I confess though that I have no hope to help you see how wrong your accusations are.

I am just as sure as I can be that Stein had no intention of hurting Sasha with the harsh and cruel things his letter contained. And I am just as certain that you had no intention of hurting me. In either case the contents of your letter were merely the reflection of your own antagonism, prejudice, and rancor that is corroding your soul and coloring everything in others of which there is a large portion in yourself. How then can I hope to reach your spirit by anything I might write you? Your letter has more than ever convinced me of the truism in the German saying, "Wenn Du es nicht fuhlst, wirst Du es nie errathen." [If you do not feel a thing, you will never guess its meaning.] If after all I have tried to bring you near to me, to make you feel that I want to be your friend, that I never had any objections to you other than your world, which is not and cannot be mine—that I wanted to take you by the hand and lead you into another, larger, more generous, more humane world—in short that I wanted to enrich your life with Sasha rather than take anything away from it—if I have failed in all that, as your letter most assuredly proves, then what will my answer give you? Nothing at all, except perhaps more bitterness.

True, for a time you made me think that perhaps you had outgrown your inhibitions, your violent dislike of me as Sasha's lifelong friend and co-fighter and [of] all his other comrades and friends. You assured me over and over again while you were in Villa Seurat that whatever might happen between you and Sasha, you would always feel you could come to me, that as a matter of fact you felt freer with me, you could be more frank, you could speak openly with me. You repeated that while you were here last year. All this led me to think that you were growing away from your past, from the narrow stifling confines of a life barren of human interest, centered only on one's family, one's furniture and silverware, one's dog. Your letter proves that I was mistaken, that inhibitions are stronger than all reason. That you are so set in your past environment you simply cannot with the best of will take anything that is liberating and free. Heavens, if you have not taken anything from Sasha with all your love for him, why should you from me, whom you have in the past and still do consider as a rival? Yes, I know I am no longer "dangerous," being a woman with white hair and "white blue eyes" (I never knew one had white blue eyes). And yet you will never outgrow your idea that I have been and will be to the end of Sasha's and my life part of him, as he is of me. You never can forget that, it seems.

My great offense and crime against you, it seems, was that I have not introduced you to my friends as Sasha's wife. Really, Emmy dear, I credit you with more intelligence than the belief that I failed to tell my friends that you are Mme Berkman only because you are not legally married. That would really be too childish to merit a moment's consideration. You seem to have forgotten that you yourself in the very Villa Seurat told me most emphatically that you do not consider yourself Sasha's wife and never will unless you were legally married, and that you do not wish to go under his name. I tried then to make you see that no ring or piece of paper could make you more to Sasha or me than what you are, but you could not see it. You were too steeped in the prejudice of your class. Anyhow, did you or did you not tell me you do not consider yourself Sasha's wife? How then should I have introduced you as such? Another thing, as far as I know Sasha has never introduced you to his or my friends and comrades as his wife. Not because he does not think that you are but because he knows how silly he would look, as silly as I would introducing [James] Colton as my husband, even if I am forced to use his name for a passport. Can't you see that [the words] *wife* or *husband* have no meaning to us? It is love that counts above everything else. And you say yourself that Sasha loves you more than anyone else. Why should you care by what name you go with his love as your treasure?

As to my attitude, dear Emmy, even if I really were all you charge me with, even if I had the antagonism against you you seem to feel, I would still be willing to accept you for Sasha's sake. I have suffered a thousand hells for Sasha; can you imagine that I would stop at taking you into my life for his sake? The fact of the matter is, however, that I have really and truly grown to like you for your own sake. I wanted to take you into my life and be your friend. I have never at any time consciously wanted to hurt you. . . . Quite the contrary, though your ideas about free love, indeed about most things sacred to me, have often driven me to despair. I have tried my damnedest to excuse and forgive, knowing as you made me know what your background has been. If you felt hurt, it must be entirely due to your notion that when one is free, one must at all times be ready to accept and agree with every nonsense one has long outgrown. I fear, my dear, your whole conception of freedom is wrong. It does not always mean acceptance; it also means the right to reject, the right to express openly one's disagreement with an old and dying world in which you continue to live and breathe in spite of all your love for the man who has sacrificed his best years in the struggle against that world. . . .

Enough, dear Emmy, and too much. You will not understand anyhow, not because you are not intelligent enough but because you are too blinded by your notions of what constitutes the value in human relationship. You cannot help being what you are and I am not finding fault with you. I accepted you as you are, though you often tried my soul to the breaking point. I knew that no one can get out of his skin. I had hoped you would also meet me in the same way. Evidently you do not. Well, all we can do is to go our way and live our lives as we know best. Someday perhaps you will understand the real meaning of friendship and then you might also understand mine. I am willing to wait until then. Meanwhile, thank you, dear Emmy, for all you say of me as the public personality, even if you find me so wanting in private.

Affectionately,
[EG]

AB TO EG, *November 23, 1931, NICE*

Yes, dear,

I saw that we lost the sweep[stakes]—well, [that] was to be expected. . . . All your letters received. But you wrote that you mailed packages on the 17th. Strange, but up to now no sign of them. Hope they are not lost. Were they registered?

Will send Sanya [Shapiro] *Now and After*—didn't know he had none —slipped my memory.

About heredity and environment—well we do not seem to get to any understanding. You always repeat that I consider heredity the only motor power of human actions. It is not true. I think BOTH heredity and environment the vital powers, and there are a number of other factors also. But between heredity and environment I consider heredity the more powerful. You, on the contrary, consider environment and early upbringing as more powerful. There are numerous instances of Indians, American, being taken away from their tribes when babies and brought up among whites. Then, when they had a chance to return to their tribes and remain there, they relapsed entirely into the original Indians. That's the power of heredity.

Beneath all our civilization and effect of environment are still the same OLD instincts—war proves that, in spite of all environment. Of course environment will have an effect, perhaps lasting, but only after numerous generations, while the instinct of the primitive is always there.

The papers are full of men killing their wives and wives strangling their men, because of some rival and jealousy. These are primitive instincts, my dear, and they still survive in spite of all environment that makes it very dangerous to kill in one's personal and private capacity. There is no getting away from that.

You ask about persons that were radical in spite of their conservative homes. Well, you prove by it MY point. Neither you nor I got their revolutionary spirit from OUR parents, nor from OUR early environment. No doubt there were some rebels generations and generations past somewhere in our families. My brothers Max and Boris (the latter still lives) and my sister all grew up with me in the same early environment. They were all conservative. But my uncle Max [Natansohn] was a rebel. No doubt he got it from some distant ancestor, as I also got it from the same source, no doubt. That merely shows hereditary influence, but the why and how of it we don't know of course.

In Emmy's case, both heredity and environment of childhood and youth have combined to make her conservative, and SUCH a combination is almost impossible to overcome. I can see that even when her reason tells her that certain existing forms are wrong, her whole nature fights against such recognition.

But we may as well let it go at that. This matter of heredity and evnironment is ALSO a matter of *feeling*, and that feeling remains. . . .

[AB—the remainder of this letter is missing.]

AB TO EG, *December 22, 1931, NICE*

Dearest Em,

It is the 22nd and perhaps you will not get this letter before Xmas. So, let this be a hearty greeting to you. And I hope the New Year may bring you at least *less* worry and more satisfaction than the year now passing.

But at heart I know that this is a mere pious wish. Our lives were and always will be the same, with wishes remaining the fictitious horses of the poor beggar. And after all it is as it should be.

Yesterday I wrote you a postal in haste, in the post office, to tell you that your last letter with the check arrived. All OK, will attend to all the "shares." . . .

You say Cohen tries to apply psychoanalytic methods. Well, this method is much overrated and overworked now. Still, Cohen has a right to apply it, the same as others. His review is at least well-meaning. We cannot expect that a reviewer should write only fine things of the book, and of course I know you don't expect it.

You object to [Joseph] Cohen emphasizing your love life [in the *Freie Arbeiter Stimme* review]. But, my dear, in your life your love life was of an emphatic nature and it is also emphasized in the book. And it should be that way. Sex has played a very great role in your life and your book would have been lacking if that role had not been mirrored in it.

You know that [Theodore] Schroeder holds that ALL human activities are due to the sex impulse. I do not go that far, of course, though *biologically* it is undoubtedly true. That does NOT mean that this urge is always conscious.

But I do believe that with women sex plays a far greater role in love than with men, GENERALLY speaking. By sex here I mean everything, affection, love, passion, all together. And I believe also that with most women in public life—women writers, poets, etc. included—it is the strong urge of sex that is the mainspring of all activity. Indeed, it is that urge that expresses itself in most of their activities. But I do not think the same is true of men—at least not to the same extent.

I don't think, for instance, that active men—in politics, movements, art, science, etc., etc.—are necessarily possessed of a strong sex urge. On the other hand, I believe that women of similar activities ARE possessed, necessarily so, of a strong sex urge. In most cases it is an unsatisfied urge. That's my impression, anyhow.

In ALMOST ALL works of women (autobiographies, novels, etc.) you will find the frank confession or hint at their unsatisfied urge. You'll never find it in any man's work. You may find in it a strong sex urge, as say in Frank Harris' works, but NEVER an *unsatisfied* urge.

Well, this is too wide a field, and my letter is getting too big. Enough for today, I must again to my translation. I hope you are getting some sleep in your new apartment. It is high enough, I am sure.

What impression did Padraic Colum make on you? Some of his poetry is very good, full of feeling images.

Well, dear, I hope you are feeling well. Is it very cold in Paris? Here very cold, for Nice, and the apartments are not heated half enough. Enjoy your Xmas, dear. . . .

Affectionately,

S

EG TO AB, *December 25, 1931, PARIS*

Dear Sash,

I found your letter of the 22nd when I came home at 3 A.M. this morning. Yes, I celebrated the birth of the gentle man who like most of us had no doubt regretted he ever was born. . . .

Of course, dear, I do not object in the least to adverse criticism of *Living My Life*. Nor do I see anything wrong in psychoanalysis, though I agree with you that it is too overrated as a means of getting at the motivation of our actions. Having always maintained the importance of sex as a dominant force, we need not argue the matter. Nor do I disagree in what you say about sex in women as a more dominant force than in men. The wherefore of it and the why we will take up another time. It is enough now that you understand these are not my objections either to [Laurence] Stallings's or Cohen's methods. My resentment is that neither has the equipment for [dealing with] psychological motivation.* They are both equally shallow. They are both puritans. Certainly Cohen is friendly—how could he be otherwise in the *Freie Arbeiter Stimme?* But his puritanism and his shallowness make him deprecate the motives he ascribes to my actions. Now, as a matter of fact my actions had never been urged by sex alone. Else why would there always have been such lacerating struggles every time I had to decide between my love for a man and my ideas? Invariably these and not my passion have decided my course. That's what neither Stallings nor Cohen have admitted. Herein, therefore, they are

---

* Stallings's review of *Living My Life* appeared in the New York *Sun*, November 20, 1931.

alike. I didn't give a damn to find the one so superficial and deliberately denying the main issue of my conscious life. But it hurt me to see Cohen equally blind. And I think it a pity that a man so lacking in penetration should be the editor of an anarchist paper. But I don't care any more. It was only for a moment, anyway. I am sure *Living My Life* will survive my critics. . . .

Affectionately,

Em

EG TO AB, January 1932, PARIS

Dear Sash,

It is cruel to add to your task of moving and putting your house in order. But you will see by the enclosed letter from Saxe that it is not for a small thing I am worrying you. I nearly fell off my chair when I read about the possibility of placing one or two articles in *Cosmopolitan*. Strangely enough, Mildred Mesirow suggested this magazine some time ago. I laughed it off. I told her *Cosmopolitan* is a Hearst publication. And he has avoided my name like the pest ever since the McKinley affair [i.e., the assassination of, in 1901]. Of course, now that Saxe has approached Burton (that too is an interesting coincidence), something may come of the suggestion.

The question is, what can one say about the "place in the world of the disenchanted radical"? Or "the position of the radical woman in Russia, in the world, for that matter, who cannot reconcile herself to the tendency radicalism has taken"? If anything, this theme seems even more difficult to handle than the first. And that because there ain't no such animal. I have tried to think of the woman outside of myself who held some important position in the various social parties who has not "reconciled herself to the way radicalism has taken." Do you know of anyone? Perhaps Angelica [Balabanov]. But even she has her party now and work she believes in and is given a chance to do. Who else? Gawd knows I would be willing to write about them. Fact is, I suspect that Burton wants me to write about myself. I dare say, I could find enough material to write a three thousand-word article, if only I could write in the popular American journalistic style. You and I know that is impossible, and useless to do something we know beforehand is likely to be rejected. It's not like the *Ladies Home Journal*, which paid a fortune, though the article was not accepted. It seems *Cosmopolitan* goes on surer grounds. It wants synopses. Well, it's too good a possibility to turn down, don't you think? You spent two months on a translation which, if it should be accepted, will never bring $750 or $1,000. . . .

I wish you were here, or I in Nice, and we could talk over the points that might be treated. It seems to me the tragedy of the disenchanted radical, man or woman, is the tragedy of our age, which has turned everything and everybody into machines. It has no room for individual values in whatever phase of human expression. It is a mob age ruled by the mob spirit, by quantity, bulk, loud and vulgar successes. Naturally no one of sensitiveness and spiritual yearning can find a place for himself or herself in our world unless they are willing to forswear their ideal, whether of a revolutionary nature or in art and letters. This is only a suggestion, dear, which may or may not be of use to you. It may prove too somber for *Cosmopolitan*. Perhaps it will be necessary to treat the American radical as never having been clear in his mind about radicalism, or sufficiently imbued by it to stand by his guns. Nearly every one of them is now in the communist ranks, or at least working with them. They have chosen compromise as the line of least resistance, which it always was. They, more than the people who have always been revolutionists, jeer at the few who will not go over body and soul to the new superstition. I have in mind men like Waldo Frank and his ilk. Something might be written along these lines, don't you think?

Then, as regards the radical woman: well, in Russia those who could not reconcile themselves [to] the way the Revolution has gone are all in prison; some like Vera Figner are too old to be active. The rest work with the regime. As regards myself, I seem to fit in nowheres, between you and me and the lamp post, not even in our own ranks. Certainly not in any other. That would perhaps not be such a tragedy if I were not still consumed with the need of activity. I am in the worst state of turmoil I have been in years. I wrote you along that line some time ago. In addition to being neither able or willing to be caught in the muddy mob stream, I also feel an alien everywhere. I am quite willing to treat this quite frankly and without reserve.

However, I can't do anything now. My head is bursting with subjects. I have to speak nearly every evening on another theme. If at least it were in English. Just fancy having to transcribe my notes into German and not yet knowing what each city wants. You know best the torture of it all. Well, dear, old pal, as usual I have to ask you to try your luck with a few hundred words on the subjects suggested by Saxe. . . .

That is a horrible business about [Nicola] Sacco's son [Dante]. But what will you when anarchists marry women who are millions of miles removed from their ideas? Look at the wives of the Chicago men . . . [or] Tom Mooney's wife, who, Bessie [Kimmelman?] writes me, is using Tom's fame for her own private ambitions. And even Lucy Parsons, who goes with every gang proclaiming itself revolutionary, the IWW [and] now the communists. Not to peask of her horrible treatment of [Albert R.] Parsons' son, whom she drove into the army and then had him put in a lunatic asylum. And now Mrs. Sacco, letting the boy go with an irresponsible man.

It gives me the creeps. Well, since Mrs. Sacco has given [that man] James the right to take the boy with him, I don't see who will be able to take him away. Besides, I don't see what the European comrades can do, being as wretchedly poor as they are everywhere. It is a complicated affair. Still, you might write Rudolf. He may know someone who would adopt the child, or he might get in touch with [Luigi] Bertoni in Geneva, or [Barthélemy] de Ligt. It would be of no use for me to write these two; Rudolf has greater pull with them.

Then there is another idea, Prince Hopkins. You know the Mesirows have their boy in his school [in England]. It is a magnificent place—certainly anything but proletarian. I am not sure Prince would take Dante; he probably would be afraid the parents of the other boys would raise a row. But he might do something for the boy, or perhaps take him in anyhow. I will get the address from the Mesirows tomorrow and send it to you. Then you could write Hopkins. For the life of me I don't know what else to suggest. As to a Sacco–Vanzetti meeting in Geneva now with the disarmament conference in session, I don't believe our people would do it. Perhaps the Bertoni group. Again I say Rudolf would be the one to suggest something. Better write him.

Often enough in my life I have longed for a child, now more than ever. But when I think of most children of our comrades I thank the stars that I will leave no one who will drag into the mire what I have always held at the heights. Perhaps Sacco's boy has been sufficiently impressed by the murder of his father and his friend to guide him through life. In that case it matters little with whom he will be for the next few years. On the other hand, the most ardent surroundings might have no effect. It did not in the case of so many anarchists' children. Why should they matter in his? It's terribly tragic. I wish I could help. But I don't know how. If I had even a small income and the boy were willing, I would take him in a minute. Without having anything to offer him, it is out of the question. Besides, the boy must be around fifteen; one really has no right to impose foster parents on him.

I must write Saxe and this is a long enough yarn. Thank Emmy for the note. I understand how busy she is. Buy her a few flowers for the new home with the enclosed ten francs.

Please, my dear, do the synopsis of one or both of the themes as soon as possible. We have tried so often to get something. Maybe we will this time. I embrace you,

Emma

THOMAS H. BELL TO EG, *January 14, 1932,*
LOS ANGELES

My very dear Emma,

I have just finished the first volume of your book, [but am] not yet in possession of your second volume. My very warmest congratulations. I am delighted with it.

I have to make a little confession to you. Some of our comrades had been reading your book as it appeared in Yiddish in the *Vorwarts*. I heard some of them—two or three of them—speak about it disapprovingly. "Too much sex. Ridiculous. Makes us a laughing-stock."

Yes, Emma, an old hand like me ought to have known better. I noticed indeed that the two or three were just that two or three who criticize and are dissatisfied with the work and attitude of our group. They mean well; they are quite sincere. They want our activities to be narrowed down to the strictly economic and the ideas to be presented in the good old way. One of them is a supporter of that "Russian" program put forward a couple of years ago. Two of them are anarchist-communists of that type, good god, which will swallow even dictatorship to bring in the society they believe in. Yes, I say, well-meaning and sincere. But the difference between them and the bolsheviki—as in the case of one or two better known comrades—is merely that they do not like the bolsheviki and imagine that they could carry out the bolsheviki ends without using the bolsheviki means.

I ought to have known. But I have to confess that though I never for a moment doubted the value of your book, I did feel just a little uneasy lest you should have been a little indiscreet. I thought it possible that your association with Harris might have swayed you a bit, and his book on his *Life and Loves* was in the back of my mind.

Yes, yes, I ought to have had more sense than to pay the slightest attention to those damned fools. It shows how even an old hand with long experience can be affected by babble.

Why, Emma, the sex side of your tale is beautiful. Beautiful all through. People who would object to any of it at all are eunuchs, hypocrites, or hopeless asses.

I do not dare to write any more, for fear of being tempted to spend my time and my little energy in a long letter instead of in the things that I have undertaken.

I am delighted with the book and believe it will be of the highest value to the movement.

Fraternally,
T. H. Bell

EG TO DR. WILLIAM J. ROBINSON, January 26, 1932, PARIS

Dear William:

Thank you for your letter and the January issue of the *Critic and Guide*. Thank you, also, for your review of *Living My Life*. True, you have damned it with faint praise, but I did not expect anything else; therefore I am not disappointed. On pain of hurting your male vanity, permit me to say that you are taking undue credit to yourself for my knowledge of birth control methods, and my lecture on "Woman's Inhumanity to Man." It is certain that you did not read *Living My Life* carefully, else you would have seen the report of my presence at the Neo-Malthusian Congress, Paris, in 1900. It was there where I first heard methods discussed, long before I knew of your existence. I certainly never heard you talk of methods, and I did not become aware of your magazine until many years later. I therefore could not have received any practical knowledge from you.

It is the same regarding your lecture on "Man's Inhumanity to Woman." Since I was not present when you delivered it at the Sunrise Club, it could not have "inspired" me to reply by "Woman's Inhumanity to Man." Really, old chap, you must not allow your conceit to run away with you. I have always been willing to give you credit for your pioneer work on behalf of birth control, but after all, you were not the only one who blazed the trail, much as you seem to think so.

Your statement, at this late date, that Emma Goldman, being a woman, naturally cannot think, is so utterly absurd that it doesn't merit a moment's consideration. Except to say that you prove that you haven't developed out of the position of the caveman. Your attitude toward anarchism, and your slipshod way of labeling everybody who does not agree with you as demented, also proves how little you have grown with the years. From time immemorial the wise-acres in the world have considered everybody crazy whose ideas they did not understand, and whose raison d'être of life and action they could not interpret.

However, I believe so firmly in free speech and press that I am quite willing that you should stick to your antiquated ideas.

Thanking you once more for them small favors about *Living My Life*.

Sincerely,
[EG]

EG TO THOMAS H. BELL, February 8, 1932, PARIS

Dear Tom,

I was very glad to hear from you, after such a lapse of years; at least it seems that long to me. I have been kept posted about your doings by Bessie

Kimmelman. I hope my little greeting to the anniversary of your activities in our ranks [fifty years an anarchist] has reached you in time.

Yes, I know what suggestion does, even to the clearest minds. I have come to think it the most vicious element in human life. Hardly anyone manages to escape its insidious effect, and those who do must make up their minds to remain alone. I am therefore not blaming you for having listened to the absurd talk about *Living My Life* from some of the Jewish comrades. They outdo the puritans in puritanism. They have so little intellectual judgment and integrity that they always go with the mob. Most of them are worse zealots than those of yesteryear. I think that our comrade, Michael Cohn, was right when he said that the objections of the Jewish anarchists to *Living My Life* were more because it appeared in the *Forward* than because it shocked them. That is partly correct. But whichever way it is, I can whisper to you that I don't give a damn. I went my way in living my life without any regard to the comments it aroused, or the condemnation. Why should I feel differently, now that the record of it is being condemned by people who have never lived?

Yes, you are right, most so-called radicals are not only physical eunuchs, they are that mentally as well, which is far worse. That accounts for their flirtation with Soviet Russia. They have no ideas of their own; therefore they bask in the ideas that come out of that unfortunate land. Then, too, they are always carried away by success, material or otherwise, and there is no denying that Russia is a success from the point of view of the power of the state. Well, it really doesn't matter.

Dear Tom, I am glad the reading of the original of *Living My Life* has shown you how inane was the impression of the crew that read the book in the Jewish translation. Nevertheless, I was surprised that you would think, even for a moment, that I could write of my emotional experiences as Frank Harris did. You see, they were never physical, alone, in my case; they were nothing but that, in the life of Frank Harris. Therefore our approach to and our treatment of sex must necessarily be different.

I am enclosing letters which will give you some idea of my doings. Remember me to all the comrades.

Fraternally,
[EG]

EG TO MARY LEAVITT, *November 2, 1932, ST. TROPEZ*

Dear, dear Mary,

Your letter of August 27th came as a great and pleasant surprise. Needless to say I had never cast you out of my mind. I knew without anybody telling me that your struggle to get your bearings after your separation from Don must be very painful. I had often wanted to write you and give you whatever encouragement I could possibly communicate in a letter, but, not hearing from you ever, I did not wish to impose my concern on you and your life. Sometimes one can do more harm by affectionate interest than by no interest at all. I have always hated to meddle between two people, and I feared you might interpret anything I might write you as such. So I kept silent. I cannot tell you how glad I am to have your letter, to know how you feel about me. I hope that neither of us will ever allow such a long span of time to pass without being in touch with each other.

Thank you a thousand times for your beautiful tribute to *Living My Life*. You will be delighted to learn that nearly every review of the book, whether from opponents or friends, has been perfectly marvelous. To my knowledge there were only a very few dissenting opinions about the quality and importance of my autobiography. I am enclosing a copy of one tribute recently received. My correspondent exaggerates, of course, still the very fact that the son of a man who was a partner of Rockefeller, whose whole background and traditions were ultra-respectable, should write as he does about my book, means volumes. Unfortunately praise does not sell a book; the best proof is the material flop of *Living My Life*. Of course it is not the fault of the work, rather is it the prohibitive price and the unfortunate moment for the appearance of the book. . . .

Yes, I remember the time when you and Don were in my place in Berlin and I was cooking a Jewish dinner for you. I readily believe that you could not visualize in the light domestic servant, Emma Goldman, the public person who was so feared and hated in her erstwhile country. This reminds me of a letter I recently received from a German friend of mine. I had stopped with his parents while in Stuttgart. He had never thought, he writes, that Emma Goldman was so feminine. I replied that for my own peace of mind I had wished all my life that I were not. People do get strange ideas about public-spirited men and women, especially the latter.

I am very glad indeed to know that you have finally found yourself, and that your relation with Don has simmered down to a friendship. It is the best proof that your love life with him had not been a failure. In nine cases out of ten the death of love leaves much bitterness, recriminations, and often hatred behind. Only the truly fine are capable of rescuing from the debacle a friendship that endures for all time. I am happy that you succeeded in that; I was confident that you would.

So glad to hear about the little fellow. As to what he will be when he grows up no amount of training and concern can decide that in advance. I was always of the opinion that all one can do for a child is to implant certainty of love and understanding, the feeling that whatever happens in his or her life they can find the strongest support and deepest understanding from their parents. The lack of such a feeling embitters the life of children. I know whereof I speak, for mine has been a ghastly childhood, as you have seen fom *Living My Life*. Perhaps because of it I feel keenly about children.

However, I do find that radical parents are often going to the opposite extreme: instead of enslaving their children, they allow the latter to enslave them. They do not seem to think it necessary to implant in their offspring at an early age the respect for freedom and the rights of their parents as well as their own. The understanding that love means give and take, and not only give all the time. But in the last analysis it is much more the outside world which molds the life of the young, and their reactions to their surroundings, than the home. I hope this may not be entirely the case with your son.

You will want to know about Sasha and myself. There is really not much to say. Sasha lives in Nice and has his own ménage. He works at correcting manuscripts, reading proofs, and typing whenever he has jobs. I have tried to become a "book broker." I have attempted to place German and Russian books in America. One book had almost been accepted when we learned that the German house did not have the English language rights. This week I have sent synopses of two other works to a number of publishers in America. I feel, however, that I will not be a success in this business any more than I have ever been in similar undertakings. You probably know that I toured Scandinavia and Germany last spring. I had hoped I might repeat it this winter but so far only Holland has responded. I am going there in January. Germany looks hopeless, though I did have a few encouraging invitations. The situation is such that one cannot say from day to day what dictator will be at the helm of the German government. . . .

[EG—what was apparently the last page of this carbon copy has disappeared.]

AB TO M. ELEANOR FITZGERALD, *November 11, 1932,* NICE

Well, dear Fitz,

I just wrote yesterday to Stella. I was waiting to hear from you about the matter, but today I decided not to wait, for you had probably asked Stella to inform me, since you had to leave for the funeral of your brother Arthur.

I could not agree to write such a book for any publisher unless I received a minimum $2,000 advance. The book might sell or not, that cannot be foretold. The advance is most important. EG's book did not sell, but at least she received $7,500 advance.

It would take me at least one year, and more likely a year and a half to write the book as I want to write it. You know what a struggle it is to relive the past and to do a really good piece of work on such a book. Nor is there anyone to help me write it. Not that I need it or would ever allow anyone to help me in writing—but I merely say that in reference to the struggle of writing the book. I have helped EG in her work, as you no doubt know. The mere assurance that someone is there to help is in itself a great moral satisfaction; even a certain security, I would say. And yet in spite of all that, EG really went through hell in writing her book. And I also always suffer a great deal when I write something worthwhile. Maybe you will be surprised to know that even in writing *Now and After,* which is not at all autobiographical, I worked like a slave and went through a terrific struggle. So bad indeed that several times I was on the point of giving the whole damn thing up. It was only sheer perseverance that forced me to keep at it.

Well, an autobiography is still more difficult to write—at least it is and would be for me. I would therefore never undertake it unless it were at least financially worthwhile. And by that I do not mean only that I should have enough to live on during the time I write but that I should also have something left over. For I surely will not be even physically able to do other work for some time after I have written the autobiography. . . .

What good would $500 be to me? I can't live on it even five months. Life is expensive here in the south and I must stay here for various reasons. First, because of my damned "papers." Secondly because I can't stand the Paris climate or any damp or rainy place. I am not so young and hardy as I used to be, my dear Fitz. Anyhow, life in Paris would be even dearer.

(And, strictly between me and you, dear, I could save money by living with Emmy and Emma in St. Tropez, but—the atmosphere EG creates is impossible. A short visit is all right, but nothing more than a short visit. I think you can realize this, dear. You know from personal experience, and you are an angel to get along with, and yet—well, you know. Incidentally, I don't know whether Stella ever told you, but the last time she was in St. Tropez she really was brought almost to the verge of desperation and spasms by the manner of EG. She vowed she'd never come back, and it was really a pity to see Stella and how she felt, and the way the atmosphere was getting more charged with friction and open storms day by day. And over what? Just over nothing. It's EG's character, my dear, and it is not improving with years. I am sorry to tell you that everyone who has stayed there for a week or more had the same complaints. EG is dictatorial and interfering, and she has a way of making life miserable for you without saying anything to which you can give a rough and suitable answer. The more is the pity. And the worst of it is that EG herself has not the least idea of it. She is a great woman in some ways, no doubt of that; but living close with her is just impossible. It is too bad, but it is so. Even when I visit her alone, I can't stand it there very long. There is no one, of course, to call her attention to those things except myself. As a good friend I do it, though very rarely. And then EG just gets mad. It is useless. But all this [is] in strictest confidence, my dear. For I know you will understand. I would not dream of saying this to anyone else.)

Well, this letter is getting too big, but I had to say those things to you, dear. For I am sure you, if no one else, will understand, and you will not misjudge the spirit that prompted the above.

I'd love a little letter from you, dear. I know fortune has not been very good to you, especially of late, but I have been wondering what work you are doing. . . . Love to you and greetings from Emmy,

[AB]

EMMY ECKSTEIN TO EG, *July 16, 1934, ST. TROPEZ*

Emma, dear,

. . . I AM TIRED, so tired, Emma, dear. I wish you were here now. You would cheer us up, Sasha and me. We need it. See, the book [i.e., the translation of Rudolf Rocker's ms.] is on both nerves already and I have not even started with typing!!!

Yes, dear Emma, one never can have everything in life one wants. I can very well believe that, in spite of your wonderful success abroad, there is emptiness in your heart. Of course, I know. One needs a heart to rest, to weep, and to be cheerful with. All those people are expecting wonders and news coming from the mouth of EG and admiration is not love.

Emma, I am SURE that you would be surprised how I have changed re my attitude to Sash. I was, of course too much rooted in that thought that a man belongs altogether to a wife. Mit Haut und Haar [body and soul]. But, if I well remember, I even was that way the last time you were with us—when I induced Sasha to go to Lyons with you, remember? So now at least there is one thing you may be sure of: You will have no difficulty in that way, that because of me, etc.

I grew older, my dear, and I feel it in many ways (though I am as gay as ever, in general). But I do (growing older) realize more and more the necessity of your both great beings clinging together. And also, I am sure that you and I will go on perfectly well. And if not (what also here and then is sure), we will not mind at all and forget about it, nicht wahr [won't we], Emma? Life is so stupid after all—one dies and EVERYTHING is finished for good, why make things harder as they are. . . .

[Regarding] my lack of understanding of what you feel for him and your not always "sweet and inviting attitude," darling, don't be angry, but I had also my troubles with you.

I tell you that now, because I am completely warm to you, and I will be, never mind what I thought and felt in the past. And when you come, sweet Emma, you will feel that I share completely my happiness with

Sasha and you. You will not believe me that I intended it at first. But circumstances all around did not give me the opportunity.

I went also through certain struggles and they made me greater and better [able to] understand the heart of others. I love Sasha more than ever but in a much broader way, you know. Not as being all the time after him, etc.

I know that we both in this regard will be perfectly happy, Emma, since I feel that my love and feeling for Sasha corresponds enormously with yours. And if even quite different because of the very difference of our personalities, dearie, he loves us both alike, you know, only that I as a comrade am regarding [compared with] you very pale, you know. But I try my best.

Emma darling, Sasha is not very strong. I have the desire and deepest hope to give him and you at least now the possible happiness there is for you both. My God, life passes so quick.

Emma—your love is certainly (re [Frank] Heiner [see p. 111]) not satisfactory but I tell you look at Gwen [Dowling]. Young, beautiful, and what has she? A man [Allan] who loves another woman. . . .

It is all an idée fixe of yours, that Heiner doesn't "see." I bet you he knows exactly how you look and that even is much more astounding than his feeling he is crazy about you, Emma. I'll explain why: When I was twenty, there came to our house a [blind] masseur, who took care of our massage. When he massaged me, he told me EXACTLY how I look in my face. It was astounding!! You would not believe how well he knew my looks and even to my *disadvantage.*

My dear, the movement of a body makes such a difference, the color. Emma, you have lovely eyes, your complexion, and you can (as I told you) be very, very sweet. Never mind age. I never did care a wink about age. Even today I would love a man of a hundred years, because it is the GEIST [spirit] I love. Why in hell shouldn't there be men like that?? . . .

No, the tragic [thing] is that he [Frank Heiner] has that lovely wife that doesn't allow you to be free toward him. I mean your feelings are against it. I do NOT agree that it would be too hurting for a while, even. Why, Emma, also your own feelings and desire for love and affection may be calmed down after a while of love life with him and discovering his weak points etc. . . .

In Liebe,
Emmy

EG TO EMMY ECKSTEIN, *July 30, 1934, TORONTO*

My dearest Emmy,

I can see by your letter that our Sash is not so well as you try to assure me. I have repeatedly written him that it is madness to work so hard as he does and so unnecessary. I cabled him yesterday to discontinue work during the excessive heat. It took Rudolf five years to write his book. It won't make much difference if it takes Sasha an extra month or longer. His health is more important I am sure. Between you and me I can ill afford to spend nearly $2 for a cable. But I am so worried about Sasha, I had to do it. It would be too awful, if anything happens to our funny man and I thousands of miles away. Not that I have any doubts about the care you give him. I am certain no one could be more loving and devoted. But it is my own feeling about Sasha which is so oppressive. If at least he will rest during August, he will be in better condition to finish the task. And having been away from it for a month will bring him back with his mind rested and refreshed.

And you too, my dear child. It must be fearfully wearing to see Sasha in such an exhausted state and so listless. You need life and play; you are by nature a cheerful kid. I am sure if Sasha will only dismiss the translation for a month, he will be in better humor too and you will not feel so unhappy as I see you are. From all angles, not the least the work itself, it is important that Sasha should lay off for a while. I hope my cable will decide him to do so.

Dearie, I have already written to my Chicago friends about a passport for Sasha. If they will succeed—I am sure they will try hard—perhaps we can do something about bringing Sasha to Canada for a visit next spring. Of course it will be necessary to have him examined by a specialist [to see] whether his heart is strong enough to stand an ocean voyage. Once in Canada we may be able to get permission to visit America. I am certain Sasha will feel differently about going there, if he will be so near the States. As I already wrote you, it is useless to even try for a permanent stay in America. But perhaps a visit for three months. In any event, you must go to America to visit your people. If we fail in our efforts for Sasha, *you will go*. We will strain every nerve to make your trip possible. Yes, I know it is long to wait. But being poor as we are and without definite security, we simply must be patient. I am sure you will be, my dearest Emmy. You have already gone through much. So you must be brave another year. . . .

Yes, darling, we grow older. And it is well, if we learn as we get on in years. But for you to say you are growing older is nonsense. You will only be thirty-two in October. I am sure not very much more, if that. I am glad though that you no longer feel I am taking away your Sash. I admit it was very hard and very painful to have to guard against every word and every look while you clung to Sasha as your property. It made life very hard for me. You see, our friendship is so rare and so old nothing could interfere with it. At the same time I felt frightful only because I could not come to Sasha with my troubles, or have him near for fear that you would be hurt. You may not know it, but I tried my damnedest to avoid coming to Nice just because I did not feel free with Sasha. Not even the last time we were together. It will be different now when I come back and you have more confidence and trust in me. I should love nothing better than a deep, devoted friendship between the three of us.

I had a letter from Frank Heiner today. I had talked to Ann Lord about you and ... she talked to Heiner about you, because he writes "whoever she is, I hail her as a kindred spirit. She loves the most wonderful man in the world, as I love the most wonderful woman." Heiner is a great enthusiast and much of a romantic. It is fortunate for him that he can create his own inner world of beauty, since he cannot see the outer world. Dearest Emmichen, it is kind of you to tell me I should not leave the great event go by. The trouble is, I cannot easily go in for an infatuation I know to be of a moment. I mean, my life is so uncertain, and so full of anxieties, I cannot bind anyone to me. The only chance I will have with Heiner will be his visit here. Afterward I may never see him again. Or if I do, it will be in Chicago with his wife and child always near. Not if my life depended on it, could I enjoy any closeness under the conditions I would meet in Chicago. Not only because of Mrs. [Mary] Heiner but also because of the comrades. I could not bear to see the beautiful feeling of Heiner or the attraction he has for me dragged through the mud, gossiped about, and vulgarized. And I am sure that would happen. After all, the world at large does not forgive a woman of sixty-five in love with a man thirty years younger. It's different about the man. Der Kerl hat immer Gluck. [Guys have all the luck.] Not that I care what people say. But I hate insinuations and remarks and smirks of any sort. Well, Heiner is coming the 15th. I will see how I feel then. To tell you the truth, I don't know whether I love Heiner or am in love with his love. It may well be that his marvelous letters of radiant beauty have carried me away. And when he will be here I will feel different. I have cautioned him that that may well prove the case. He is therefore prepared for it.

Emmy dearest, you say Sasha is taking the medicine the doctor gave him. What medicine? I suppose you went to a doctor with him when you were last in Nice. I am so uneasy and worried. Sasha is ridiculous not to let me know how he feels. Not to know anything is worse. It lies like a stone on my heart. So please, my dear, tell me frankly what is the matter with Sasha? Is it just fatigue or his heart? I really *must know*. If Sasha is in the least danger, I will return right away. I can borrow some money for the trip. I simply can't bear to be so far away, if there is anything serious the matter with Sasha. But if it is only the translation, then he must let it go for a month. It would revive him wonderfully just to dismiss the damned book and rest and loaf. I have asked Stella to send him $75 and $50 was sent to him by our new dear friend, Jeanne Levey. This money has nothing to do with the translation. You and Sasha could therefore use it for a holiday during August. I am writing Sasha to this effect.

Dear, dear Emmichen, don't feel bad; just you take it easy, and get the Sandstroms to take you and Sasha to the beach, for a picnic or something of an outing. I embrace you with love,

[EG]

EG TO AB, *September 13, 1934, TORONTO*

Dearest Sash,

It was good to get your newsy letter. I fully agree with you in what you say about Spain. There is even more than bull fights to indicate the backwardness of the Spanish people. That is the status of woman. I could understand the church and the middle class keeping her in complete subjection. But imagine our own comrades still in the old ideas. Sanya [Shapiro] told me that a large percentage of our young comrades are infected with venereal disease because they are forced to cohabitate with prostitutes. No girl is permitted out of sight of her parents. Neither would our young comrades have anything to do with girls, unless they are ready to marry them. No wonder the women when they got the vote gave the reactionary elements a majority. Heaven knows the French comrades have by no means a free attitude toward women. But they are miles ahead of the Spanish. In fact Sanya told me the comrades refuse to have women attend their meetings. You probably remember Hildegarde, an awfully nice girl who used to be with [Augustine] Souchy and Therese a great deal. Well, she is the sweetheart of Orobon [Fernandez]. In Germany she was active in the youth and anarcho-syndicalist movement. In Spain she was not permitted to do anything. She complains bitterly to Sanya about the backwardness of our comrades toward her and all women. I don't see how our comrades in Spain hope to advance much, if they keep their women down so much. Anyhow, I agree with you that both Nettlau and Rudolf are too enthusiastic in re Spain. I suppose it is their despair over the world situation that makes them cling so to the possibilities in Spain. I plan to spend next winter there to see for myself. . . .

Dearest, you guessed it right about my affair with Frank. True, the two weeks of his visit were like magic. I don't remember the time when there was such peace and joy in my life. BUT they are probably the first and last two weeks I will have with him. Even if I should succeed in getting to the States [again], my visit to Chicago will have to be brief. And what with nightly lectures, the comrades to claim my time, and Frank's wife so near, there will be no chance of any intimacy or privacy with Frank. Besides I am not hopeful about America. Of course Frank might again come here. But that will not be until next spring before I sail back to France. It is a long time to wait when one has just entered a new world. Altogether the odds are against us that we should hope for another reunion of such harmony, peace, and happiness of the two weeks here. Frank is an optimist; he had to develop that or he could not have conquered his difficulties. He is even sure he will come to France. His ardent wish is father to his thoughts. But I have been too battered by life, especially my love life, to hope for much more than I have already received from Frank. I suppose I will get myself in leash. But just now I feel all smashed up. I am no fool, as you well know. Not for a moment did I expect that Frank should tie his life to mine, even if he had no wife whom he cares a great deal about. His whole life is before him; mine is on the downward road. He belongs in America, where I cannot be. And he must work on his degree to be able to establish himself in some independent position, since he is poor, has responsibilities, and I can offer him nothing except love much deeper and [more] radiant than I have felt for a long time. You see then, dush, that I have no cause to be happy, though I am grateful to the stars that helped me discover Frank and have two marvelous weeks with him. At least if I should not see him again, I will have the satisfaction of having given him to our movement. That is something. . . .

Give my love to Emmy and a huge chunk for you, my own dear old pal,

Em

EG TO DR. SAMUEL D. SCHMALHAUSEN, January 28, 1935, MONTREAL

Dear Samuel Schmalhausen:

Thanks for yours of the 21st. I know I am a sinner. I should not have waited for you to remind me of your book *Woman's Coming of Age*. Truth is, I was through with the volume two weeks ago, but I waited from day to day for a free moment when I might write you about it. Now I will delay no longer. . . .

About your essay [in the symposium]: I am delighted to know that one of your own sex is so understanding of the different effect of the sex act on the male and female. Singularly enough I have maintained, since my intellectual awakening, the same thought. Namely, that the sex act of the man lasts from the moment of its dominant motivation to its climax. After that the brute has done his share. The brute can go to sleep. Not so the woman. The climax of the embrace, far from leaving her relaxed or stupefied as it does the man, raises all her sensibilities to the highest pitch. All her yearning for love, affection, tenderness becomes more vibrant and carries her to ecstatic heights. At that moment she needs the understanding of and communion with her mate perhaps more than the physical. But the brute is asleep and she remains in her own world far removed from him. I know this from my personal experience and experiences of scores of women who have talked freely with me. I am certain that the cause for the conflict between the sexes which continues to exist regardless of woman's emancipation is due to the differences in quality of the sex embrace. Perhaps it will always be that way. Certainly I find very few men who have the same need, or who know how to minister to that of the woman. Naturally, I felt elated to read your analysis and your conclusion which actually express what I have felt and voiced for well nigh forty-five years. Altogether, *Woman's Coming of Age* was a treat. I really have reason to be proud of myself [for] having voiced many ideas expressed in your volume so long ago. I should be able now to sit back and rest on my laurels and let you and the other youngsters continue when it is all safe and sound.

You will forgive me when I say that you are like the cow that gives good milk and then kicks the bucket. In the second half of your essay you undo what you say in the first. You end up like a good old German Philistine in your contentions about marriage and honest-to-god monogamy. As to your reference to "anarchist egotists," that is not only dragged in by the hair, but is in tune with all Marxists' attitudes to anarchists and anarchism. The most intelligent and fairest of them merely repeat the vindictive charge of their masters, Marx and Lenin. I confess I was surprised to find a man of your breadth of view use the term "anarchist egotist." Where did you find such creatures? Was [Peter] Kropotkin an egotist? Was [Elisée] Reclus, [Errico] Malatesta, or Berkman? In point of fact, Kropotkin and Reclus were rigid monogamists. I doubt whether they ever had any other experience except with their wives. Their opposition to marriage was not due to their desire to sleep with another woman every night, as you would make all anarchists appear. It was their opposition to the state and state interference. But I cheerfully admit that I do not see in monogamy the only mode of relationship between the sexes. Whatever it is to be depends on the temperament, on how far one is sexed, and how great one's need for love and sex expression. One cannot dictate that by Marxian dialectics or the GPU [i.e., Russian secret police].

Altogether, I consider it unfair, to say the least, to constantly confuse anarchy with the capitalist system as chaos or charging the anarchists with being bourgeois sentimentalists or, as you charge them, with being anarchist egotists. Leave that to the politicians: unscrupulousness is their stock in trade. I take it that you consider yourself a scientist. It is, therefore, unworthy of you to employ the same lingo.

I don't know what the communists and their devotees would do if they couldn't always revert for their arguments to the Russian Pope, Lenin. Now, I don't gainsay his knowledge of Marx, although the methods he had employed to impose Marxism on the Russian people would turn the dear old man in his grave, if he knew, and certainly make his nice beard rise to the very heavens. Anyway, Lenin knew his Marx, but I am quite certain he knew nothing about sex. He was as barren of that as his comrade George Bernard Shaw and I am sure as little worried with it as he. Lenin was as cold as a cucumber and while no doubt he loved Krupaskaya, it was in the sense of comradeship and not sex. Whatever intensities he had were centered on his idée fixe of the dictatorship for which he not only destroyed millions but was willing to destroy many millions more. . . .

Cordially,

[EG]

EG TO MAX NETTLAU, *February 8, 1935, MONTREAL*

Dear, dear friend,

I have your letter of January 12th. I am terribly sorry to have hurt you. Believe me, I had no intention to do it. I understood perfectly that in referring to the "innermost wish" of the Spanish woman to have broods of children you were teasing me and that you meant it as a joke. Those who know me more intimately than you, dear comrade, know perfectly well that I appreciate humor because I have a considerably developed sense of it myself. How do you suppose I would have survived my struggle, if I lacked that sense? But there are certain things which somehow don't lend themselves to joking. And one of them is the male contention that woman loves to have broods of children. Please don't feel hurt again when I tell you that like the rest of your sex, you really know nothing about woman. You take too much for granted. I would have to talk with Spanish women myself to get beneath the age-long tradition which has put her into the sexual straightjacket. I am sure that I would get quite a different picture than you have painted of her.

You charge me with having a hasty and superficial opinion about the Spanish mother from my short visit in Spain. You forget, dear comrade, that I had been thrown together with Spanish men and women in America for over a period of thirty-five years. We had quite a Spanish movement when [Pedro] Esteve was alive. Not only did I know all the comrades merely in a public way from meetings and gatherings, but I knew their private lives. I nursed their wives in childbirth and I was with them and the male comrades in a special way. Long before I went to Spain I knew the relation between Spanish men and women. As I knew the relation between the Italian men and women. My visit in Spain merely verified all that I had learned from them over many years. And what is it that I have learned? It is that all Latin men still treat their wives, or their daughters, as inferiors and consider them as mere breeding machines as the caveman did. And not only the Latin men. My connection with the German movement gave me the same definite impression. In other words, with the exception of the Scandinavians and the Anglo-Saxons, the most modern is the Old Adam in his inhibitions to woman. He is something like most Gentiles are to the Jew: when you scratch deep down to their inner being you will find an anti-Semitic streak lurking somewhere in their make-up. Now, of course, dear comrade, you call that "terrible Russian rigorousness and severity." Aside of the fact that you are the only one of my friends who has discovered this trait in me, I wish to say it is nothing of the kind. When one feels deeply, one's expression sounds "rigorous and severe." And I do feel the position of woman very intensely. I have seen too many tragedies in the relation between the sexes; I have seen too many broken bodies and maimed spirits from the sex slavery of woman not to feel the matter deeply or to express my indignation against the attitude of most of you gentlemen.

All your assurance not withstanding, I wish to say that I have yet to meet the woman who wants to have many children. That doesn't mean that I ever for a moment denied the fact that most women want to have *a child*, although that, too, has been exaggerated by the male. I have known quite a number of women, feminine to the last degree, who nevertheless lack that supposed-to-be inborn trait of motherhood or longing for the child. There is no doubt the exception. But, as you know, the exception proves the rule. Well, granted that every woman wants to become a mother. But unless she is densely ignorant with an exaggerated trait of passivity, she wants only as many children as she can decide to have and, I am sure, the Spanish woman makes no exception. Certainly habits and traditions play a tremendous part in creating artificial desires that may become a second nature. The church, especially the Catholic Church, as you know yourself, has done its utmost to impress upon woman that she must live up to the dicta of God to multiply. But would it interest you to know that among the women who apply to birth control clinics the Catholics, regardless of the hold the priest has over them, represent a very large percentage? You may suggest that in America they have already become "infected with the horror of horrors" of limiting the number of offspring. Well, I would be willing to put it to a test, if it were possible to reach the women in Spain with lectures on birth control and birth control methods. Just how many would demonstrate your romantic conception of what they want or my suggestion of "artificial" limitation of offspring? I am afraid, dear comrade, you would lose the bet.

Your interpretation of matriarchy as meaning that the mother must keep her sons tied to her apron strings, accept his earnings, and act the generous godmother in giving him pocket money, was to say the least very amusing to me. To me this merely indicates the unconscious revenge of the enslaved female on the male. But it doesn't indicate the least freedom of either the man or the woman. Besides, matriarchy means more to me than this cleavage which exists between mother and son or father and daughter. Where such conditions exist no one is free. . . .

Aside from all these considerations, it is the continuation of the conservatism of woman which has undoubtedly been a great contributory force to the reaction in Spain, the complete collapse of everything worthwhile in Germany, and the continued existence of Mussolini. Or will you deny the fact that the first thing after the Spanish women were given the vote was to vote back black reaction? Or will you deny the fact that the German women have been driven back to the Kirche and Kinder without as much as a protest? Or that the Italian women have been hurled back at least fifty years into their old position as mere sex objects? Heaven knows, I hold no brief for the American woman. I know the majority is still as conservative and as much in the clutches of the church as the women of the countries I have mentioned. But I do insist that there is in America a large minority of women, advanced women, if you please, who will fight to the last drop of their blood for the gains which they have made, physical and intellectual, and for their rights to equality with the man. Anyway, dear comrade, it seems futile to argue this matter between us. We will never agree. It is a commentary, however, on how little theories fight inhibitions. Here you are an anarchist, firmly believing in the utmost freedom of the individual, and yet you persist in glorifying woman as the cook and breeder of large families. Do you not see the inconsistency of your claims? But the inhibitions and traditions of the male are too deep set. I am afraid they will continue long after anarchism has been established. . . .

My chances of getting another visa from America are very dubious. A new reactionary campaign against all aliens was begun by the yellow Hearst papers and as a result the administration is more timid than ever. A polite expression for cowardice. But since I cannot sail back now owing to lack of means, another attempt will be made by friends in New York. I am not at all hopeful. In fact, I feel certain that I will have to sail back to France early in May. If only I could be active there, but that, of course, is out of the question. I would fly out in twenty-four hours. The anti-alien spirit is spreading all over the world like wildfire. To me the deepest modern tragedy is the homelessness and hearthlessness of all political refugees. Well, one cannot make plans now. One just drifts from day to day. . . .

I know you are too generous to harbor a grievance too long. You must not be angry with me for having called you antediluvian. I meant no hurt, but I will fight you to the last stitch on the question of woman and her great desire to have broods of children.

Affectionately,
[EG]

Sixty: "Fedya" (Modest Stein), EG, AB, and Mollie Steimer at Emma's birthday party   FLECHINE/IISH

EG's cottage, "Bon Esprit," St. Tropez   R. DRINNON

Exiles on an errand, perhaps in Nice, 1930s

AB and Emmy Eckstein, ca. 1929   FLECHINE

On the run: AB in Antwerp after his expulsion from France, May
1930   IISH

From the presentation copy of *Living My Life*, to her "husband"

To James Colton —
brave comrade
and staunch friend
Affectionately
Emma Goldman
Paris. Oct 1931

EG speaking from a platform, probably Hyde Park, 1930s

BROADWOOD HOTEL AUDITORIUM
BROAD AT WOOD STREETS   PHILADELPHIA, PA.

WEDNESDAY Feb. 28
8:15 P. M.

WELCOME HOME TOUR

HEYWOOD BROUN,
Chairman

EMMA GOLDMAN

After 15 Years Enforced Exile.

who will lecture on her famous autobiography

LIVING MY LIFE

RESERVED SEATS: 50c, 75c, $1, $1.50, $2 (PLUS 10% TAX)
ON SALE
EMMA GOLDMAN COMMITTEE, 310 N. BROAD ST.

Homecoming interlude,
February–April 1934

Nice, June 27th

Dear, this is your birthday. Sorry I can't be with you. Some other time, I hope. Nothing new here. Both feeling some better. Will call you up later in the day — 12 only 7 a.m. No autobuses yet. How is everything with you, and the visit of the C. family? Got yours of the 25th will answer your points — by only I hope you have nice day there (the weather uncertain here today) — enjoy the day. affect S.

On EG's sixty-fifth birthday they wrote each other for the last time; AB's postcard arrived after his death

IISH

June 27th 36.
My Dear. Whom else should I write on this day but you. Only there is nothing to tell. I keep thinking what a long time to live. For whom? For what? But there is no answer. Useless to rake one's brain.

I have asked Michael and his family to lunch to day. One thing, I can still find relief in housework and cooking. Need I tell you that I miss having you on this day? And Emmy who would have enjoyed the chicken. But if you feel better and are gaining strength I do not mind the disapppintment.
Indeed it would have been a grand surprise. And your room so nice and clean and inviting. It looks sad to day. Imagine I had a wire yesterday, you'll never guess from whom? From Demi Coleman to my birthday. Wonderful that she should remember. She is evidently in England. Cannot make out the name of the town.
               Let me hear from you how you are Sasha
dear.   Affectionately.   EMMA
Greetings to Emmy.

5

Living the Revolution

Paris and Montparnasse. Types and doings. The Latin Quarter: artists, bohemians, and their various "movements." The expatriated of the world.

I am suddenly expelled from France [May 1930]. Mysterious enemies. An involuntary journey to Belgium and my arrest on the border. I am ordered to leave but remain "underground." Adventures with diamond speculators and contrabandists. . . .

Back in France. Soon again requested to leave [November 1930]. Expelled again and again [June 1931]. . . . Nowhere to go. . . .

Alexander Berkman, *An Enemy of Society*

IT is nice to think that one of the best books to come out of World War I
had something to do with Emma Goldman's letters. For having a friend
who had written her about soldiers at the front, and for his own mild
insubordination against the discipline of the Norton-Harjes Ambulance
Corps, E. E. Cummings was sentenced to *The Enormous Room* (1922),
which turned out to be just the right setting for the nausea he had come to
share with his friend William Slater Brown and with so many other former
enthusiasts of the Great Crusade.

As the story goes, a whole generation of the sentient young was "lost"
to Paris and the Left Bank. Certainly Americans came in considerable
numbers, as tourists or expatriates. "Never at any time have I seen so many
Americans abroad," Emma wrote her niece Stella on arriving in Paris in
1924. On one August evening, for instance, she was greeted at the Dôme
café by Arthur Bullitt and Louise Bryant—she had not seen Louise since
1920 when the latter had collapsed after Jack Reed's funeral in Moscow's
Red Square; by Charles Erskine Scott Wood, the poet and libertarian
lawyer who had come to her defense in many a battle; by Frank and Nellie
Harris, by the painter Marsden Hartley, by Mark Dix and his wife—"in
short," Emma reported, "everybody is here." Even as late as 1931 she
could still have a good time in Paris with clumps of her erstwhile compa-
triots: "The girls had a wonderful time at the party Virginia and I gave
them in the Hersh studio," she wrote Berkman:

> Cecil and I came back at 5:30 in the morning. Patsy and Florence came
> home at seven. They were with Fredrickson and another man at Mont-
> martre where they danced until that hour. Tomorrow is their last night.
> Fredrickson, Bear, and the guy who was with the girls yesterday (he is dead
> gone on Patsy) are taking us to a Negro place tomorrow night. I fear it is also
> going to be an all-night affair, after which they will be taken to the train.
> They have five days on the steamer to sleep it off. But I don't intend to keep

such hours—me for my bed at about two, which would still give me six hours' sleep.

Thus the feverish pace, jazz, red burgundy, early morning hours, black coffee, "flaming youth," and their sixty-two-year-old fellow traveler—actually, as you will have observed in Part Four, Emma and Berkman had what almost might be described as a conservative view of the rootlessness of some of their young friends and the shallowness of their affairs. As she wrote him in 1936,

> I suppose the [international edition of the New York] *Herald Tribune* carried the news of Louise Bryant's death. The last time I saw her was at the Sélect when two drunken Corsican soldiers carried her out of the café. What a horrible end. More and more I come to think it is criminal for young middle-class American or English girls to enter radical ranks. They go to pieces. And even when they do not reach the gutter, as Louise did, their lives are empty. They receive nothing from the particular ranks they enter; they certainly give nothing to them. And they become unfit for ordinary human relations. As wives or mothers, they are altogether misfits. Of course, Lincoln Steffens was right when he said about Louise [that] she was never a communist, she only slept with a communist. That is unfortunately true of the majority of girls, whether they sleep with communists or anarchists. It is very sad, I think.

Berkman liked Kay Boyle and admired her work, was friendly as well with Caresse Crosby, Laurence Vail, and other writers of the *transition* group, and could count, more or less, on their support and protests when the authorities moved to expel him from France. He translated one of Eugene O'Neill's plays for the Moscow Art Theater and both he and Emma were on friendly terms with Paul and Essie Robeson, Jimmy Light, and the remaining members of the old Provincetown gang. Evelyn Scott was very dear to Emma, as their exchanges show; Edna St. Vincent Millay, Lola Ridge, and other poets and novelists of their generation had her friendly respect. But her attitude was a good deal like that of Sinclair Lewis, who had been her friend since the old days when he used to drop by the *Mother Earth* office in New York. In his Nobel acceptance speech of 1930 Lewis saluted the younger writers and congratulated them for their rebellion against gentility and commercialism, but made clear he was of an older generation and of a different tradition. So too were Emma and Berkman sympathetic and friendly but separated from the expatriates by their years and interests. With a few exceptions such as Kay Boyle, as Malcolm Cowley reminds us, most members of the Lost Generation "found" themselves through repatriation shortly after the Crash. But the two older rebels were not undone by the failure of the religion of art, since they had never been believers; they were not playing at exile and free to return when the postman stopped delivering checks from home; and they were not international revelers—there was no way for them to catch a steamer and "sleep it off" on the five-day passage.

Not the crazy rush from café to café but other grimmer images were true to their lives as real exiles: that of Emma walking up the steps of the British Museum to plunge into that "bottomless tank," as she called it, for her work on the Russian dramatists and the slim possibility of some small income therefrom; that of her rushing around Berlin in March 1932 trying to run down the address of "a new literary star on the German firmament who goes by the name of [B.] Traven" and who just might, if he could be located, give Berkman permission to translate his novels; that of her disappointment over the financial failure of *Living My Life* and, ironically, the measure of encouragement she received from being expelled from Holland in 1933—no harm done, wrote Berkman, "evidently you are still dangerous"; and that of her staggering persistence in lecturing to handfuls of people to open up a "field" for herself in England, in Canada, on the Continent. Both lived on the edge of want during these years and, at the depth of the general crisis, tried everything from putting up tents at St. Tropez for nonexistent tourists to buying sweepstake tickets with the wrong numbers.

Though Emma shared what she had, Berkman sometimes lived over the edge of want: "We have been sitting here for almost two weeks without a cent," he wrote his absent comrade in 1934. "Some days we did not have even enough to buy food. Nor even for carfare." But a friend he cabled responded with the rent money, some other money came in for his editorial work, and Emma's check for sixty dollars arrived in the mail:

> Anyhow, I am rich now. You would have laughed to see us here, outside raining, chilly and no heat any more in the house, and literally no carfare to go to the city. And Emmy coming up with a large black bread and some butter and cheese, taken in the grocery store here on credit, and she singing all the way! It is good she inherited her mother's irrepressible Austrian cheerfulness, for I admit I have not been very cheerful of late. . . .

And of course all of this made a mockery of the communist charge that the two were living high on the Riviera off the proceeds of their betrayal of the Revolution.

Along with their poverty came the challenge of growing into old age with declining vital powers. (Both in fact faced the consequences of age, though Emma seemed not to and, as if she were a Kazantzakis hero, complained bitterly of "the fire that is consuming me at my age.") Finally there were Berkman's continual difficulties with the authorities over his lack of "papers" and the expulsion orders fully discussed in the letters below. As Emma wrote Ellen Kennan in 1932, every three months the renewal ordeal came around again and "it has been sheer agony each time, the dreadful uncertainty, the wait, the wear and tear of his not being able to budge from Nice, which is his domicile. In addition, Sasha had trouble with his health this winter." All this was enough and more than enough to lead one into immediate agreement with Berkman's tight-lipped observation: "These are not cheerful times."

Yet their letters are anything but depressing. They reveal the two, estranged from hearth and kin, helping each other survive spells of dejection and always holding on to their refusal to be reconciled to the wretchedness and injustice in the world. And that at a time of rising dictatorships, general reaction, economic breakdown. As Emma put it in a letter which appears in this part, "you are right, dear heart, the masses are anything but hopeful. And yet we must go on in our work. We are voices in the wilderness, much more so now than forty years ago. I mean voices for liberty. No one wants it any more. Yet it seems to me that just because of the present mad clamor for dictatorship, we of all people should not give up." Of all people they did not: When Berkman could no longer cling to their vision and serve it actively, he "cleared out" as he had promised he would. Emma was left behind to live out four more years of it and thereby bring the revolution that much closer.

How they brought off such a profoundly cheering moral triumph no doubt had much to do with their belief in freedom. It is certain that both thoroughly grasped the nature and dimensions of the challenge they faced. Berkman, for instance, more than qualified as an expert witness for his observation to the imprisoned Mooney: "It is far easier to die for one's faith than to suffer for it day in and day out, for long, endless years." Still, how one comes by such rare strength is mysterious, as Emma's nephew Saxe Commins observed in wonder:

> Your faith was strong enough to survive doubt and disaster, events and lapses. How do you do it is what I'd like to know. I am not satisfied with the easy answer that a fervent ideal is all that's necessary. Nor am I silly enough to expect any kind of an answer to the unanswerable. (May 29, 1934)

Unanswerable maybe, but there are clues below.

EG TO AB, May 2, 1927, TORONTO

My own Sash,

I left my writing glasses at the home of one of our comrades last night, so I must write you by hand. Besides, it is more intimate for a birthday letter. Isn't it?

Dearest chum, what am I to tell you on this your 21st anniversary since you came to life again? It is unnecessary to tell you how rotten I feel that I will not be with you this year. My one consolation is that you will have a few very devoted friends with you on the 18th. That you have Emmy—that this year at any rate you will not be so lonely as I am here.

What the 18th of May has meant to me all these years you know only too well. You know also that whatever may have come between us, or whosoever, you have been, you are, and you always will be part of myself, part of all I have hoped for, believed in, strived to achieve, my own beloved Dush, friend and co-fighter. You may not have been aware of it, Sash dearest, but you have been the greatest force in my life—your welfare, your aims and your dreams, as far as you let me share them with you—my deepest concern.

All sorts of people have been in my life, but your coming into it August 15th, 1889, at Sachs's restaurant, has marked the beginning of a friendship—the stirrings of an affection which has only deepened and strengthened with the years. It is as abiding today—in fact more so—as it was years ago and until the end of my life you will remain the great and inspiring force, urging the best in me toward the light. But you know all this yourself, why tell you it again?

Dearest boy, this is the first time in many years that I am too poor to send you a birthday gift. It hurts like hell, but it cannot be helped. You will get my loving and cheering greetings through Emmy, but I had hoped to send you something that you could spend for yourself. Well, the will is strong but my capital is weak. I know you will not mind. . . .

About myself there is not much to say. Moe [Morris Goldman] goes back to New York today and I shall feel more destitute than ever. I am not looking forward to a joyous summer. I have met a few pleasant people, but they are not the kind one can feel intimate with outside of the work I am doing. Our own comrades are friendly enough but so very narrow in their outlook on life. I do not know of a thing I have in common with them except propaganda. I am sure that they see no other phase in my character except what I can give to what they consider "the movement." The one person I have grown to care about a great deal and who might have helped to give cheer and color to my life here this summer is very ill at present and not within reach. It is our old friend Leon Malmed. He has had a complete breakdown from his ridiculous business transactions. Just how serious his condition is I will only know when Moe gets to Albany and sees Leon's physician. He stops off on his way to New York. So you see, dear heart, that I have no luck with my love affairs—such is one of the ironies in my life. . . .

Dearest, have a good time on the 18th and drink a silent glass to our friendship, which is unlike anything in the world, in this material world. The poets used to sing about such abiding love and devotion as ours. Is it that such friendships no longer exist? Is that why no one writes about them?

I embrace you tenderly. I will be with you on the 18th—in thought anyway. Much much love, your old sailor,

E

EG TO BEN CAPES, July 8, 1927, TORONTO

Ben, my dear,

Your letter of June 26th and the one of the 4th with Nettlau's letter enclosed, reached me safely. I can well imagine how outraged you felt over the savage treatment of that poor Negro boy who is working for you [in St. Louis]. Even reading your account made my blood boil. It brought to my mind how much more terrible is the position of the Negro in America than that of the Jews anywhere in the world. Of course there are pogroms and persecution of Jews going on all the time, still it is not so constant and so brutal as that of the Negro. And the whole world is outraged when something particularly wanton takes place. Witness the amount of publicity given the hazing of the Jewish interns in the hospital in New York. But the cruelty to the Negro goes on and on and no one gets particularly excited even. It is fierce. . . .

[EG]

EG TO AB, August 19, 1927, TORONTO

Dearest,

I have neglected you for some time, haven't I? You will have to blame it on my moving and even more than that the terrible restlessness which has gotten in my system since all hopes for Sacco and Vanzetti became meaningless. I cannot tell you how utterly wretched I have been these weeks. Our whole life and all we did stood out with such force it just robbed me of all peace of mind. The horrible feeling of futility, if now after forty years of so-called advancement [since the execution of the Haymarket martyrs] Sacco and Vanzetti will be sent to their death by such rank prejudice as was displayed all along by [Judge Webster] Thayer. Just this minute I was called up by one of our comrades who told me the noon papers have it that the Massachusetts Supreme Court again denied the motion for a new trial. It seems inhuman to go on torturing the two victims, instead of letting them die in peace.

Last night we had our meeting; it kept me busy for a week organizing it, since our own comrades are a hopeless lot, at least now. . . . However, we had a packed hall. I had to give a complete history of the case because most people here really knew nothing about the matter except the snatches given to them in the papers. So I even had to go into the various testimony, reading the largest part to make it accurate. Still it went off all right. The appeal for the defense brought $51; it should and would have been double, if the audience had not started out the moment I finished speaking. As usual, the collectors went about their business badly. The enclosed wire was sent to [Governor Alan T.] Fuller, [President Calvin] Coolidge, and Sacco and Vanzetti, merely as a protest from the audience. You will see by the mild tone that I did not draw up the wire.* Well, the meeting was merely a plaster for one's own aching heart; it can have no bearing on the fate of Sacco and Vanzetti. Nor does it satisfy me. I feel I have been terribly amiss because I have done nothing before for the two boys. If there is any excuse at all, it is the bitter struggle I have to make almost single-handed in this cold and alien country. Somehow it was easier when I could make the struggle with you, but now, alone, it is hard, Dush. . . .

About my lectures, I am very worried; your suggestions are good, dearest, but the working out of these suggestions is the difficult thing. Frankly I have not the remotest idea how to go about it. I suppose it is because I do not feel the subjects, hence cannot work them out. I have again been convinced by my last night's talk that only when I am intensely aroused can I speak well, or prepare my talk interestingly. Just mere theories do not move me. Take the idea of Russia, I could not just merely talk along the lines you suggest in yours of the 27th, since I am not able to give even a remote idea what is likely to happen there. Also it is rather hard to talk about Russia now with the whole White pack at its throat. I have decided to avoid the subject for the present. You understand, I do not want to hide anything about Russia, but neither do I want to add fuel to the present situation. I am enclosing a tentative list of subjects which I have submitted to the committee. I mean to substitute some of those mentioned. I think several of the topics are most timely. There is again the war spirit in the air and the question of crime has again become a vital issue in connection with the Sacco-Vanzetti case and the terrible fact that people here are constantly being sent to the lash—can you imagine such a dreadful thing at this late day? Anyway, I will be able to pull through some of the themes but it means a terrible lot of grind which is doubly hard because I have absolutely no intellectual companionship here and must sort of dig everything out of my own brain. . . .

Dear, this is a gloomy letter, perhaps I should not have written today, I feel dreadfully depressed with the latest development in the Sacco-Vanzetti case. But if I do not write today, I will again have no time. I know you will forgive the gloom. I think of you constantly, my dearest, own Sash. And I miss you more than I can tell you. I embrace you, dearest,

E

P.S. Dearest, I read your Sacco-Vanzetti article in the *Syndicalist*. You are wrong when you say there are no such voices as [Émile] Zola's in America for Sacco-Vanzetti. You are right only in the sense that no one in America who has voiced their cause is as well known in the world as Zola. But as far as the support of the case is concerned, it has been the most amazing thing

* The "enclosed wire" has apparently not survived.

to me, not one but hundreds of the leading men and women in America, in the universities, churches, lawyers, writers, in fact everybody, have for years now made their voices heard and have written on the case. In fact the protest in America is tremendous. Alas, not from labor. The same old story, the workers lag behind. Only recently a campaign has been started which is backed by every leading writer in the States. Then [Oswald Garrison] Villard has been working on the case for several years. Now he's gotten [David] Starr Jordan, Prof. [Alexander] Meiklejohn, and ever so many others to help; as to [Felix] Frankfurter, he and a group of professors have been at work for a long time. It is Frankfurter's series of articles reviewing the case and published in the *Atlantic Monthly* which aroused a great many people. Altogether the response has been more widespread and more numerous than the [Alfred] Dreyfus case created. There is no doubt about that. Of course, if American labor had come to the rescue, it would have been different, but labor is the most reactionary element in America. And the rulers in the States are more powerful and care least for critical opinion. The same protest in Europe would have put the fear of god in judges and jurors. In America they don't give a damn and Sacco and Vanzetti will probably have to die. That is the superiority of democracy, if you please.

AB TO TOM MOONEY, *September 5, 1927, ST. CLOUD*

My dear friend Tom,

I hope you will forgive my delay in acknowledging the receipt of your letters of 8/5 and 8/13, with the enclosed documents. You understand, of course, that these last weeks have been very strenuous: much of my time has been taken by the Sacco-Vanzetti work.

Need I comment upon the terrible tragedy? I am sure you know how we all feel here about it. The conscience of the entire civilized world has been outraged—the voice of humanity has found no sympathetic echo in the hearts bent upon class verdicts.

I feel sad and not in a mood for correspondence. I shall today merely reply to some of the contents of your last letters.

I am very glad to have the documents of your case—I shall make the best use of them that I can. In fact, some use has already been made of them. Your case was dwelt upon here in connection with the one mentioned above, both at very large gatherings and in the press. I shall not neglect any opportunity to get people more acquainted with the circumstances of your case. Rely on that. . . .

You may be sure that I shall spare neither time nor effort in doing what is in my power to aid your liberation. It is high time that you, as well as

[Warren] Billings, were out. More than high time. You should have never been in, were there any justice in the world. . . .

Yes, I shall certainly not forget you, nor Billings, nor Matt [Schmidt] and the others. And wherever I can, my help can be counted on in the right cause. Best greetings, as ever,

[AB]

EG TO EVELYN SCOTT, October 17, 1927, TORONTO

Dearest Evelyn,

. . . Dearest girl, your letters are always a great comfort to me. Your beautiful spirit and your great gift for painting in words are a great delight. But there are some things contained in your last letter that I cannot agree with. For instance your suggestion that nothing is lost in the world. From an evolutionary point of view you are no doubt right, but realizing that each of us contributes a millionth fraction to the sum total of social changes can be no comfort to those who give out of themselves passionately and to the very limit of their being. One wants to see some result. I don't mean in a material sense, of course. I mean that giving in social ideas is like planting seeds. One wants to see the fruit of one's efforts. One wants to behold if only a little flower from all the labor one has had in digging in the soil. Don't think that I am pessimistic. I am merely facing facts, and what I see convinces me that individual effort is really of very little consequence to the evolutionary forces in the world.

Then there is your suggestion that the people who went to Boston to protest did so much more because of their inner need to express themselves than because they thought they would help Sacco and Vanzetti. I agree with you there, my dear. But at least they were able to protest. They were able to express their intense wrath against the crime of Massachusetts. Besides, I do not believe that their efforts did not help Sacco and Vanzetti. I am sure that what was done for them gave them courage to hold on to the very last, and to die as bravely as they did. I think there is more truth than fiction in the saying that "man is not made to be alone." Loneliness whether in life or in the face of death seems to me to be the most difficult thing to endure. Indeed I think it requires much more courage and deeper faith to live and die alone than it does when you have the support of kindred spirits. Without thinking for one minute that Sacco and Vanzetti would have lacked the courage to die had no one supported them, I do wish to say that their death was no doubt made easier because they knew they had support. No doubt they exaggerated in their own fancy the strength or the scope of the support they had, or the effect their death would have upon the spirit of their ideals. Nevertheless, they were encouraged by the campaign made for them. So, in the last analysis the people who did protest were really a great help to Sacco and Vanzetti.

My tragedy in their case was that I not only could not satisfy my own need of crying out against the wanton murder, but that I was unable to be of any spiritual help to them; to make them feel that I am one of the numbers who came to their assistance. You certainly are right that the killing of Sacco and Vanzetti was only a drop in the oceans of crime "committed by law against individuals every day"; and you are doubly right when you say that one cannot have much faith in people for whom crime must be dramatized—people who remain indifferent to the vile sins committed against human beings and only cry out against one outstanding sin. They certainly are not to be depended upon. It is nevertheless true that all of us are much more intensely and vividly against a "concentrated sin" or social offense, I would rather call it. Such an offense has a more immediate effect on our sensibilities. It is on a par with some great misfortune which we see as against the one we read about, perhaps because it reaches our sensibilities in a more direct form. I do not know. But I do know that such a specially cruel and heinous crime as the killing of Sacco and Vanzetti must grip one with greater force than the million little offenses we know about. I know it has gripped me in that way. . . .

While I have not written you for a long time, you have never been out of my mind. Often in the early morning hours after crawling into bed you stood vividly before me and I wondered how you were; how you are getting along with your work; how your handsome son is; and many other things. Please write, my dear. It is always a great treat to hear from you.

Lovingly,
[EG]

AB TO EG, April 11, 1929, ST. CLOUD

Dear,

I wish you would write as easily and fluently your book as you write letters. And maybe you can get yourself into that condition. Try it.

Your letter to *Freie Arbeiter Stimme* re [S.] Yanofsky is extremely good. You have covered the points well. I have added some lines and mailed the first copy.

Am enclosing the other copies here. Not very clear they are, because my machine is too light for copies. I have kept one copy here, but it lacks the FIRST page. You could have the first page typed and keep it, so that you can make use of the other copies I am sending you here. Though I don't know what you could use the other copies for. It is no good for other papers.

I forgot to mention in my article that Siegman, now President of the

Amalgamated Clothing Workers, used to be a member of the Anarchist Federation. In fact, he was assistant secretary, while I was secretary, during the [Selig] Silverstein bomb period [1908]. I don't know whether you have yet received the *FAS* containing Yanofsky's reference to that bomb.

Well, maybe it is good for you to do physical work in the garden; it may help you with the intellectual work. I love to work in the soil, not too hard of course, but this year I am planting little here, almost nothing, because seeds and plants cost money and I don't want to invest anything, as I am sure to give up the place in October.

CHECK received. Thanks. Will do for the present.

About making a kind of will, to which you refer in your last—well, of course, you are in a position where it may be necessary. On the other hand, I could not make one, because all I own is my writing desk, a stove, and a few books. Not worth mentioning. But you ought to see about your mss. and the place there. Of course, I am sure you will survive us all, knock wood, but it is well to take no chances.

Your suggestions about appointing Rocker and Stella etc. are OK. My only objection is your proposing to make Henry [Alsberg], myself, and Demie [Coleman] the "executors" of your mss. Demie does not belong there. She is a fine girl and all that, but you know that neither Henry nor I will agree with her on the question of the book and its contents. To appoint her together with us means only to create trouble. Better make it Rocker in place of Demie.

But anyhow, I hope and think that paper will not have to be used. Certainly I don't mean to survive you. Between ourselves, I have had enough of life. I am not active in the movement and I don't see any special purpose in continuing. Especially when one has no income and no means of getting one. I feel rather tired, and certainly not disposed to continue simply in order to write articles that may possibly bring in a few dollars now and then. Nor have I any ambition to write an autobiography or any other book. This is all confidential, of course, and it is not a question of today or tomorrow. In the first place I want to live long enough to help you revise your book, for I am vain enough to think that no one can do it as well as I, even if you have your doots about it, and perhaps justly so. So that sufficient unto the day.

Well, I have terribly delayed the *Bulletin*. Must get at it in order to finish it. So enough for today.

Affectionately,

S

EG TO ARTHUR LEONARD ROSS, April 29, 1930, PARIS

Dear Arthur,

On Saturday I sent you the fifth and last installment, minus two chapters, of my ms., and I also wrote you at length. No doubt both will reach you before this letter. Today I am writing because I have finally ascertained that it will be all right to use my expulsion experience for publicity. That you may have the exact facts of the case, I summarize them here:

March 1. I was visited by a detective and taken to the headquarters of the police department. There I was confronted with an order of expulsion dated March 26, 1901, and signed by the Minister of Interior Waldeck Rousseau, who has been dead for nearly twenty years. The order had been issued after I had returned to the U.S. I left France in November 1900.

Secondly, under the pretext of taking me to see a high official I was taken to a secluded room, photographed, fingerprinted, weighed, and measured. It would have done no good to protest, because even if I had cried [out], no one would have heard me. When I came back, I was told I would have to leave the same evening. I assured the police that I would not go, and then they gave me ten days' time.

I turned the matter over to Henri Torrés, the famous attorney, and he succeeded in having the order revoked. The new order issued to me, which acts as a stay but does not specify whether it is permanent, is signed by Tardieu, present Minister of the Interior and Prime Minister.

In using the material for publicity it might not be a bad idea to point out that France, even if it makes a stupid blunder, does rectify it, which is more than can be said for the U.S. . . .

Affectionately,
[EG]

AB TO MICHAEL COHN, June 6, 1930, PARIS

My dear Mac,

Well, I am back in Paris! After more than a month's effort upon the part of EG and of all our numerous connections in France, we succeeded in getting permission for me to stay—but just three months in France. We hope that upon the expiration of that time a prolongation can be secured.

Now I have my hands full: 1) must secure my carte d'identité, just as if it is the first time I am coming to France—even more difficult, because my dossier shows that I had been expelled; 2) must have a new passport—also not an easy thing for one in my position; 3) most important of all, must get the order for my deportation or expulsion ANNULLED.

The last is the most difficult thing to accomplish in France. Generally an expulsion order remains in force thirty years. In EG's recent case, the order proved to be twenty-nine years old and issued by an administration long since politically and even physically dead. Even at that it took a lot of time, money, and effort to annul it. Now, in my case it is much worse, because it was issued by the PRESENT administration and of course it does not care to reverse itself. It may take a very long time to annul it, if at all. Maybe a year or more. Meanwhile I live in constant anxiety lest a new bolshevik denunciation should result in a second expulsion. And THAT would mean forever, because two expulsions from France mean that.

Well, all this involves constant work in that direction.

My stay in Belgium and particularly my return were a veritable odyssey, full of exciting moments. After the Ministry here gave permission for me to remain three months in France, I needed a French visa to return here. But the consul (French) in Brussels refused to give me a visa. At first the authorization from France failed to arrive and then the consul told me that even when it does arrive, he will not give it to me.

There was a situation for you! Permission to BE in France, but no chance to get there! On the French border they would not let me pass without a visa and I could not get that visa. What to do? Well, I got acquainted with some diamond people in Antwerp, got friendly etc., and finally managed to get over the border with their help. One Holland Jew [M. Polak], a rich man, proved himself a corker. Took me on his own responsibility etc. And I a perfect stranger to him! It has increased my faith in humanity, I can tell you.

Well, as I am writing this, my dear Mac, I keep wondering and in frankness I must tell you: I am wondering whether I am not boring you with all these matters, vital as they are to ME. Why do I have such thoughts? Because not a line had reached me from you since I informed you that I had been expelled and that I found myself in an illegal condition in Belgium, without money, friends or any passport and visa there. I wrote to you from Antwerp on May 2, the day I arrived there. And till yesterday there was not a single word from you about the matter. I must say it did not impress me as if the thing worried you much. Moreover, you knew in what danger I was all the time in Belgium, because I was forced to get there without a visa, which is punishable by imprisonment and return to Russia, in my case. You know—because I had written you—that I was taken out of bed at 6 A.M., on May 1 and without any warning or time to prepare I was rushed out of the country on the SAME day. You knew that I was without money and that I had no friends in Belgium, except one address of a man I had met just for a few minutes in Paris once. In short, I was really in a very terrible condition, and—when I say TERRIBLE, then it is even worse than it sounds, because I have been in tight places before and I am not given to complaining or exaggerating a dangerous situation.

Well, in spite of all that, not a line from you and not a cent. You have been my friend and comrade for years, dear Michael, and you have always been generous with your aid to me—and THEREFORE I cannot understand the reason for such apparent indifference on your part. I am speaking frankly, and I hope you will pardon me. You have often told me to call on you when in need, and this time I did and there was no answer. I admit I am fearfully disappointed, even shocked.

Of course there may have been good reasons for your silence, and therefore I am going to reserve a final opinion on the matter till I hear from you again.

Now the situation is this: it seems that Moscow is back of the whole trouble. I am accused of "political" work because I am the treasurer of the Relief Fund for Russia! I am going to see a certain person—the one who unmasked Azev—I don't want to mention his name*—he is here in Paris and I will ask him to unearth the real forces back of my expulsion. For certainly France has NO cause whatever to expel me, since I have never participated in any political activities in this country.

Yesterday EG received the letter you wrote to me and the check for $100 that you sent. I want to thank you for it. The letter was written by you on May 28 and check bears the date of May 29!

I don't know a thing about the [Joseph] Cohen-[Rudolf] Rocker controversy. I could not get the *Freie Arbeiter Stimme* in Belgium, nor did I care to receive there any radical literature. All my mail has accumulated here in Paris, and as soon as I get a bit of time I shall read it all. Meanwhile I am busy running after the bureaucrats for a carte d'identité (my old one is confiscated) and for—a passport. I simply MUST secure a passport, for in case I am expelled again I must at least have something on which I can go to some other country. At present I have nothing, all my papers either confiscated or no good.

Too bad you did not send me a letter to your freind in Antwerp. Even if he was absent, the letter might have helped me to get at some other diamond people. They have a lot of influence there.

Well, enough now. I have an "engagement" with the Préfecture. I wish you and all yours well,

[AB]

---

* In 1908 the well-known Social Revolutionist Burtsev brought charges of treachery against Azev, the leader of his party's battle organization. A Jury of Honor, on which Peter Kropotkin and two other distinguished revolutionaries served, considered the evidence in Paris that October and ultimately established that Azev was a double agent who had successfully plotted the assassination of a number of high Russian officials while simultaneously acting as an informer for the Czar's secret police. Berkman was thus going to see Burtsev, in all probability, for it was he who had "unmasked" the spy. He could assume that Cohn, a long-time anarchist, would know immediately whom he meant.

EG TO AB, August 23, 1931, ST. TROPEZ

Dear Sash,

Talk about a mystery case. Yours is certainly the most complicated of any I ever read. Every day it develops new sides and only the stars know when this is going to end. More and more I am convinced that someone is back of all your trouble. No, not the commissars here. Ridiculous. All the reports of the two skunks here could not drag out your case and give new excuses why you are not to be left in peace. It must be somebody who, now realizing that your case has aroused interest, is busy inventing new stories to get you discredited. Else where would the chef [-de-cabinet] have gotten the idea of Canada and the U.S. government [and the absurd report that you killed a man on the Canadian border]? I quite agree with your letter to Vera that rotten as the U.S. government is, it has no reason to get you removed from France at this late day. I could understand, if you had been busy all the time in exposing conditions in the States. But why should it now want to induce the French authorities to put you out? The whole thing is pure invention like all the rest so far brought against you.

What puzzles me is that [Roger] Vitrac should have found it necessary to call on the chef-de-cabinet. I was under the impression that he was going to find someone who knows [Pierre] Laval. After all, it is Laval and no one else who can stop the whole outrageous persecution. Why did Vitrac change his intention? Well, it is awful that we are both aliens here and must depend on all sorts of ineffectual people, instead of raising a campaign ourselves. I can't tell you how this eats into my heart and gives me no peace here. But whom to see or what to do? I can't think. . . . I have already written you once that I would go to Paris at once if you think I might achieve something. There is no other matter so important to me than that your case should be settled once and for all. . . .

Affectionately,
E

AB TO EG, August 26, 1931, NICE

Dear Em,

Yours of the 23rd just arrived. The 23rd was Sunday, and you say that the Lavers [Tommy and Nell] will come here a week from Thursday. Do you mean then they will come to Nice *Thursday, September 3rd?*

If I have figured it out wrong, please let me know at once.

Now, as to my case. Yes, you are right, it is rather mysterious and "the plot thickens," as the old novelists used to say.

It looks strange that the trouble should come from the U.S. And yet,

Abramov also mentioned that the only thing the Sûreté has against me is the record from America. So it looks as if [Roger] Vitrac and [Pierre] Rénaudel have been told *the same thing*, but from different sources.

I don't think that the U.S. would be interested enough to push the case against me here. But naturally the French have asked the U.S. for my record. There is an international police bureau and they exchange information on all such matters. So, France of course has my complete American record.

But *that* does not explain why they started four years after they knew all about me, four years after I have been living in France.

Now, about this Canada matter. That seems the most serious part of the situation. That Vitrac was told so, I have no doubt. Of course, the chef (whoever he is) may have gotten Canada mixed with California. But here is a strange thing. Kay Boyle told me two weeks ago, or more, that Waldman (who was married to Peggy's sister) saw some very prominent French writer and tried to get him to sign the paper for Laval. I forget the name of the writer, but he is very prominent. He said he would, *but* he could not because he had heard that Tostogub [i.e., AB] had killed a man in Canada. Kay Boyle was here yesterday and she repeated this to me again.

Now, this seems very strange. I don't know where that writer had heard about it. But now that the chef told Vitrac about it shows that there must be some such item in my dossier. It could not well be that it is merely a confusion of Canada with California.

I have a very faint recollection that a similar insinuation once appeared in an American or Canadian paper. I have read it somewhere, years ago. It is just possible that that newspaper story got into American police records and in that way it was transmitted into my French dossier. That's merely a guess, of course. Yet the fact remains that such a story IS in circulation somewhere.

How closely the police follow all newspaper stories of this character I experienced in Paris the last time I was there. The item in *Les Temps* about my alleged anti-military activities appeared in a very obscure place, just three lines in small type.* When I was told about it I could not at first find it. It was hardly to be noticed.

Yet, the paper was out about six in the morning. At eight the Sûreté Générale phoned to Rénaudel about it. He went over there and the chef of

---

* On July 6, 1931, the Chicago *Tribune*, Paris edition, reported that "the Communist writer Alexander Berkman" was ordered out of France because of his "anti-militarist propaganda in Toulon." Berkman labeled the item "an ABSOLUTE LIE. I have never been in Toulon except once, two and a half years ago, in the company of my St. Tropez neighbor, a French landowner." Despite the fact the *Tribune* issued an apologetic retraction, the French daily papers of July 7 picked up the item and gave it their own twist—in *Les Temps* Berkman became a "Bolshevik agent" who had been active "among the sailors on the Riviera." The Ministry of the Interior responded immediately to this unfounded and perhaps planted "news."

the Sûreté took the item so seriously that he told Rénaudel that no continuation would be given me and that I had to leave the country.

It was then that I wrote you that things looked rather bad. When Rénaudel saw me after his visit to the chef, he was very discouraged and he said that there is no hope at all. The only thing was to catch Laval somehow and get a special order from him. Well, he succeeded in doing that, because Laval had to be that day in the chambre and there Rénaudel caught him and got a note from him ordering three more months for me.

Now, I explain this to you just to show you how closely the police watch the papers. And I am sure the police in other countries do the same and when they see some item about such matters in the papers they simply cut it out and add it to the record of the man in question. It is possible that in *this* manner the newspaper story about Canada got in the police records in Canada and in the U.S., and then it was transmitted with my other records to France, and no doubt also to other countries.

Well, all this may be speculation, but I am sure that that is the way these records are "filled in," and in this manner the police can show that they "know everything."

But however it may be—the fact is, that there *is* such a story being told, and no doubt it comes from the Sûreté in Paris. . . .

No, dear, it is not necessary for you to go to Paris on my case. Of course I know you'd do anything possible, and I appreciate it. But I prefer nothing should be done by you or me just now. We must see how that thing of Vitrac will develop. He is trying to reach a man who can see Laval personally. Anyhow, when the time comes and it is necessary to go to Paris, I will have to do it myself. I know many people there and especially will it be necessary that I see Rénaudel personally, later on.

Well, enough of this. For the present there is no use worrying. . . .

Affectionately,

S

AB TO ROGER BALDWIN AND ROBERT REINHART OF THE INTERNATIONAL COMMITTEE FOR POLITICAL PRISONERS, October 1, 1931, NICE

Dear friends:

Pardon my writing to you a joint letter—I am fearfully crowded with work, and that will save time.

The enclosed letter will inform you as to the present status of my case. So far, so good.

Now a word about the "powers" behind my case. We have the information from officials very high in authority in the Ministry of the Interior that it is the U.S. that is pushing the case against me. Details are of course almost impossible to obtain. One chef claims that Paris received the information from the U.S. that I had "killed a man on the Canadian frontier." Another said that "it is the Frick case." Just imagine!!! They are giving varying explanations (to persons intimate with them), but all to the effect that it is *to please the U.S.* that I am expelled from time to time.

The ten-weeks' delay in forwarding my documents from Paris to Nice has been explained by a high Paris chef as due to the following reason: Paris wanted the U.S. to know that I was expelled and therefore no *official* record was made of the three months' stay given me in July. Nice was notified about it by Paris *by wire* and told to let me stay for the present without documents. But Nice was to have *no official record* of it for some time.

It is hardly probable that any private American busybody or some individual Secret Service man (as suggested by Roger) should have so much influence with the French Government. At any rate, it would be interesting to investigate this matter at your end.*

Now, another thing. I should very much like to have your opinion on the following suggestion: Would it be advisable for your organization to have a committee call personally on Laval during his presence in Washington, to appeal to him in my case? Of course, such a committee must necessarily consist of some very prominent men, as for instance Professor [John]Dewey etc.

* Chances are that Berkman and Emma were too hasty in rejecting the possibility that someone in the U.S. was behind the mystery. First an order expelling Emma, dating back to 1901, was pulled out of the files and resuscitated. Then Berkman was repeatedly subject to deportation orders lodged, according to good information, "to please the U.S." Now if someone in America was indeed responsible for this continuing harassment, no one was more likely than their old enemy J. Edgar Hoover, who had since taken over the Federal Bureau of Investigation and who thus had immediate access to the international police bureau Berkman mentioned. Hoover's proprietary interest in Emma surfaced in 1934, when he assigned agents to keep her under surveillance during her three-month tour and used their reports as the basis for a memorandum to his superiors indicating his worry that "her activities in this country at the present time are in violation of the agreement upon which she was permitted to enter." A still better bench mark of his stake in the two rebels came out during his appearance in 1936 before Senator Kenneth D. McKellar's Subcommittee on Appropriations. Pressed by unfriendly questioning to relate what he *personally* had done to apprehend criminals and subversives, Hoover came up with only three cases:

> McKellar: Did you ever make an arrest?
> Hoover: No, sir; I have made investigations.
> McKellar: How many arrests have you made and who were they?
> Hoover: I handled the investigation of Emma Goldman and prosecuted that case
> before the immigration authorities up to the secretary of labor. I also handled
> the Alexander Berkman case and the case of Ludwig Martens, the former
> bolshevik ambassador to the United States.

Even if Emma and Berkman had pretty well forgotten the colorless functionary who had helped hustle them out of the country, Hoover had by no means forgotten them as his two first and most important "cases." And a concerned word from him to his French counterparts, by way of commendable follow-up, was quite sufficient to thicken their plot.

On the other hand, the Washington officials, learning the purpose of such a committee, might still further prejudice Laval against me. I leave it to your judgment, my friends.

Mr. Reinhart has asked Harry Weinberger about the signatories of the Laval protest in Europe. I have not the complete list, the latter being in the hands of the French committee. In Denmark Karin Michaelis has written a strong appeal to Laval and she is now collecting signatures in various countries for it. She expects to secure the signatures of: Selma Lagerlöf, Knut Hamsun, Romain Rolland, Jean Richard Bloch, etc. Also: Heinrich Mann, Thomas Mann, Ricarda Huch, Lionel Feuchtwanger, Käthe Kollwitz, René Schickele, Annette Kolb, etc. Also [Albert] Einstein.

In France some of the signatures already secured are: [Georges] Duhamel, Charles Vildrac (writer and dramatist), Roger Vitrac (writer), L. Durtain, Bernard Grasset (one of France's best publishers), Georgette Leblanc (former wife of [Maurice] Maeterlinck)—incidentally also Cecil B. de Mille, Anita Loos, John Emerson, who were seen in Paris.

Since the protest to Laval is not to be presented until after his return from the U.S., we have more time to work on it and to gather signatures. I shall, of course, keep you informed of whatever new developments there might be in my case in the meantime.

Thanking you both, as well as the members of your organization, for all your efforts in my behalf, I remain,

Fraternally,

[AB]

AB TO EG, Wednesday, 10 A.M. [ca. October 1931], NICE

Dear,

Enclosed gives the situation. I have worked my head off and am tired to death and still rushed.

Just wired you to meet me as arranged before. I am leaving tomorrow evening, Thursday. Will be there [St. Raphael?] about 1:15 or 1:25 P.M. We could lunch there together. Come alone and go by autobus, if possible.

About other matters personally. Will also write this evening, if I get time, and you may get the letter after you have seen me.

Do not say anything to any newspaper man there may be around there about my coming.

Now, you are a dear and devoted soul, but somehow you cannot get to understand me in spite of forty years. You should know by this time that I have a head on my shoulders; that I make no statements unless I know what I am talking about; that when I HINT a thing, it means that I am almost sure of it; that I am so careful that I habitually say "MAYBE" when others under the same circumstances would say "SURE."

This refers to EVERYTHING. And therefore it is rather strange to have you point out my "inconsistencies" or tell me that YOU know a certain thing is perfectly all right after I had hinted that it is NOT.

My "inconsistency": I told you not to refer to certain things in Paris and you reply that in the same letter I spoke of such things in reference to the fifty francs I gave that fellow in your place. It is too bad that I have to explain all this to you, and I am awfully busy. But you often take the same tone, so I must make it clear, and I hope it will be of some future use.

Your suggestions for Paris in the above matter were some things I would know myself, and were moreover not to be written. If I did the same in re your place, it was because I WANTED the thing to be read, if my letter miscarried. That's the difference. I told about it to various persons here who should know it.

More about this in person.* For the present: your neighbor is very naive and his faith in the man is entirely misplaced. Say nothing to him till I see you. The whole trouble comes from the fellow who took the place of the cur who made the trouble for you, originally. And remember again that when I say something, it means something. This is no "maybe" any more. I have it directly from the very highest authority, and from different branches of it. It is absolute and final.

It was therefore that I hinted to you that you better meet me. You replied in a piqued tone that you did not see why so and so and so and so and that it was all right for me to come as usual etc.

Well, I would ignore this attitude of yours. But I ignored it before too many times; ignoring it longer causes only misunderstanding on your part.

It was the same attitude on your part—though in an entirely different matter, yet in the same SPIRIT—that caused you to be piqued and even write me one of your famous letters in connection with my surprising you on the 27th. An entirely different matter, as I say, but the same SPIRIT, and a wrong one, my dear. I ignored the matter then, but I see it is a mistake to ignore such things.

Well, take this in the right spirit, dear, and don't always misunder-

---

* Berkman's obvious anger over what he regarded as Emma's lack of discretion was complemented by an equally obvious fearfulness that this letter would fall into the wrong hands. Hence he hinted at certain things, alluded obliquely to others, and refrained from the use of names. As a consequence the origins and specifics of his outburst remain obscure. The "enclosed" he mentioned in his first line above was perhaps a copy of his letter to Baldwin and Reinhart of the International Committee for Political Prisoners. The "there" he proposed in his second paragraph was probably St. Raphael, a rendezvous point when they could not or did not want to meet in St. Tropez. The "neighbor" in this paragraph was probably their friend Sandstrom. The successor of "the cur" was probably the current Var Préfect, who appeared in other Berkman letters as a "skunk," or "the main skunk," or "that rat."

stand. About other things later or in person. Affectionately, AS USUAL, of course,

S

P.S. Work of petition etc., must go on, of course.

EG TO AB, *Friday morning* [ca. *October 1931*], *ST. TROPEZ*

My dear,

The hour or two I will have with you will be too precious to spend on explanation of my sins, which never do explain anyway. I am only writing this to forewarn you that another one of my "famous" letters must have reached Paris too late to still find you there. It will be forwarded, of course. May I ask you as you have me to take it in the right spirit.

I am only too well aware of my shortcomings, my dear, errors I often make. The cause of the many misunderstandings between us, however, is that you consider yourself beyond reproach. I don't mean to suggest that you are not also aware that you too are but human. You are too honest not to admit that to yourself. But there is a strain in your being, call it pride, stubbornness, or hardness, which has never let you admit any wrong on your part.

However, if a life's service to the uttermost, a friendship that has never known bounds, a consecration that withstood a thousand hells have not proven that the motor power in my forty-two years with you, what can feeble words hope to achieve?

"Piqued": Ah, if only it were that, the things you say and often do would cause less pain. But you have judged by surface things. Deeper motives have remained a book with seven seals. And will to the end of our lives.

A head on your shoulders, always sure of what you do: Did I have to be told that? But Sasha, dearest, the wisest err at times. May not the innocent in heart suggest such a possibility? After all it is time that you know that my profoundest concern in life has been *your welfare, your safety, your peace and happiness.* If I do not always get your "hints," it is because I tremble lest the already shaky ground under your feet may crumble altogether, as for instance your article, which if it had appeared, would have done you more harm than the wretched *Tribune* story. Do I deserve admonition as if I were [my great-nephew] David's age, or bitter words from you for that? I have demonstrated my undying faith in you all through the years and even where I had to dissent from what seemed to me childish undertakings, I have never impugned petty motives for your exploits. I knew that the greater and stronger the human being the more often is he likely to commit mistakes, or if not that, at least slips of incalculable consequences. But as I said, you are too honest not to know that in yourself, as you do in others, though you cannot and never have admitted it to me.

Never minds, my dearest. Nothing is of moment to me except the fervent hope that you may not again be harassed and driven, that you may find tranquillity and peace to live and work, that life may grant you the years still before you in harmony and joy. I have never been moved by any other motive, whether in my "famous" letters to you or our talks but that. Funny you who are so original had never come on that term until you heard my darling Stella dramatize her hurt. Funny indeed from one who is so level-headed and not given to making a mountain of a molehead. But let that pass. I only implore you in your own words, take my "famous" letter which will reach you in Nice in the right spirit. In return I promise you to write fewer letters, famous or otherwise. There is no use, so why cause you chagrin.

I embrace you once more and wish you a joyous homecoming, some rest if possible, which you must be terribly in need of. Your devoted soul. Thanks for them kind words,

[EG]

P.S. Give Emmy the enclosed clipping which she sent me and tell her I will write her when I too have had a little rest, rather sleep, after the two weeks of fretful and sleepless nights.

AB TO EG, *Friday evening* [ca. *Fall 1931*], ST. TROPEZ

Well, dear,

Just had dinner and now I want to talk to you a bit.

Well, you need not laugh over my dinner, either. Maybe you have no faith in my cuisine—well here it is:

Oysters à Côte d'Azure (sardines)
Soup à Sitting Bull (I make it sitting, with viando)
Steak à Frankfurt (hot dogs, in boite)
Dessert à St. Tropez (preserves here)
Coffee à "Bon Esprit"
Fruit au Jardin

That looks like something, doesn't it? It was fine.

But the coffee gave me a little trouble, as there is no percolator here. Made it in one of your teapots, of your new set on the shelf above the icebox. Poured boiling water on the coffee and let it draw. Was splendid, even with the floating black spots. Nothing missing, you see.

Well, the place is in bloom, roses, chrysanthemums (or whatever they are called), geraniums. Weather was fine, but now mistral started for good. Tried to start since yesterday. But the moon is out in force.

There is so much to read here, and I have to look up some old manuscripts etc., that one could spend the whole winter here, or at least till the rains start. I don't mind the wind, though it seems to affect my legs. They started to hurt as soon as I arrived, for yesterday there was also a little mistral. But that is nothing. The jaw is getting better.

However, with my teeth I prefer to eat alone. I say this because Mrs. Sandstrom invited me to eat with them. Very nice of her, but I declined. I can eat here when I want and I only dirty ONE dish and one spoon. Very simple housekeeping, I can tell you. . . .

I see here Dreiser's *A Book About Myself*. I thought I saw the *Genius* also, but maybe it was this book. I'll look around for it.

It's blowing like hell. I have a fire, of course, and it is comfortable.

Let me know what's doing in Paris and about yourself. Are you getting any replies about lectures? And how are you feeling?

Affectionately,

S

AB TO EG, March 4, 1932, NICE

Dear,

I rushed my synopsis for your radio talk to you and I hope it may reach you in time Sunday morning.

I thought the synopsis rather interesting—when I wrote it. Well, I still think it is, but maybe it is not just the thing needed just now for the radio.

In the first place, you will need a lot of time for such a talk. But it is never advisable to talk on the radio more than half an hour—maximum. The listeners-in don't see you (as an ordinary audience does), they miss the personality of the speaker, his gestures, expression, etc. And therefore I think the listeners-in might get tired hearing TOO long a talk. Even half an hour seems to me too long. TWENTY minutes ought to be enough, especially for one who talks fast like you. (You should take care not to talk too fast—for the radio machine may get your words BLURRED and not clearly heard.)

. . . That they want you to talk on anarchism—well, it's hard to say why. I don't believe it is because there is really an interest in anarchism in the U.S. That would be too strange—there is no sign of it anywhere. It is more probable that the directors in the U.S. feel they should give new and striking programs. Or there may also be someone among them who has a leaning to radical subjects. No telling.

I wonder how your lecture before the women came off, and how your throat and voice were? And the swelling of your face and lip? I hope it is getting better. These things may get dangerous, if neglected.

Here nothing new. Both under the weather and Emmy very bad. She wants to thank you for your nice note. She feels sometimes so rotten she rolls around here on the floor. Something pressing against her bowels and she thinks her stomach is down again. But there is nothing to be done for it except maybe to put her into a clinic for observation for a few weeks. But they tell me that the clinics here are very bad. Besides, there is no money for it. It's hell, of course. But she takes plenty of oil and diets—eats hardly any bread or meat now—eats little and is falling away. Some days she feels a bit better, some days worse. I try to keep her busy and am dictating to her the translation of Valya [Gagarin's] stuff. She has no paid typing now anyhow. . . .

I hope you feel better, dear. Don't worry, if sometimes a few days pass when I don't write.

Love,
[AB]

EG TO AB, *March 6, 1932, BERLIN*

Dearest Sash,

You are a comfort, so dependable and quick. Thank you, my dear. Everything arrived yesterday, all the copies of titles and the outline. One was especially good, if only you had not stopped short and started on the other. But it does not matter. I have combined the two and have added something of my own for the radio. Not as a final thing of course, just as a suggestion. Mollie is typing it. When she brings it, I will see how it reads and perhaps send [César] Searchinger a copy. . . .

You will be glad to learn that the swelling of my face is gone. I still have a little pain in my jaw. But it is nothing to the agony of last week. It was neuralgia I am sure. I feel better all around except for my cough. Nothing seems to affect that. The physician who treated me is a lovely person, something like Moe, but very old-fashioned. He prescribed oceans of medicine. And it did no good whatever. Well, the cough is nothing new. It's terribly annoying and makes me weak all over. But it is nothing to worry about.

Yes, I wanted to gather material and interview people. But my illness kept me indoors ten days. And now I haven't the time. I mean to do that either when I return from Erfurt the 26th of this month, or on my way back from Scandinavia. It will be just as well because now everybody thinks of nothing else but the elections, which take place next Sunday. People are in a terrible ferment here, the political waves running over everybody's head. It's impossible to talk to anybody about anything outside of political issues. And that of course I cannot do. It occurred to me it would be great fun to interview Hitler. Of course I'd have to do it under my good old Scotch name, Colton. It ought to prove first-rate stuff for an article. Don't you think? I will see if it can be accomplished before I go to the provinces. After next Sunday there may be no touring any more. Certainly not, if the Hitler gang gets in. . . .

Dear, old chum, was it necessary to suggest that I should recommend you for a radio talk, if mine goes through? That was my very first thought when Nic Mesirow returned with the news that the Columbia [Broadcasting] Company is interested. In fact, I never think only in terms of myself when anything is proposed in the way of writing or work. I always think of you and me, honey boy. If only my talk materializes. The human heart is contradictory. I dare not hope, yet I do of course. Indeed I will write you, if anything comes of the matter.

Dear, I will send you Mesirow's letter tomorrow—I must reply first. I have just come back from the most impressive war film I have seen. Much more impressive and disturbing than Remarque's ["All Quiet on the Western Front"] or "Journey's End." The art in it is sublime and its message far more convincing because there is little talk. There is only dumb humanity. It is called "Niemand's Land" and deals with the effect of the war horrors on five soldiers, a German, a Frenchman, an Englishman, a Jew, and a Negro. I tell you I was so gripped I shook from head to foot all through the performance and for hours after. Rudolf [and] Milly, Mollie and Senya were with me and we were all terribly affected. Rudolf agrees it is the most marvelous anti-war play, its effect simply staggering. I wish you could see it. . . .

I will write again before I leave Berlin. And I will send you a check, dear. I have asked you three times if you are short. I see you do not reply. Never mind. I will send it anyhow. Everybody sends regards,

[EG]

EG TO AB, *March 14, 1932, DRESDEN*

Dearest,

The comrade I am stopping with lives an hour's car ride from the center of town and ten minutes' walk to the next letter box. I have just come back from a long tramp. I am too tired to drag myself back to mail this today. Besides, I want to wait for today's mail which I will not get until this evening at the meeting. Well, there is no such hurry. . . .

I wrote you yesterday that I found the deportation ms. Well, I read it again. It is absolutely no use for the radio. I have been thinking a good deal during the night. I have come to the conclusion that deportation is really of minor importance now with impending war and the world crisis. If I had

a half hour to talk over the radio, it might be worth bringing in deportation. But the allotted seventeen minutes seem entirely too precious to
waste. Don't you think? I feel that I ought to have a few introductory
remarks about the thrilling experience of sending my voice across [the seas]
while I myself am unable to return.* Then speak of my continued interest
in America now more than ever because of the collapse of her so-called
prosperity. Then talk of its cause, which is everywhere the same and
connect this with the [disarmament] babble in Geneva and the impending
danger of a new war. And close with anarchism as the only way out from
the world muddle and distress. The whole talk might be of a personal
nature, expressing my reaction to the world events and how they have
strengthened my social ideal a thousandfold.

In regard to the League of Nations and its futility, I am sending you the
new *Syndicalist* in case you did not get it. It is a first-rate number. But two
articles are altogether splendid. One is Rudolf's "Paris and Kronstadt,"
and "Die Masken sind Gefallen," by [Arthur] Mueller Lehning. This I
consider a brilliant analysis of the Geneva fake. In fact, I have been
thinking along this line for my talk. I don't mean all the statistical part, just
the exposure of those fakirs who know in their hearts that no government
inclusive of Russia means or intends to disarm, yet they perpetuate the
fake because of the sinecure it means to them. I am sure you will be able to
make this part as strong as Mueller Lehning's, or even more effective: I
want to stick in the bones and minds of the listeners how they are being
faked, misled, and prepared for the next slaughter.

Then about the crisis, that too ought to be in sledgehammer language
to take the breath away. It's the only method to make the millions of dubs
take notice. If only I did not have to chase from town to town, I would
write out a rough draft. I simply haven't a moment until I get back to
Berlin. And that means a loss of eleven days. It is just possible that I will
not need the stuff until later in April. But what if I should receive word to
be ready for the 4th? I'd be in a stew then. And so I have to ask you to try
again along the lines I have suggested here. It's got to be complete in short
terse sentences. Please try your luck. . . .

All I can say is I will be glad when it is all over and I can be back in "Bon
Esprit," and have you there for a visit, if only for a few days. I will add more
in the morning.

March 15th. Good morning, my dear. There was no word from you
yesterday. I hope it is not because your cold is worse, or poor Emmy is also
worse than she was. . . .

Well, dush, you need not rush with the text; it's all right if I get it at the
end of the month. It is not likely that the broadcasting will take place

---

* AB penciled "NO" in the adjacent margin.

before April 4th, maybe not then even, or not at all. We must expect the worst; perhaps a little good will come.

Have had a letter from the Seligman [bank] people; my whole capital up to date consists of $387. A fortune, isn't it? Even the strictest economy won't take me far. More reason why we must earn money. I wish Saxe would answer. I keep on wishing. It's the only thing one can do. Although the Seligman note is dated the 11th, there is no mention of the 4,500 francs Modska is supposed to have cabled. I have to write them again to find out. I was to pay up the balance for "Bon Esprit" today. I have written Sandstrom to tell the lawyer it will be delayed for a few days. I hope there is no mistake. I am so tired of having to fret all the time about the mere necessities of life. Well, it cannot be helped. Much love, my dear. Best of wishes for Emmy's improvement.

Emma

AB TO EG, March 31, 1932, NICE

Dear,

Am enclosing here the FINAL typing of the radio talk. I hope it is OK now. The reworking came rather hard, because it is difficult to get in a clear definition of anarchism and also an explanation of the economic forms etc. in a brief space.

I am afraid that the thing may be a bit too long. You can find that out by reading it aloud to yourself on the watch. If too long, you can cut out a word here and there.

I had Emmy type it very clearly, with wide margins and big spacings. I hope it is clear enough for your tired eyes. But you must read it over a few times so as to familiarize yourself well with the thing.

By the way, in case you have no pronouncing English dictionary there: the word PAEANS is pronounced pee-ans (the pee as the word *me*). . . .

Yes, Kay [Boyle] sent an invitation for the second [of April]—at 5 P.M. at her place, but I won't go of course. I think it is stupid to make a special celebration because of her wedding two years after the fact. I am sending her a wire: "MAY LOVE LAST IN SPITE OF LEGAL BONDS AND SANCTION."

Well, dear, how are you and are you getting a rest? I know you have scores of people to see and things to arrange. I hope something will come out of it all. We sure need it badly. And if the radio talk don't go through, then we sure will be on the bum. . . . Love to you, dear,

S

AB TO EG, *Thursday P.M.* [ca. *summer* 1932], NICE

Well, dear,

For a little talk with you. You ask about the system of the clinic.

You go in and they ask you what you want. You say a boil or a feruncle. Then they send you to Dept. D, and you find you are in the syphilis ward, where skin diseases are treated. You stand in line, get to be examined, they examine one patient while they lock you in—actually—in a hole of a room to undress. Then they unlock you, look at your wound or boil, and give you a laissez passer. You are to wait again, then you are called in to Room 4, and there is a doctor who looks like a chimney sweep. No nurses, nothing. They are in the room where you are first examined.

Well, in the hallway waiting are boys and girls, all prolets [i.e., all proletarian], badly dressed and just from work, with turned up sleeves and even in aprons—that's the syphilis clientele and among them a girl of fifteen and her "man," both sick.

And so on. Finally I am called in to the "chimney sweep." Emmy says he looks just like a chameleon. And indeed he has round eyes that seem to change color and when he talks to you or looks at you he turns his head sideways, just like a chameleon, or like one of those lizards that hunt the bugs on the big veranda at "Bon Esprit," right under that electric light. You remember, we watched them last summer.

He has a rough exterior and talks gruffly and loud but at heart he really seems good. Well, anyhow, "Are you a writer?" he asks. He got my name etc. from the examining room. "Yes." "Well, why do you come here for free treatment?" "C'est la crise," I tell him. Then he is satisfied, apparently that foreigners also feel the "crise."

Well, he tears off the sticking plaster and cotton that I have put on my boil, the same as they do in prison. But I had taken the precaution to shave off the hair on my chest around the boil, so it is not so bad. Then he wants to know who has been treating me and I tell him I did myself. Then he goes to work and does not talk any more. He fools around a bit about the boil, washes it with ether, puts some black stuff on it, like vaseline, puts sticking plaster over it, etc. I ask him if it is a feruncle (boil) and he says no. "It is not syphilis?" I ask, though I know it is not, but just to get him to say something. He says no. Then what is it, I ask. He has a manner of not hearing your questions. I ask again, louder. He looks at me and does not reply. I can't help laughing at his manner and he laughs with me.

"This is not very pleasant," I say, as he tears some more plaster off my chest. "You say I am not pleasant?" he asks. "Oui," I reply. And he thinks it a great joke and laughs.

So it goes every day. The first day he took my "pee-pee," as he said it, but I never heard anything more of it. It is the usual procedure, I suppose.

He is a funny cuss, but he is treating the boil all right. By the old system, of course. It has to develop and get ripe, he told me today. It is developing very slowly though, and it is as big as a good-sized apple. Hurts like hell all the time, hard to stand or sit. The worst of it, I can hardly do any work, every movement hurts. . . .

Well, now I told you a lot about it, so don't expect me to write about it again so soon. It is nothing serious, bad blood, that's all. I have cut out all meat. I eat little now anyhow, no appetite, and I will put myself on a diet of cooked vegetables and boiled fruit (compots). . . .

How is your own physical trouble, dear? You have had enough visitors there of late to keep you cooking and serving. I think you need a rest. As to Emmy, she must stay here now till I am better. . . .

LATER, it is Friday P.M.—there are other things I want to write about, can't now. Will write tomorrow or this evening. Must close.

Affectionately,

S

AB TO EG, March 5, 1933, NICE

Well, dearest Em,

Maybe I can write you a more decent letter today. Been in bed a couple of days with a bad cold. And Emmy also on the bum, worse than in the last eight months. Hope she will improve soon. . . .

Dear, I am rather anxious about your decision to go to Germany. I don't know who those people are who have invited you, but I think it were best for you to consult Rocker etc.* From here out, judging by the papers, it looks to me that radical meetings are now out of the question in Germany—at least in Prussia. In other places also—the papers report—the nazis have the upper hand.

I am sure that even if the organizations that invited you are just liberal or artistic, the moment it becomes known that EG is to speak, they will stop the meeting, if not worse.

The social democrats there have fully earned what they get now. They themselves helped to crush the Revolution and afterwards the revolutionary spirit. They had a chance to do something for years and they just helped the bourgeoisie. Now they will reap what they have sown. And of course the communist bodies will be exterminated.

There must be about fifteen million or more of communists and social

---

* On December 1, 1932, EG had reported receiving "a letter today from den Deutsche Verband für Geburtenregelung und Sexualhygiene [the German League for Birth Conrol and Sexual Hygiene] that they are planning a tour for me in March. That after I had definitely given up the idea of Germany. Who says that patience and postage stamps do not bring results?"

democrats in Germany, yet there seems no sign of uprising. Of course it will come to some minor clashes here and there, but history repeats itself. Hitler and his gang have at once raised the iron hand and it seems to me that always succeeds with the masses. I must tell you, dear, that the longer I live the less faith I have in the masses. They will follow those who are successful—those that will act like Stalin, Mussolini, or Hitler. It's dictators that the mass loves and follows. And it is evident that in France, England, and even in the U.S. there is a strong popular call for a dictatorship. In the talks of people on the street you can hear that even the Frenchmen, afraid of a Hitler-Germany, secretly envy Germany "their strong new man." Americans talk the same way—of course, Americans of a certain kind, but it is significant.

Today is election in Germany and I suppose Hitler will get a strong majority, especially since the communist and social democrat papers are suppressed and can't do any election agitation. But even if Hitler does not secure a landslide, Hitler will remain in power one way or another. That is easily done once you have the power in your hands. Well, the whole damn thing everywhere looks rotten.

The *Syndicalist* asked me to write something for Rudolf's sixtieth birthday, but it seems to be silly to write about such things these days. Maybe the *Syndicalist* is already suppressed at that.

Enough for today. I hope your meetings will be good. It is surely more useful to lecture in a country that is more or less psychically normal, like England, than to waste time and words on a people gone mad with Hitlerism.

Affectionately,
S

EG TO AB, *March 8, 1933, LONDON*

Dearest Sash,

I am so tired chasing windmills I decided to stay in today to write you and mend my pants. Everything gets so torn when one is en route. And as I have no money to buy new things, I must sit me down to put the old rags in order. But first comes you, of course. . . .

Yes, dear, hard as it is to admit even to myself, I am beginning to think that my enthusiasm, or rather my expectations, which seemed so much likelier of attainment this time, look discouraging. As eight years ago, there is no lack of social engagements. I could live for months and not have to spend a penny on food. But that is as far as the interest goes. I am tired to death from all the people I have already seen who claimed interest. But I see no indication of any real support in what I have come here to do. Our own people are as everywhere ineffectual. Besides we have no one of any ability whatever. The groups consist of living corpses. There are not more than three young people in the groups. They are eager enough to be of help. But they lack judgment and organizing ability. The only worthwhile worker is Mace. He got all the publicity and whatever interest I found. But the man has been out of work for two years. He is terribly hard up. And I have no money to back him in the work he does for me, at least the expenses for telephone, bus fares, and what not. Naturally I had to do something to reimburse him, since the comrades do not think about such things. And Mace is too sensitive to present them with an expense bill. Anyhow, things do not look very bright. . . .

You are right, dear heart, the masses are anything but hopeful. And yet we must go on in our work. We are voices in the wilderness, much more so now than forty years ago. I mean voices for liberty. No one wants it any more. Yet it seems to me that just because of the present mad clamor for dictatorship, we of all people should not give up. Someday, sometime long after we are gone, liberty may again raise its proud head. It is up to us to blaze its way—dim as our torch may seem today, it is still the one flame.

I agree with you it is futile to think of holding meetings in Germany. And foolish to think of going there. But dear Dush, if "Der Reichsverband" will really go ahead, I cannot let them down, whatever the consequences may be to me.* I am sure you will understand that, if no else does. But as I said, I am confident I will not be called upon to make good my promise. For the present then there is no need to worry. . . .

I can't take time to go over this, dear.

Affectionately,
E

AB TO EG, August 10, 1933, NICE

Dear,

Here is the first ROUGH sketch of your article for that book on THE AMERICAN MIND.

You DID NOT send me the letter of that man [editor McKnight]. I am sure you will find it among your papers. You had read it to me when I was in St. Tropez, but I'd like to read it over again to be clear about just what he wants.

As it is, I don't know on what subject he asked you to write. I believe he wrote that you may choose your own subject, but you have so far not told

---

* Fortunately, her tour was canceled by the Birth Control League. It would have been more than a little awkward for her to have attempted lectures on that subject after March, when Hitler assumed power.

me what your subject is to be. You noted down a few points in your last letters, but the subject you did not state.

Another thing, I don't know how big the article is to be. The enclosed sketch will amount to about 1,500 words.

It can be enlarged, of course. Make your notes on it, if you want it changed or enlarged. The copy you may keep, as I have another one. But if you make your notes ON the copy, then send it back. Otherwise make it clear just what places need changing or enlarging.

You may not like the first part, where I speak of the non-existence of the national mind. If you leave that part out, then you must take some definite subject to write on. The "achievements" of America or of the American intelligentsia is a poor subject. America has achieved a lot in mechanical and industrial things, but that is no subject for you or me to write on. It is well enough known and needs no special article about it. As to the "achievements" of the American intelligentsia, I know of none. They have achieved absolutely nothing in any field that is worth mentioning.

What have they achieved in a social sense? Just nothing. There is not even a single social movement worth speaking about.

Have they achieved anything special in culture? I don't know what, except some pale reflections of European things, things that Europe achieved long ago.

What have they achieved in literature? They have a single dramatist, O'Neill, and he is "great" only because there is practically no one else in the U.S. I consider O'Neill's dramas well done, but touching only the surface of either human emotions or social aspirations. He is far from being great or even outstanding when compared with really great dramatists, as for instance with "Die Weber" of [Gerhart] Hauptmann. Hauptmann is played out and reactionary now, but that does not alter the fact that some of his former works are really great. And O'Neill has not done a single thing as deep and strong as "Die Weber."

In other forms of literature—what has America achieved? A superficial clown like [H. L.] Mencken; a windbag and turncoat like [Walter] Lippmann; a dull propagandist like Upton Sinclair; a very average writer like Sinclair Lewis, who today satirizes American middle-class life—something that in other countries has been done fifty years ago, and done better.

In music and art—what has America achieved that has not long ago been done in Europe and done better? I think that the only thing America achieved is a new form of architecture. And that is all, outside of industry. . . .

It is rotten that the tents cannot be rented. I am afraid there is no hope for it; surely not this year any more. The investment was just a waste of good money; still, it had to be tried. There is no help for it. . . .

                                             Affectionately,
                                                  [AB]

EG TO AB, August 12, 1933, ST. TROPEZ

Dear Sash,

. . . First about the rough draft you sent. You certainly caught the thoughts I had sent you.* For what you wrote is exactly what I had in mind. The article needs to be enlarged, of course. Some things left out to make room for more vital thoughts. But on the whole the draft expresses most of what I want the article to represent. You say I did not state what subject the article is to represent. Well, it is to be not the achievement of the American Mind but its lack of it. In other words it is to show how very miniature and immature the American mind really is. You have already done that admirably. However, I think you have not dwelt enough on the immaturity of the American intelligentsia, its tendency to hang on to every fad and pseudo-fundamental discoveries. Especially along socio-political issues. Mainly do I have in mind the love feast of the American intelligentsia with Soviet Russia. You have touched upon it. But not enough. I wish you could have read the book sent me before I got back. It is called *Recovery through Revolution*. It is also a symposium and has been gotten up by [Samuel] Schmalhausen. Of course none of the [outstanding?] American writers has contributed. But those who have, besides being socialists in their analysis of our wrongs, point to Russia as the last word of recovery through revolution. It is to laugh. The writers, on the other hand, except for Sinclair Lewis, have nearly all been caught in the toils of the Moscow regime. You will see by the article on "Proletarian Literature" I sent you that Dreiser is beginning to wake up from his soviet drunk. The others are still under the influence of its dope. What I want most to bring out is the fact that the American intelligentsia do not accept a thing out of conviction derived after fierce inner struggle or painstaking study and knowledge. Not because it is an ideal reviled and repudiated by the rest of the world. But as a fad and when it has already been respectabilized. As I said you have already mentioned this but I should like the matter treated at length. It is important enough to do so, I think.

In showing up the superficiality of the American mind I don't want to deny what has been achieved. And here I do not agree with you, dear Sash. It is true that nothing REALLY GREAT has been achieved. But that is because of the general poverty of greatness in the world. America does not stand alone in this. It is nevertheless a fact that in the sciences, in psychology, education, architecture, the stage, the drama, poetry, yes, and literature, surgery, and many other fields, America can register very notable achievements since 1900. What if Sinclair Lewis writes only of middle-class American lives? After all, that class is dominant and its exposure and analysis are of importance as social factors. [Ivan Aleksandrovich] Gon-

---

* "Strange. Rather funny," was AB's marginal observation.

charov too wrote of the Russian middle class. Did that make him superficial? After all, each country must create out of its own soil in art and letters. And the writers of America have been doing that. Nor is it true that Mencken is a clown. More than any other American, Mencken has pleaded for libertarian ideas. And he has stood his ground when others of the intelligentsia had failed. I admit he has deteriorated. But that does not lessen his contribution and inspiration of young writers. On the other hand America is foremost in the world in its attitude to the child and education, in its criminal psychology, never mind its lack of influence on the conditions in prisons. Lastly is the achievement in the frank treatment of the emotional phase of life, the reaction of prisoners, and a lot more. However, since others will write about that, I want to stress the lack of achievements in the social and human sense, in the grasp of the essence of the social struggle, ideas other than the respectabilized socialist schools, anarchism for instance. True, anarchism as a social philosophy is still very little understood in all other countries. Still, American intellectuals are most ignorant even of its historic part. I want the article to point that out, to stress how much under the influence of the newspaper idea of anarchism the American intelligentsia is, and how cowardly afraid it is of the very word and its true meaning. . . .

Affectionately,

E

AB TO EG, *August 15, 1933, NICE*

Dear Em,

I am glad that you liked my sketch of the "Miniature Mind." I did not really think that you would like either my attitude or philosophic considerations on the matter of a "national mind." But if you agree with me on the non-existence of a national mind, then so much the better. But I should not be surprised if you are attacked for such a heresy. But that's nothing, of course.

Of course the sketch must be somewhat reworked and filled in. I am not sure, however, if I can do it according to your ideas, except where our ideas agree. I'll see what I can do. For I do not at all agree with you that America has achieved anything since 1900 in the fields you mention; that is, achieved anything from OUR standpoint. No more than Europe has achieved anything.

It did achieve something in architecture, as I already mentioned to you in my previous letter. But even that it did not achieve since 1900 but long before—when the idea of the skyscraper first was realized. Since then they have simply developed the same idea to greater heights, so to speak, built larger and bigger skyscrapers; used more steel and concrete and more glass, to the exclusion of the materials used before, such as wood and iron. But that cannot properly be called a NEW achievement.

As to surgery, which you mention—Americans have an inventive and a pioneer—that is, daring—spirit. They have invented new tools in surgery as in industry, and they have dared to use the new tools in operations. That belongs to the American ability for things mechanical. They have certainly made great progress in all those lines (surgery, surgical dentistry, etc.) but I do not think that those things can be regarded as "achievements" in the sense of the McKnight symposium. And surely not in the larger social sense.

Such achievements are aplenty, in every country. It is just the ordinary development of the various fields of human endeavor. It is not for us to dwell or enlarge upon such achievements. [Guglielmo] Marconi, for instance, has just invented an apparatus for ships that will automatically warn the captain of hidden dangers, of underground rocks, sunken ships, or of any danger in the way of the ship; it will even give the exact distance of the danger from the spot where the ship is at a given moment. A wonderful invention, a great achievement in the ordinary sense, but by no means an "achievement" in any fundamental social sense. And I think that you can speak only of real achievements—that is fundamental social achievements. . . .

The idea of comparing Sinclair [Lewis] to Goncharov! Goncharov did what Sinclair does in his satire on the middle class, but Goncharov did more: in his works you feel the rottenness of the whole of Russian middle-class life and of its very foundations. While Sinclair never goes beyond the exposure of the pettiness of provincial American life. He is careful not to touch any basic institutions and conceptions.

As to Mencken, I surely consider him a clown. He was never more than the "smart Aleck" of American literature, who indulged in clever, and sometimes only in would-be clever, puns on the professorial mentality, on the American prudery and provincialdom, etc., etc. But though Mencken is personally undoubtedly socially conscious, he always avoided a criticism of the fundamentals of our civilization. That would have labeled him an anarchist, and I am sure that he always avoided such fundamental criticism *consciously*.

Well, my dear, we will most likely not agree on this, as we do not agree on most things. That brings me to a different matter, but one really directly related. You say, for instance, in your last letter, why I "take you up on a word." Because back of the "word" is a world of feeling and attitude. And it is that feeling and attitude that I mean to call your attention to, when I "take you up" on a word. I have indeed repeatedly called your attention to your careless use of words; but words are not merely words; they express feelings and thoughts. And your careless use of words has very often caused much misunderstanding. You surely must know this from your own correspondence.

Your letter to Evelyn Scott is a case in point. You wrote her, for instance, that because of my American record my coming back to the U.S.

is entirely out of the question. (Or words to *exactly* this effect.) Now that means in English that there is no chance of my returning to the U.S. But you know very well that when you write like that, you give the direct impression that I am as eager to return to the U.S. as you are, which is absolutely not true. As a result of this, most people who know that you want to return also assume that I am just as eager to return. It is therefore [as] I told you in my recent letter that I do not want to return *under any conditions.* You might as well ask me whether I would go to Mars, if invited by the Martians. We are not speaking of the impossible, but only of the reasonably possible. That means, that as long as capitalism and government exist in the U.S. (and they will exist a long time yet, much longer than I will live), I would not return, nor want to return. Nor could I, even if I wanted to. But you should not leave the impression that I would like to return under existing conditions. For under existing conditions I could not return "under my own conditions," as you put it. There is no such a thing. You could return only by having people pull some political wires, even if you personally had not to make any pledges. But I would not return even if I *could,* under similar circumstances. . . .

Well, there is no news here. As hot here as in St. Tropez, every bit of it, and hot as hell in the house. No rain here for weeks and weeks. And no sign of it. It is all right, so far as sunshine is concerned, but I am afraid it is very bad for the crops.

The tents—no, I have no hope of them, either this year or next. Let them stand, however, for the present. There is plenty of time to take them down.

Affectionately,

S

EG TO AB, August 18, 1933, ST. TROPEZ

Dear Sasha,

. . . You are so obsessed by the idée fixe that we do not agree on most things that you actually took it for granted that I would reject your point of view on the national mind. What interests me is where you got the notion that I stand for such a thing. Can you mention an instance in all the years we have worked together where I by pen or word of mouth advanced this idea? True, I hold that every country develops traits in its people which another country does not. Thus you will agree that America has produced certain traits and characteristics which neither Germans, Frenchmen, or Russians have. In this sense one speaks of German, French, Russian, or English literature, or culture. And in this sense too, I hold that writers like Sinclair Lewis, or Dreiser, or the others must needs write differently than writers in other countries. Their difference is only the angle most pressing in the country. Thus the development in America started from the individual and emotional as a natural consequence of puritanism and the individualistic struggle against the elements in the U.S. In European countries the starting point had been the political and the social, hence the social literature. But because I hold to this it does not mean I stand for a national mind. Really dear, I am inclined to think you hate to find that I do agree. Well, it happens that I have never expressed anything else about the national mind except that it is non-existent. As I said, I cannot make out where you suddenly got the notion that I think otherwise.

No, there is no use in arguing American achievements. Certainly not on paper. I do, however, wish to say that you are dogmatic in your denial of them. But then, you are dogmatic in many other things. For instance, you tell me I make wrong uses of words because I had written to Evelyn in re your not being admitted to the States. Only you, my dear, interpreted my word and meaning in the wrong way. Evelyn certainly did not. You say while you know that I would return to the States only on my own terms I am still willing my friends should pull wires which you are not. Dear, old Sasha, you do love to ride the high horse of consistency, don't you? Well, the trouble is, you are no more consistent than I or anyone else. You would have nothing to do with the application for a visa. Yet you spent a fortune in bribing the police in Berlin and being at their beck and call. And were you not willing that your friends in Paris should wire pull to get your expulsion removed or a stay in France? The fact is, my dear, since the war no one can ride the high horse; every one of our steps are being dictated. So why such fuss about America? You will not have a chance to refuse any more than I will. But if such a chance were to come and I could go on my own conditions, I frankly admit I would. And what is more, so would you. I know it does not seem so to you now. But then, dear heart, many things that did not seem possible had to be done, by you as well as by all of us. You know it as well as I.

If this reaches you before you have made the final typing, I wish you'd leave out the reference to Lincoln Steffens's part in the McNamara case. I had forgotten that he had written me while I had been on *LML* that he had merely carried out the suggestion of [Clarence] Darrow and others. And a lot more. I don't like to charge him with the stupid effort now. But it is all right to quote from his autobiography in re bringing the rich and poor together. I thought of this last night. I hope I am not too late.

Affectionately,
[EG]

AB TO EG, August 22, 1933, NICE

Dear Em,

I hope you got the copies of the article for McKnight's anthology and that you liked and sent it out. I forwarded you one first copy in a letter and three carbon copies in case you need them.

Could not write before: had to put the finishing touches on [Emil] Bernhard's PRISONER, which he thinks he can place in London. Rereading it again, I had to admire the skill and force with which the characters are drawn. It is really a great powerful play. I wonder whether you remember it.* I am only sorry he made his hero a Tolstoyan. But I think Bernhard himself is one, so that explains it.

There were several points in your last letters which really need answering. But it is fearfully hot, and I know neither of us will change his opinion. So it is really useless. But one or two points I do want to refer to, briefly.

Every time I say something you don't like, you answer that I have an "obsession" about it, or an idée fixe.

As to your long argument that you do not believe in the national mind—who said you did? I happen to have a copy of my letter about it. I wrote there: "You may not like the *first part*, where I speak of the non-existence of the national mind." I was speaking of the PART, not of the "mind." Because that part is not written in your usual style; there are even expressions there that you never use, and therefore I assumed that you would not like that part. But since you did, so much the better.

As to consistency—your comparisons are entirely illogical. As an anarchist I should not support the government in any form. Yet I write letters and buy postage stamps from the government. Or I pay (when I happen to be in a hotel) the government tax, etc., etc. I pay or I do these things when I MUST. Not of my own choice. It is therefore also that I managed to stay in Germany, or that I make my applications here for renewals. Because I MUST, having no other choice and having no place to go to where I would not have to do these things.

But to try to get to America is a DIFFERENT thing. There is no *must* about it, and that is why I said (and repeat) that I would not do it. "On your own terms," as you put it—that's nonsense. You know you'll never get to the U.S. on any terms but what the government will make. I know you would not accept certain terms—still, you let Isaac Levine "try"; that is, you knew he would go straight to Washington to pull wires; that is, to secure some terms. Whether you could have accepted those terms or not,

---

* In 1928 Berkman had translated Bernhard's five-act play about a prisoner in Siberia and the Provincetown Players staged it shortly thereafter.

that is another matter. But I would never consent to go to the U.S. through anyone trying to do something in Washington.

So you can see that there is no comparison between things that one MUST do and other things that one does not have to do. Of course you might say that desire for activity and economic reasons are also a MUST in a certain sense. Maybe, but it is not the same kind of MUST as when you have no passport at all and not even an identity card, so that you can't actually go anywhere at all in the world and you are compelled thereby to compromise by applying for renewals or bribing the police. There is a big difference, you know.

Well, otherwise things are quiet here. And nothing new of course.

Affectionately,

S

EG TO AB, August 23, 1933, ST. TROPEZ

Dear,

I have been in such a mad state of depression for a week and so restless I wanted to lock up the house and run. Indeed I would have done so had I been able to call off Nellie Lavers' visit. But I did not have the heart to disappoint her since she is looking forward to her holiday here with such eagerness. She and her friend arrive Sunday evening. Then too, I had two boarders for two days. Two American boys, students, friends of the Mesirows [Nic and Midge]. She had written me that they were coming for several weeks and would want a tent. Well, they had spent so much time on their trip already they could only remain here two days. They left this morning. Nice Jewish American boys. Anyhow, here I am still and will remain until the end of September.

I started really to let you know why I had not written you all this time. I just couldn't. My head felt pressed down by an iron ring. The occasional attack of insomnia added to my misery. I can't say I feel much better today. But I did not wish to keep you wondering what might be the matter. . . .

Yesterday was the sixth anniversary of Sacco and Vanzetti's death. I wonder if they had been remembered even by our own comrades. Human memory is so fleeting. The thought of them added to my depression. It made me feel how crazy I am wanting to keep up work for our ideas, when nothing changes in the world. What is the use of it all? I wish I could at least make my peace with the world as behooves an old lady. I get disgusted with myself for the fire that is consuming me at my age. But what will you? No one can get out of his skin. . . .

Have you read about the University of Exiles started in New York? Perhaps it means nothing to you. To me it is a wonderful thing. That it should happen in America sort of reconciles me to some of the idiotic and infantile things Americans do.

Enuf for today. I hope you keep well and get lots of sunshine. How is Emmy's stomach trouble? I hope it keeps getting better and better every day.

Affectionately,

[EG]

EG TO AB, November 26, 1933, PARIS

Dearest,

... Now as to my Dutch experience. As I have already written you, my lecture last Thursday in Rotterdam had been forbidden by the authorities. I spoke Wednesday in Amsterdam in a trade union house where only members had come. I suppose that accounts [for] why the police did not come. They had simply not known about the meeting. But they were on hand at Apeldoorn, about three hours from Den Haag. They took me to the police station and informed me they have an order from the ministry to send me across the border. They were going to do it the same evening. But I insisted I must get back to Den Haag to collect my things and my return ticket. They consented to send me back to the Haag with a detective. There I was received by the Haag police. But my host had also come. And as the Coopses are representative people [i.e., established] in Holland the police consented to let me stay overnight with my friends. They came at 10:30 Friday to see that I got safely into the train. Well, four meetings had been ruined. I don't even know whether the comrades will be able to pay my fare and expenses, which amount to about four hundred francs. Wim Jong, who had arranged my tour, was to speak in my stead in all the meetings yet to be held and he has promised to get some money for me.

Of course this is not the worst. It is that the last country in Europe where I thought I might be active at least a couple weeks a year is now also closed to me. It is awful and most discouraging. I confess I am worried now about Canada. What if I am not admitted there? Or if I am also to have all lectures stopped? Imagine spending all the money and working so hard to make the trip for nothing. Frankly, I am worried. I had hoped to really rest and enjoy my crossing. I fear that's all gone. This brings me to what I wrote you in the summer that trying to get back to America is really a question of life and death to me.

Well, dearest own Sasha, I am still as pessimistic about my reentry as you are. Still the work has been going on. I did not wish to bother you with it because you were opposed to it being tried in the first place. I am now enclosing a letter from Roger [Baldwin] and one he had written to my friend Mrs. [Mabel Carver] Crouch, the woman who had started the campaign. You can see that the Department of Immigration and Labor [*sic*] has declared they have no legal grounds to refuse me a temporary visa. Roger therefore thinks it will be a question of policy. And inasmuch as the Minister of Labor Frances Perkins is considered most liberal and is known by Stella and a lot of other of my friends in the States, they are hoping to get her to consent. With that in view, Mrs. Crouch has organized a strong committee that is to write Perkins and ask her to readmit me for a short period of a visit and some lectures. In fact I have already several invitations, as you will see by Stella's letter. Roger thought that was necessary to impress Perkins.

I had almost decided to follow Roger's advice to apply for a visa at the American Consulate here. But since my expulsion from Holland I came to the conclusion it will be better to wait until I have entered Canada. I feared it might leak out through my application for an American visa that I am going to Canada. And I may not be admitted. Roger now writes it will be easier to negotiate from Canada. At any rate there is no hurry. I repeat I am not hopeful. But it is like buying a lottery ticket. We have no hopes. But we try anyhow. The fact that I do not have to hedge and trim, that I can openly declare that I had remained what I had been makes the application for an American visa and the effort easier. So don't be too hard on me, my dearest. It is really my last resort to justify my life before myself. . . .

I am so happy to learn you and Emmy are better. May it last. Give her my love and say for one who hates being photographed as much as I, it is a great proof of my affection for her to have consented to take my hands [i.e., have them photographed] at a time when I am crowded with engagements. Much love to you, old chum. Will add a line if I hear from you tomorrow. Good night, my dear,

Em

AB TO EG, *November 27, 1933, NICE*

My dear Em,

So you are expelled from Holland! Well, that is very good. No harm done, and I know it has put new fighting spirit into you. But to think that a Scheiss [shit] country like Holland prohibits a talk on dictatorship and expels you—a British citizen!!!

No, I do not think you will have trouble on the border of Canada. At least I hope not. But whether Canada will permit lectures on dictatorship is also questionable. Yet I believe they will not interfere. Still, if they do, the TITLE can be changed, if necessary, but the same contents kept. I know you will be clever enough, as always, to manage it OK. . . .

S

AB TO EG, *December 31, 1933, NICE*

Dearest Em,

This is the last day of the year and I want a little talk with you. May the next year bring more satisfaction—to you, to me, and to all of us, and to the world in general. The world really had nothing to laugh about in 1933. . . .

Now, dear, about the U.S. Of course, you know my opinion. However, I may prove wrong and they may let you in. Yet I doubt it very much. Roosevelt and his administration have enough criticism against them. He'll hardly want to give the other political parties a chance to kick about this matter. Of course, I know it is not he but his Secretary of Labor that is to decide the matter. But that will amount to the same thing.

However, if you do get in, I shall be pleased on YOUR account, since you are so keen about it.

But, dear, do not forget what I told you on previous occasions. You said then, as you often say, that I would change my mind. No, dear, I have not and will not. As a matter of fact, I feel even stronger about it than ever before. I DON'T WANT to go to the U.S., on any considerations. Please remember it.

Why do I refer to it? Because in one of your letters to Baldwin you wrote that it would make you happy to be back in the U.S., but that your happiness would be complete if I also were there with you.

That is a direct hint to start efforts for me in that direction. In any case, it is MOST MISLEADING, for it gives the impression that I am also eager to come back. Many people have already written me assuming that I also want to come back.

Well, my dear, I DO NOT and will not even if I could come back by just applying to the American Consul for it. I hate America now and don't want ever to see it again.

So, please, do not give the impression that I want to come back. . . .

Well, dearest sailor, may your wishes come true and may they not bring you disappointment. I hope the lectures will be a success. Don't worry about them—I am sending on whatever [notes] I can.

Love,
S

AB TO EG, *January 14, 1934, NICE*

Dearest Em,

I just want to send you congratulations on having achieved your great longing. For I have just now received your cable that the visa was granted.

Well, I was wrong. I did not believe you could get in without having some political strings attached to it. That is why I was not in favor of your even trying it. But of course everyone should follow his own judgment.

Well, I am glad on YOUR account. It opens a new field of activity to you, for your place is the platform, of course. Now that they let you in, even if only for three months, I think it will not be difficult to prolong the term. At any rate, they could not well refuse a visa again some months later, or next year. In the course of time you could probably stay there as long as you want. . . .

Well, when you are in New York give all friends my greetings. Don't let them get the impression, however, that I also want to come there. . . .

This is in haste. Today is Sunday, my rest day, so I must prepare that article for the encyclopedia. But I am sure they won't take it, as I have to say things against the German socialists and their indirect aid, and even direct, in preparing the way for Hitler. Love to you and much joy in your return to the U.S.,

S

EG TO HENRY ALSBERG, April 9, 1934, ST. LOUIS

Dear Henry,

. . . My tour outside of Chicago continued the worst flop I've ever known. Not even in the beginning of my lecture period have I had such dismal failures. City after city, with huge halls, and only a handful of people present. It was heartbreaking, in this city as well as everywhere else. Chicago proved that there is nothing the matter with my appeal to the public. There was everything the matter with [James] Pond's management [of the lectures]. The comrades in Chicago organized four meetings attended by eighteen hundred people at some and not less than a thousand at the others. They sensibly charged 45 cents admission and kept expenses down. The result was magnificent. What is more to the point was the quality of the audiences. The meetings in Mandel Hall and Lincoln Center were attended by students as well as many of the faculty. The meeting in the New Masonic Temple was almost exclusively of a working class quality, mostly young and vivid people. I should have despaired utterly were it not for the one bright spot in Chicago; but even that cannot help my despair over the bungling of the grandest opportunity of a lifetime. If I do not get an extension, I will have to leave America as poverty stricken as I was when I reached here, with hardly any impression left behind. More reason why you and my other friends should not have lost three weeks in rousing interest in the continuation of the ninety days. . . .

Affectionately,

[EG]

EG TO AB, May 15, 1934, MONTREAL

Dearest own Sash,

While I am dead tired from last night's meeting and must speak again tonight, I want to send off a few lines to catch the "Olympic" which sails Thursday, the 17th. . . .

Dearest, I don't believe that you can no longer write articles. I think it was your exhaustion from the [Harry and Lucy] Lang book. And also that living in exile does dry up one's spring of interest and activity. I know it from my own experience. In all the years in Europe I have not felt so vital or alive as I did while in the States and even in Canada. I guess it has as much to do with the interest one meets in social affairs as it is that I feel at home in America. I am certain you too would feel reawakened and your faith strengthened. There is much truth in the saying Der Appetite komt mit dem Essen [Appetite comes with eating]. When our interests are alive our capacity grows [and] our mentality revives. Living in the enervating atmosphere of the south of France, removed from every activity, it is not surprising that you found it so difficult to write the articles. Then too you had no material on hand of any sort. At any rate, I know you can write and you will again more easily when you have some let up of material anxiety, and worry over other people's bad writing [i.e., the Lang ms.]. . . .

Goodby, for today, dearest. Love to Emmy and loads of it to you,

E

EG TO AB, May 27, 1934, TORONTO

My dearest Sash,

. . . To come back to the material for the individual. Dearest, you wrote me yourself that one of the reaons why you had found it so difficult to write the article was you had no material. Nothing in the library in Nice, etc. That's why I sent you the [Horace] Kallen book [*Individualism* (1933)]. I know one has to have one's own ideas to start with. But a work like Kallen's can suggest and clarify our own thought. That's why I sent it. I hope it helped you, if only to refresh your mind of the American traditions. They certainly were anarchistic. By the way, you wanted Voltairine [De Cleyre's] article on the same subject. So you do need, as well as all of us who speak or write, something someone else has written. Naturally, the material must be somewhat in keeping with our own ideas. Well, I consider Kallen's treatment of the place of the individual in the light of

American traditions far more illuminating than Voltairine's and more informative.

That brings me to your prejudice about things American. For instance, your reference to Evelyn Scott in your letter to Stella as being far too good a writer for America. Either you have not kept informed of what is being done in the States, or your long absence has sort of dimmed your judgment. Fact is, dearest, Evelyn writes as she does because of her American background. No other country could produce just such writing. And what is more to the point, some of the best writing of our time is being done by Americans. I could name you a dozen, some very young people who have just begun to write, who are doing better work than Europeans. You have enthused so much about Kay Boyle. Well, she is an American. Not that I consider her as good a poet as Vincent Millay or Lola Ridge, or as deeply socially aware as Evelyn, and others. Still, she writes better than some of the English writers. And who else, except perhaps the younger French, are in Europe, with Germany dead as a doornail? I am sure, dearest, it is your long absence from the States that does not let you see what is really going on there.

I leaned in this direction myself until I returned and could see with my own eyes just what is being done in the country in all sorts of ways. True, America remains naive, childish in many respects in comparison to the sophistication of Europe. But I prefer its naiveté: there is youth in it, there is still the spirit of adventure, there is something refreshing and stimulating in the air. Europe is hoary with age; it sticks in its centuries of traditions; it dares nothing. The very experiment of Roosevelt, childish as it is, has the adventurous spirit of the country. For what statesmen in the world would have undertaken Roosevelt's scheme without immediately slamming fascism on the country? Don't think I have any faith in the New Deal. It is a failure already. It has helped the big robbers, of course, though they are allied against Roosevelt because he has dared to declare that the workers have some rights. They were so used to having it all their own way, they cannot forgive Roosevelt for putting the workers on their mettle. No, the New Deal has not and could not succeed. But it has put new life into the workers. Proof for that is the truly grand influx into the trade unions; the numerous strikes fought not with kid gloves; the open and outspoken attitude toward revolution. Roosevelt has unwittingly awakened the whole country to a deeper social awareness and freedom of expression. But that is not what I want to stress. It is that America brings out adventure, innovations, experimental daring which, except for Russia, no European country does. And it is this surcharged, electric, and dynamic atmosphere which permeates its writers, poets, and dramatists. You'd rub your eyes if you could see some of the plays now given on the American stage. Or the marvelous productions. Not only now, but nowhere since the war have I seen in any country such vitality in scenery and production of plays. Believe me, I am not carried away by mere appearance. Only I was able to see what one cannot do [or see] when so completely removed from the atmosphere of a country as we have been and you still are.

Dearest own Sash, I am so delighted you and Emmy have gone to "Bon Esprit" and that you may make use of it for the whole summer. I have already written you that Kinzinger, the artist, has decided to go to Spain. But even if he had wanted to rent our place, I should not have cared to let him have it so long as you can be there. Why, nothing is so important than that you should have all the sunshine you need. Yes, I know you might have it in Nice, if you had the time. But even then you'd have to go to all the exhausting process of dressing for the beach. In "Bon Esprit" you can run around naked and step right into the sun. In fact, work on the terrace all the time. . . .

You and I have no luck, dearest. I tried so hard to get the translation rights for [B.] Traven's *Totenschiff*. His publishers, Der Gutenberg Verlag, told me he was absolutely opposed to having anything published in America. Furthermore, he was impossible to reach. He answered letters once a year or so. Well, Hitler must have changed Traven's mind, because Knopf got out his book. I was never more surprised than when I read the review of *Totenschiff* in the [New York] *Times* and of Knopf as its publisher. . . . Just our rotten luck to have everything literally taken out of our hands that succeeds. That's why I understand so well, dear heart, the difficulty you find in writing original stuff. Our failure would dishearten the staunchest souls. Yet I feel we must not give up, especially where actual and assured orders are concerned. I am convinced you would not have found it so trying to do the individual had I been there and we could as always exchange ideas and go over the attempt. It's all right, my dear, I will do my best to rework your notes into something, especially if you should really send on a little more as your wire promises. . . . Goodby, dear heart. I embrace you with love,

Em

AB TO EG, *June 3, 1934, ST. TROPEZ*

Dearest Em,

Your long letter from Montreal of May 21 received yesterday. (Sunday is my letter-writing day; can't afford it during the week.)

Also copy of your letter to Joe Goldman and the stamps. Fine that you sent the latter. Never saw them before, particularly that special delivery stamp and the ones with the woman on it, in memory of mothers, etc.

Well, dear heart, when one is so far away as you, letters often cross themselves or arrive after the points in reference have long ago been answered. ...

Well, anyhow, dear, by this time you have the cable and also the little article on the individual I sent you to Toronto. I am sure that together with what I had sent before on the individual and the notes you have made yourself on the subject, you will be able to have a good article. I only hope it will be accepted.

Well, I am surely flattered about what you say about my ability to write. I know you always had a rather too good opinion of it. Anyhow, I am glad of it: I don't mind at all my friends exaggerating my abilities. See?

But seriously, I DO hope that both articles will come out OK, and what is even more important, that they will be accepted and paid for!!!

As to being isolated etc. Of course there is much truth in it. Yet it is also a fact that people have never given me much in point of thought and ideas. But the exchange of ideas is important. Some inspiration of course one gets OCCASIONALLY from some book or person. I prefer books, though. I get, as a rule, a great deal more from the New York *Times Literary Supplement* [or *Book Reviews*] than from many another source. Unfortunately I seldom receive it. I have just written to Stella and asked her to send me her own old copies.

And dear, when you have some old magazines, such as the *Nation*, [*New*] *Republic*, or that illustrated communist monthly, send them to me when through.

Kallen's book I returned to you, to Toronto, registered. Hope you got it at the same time as individual article. Let me know. ...

I embrace you, dear, and hope you may not find the trip in Canada too hard, and that you also find some joy with [Frank] Heiner.

Affectionately,
[AB]

AB TO TOM MOONEY, *February 6, 1935, NICE*

My dear friend Tom,

It was good to hear from you again, and your letter of January 10th gave me more joy than I can tell you. For it is such a fine expression of my good old Tom, who is to me one of the most courageous, steadfast, and devoted men it has ever been my good luck to meet. I know what it means to spend so many years under the conditions under which you live—exist, really, is the proper word for it. And I know what strength of character and devotion to one's cause is necessary to remain unbroken in spirit and true to oneself.

I am not given to flattery, but it is out of an inner urge that I must tell you that you are to me one of the biggest and finest men I know. It is far easier to die for one's faith than to suffer for it day in and day out, for long, endless years. And to suffer not only the persecution and humiliation by the enemy, but—worse yet—lack of understanding and sympathy on the part of some friends, as has always been the fate of martyrs.

And now to your letter. First of all, dear Tom, do not let it worry you for a single moment that you cannot write to me as often as you would like to, or that you cannot always reply to my letters. It is a wonder to me that you can find any opportunity at all for private correspondence, for I know how limited your facilities for writing are and how many much more important things you have to attend to in the line of writing. So, do not let this add to your worries, and know that I shall never misunderstand. . . .

As to adding those things to which I have referred, it would make your pamphlet a *book* of goodly size. For the story of those first days in San Francisco, after your arrest, would take a lot of space, if it is to be told as it should be told—in an intelligent and comprehensive manner, giving all the illuminating facts of the situation: the general San Francisco atmosphere at the time, the various labor phases, the specific psychology of the city at the time, etc., etc.

The coming together of the first defense committee, its difficulties in the face of the silly general panic, the need of funds to secure even the most elementary public hearing for the arrested, the attempt to get a hearing from alleged labor friends scared stiff by preconceived notions and their prejudices against those accused simply because they had been accused—in short, the initial struggle against human stupidity and prejudice, against cowardice and downright insincerity—the adequate description of it all would make most interesting and informing reading, but it would require time to write it and would of itself make quite a book.

Then the other chapters in this drama: the eventful trip to New York to secure defense counsel not prejudiced for or against those arrested by the San Francisco atmosphere and labor antagonisms, to secure such impartial and *able* counsel without having a cent to offer them for their expenses and services. To interest the labor organizations of New York in the case, of which *not a word* had till then been heard in the East. The struggle in New York with some socialist and "pure and simple" labor elements who were opposed to getting mixed up with "a local fight" in San Francisco. Then a trip throughout the country, talks to hundreds of labor unions, big and small, who were either not interested or positively antagonistic, and yet who were gradually induced to give not only moral but also financial support. Well, my dear Tom, familiar as you are with the red tape, the methods and attitude of unions, you know what a Herculean job that was.

Then the chapters of getting word to the Russian proletariat about happenings in San Francisco, the monster meetings in Kronstadt and Petrograd in the case of "Muni," and how the matter reached Wilson through Francis, then U.S. Ambassador in Russia, who was visited by a determined delegation of Kronstadt sailors and soldiers. Incidentally, their interpreter [Louise Berger] on the occasion was a close friend and comrade of ours, a girl from New York, who had returned to her native land soon after I arrived in New York from the West.

Well, all this and related matters would indeed make a book. So, you understand, Tom, why I could not go into details about these matters in my recent letters to you, or to suggest them to be incorporated in the pamphlet. As I have already said, they are not absolutely essential to your story (for the pamphlet) and they would turn your pamphlet into a very large volume. Outside of this, I found nothing missing in the pamphlet and no important changes to be made.

If I refer to these phases of your case now, it is because your last letter suggests that I write my own story of the case. A good idea, no doubt, and I should certainly be very happy to carry it out. Unfortunately, I am afraid I shall hardly ever be able to get to it. My health has not at all been satisfactory for a long time now, which means reduced ability to work. And all my time is taken by translations to make ends meet, and by similar things that are necessary and done gratis.

Between you and me, Tom, I have for years had in mind several books that would probably prove both interesting and useful reading, but the world outside is also only a prison, on a larger scale, and one is no more a free agent in it than you are within the walls of San Quentin. And life outside is, especially these days, similar in a certain respect to life "inside." The longer one stays in it, the more unbearable it becomes. There is no "getting used" to it for those who have spirit and a sense of social justice.

While I am on the subject, let me mention that I have for several years now had in mind a book, in a not too serious vein, that would be mostly autobiographical and necessarily reflect also the various social movements of my time. I would call the book I HAD TO LEAVE, and maybe this title will convey to you some idea of its planned spirit and contents, for from early childhood, even beginning with school and the parental home, I always "had to leave," an undesirable citizen always, and desired only in places which they did not want me "to leave.". . .

As to general conditions in Europe, I am sure you are keeping informed, for I remember what a great reader you are. I only hope that you have permission as well as time to read all that you want to. The crisis is felt very badly on the Continent, and particularly so now in this country. A great many men and women, exiles from other lands, have come to France; but owing to the growth of unemployment among the natives, the foreigners are now subject to ever greater restrictions. Practically speaking, they are now entirely unable to hold jobs: special laws have been passed about it. You can readily understand what it means to the thousands of exiles from Russia, Germany, Italy, Spain, and other countries, who are penniless and unable to go to other countries for lack of "papers" and visa.

On the other hand, the cost of living is very dear in this country, and for that reason a great many English and Americans, former residents in France, have left for other shores. Nice, for instance, is entirely deserted. I used to have a great many friends and acquaintances here, among Anglo-Saxons. Now we know hardly a soul in the town. And it really holds true of the whole of France. . . .

Yes, surely I know something about the monopolistic tactics of the Communist Party, to which you refer in your last letter.* Bob Minor, whom you mention, used to be one of my very dear friends, but I have not heard from him since I met him in Moscow. He did not like my saying to him that the possession of a red card works more miracles than a lifetime of devoted revolutionary activity. It was in reply to his question why I was not present at some official conference going on at the time in Moscow, and to which I could gain no admission, since I had no red card. Nor did he like my refusal to accept from him the leavings of the fine repasts he and other delegates were getting in order to give these leavings to the anarchists imprisoned at the time in Moscow and who were on a hunger strike in protest against being imprisoned without any charges against them.

Our people were then twelve days on their hunger strike and the bolshevik authorities felt ashamed at the situation, for almost all of those prisoners were men who had suffered under the Czar and later fought with the bolshevik shoulder to shoulder on the various fronts. Among them were some of our best and dearest Russian comrades and some former American exiles. Many of them I knew personally as most loyal and devoted revolutionists. But though cooperating in educational, military, and economic matters with the bolsheviks, they remained true to their political views. It was for *that* they were in prison.

Well, then, the bolsheviks were afraid our people might hunger-strike to death, for they were determined men. The authorities were anxious to break the strike—now you understand why Bob Minor brought food from the first-class hotel in which he was staying in Moscow (as a guest of the government). There were all kinds of delicacies there while the people were starving, actually—I mean the people of Moscow and other cities. Wagons of fresh-baked white bread, and of meat, used to stop every

---

* In his letter of January 10, 1935, Tom Mooney, still number 3192 at San Quentin, asked Berkman for his help—he wanted AB's account and that of "all others who took an active part in those early days when the going was rough"—and then further along apologized that the "pamphlet *Labor Leaders Betray Tom Mooney* does not do justice to you and your comrade—the reason is their (Communist Party) hatred of both of you for what you said about the U.S.S.R. in *Living My Life*. They—that is, sources friendly to their party—prepared the pamphlet and that explains your exclusion." Mooney stepped back from the controversy, but did hazard the opinion that, in spite of all the communists' shortcomings, "if they can be called that, they are building a future society from which will come great things." It was to this apology and contention that Berkman responded in the paragraphs that follow.

morning at the Hotel Lux (that was its name) and hordes of little boys and old women used to hide in the doorways of the houses nearby and watch for a chance when the armed guards, accompanying the wagons, would turn their back, so they could snatch a few bread crumbs that had fallen to the ground—and be arrested for it when caught.

I lived in a side street nearby and I used to see that sight and many other similar ones. Well, Bob did not like me telling him about these things. And of course, those things were merely symptoms of the whole rotten situation. And naturally, I refused to help Bob break the hunger strike of our people in prison.

But returning to Bob Minor. He is a good boy, and his tragedy is that instead of sticking to his last (for he is a good artist), he turned to politics, of which he understands nothing. He is neither by temperament nor mentality capable of taking an unprejudiced and big view of a social situation. . . .

But you refer to U.S.S.R. as the only hope of the world. My dear Tom, how I wish I could share your opinion, for it must be very comforting. Unfortunately, I know too well what is going on there, for I am in touch with that country and I know Russian, which enables me to follow Russian developments with more understanding than would otherwise be the case. It is not the Russian shortcomings, of which you hint, that matter. Tenfold greater shortcomings could be overlooked, if they were really "building a new world," as you put it. Terribly sorry as I am to tell you, the fact is that what they are building is a very, very old world that has been dead long ago. They are reviving feudalism of the worst kind, and their example has to a very great extent been responsible for the doings of the Mussolinis and the Hitlers in other countries. I am sorry to say it, but it is only too true, most unfortunately.

Do you think I would have for a moment considered leaving Russia, if I could have seen even the least sign there of anything approaching the "building of a new world"? I am sure, they treated me with silken gloves and offered me the best and most lucrative positions, so surely I had no personal reasons for leaving and going into perpetual exile. But to accept those offers meant self-betrayal, which I refused to do.

It is not the shortcomings of Russia that I am speaking of. It is the very principles of their "building" which are reactionary to the core and which inevitably lead to the destruction of the best that there is in human nature. It is too big a subject to discuss here, Tom. I have written enough on the subject, and among other things also my book, *The Bolshevik Myth*, but probably you have no access to such literature. I can only say here one thing, and that is the essence of the whole question about Russia. You cannot educate men for liberty by making them slaves. That is the sum total of all the lessons of history and of human experience. THEREIN is the trouble with the bolsheviki, and not in their shortcomings. If you had the least inkling of what a young generation of careerists, adventurers, and unprincipled and fanatical worshipers of the "leader" and of the "party" there has grown up in Russia under the bolshevik regime, you would know what I mean. . . .

Enough, and more than enough, for today. I have never received a copy of *Labor Leaders Betray Mooney*. I wish I had it.

My best wishes for your health, dear Tom, and for the success of your heroic efforts. Do give my warmest fraternal greetings to Matt [Schmidt] and J. B. [McNamara]. They are brave old warriors. I wish I could also write them from time to time, but the pressure of daily work makes a large correspondence impossible. But do tell them that all my sympathy is with them and that I often think of them.

LATER. Dear old boy, I was going to ask you by no means to send me the money you mentioned in your letter, but while I was writing these pages the letter carrier came and brought the $25 you sent; or rather French money to the amount of 370 francs and 37 centimes.

I am GREATLY moved by what you did, dear Tom. The spirit of it is an expression of your true character, and I cannot tell you how much I appreciate the motives that prompted you. It is just wonderful. It is really almost incredible for the nobility of it.

But I hope, dear friend, that you will not misunderstand when I tell you that it is entirely impossible for me to accept it. Inherently impossible. Believe me, I appreciate *most deeply* what you did, and I know that you are understanding enough not to misjudge me for declining to accept it. Why, old boy, it is simply incredible that you should have even thought of such a thing, really!

We live here far from the center of town and there is no post office in the neighborhood. Nor do we go every day downtown. But in a day or two one of us will go down, and we shall send the amount back to Anna [Mooney]. Again I ask you, dear Tom, do not misunderstand it. That such an idea ever entered your mind is a thousand times of greater meaning and value to me than the gift itself. And I heartily thank you for it.

And now it is really time to close. My affectionate greetings to you and your co-workers. And courage, always courage, of which I know you have plenty. I am sure that the last word has not yet been said in your case.

Fraternally,

S

EG TO AB, *February 23, 1935*, MONTREAL

Dearest Sash,

This has been a rich week, made so by your letters. Two of the 4th and

5th came Tuesday and the one of the 8th with Emmy's letter included came yesterday. I have not had so many letters from you in one week for a long time. You bet it helps to stand much of the misery this town has given me. . . .

Yes, that is pathetic that Tom Mooney should send you money for the work he asked. Naturally you have to send back the $25. It is the first time I have to agree with you that the money must be returned. At other times it seemed uncalled for. I mean if the comrades who value your contribution to our movement knowing that you are hard-pressed send you a gift, I cannot see why you should resent it, as you have on several occasions. It is not as if you lived in saus und schmaus [the lap of luxury]. However, that is more a matter of feeling, than reason. But in Mooney's case it is imperative not to accept anything. It is too bad that you cannot now write about his case. But the historic end of it is not going to run away. Perhaps you'll be able to do it when you have finished Rudolf's job. I am glad Mooney finally woke up to ask you to do something. All these years he and his helpers have studiously avoided mentioning your share in the case. Perhaps death is preferable to endless years of a living grave. But it is certain that it was you who saved his life: your efforts resulted in Wilson's plea for commutation of the death penalty. Not that you or I care that no mention was ever made of that by the different people who entered the campaign for Tom. Still it is cheap. So I am glad he finally realizes that it was shabby to ignore your marvelous consecration to his case. . . . Goodby, dear heart. With lots of love,

[EG]

AB TO MICHAEL COHN, *March 15, 1935, NICE*

CABLE VIA WESTERN UNION BROKE AND IN DEBT GIVING UP APARTMENT URGENTLY NEED SEVENTY FIVE DOLLARS PLEASE CABLE AMERICAN EXPRESS

SASHA

AB TO EG, *April 8, 1935, NICE*

Well, dearest girl,

Life is really a tragic joke. We had notified our landlord that we leave the apartment, we packed all our things, and everything was ready to move to St. Tropez. Every day we expected a reply from Draguignan and so three weeks passed and of course I could not work under those conditons. We were ready to vacate at a moment's notice. Finally the police here called me, as I have already written you. They told me there is an enquiry from Draguignan and that permission will be granted to settle in St. Tropez. Then more time passed and finally Emmy was called and got her permission. Then more time passed and on Saturday my "man" came up and brought a paper to inform me that I was REFUSED permission by Draguignan.

Well, there you are. So now we have started to unpack again and we are making arrangements with the landlord to stay here. Fortunately he is not taking advantage of our situation. In fact, we got him to reduce the yearly rent from 2,800 to 2,600 [francs]. He even promised to fix the toilet, which is leaking, and make other little repairs.

It means then that I am virtually a prisoner in Nice, or in the Alpes Maritimes district.* Of course, I can go out for a visit to St. Tropez, but it would not be good policy to go out right now. Of course, first of all, I MUST keep a *permanent* residence in Nice. You see, dear, you were right in advising us to keep the apartment. I had at first also intended to do so, but we were financially so hard up that it was really impossible. Therefore I made the application to Draguignan. The money from New York and your cable came much later; that is, long after the application had already been made.

Anyhow, it has its good side also. For now we KNOW that I cannot change my residence. We might have planned some day to move to Paris or to some other place, but now we know that we must stay here—at least I must. . . .

As I write this, Monday, 6 P.M., Emmy brings up TWO letters from you, of March 26 and of the 28th. They certainly contain a great deal of information, especially about the money sent to me.

Regarding that: I had received $75 (the amount I asked) from Cohn, and I wrote him a word of appreciation. Two weeks later I received a letter from the manager of the *Freie Arbeiter Stimme* and also a line from [Mark] Mratchny telling me that it is the *FAS* which is sending me the money.

Now you write that Cohn had paid the *FAS* back the money they sent me. So it is Cohn after all who had sent it. Well, I have thanked both Cohn and the *FAS* for it, so it is OK. But I am really surprised to know that Cohn is so short of money that he had to borrow the $75 from friends, or to get them to contribute the amount. . . .

* Recent French laws required aliens, before giving up their residence in a certain district, to secure permission from the Préfecture of the district to which they intended to move. Thus AB, living in Nice, was in the Alpes Maritimes; to move to St. Tropez he had to receive permission from the Var Préfecture. Under the new laws, if Berkman wanted to leave Nice for one day, he had to get a "visa" from the police and then immediately register at his destination—he was thus virtually a "prisoner in Nice," under what amounted to city if not house arrest.

The letters you mention (of your own) I have received, also the WILL, as well as the money order for $30. Several days ago the post did not have yet any notice about that $30. But it is probably there now. Yesterday was Sunday, so I could not go there, and today I worked. I'll go down tomorrow.

You think I am impractical for not asking for money before I run short. Well, dear, that is very simple. It is hard to ask for money, so one waits till it is absolutely necessary. And besides we always try to sell things. That is, Emmy does, as I am no good at it. Living on bread and tea is not so terrible, after all. But the fact is that some days we either had the bread and no tea, or the tea and no bread! But one has to take it in good grace—under such conditions I always think of the days in Russia when we were there and [what] we saw there. As to the radio, that is all right about your suggestion to sell it, but the trouble is people don't like to buy a used radio, for there are new kinds appearing on the market every day almost, improved ones by which you can even hear America. Moreover, the radio has been on the bum for some time now. Either the lamps are burned out (and those lamps are expensive, from 50 francs up apiece) or there is some defect in the thing itself. It has not "worked" for a long time now, and such a thing cannot be sold of course. The same about my new things. Sure, dear, I understand how you feel about them [i.e., radios]. Well, anyhow, now we are "flush.". . .

I must send this out tonight or it will not catch the "Berengaria," which sails on the 10th. So enough for today, dear. Cheer up, dearest girl, and soon I hope not to need to write letters to you. It is unsatisfactory at best. I take you in my arms, dear heart.

S

AB TO STELLA BALLANTINE, August 14, 1935, ST. TROPEZ

My dear Stel,

It is a long time since you had a letter from me, dear girl. One damned thing after another, you know, so that the days pass without one having done what his heart really longs for. . . .

But today I feel, as in the good old Pennsylvania [prison] days, that it would [do] me good to have you actually receive my communion with you. Not that there is anything wonderful to tell you, except the wonderful news that I am free of the Rocker translation. . . .

News there is none. EG arrived from Canada pretty much exhausted, more mentally perhaps than physically. Emmy had gone to St. Tropez two weeks ahead of me, and when I arrived here (just one day before EG) I found the house all spick and span, every room including the "boudoir"—outhouse— whitewashed and painted, Emmy herself having done all the painting, very beautifully and artistically. EG, however, seemed too tired out and oppressed to notice much of it. Indeed, I felt that she was more oppressed in spirit than at any former return home. Most probably Chicago [i.e., Frank Heiner] was the cause of it. At any rate, the surprise of the renovated house and cleared garden, the most warm welcome, etc., failed to raise her spirits, unfortunately. You know our dear Emma—and even Emmy's spontaneous cheerfulness and my "celebrated" jokes were powerless to lighten the atmosphere. Indeed, I believe that the cheerfulness was resented as aggravating to a serious attitude toward life. It's too bad, of course, but there is no cure for it. Things must take their course, in their own natural manner, so to speak. . . .

As to myself, here you have all about me in this letter. Have been a bit under the weather of late, but nothing serious. On the whole, with social conditions as they are throughout the world, with poor health and leading a rather useless life, socially, I often get to feel rather tired of the whole tragi-comedy. There is no limit to man's stupidity, and it isn't even interesting any more to watch the eternal repetition of this universal cinema. . . .

Love to Teddy, Ian, and Davy. I hope all is going as well as can be expected. Poor Mods [Modest Stein] is also having plenty of troubles. I hardly think he will be able to come this year. Yet I should like to see him again. Much love to you, dear Stel,

[AB]

EG TO AB, November 19, 1935, LONDON

My dear, old Dush,

As a greeting to your sixty-fifth birthday it is fitting that I should tell you the secret of my life. It is that the one treasure I have rescued from my long and bitter struggle is my friendship for you. Believe it or not, dear Sash. But I know of no other value, whether in people or achievements, than your presence in my life and the love and affection you have roused. True, I loved other men. I love Frank [Heiner] with a silly, but nonetheless intense emotion. But it is not an exaggeration when I say that no one ever was so rooted in my being, so ingrained in every fiber, as you have been and are to this day. Men have come and gone in my long life. But you, my dearest, will remain forever. I do not know why this should be so. Our common struggle and all it has brought us in travail and disappointment hardly explain what I feel for you. Indeed, I know that the only loss that would matter would be to lose you or your friendship.

Such an abiding feeling could be better explained if you had always been all kindness or understanding. But you were not that. On the contrary, you were and are still often harsh and lacking in comprehension of the inner motivations of my acts. But all that is as nothing [compared] with the force you have been from the moment I first heard your voice and met you in Sachs's café and all through the forty-five years of our comradeship. I seem to have been born then as woman, mother, comrade, and friend. Yes, I believe my strongest and most compelling feeling for you is that of the mother. You have often resented that, saying you are no mollycoddle. Of course, you failed to understand that it was not my desire to impose my mother authority on you. It was the ever-present concern in your welfare and the equally present fear that something might befall you that would tear you away from me. Terribly selfish feeling, isn't it, dear heart? Or is it that you had bound me by a thousand threads? I don't know and don't care. I only know that I always wanted to give you more than I expected from you. Indeed, I know that there is nothing I can think of that I would not joyfully give out of the fullness of my being to enrich your life.

Feeling as I do for you, it was bitter hard to go away before your birthday. I wanted so much to remain and celebrate it with you and Emmy. But I feared my presence might interject some discord. Not that any one of us would do so deliberately. On the contrary, we'd try hard to avoid it. And because we would be careful, it perhaps would have happened. However, what difference does the physical presence make? I feel bound to you spiritually. And it is this which keeps you ever present and real to me even when we are separated by thousands of miles. So it is all right my being away from you on your birthday. I will be with you in my thoughts and with my heart. Strangely enough, I will be lecturing Thursday. I wish it were on a subject that had some bearing on your life and work. For I always wanted the whole world to know about you. But I am speaking on the international munitions clique, the traders in death. Still that won't prevent me from thinking of your birthday and feeling you real close to me. . . .

Goodby, my dear, dear Tolstogub. With all my heart I wish you a grand birthday, very much improved health, and some interesting and vital work that would relieve you of economic stress and anxiety. My love to Emmy. I embrace you tenderly,

Emma

AB TO EG, November 24, 1935, NICE

Dearest Em,

It is certainly time I write you a decent letter. But I have been trying to do so for several days, yet something always interferes. Just now as I began this letter, the lights went out in our apartment, and it took a while to fix them. But in reality my delay is due to my monkeying with the two shelves

I got from Nellie. Had to put them together. There are many pieces in them—they are standing shelves, you know, like étagères—and some pieces are missing, so I had considerable difficulty in fitting things etc. And I find that after some physical work I am rather tired and can't do anything else. Maybe the weather is also responsible for it. It has been raining for days and days, though the sun also shows up now and then.

Anyhow, what I mainly wanted to tell you is that of all the letters received, yours is the most beautiful. Naturally so, everything considered. But it is the most beautiful letter, perhaps, that I ever had from you. . . .

Nellie just came in and I have some letter on business to write for her. So must make it short. More anon. Love.

Affectionately,
Sash

EG TO AB, *January 25, 1936, LONDON*

Dearest,

I wish I could write something cheerful. But my usual gloom has been increased by the widespread fake grief displayed by the whole city over the death of the king. It is simply unbelievable. Not only the average Britishers, the Tories or Liberals, but also the entire labor and radical ranks have closed down everything because of the death of George V. All meetings and public affairs have been cancelled by the Labor and Commnist Parties. Even the idiotic Arbeiter Ring has called off a meeting that was to have taken place yesterday. But for the protest against such cringing chauvinism, it would have been better to call off my lecture last Thursday. For only about thirty people were there, mostly our own, and the few outsiders came dressed in black. But of course, I insisted on our meeting being held, though I knew it would be a flop. I was not mistaken.

The irony is that we worked hardest for the lecture last Thursday and a small fortune was spent to circularize about three hundred people, not to speak of the expense and the amount of work [Ralph] Barr put into the venture. Poor Mace, when he wrote that I should postpone my coming here because of the royal wedding and the elections I thought he was crazy. I could not imagine a whole people prostrate before royalty, so absolutely held in awe by their king and every fart coming from him. As to his death, I tell you it is amazing. The whole vast city of London has been turned into abject gloom, everybody is in black, every shop window in black and purple. Yesterday I had to meet someone in the tea room of one of the hotels. The place was jammed with people in black and an organ playing mournful tunes. It was so depressing I gave a sigh of relief when we got out. Needless to say, most theaters are closed until after the funeral. [Fritz] Kreisler's concert, which I was going to attend tomorrow, has also been called off. But why wonder at that when the radical Jews are such apers of the rest? I believe outside of our few comrades, the rest is dissolved in crocodile tears and laments over the beloved, fatherly, and most humane king. And here am I trying to penetrate the minds of the English people. What a god-damned fool. . . .

Emma

AB TO EG, *March 5, 1936, NICE*

Dearest Em,

Here I am at my little machine again. The FIRST typed letter for YOU, and it is time to write you a decent letter.

Now, dear heart, you probably feel confused about my contradictory postals and letters about Emmy and her condition. So I shall try to make the whole situation clear now in this letter, both in re myself and concerning Emmy.

So here goes. Emmy had a very thorough X-ray, several of them, for the different organs. She was naturally very nervous about the decision, and so the doctors told her it's all right, no operation necessary. And of course you can imagine that we were both happy about it, and I immediately wrote you some postals about the good news.

But that was only to put Emmy at ease. You understand, dear. The doctors wanted only to quiet her fears. But the next day they told her that SHE DOES NEED AN OPERATION. The main surgeon in her department in Pasteur Hospital is Dr. Casiglia and he has a very big reputation. He found that the mouth of Emmy's stomach has switched to the *right* side (while normally it should be on the left side). That is the cause of the pressure on her intestines and Casiglia said he is confident he can make a new and healthy woman of her. He said the operation is NECESSARY. Lavements (washings) are all right, but they can never replace the mouth of the stomach in the proper place. . . .

The ONLY important thing now is that you should be here when the operation takes place. For that reason we want to ask Casiglia whether Emmy can wait one month with it, for by that time you will be able to be in Nice. Emmy feels that she would have so much more courage and faith, if you were here at that time. Her faith in you, your strength and affection and your ability to communicate your strength to others is really touching. . . .

I am feeling all right and gradually improving. I also have to gain strength for the second operation.* Now, the point is this. I require a lot of attention. I am supposed to sleep in a sitting posture and even during the

---

* In February Berkman had undergone an operation on his prostate gland.

day I need this and that, a rub down, or a washing, and things handed to me so that I should not have to move about much, etc. And Emmy is proving a wonderful nurse and is just splendid in that way. I also need certain kinds of food, vegetables and light things, and Emmy is preparing them for me just the way needed and in short is most capable. I don't need to tell you that she does it all in a most loving manner, and she has arranged her day so that she should not tire herself and have time to take care of herself and rest. We don't want a strange person in the house to help Emmy. The washing she will give out and so she can devote her time to me and to herself without working hard. So in this point everything is fine.

But in case Emmy should have to have the operation in a week or so, then things will not be very satisfactory for either of us. She will have no one to visit her or help her or bring her anything at the hospital, because I am not in condition to walk about. I must either lie down or sit down most of the time. . . .

Of other matters by and by. I hope your meeting on the 31st will be a great success. Must close now to mail this letter. With constant thoughts of you, dearest Em, I embrace you lovingly. As ever the same, even if non-pissing,

S

EG TO AB AND EMMY ECKSTEIN, *March 9, 1936,* LONDON

My dear ones,

It was indeed a grand surprise to get your typewritten letters. I hope they truly indicate that you are both feeling much improved. Because if it meant considerable strain, I'd rather have short scribs by hand. Meanwhile, I enjoyed your detailed account of your condition. I have written you both Saturday that I will get away as quickly as possible after my last lecture March 31st. I will only stay a night in Paris to get some rest. And if my last lecture is successful, I may even fly to Cannes. That would save two to three days. In any event, you can rest assured, my dearest ones, I will be with you the first days in April. I am now waiting to hear what your physician, Emmychen, had to say about the postponement of the operation until the first week in April. I hope he will agree to that. Though I don't see why he shouldn't consent in view of the fact that your condition is of long standing. I am only sorry that you should have to suffer another month, my poor little Emmy. But otherwise it does not seem to be such an emergency, does it? Well, you will have to abide by what your surgeon decides. I do hope though he will let you wait. I want very much to be present and with you after you come out of the anesthesia. I want with all my heart to give you all the assurance and strength I can. But do not credit me with being superhuman, my dear. Anyhow, be of good cheer and brave heart until we meet. And then some more.

Your condition, my Sash, may be such that the second operation is imperative. Yet I hope you too can wait. It gives me the jitters to think that it might be urgent. Fact is, I am between two fires. I cannot bear to have you undergo the operation without me. And I am afraid your condition demands an immediate operation. I can only hope that the latter is not the case. You could go back to the hospital almost directly [when] Emmy comes out of the operation. I could then visit both of you at the same time and look after your comforts. I do not see why you should have to remain in the hospital a month. You say yourself one cannot recuperate there. It seems to me that it would be much better for you if you could leave directly after the main care, dressing your wound or whatever you are getting now. You could have the man who comes to you now do the same after the second operation. However, we need not discuss this now. Naturally you must not do anything rash that would harm you. The main thing now is whether you can wait until I return. I hope fervently you can, my dearest Sash.

My dear, don't get frightened about what I am going to tell you. Your old sailor had a very narrow escape of the kind of death she never thought would come to her. I went to spend the weekend with the Suttons. They have a very nice home, but like all English houses it is blood-freezingly cold. Before I went to bed Mrs. Sutton lighted a gas fire. I thought it was an electric fire like the kind we have. Well, I read until very early morning, then fell asleep. I felt in my sleep that something heavy was oppressing me and that my head ached violently. I tried to waken but couldn't. Finally I tore myself out of sleep and found my room filled with gas. Fortunately Mrs. Sutton had left my window wide open. Or the silly and futile struggle of life would have been over. Strangely enough I wanted to shut the window before I retired because the night air in England at this time is even more penetrating than in the day. But Mrs. Sutton had given me a mountain of blankets. So at the very last second I refrained from closing the window. Strange, isn't it? Anyway, I felt sick as a dog all yesterday and even today I have my nose full of gas smell. Talk about Dutch luck. Frankly I am not keen for such an end to happen just when you and Emmy need me so much. Otherwise it might have been an easy escape from life with all its rotten conditions. Evidently it was not to be. I suppose the struggle must go on. . . .

I still have an awful lot to do to get ready and oceans of letters to write. So I must close. Goodby, my dear ones. With loads of love,

E

EG TO AB, *March 15, 1936,* COVENTRY

Dearest Sash,

I wrote Emmy yesterday with only a greeting to you. I have a little time before dressing for my lecture so will write you. I will add a line to tell you the outcome of tonight's affair. I understand the drama organization in this town has a thousand members and most of them will attend. Gawd, if only I could have more such bodies to speak for. How much misery that would save me. Perhaps when I have once established myself. When. I fear it will take many more years than I have before me. And the way so far has just been hell. . . .

My main concern now is to get to you and Emmy and help you two back to health. I hope I will succeed.

Goodby, my dearest. Love to Emmy. Must dress now,

Emma

[P.S.] Monday morning

Here I am, my dear, waiting until train time to return to London. The meeting last night brought back America very painfully. About 1,000 people in the theater more responsive than any audience I ever had. The group at the Repertory in this city is also more human and sociable than most such groups I found. It gave me a feeling of the past in a similar atmosphere in the States. If ony I had two such engagements a week, life in England would not be so paralyzing. You know better than anyone how enervating it is to have to attend to every detail yourself, eat your heart out in dealing with people who lack a large outlook, and then speak before a handful of living corpses—it's been that in every meeting in London and it's just been hell.

Last night's affair made up for much. It holds out a ray of hope that I might build up something when I return next fall, yet who knows how this rotten world will look next fall? Say what you like, my dearest, but more and more I am coming to see that Nietzsche was right. History is nothing else but an eternal recurrence. The masses everywhere are as ready to fly at each other's throat and tear each other limb from limb as in 1914. They have learned nothing and we fools go on believing. In my case it may really be habit more than faith or some form of rationalization of the growing void in my life that needs something to hold on to.

Forgive me philosophizing when you are ill but whom else should I write about the things that occupy my mind? I do hope your condition is improving. . . .

Love,

E

AB TO EG, *March 18, 1936, NICE*

Dearest Em,

I meant to write to you *today* anyhow and this morning I got your handwritten letter from Coventry and it has been a long time since I have had a letter that gave me so much joy as the news of your great meeting before the drama organization. That was wonderful, and certainly encouraging, and I know it must have done your heart good.

Dear, you have made a heroic struggle—I mean, all your life has been a heroic struggle, but I am referring particularly to the present tour in England. This time you were more single-handed in your efforts than ever before, I think. What with the absence of active comrades, disillusionment, war clouds, and the great poverty of the crisis—why, our struggle in the U.S. has never had such handicaps as your present struggle in England. And yet I think you have accomplished wonders—the mere fact that you have kept it up for over four months is proof of it. Well, dear heart, I can tell you frankly that I don't know anyone else who could have carried through such a struggle against such terrific odds. I know I could never have done it. . . .

I hope you have entirely recovered from your cold and also from the effects of that gas that you inhaled so unwittingly and generously. Take care of yourself, dear girl, and rest up a few days, either in London or Paris, before you return here. Of course you'll stay in the apartment here. It is really very nice and handy for buying things etc. and quite comfortable. It is a little out of the center of the city, but then one does not need the center very often. And as to the hospital, the connections are all right. But sufficient unto the day. . . .

Yes, dear, you are right, history repeats itself and now we seem to be just where the world was in 1914. This Hitler business does not presage any good. There may be no war very soon, but in the course of time—maybe in a year or so—it is likely to break. Well, it is no use looking into the future. . . .

That is all for today, dear. It is the 18th, but there is not much to congratulate oneself on, is there, dear? Except that after all those years, long and hard years and fearful changes in the world, our old friendship has remained unchanged, and indeed [is] stronger and more understanding and intimate than ever. And THAT is a very great deal.

S'long now, dear chum. Emmy sends love. She has not been much in a letter-writing mood of late, but hopes you will excuse her. She is picking up a bit of weight, which she will need before long. She asks me to tell you that she could use two nightgowns, but they should be *with long sleeves,* warm ones and *simple,* for in the hospital they do not allow the women to wear any fancy nightgowns. I embrace you affectionately, ever your old,

S

AB TO EG, March 21, 1936, NICE

Dearest,

... Emmy feeling pretty good today and I also. Hope things are going a bit satisfactory with you, dear heart. You are the greatest revolutionary fighter that ever lived.

By the way, dear. The enclosed from Spain came yesterday per Sanya [Shapiro]. Did you get such a letter also? Maybe they don't know your address.

I would reply: To question #1: yes, it is a principle of anarchism. To #2: *no*. To #3: Anarchists cannot participate in political activity for any reasons. Would in the long run be useless and defeating our true purposes.

But there is one question in my mind. In this last election in Spain the revolutionary syndicalists (our people) seem to have voted with the other radicals and thereby gained a majority over the reactionary elements. If they had not, it is sure the fascists would be in power there now.

Now, I do *not* believe in the old stupidity that "the worse the better." We *need* as much political liberty as possible *even now*, in order to propagate our ideas. During black reaction the revolutionary movements are simply destroyed, as in Russia, Germany, Italy, etc.

Now, then: The question arises, is it logical to oppose our people working politically in elections *with* the other revolutionary elements (revolutionary socialists and communists) *against* the common enemy of fascism?

I want to know what you think of it before I reply to Spain. Let me know soon as possible, dear. Just briefly, for I know you are busy—obviously, I am opposed to cooperating with the communists. But in Spain it seems that the present victory of the radical elements is due to our people having helped them with their votes. Must close. Much love to you from Emmy and your,

S

EG TO AB, March 22, 1936, LONDON

My dearest old chum,

That was a beautiful letter you wrote me the 18th. Not that I did not know how you feel about my struggle and about my work. But a fellow does sometimes long to hear that one's nearest and dearest realizes the struggle and appreciates one's efforts. I don't much give a damn if outsiders, or our comrades fail to understand, or to care. I do not even care so much about anybody's opinion, as I do about yours. Then too, one begins to value [more] the few most precious friends of a lifetime when one goes on in age than one does in one's youth. Youth has all of life to live and is so callous and indifferent to time and relationships. But when one gets to my age, one clings more hungrily to the few unchangeable friends. That's why your letter gave me such a lot of joy. I felt it was almost worthwhile to go through the pain and the misery of four months to have you say such lovely things about me. I hope to give you a special hug when I come back.

I cannot agree with you, my dearest, when you write that you could not do what I have done. Of course, dearest Sash, you could not do it now, sick as you are. I also could not have gone through such an ordeal but for my iron constitution. Nothing seems to harm that. Not even a frightful cold and the worst kind of a cough I had in years. Such things roll off me like water from a duck. A few days' warm weather and I am again feeling all right. With such a constitution, it is no virtue to go on against all odds. And I know you would. Did you not prove it time on end? Have you forgotten how ill you were before you got to the "Buford" and how energetic and active you became when confronted with necessity? . . .

I do hope I will have a wire from you not later than Tuesday so I can settle about my going, whether it is to be by boat to Marseilles, or by train to Paris and two days later to Nice. As I wrote you, I am very worried about the delay of your operation. I should think the man who comes to change your tube and bandages or whatever he is doing ought to know about the second operation. I hope you have not in anyway injured yourself by waiting so long. I am looking forward to your wire.

Soon, dearest, I will take you in my arms and take care of you.

With love,
Em

P.S. Sure, dearie, your apartment is very nice. It is only that two sick people need separate beds. So I do not see where you and Emmy are going to put me. When you will both be in the hospital, it will be easy. But I hope you will not have to be there very long. The main thing will be the convalescence at home and the care. Well, we will see. I am entirely at your and Emmy's command. When you will both be well again I can again become the boss.

EG TO AB, *March 24, 1936, LONDON*

Dearest Sash,

Yesterday morning I got your letter of the 21st. I had to rush away to meet some people and attend to other matters. And also I wanted to think over the idea of anarchists participating in elections. On my return last night I found your wire. Then this morning came yours of the 22nd and a post card. I will now try to answer the whole lot. First of all though, I feel so relieved that your condition is not so grave that a day or two more would injure it. I confess I am really tired as a dog. . . .

No, I did not get anything from the Spanish comrades. I dare say they did not know my address. It does not matter. I agree with you in your replies to the three questions. So if you wish, you can sign my name to the reply you will send them. Or if they care to have my opinion, let them send me the questionnaire to your address. I will reply when I come.

Dearie, while I fully agree with you that it is stupid to maintain that conditions and situations must get worse before they get better, I cannot agree with the suggestion that anarchists should in grave times cooperate with communists in elections. You probably remember the controversy between [Errico] Malatesta and [Saverio] Merlino. Of course fascism wasn't known then. But black reaction was. And it was Merlino who argued that anarchists by joining the socialists during elections would help defeat the reactionary gang. I don't know whether you remember Malatesta's reply. It was to the effect that the anarchists would, as they had always done, merely get the chestnuts out of the fire for the socialists and liberals. And they would injure their idea beyond repair.

Now, I do not mean to suggest that you and I must follow Malatesta's ideas in the matter. But it happens that I myself consider it not only inconsistent with our views on vesting power to politicians by means of voting for them. I also consider it highly dangerous. We insist, do we not, dear, that the means must harmonize as far as possible with the end. And our end being anarchism, I do not see how we can very well unite with any political party. Especially with the communists, knowing as we do that their dictatorship is by no means different than [or from] that of the fascists. In Spain there was also [Francisco Largo] Caballero, who had not only fought the CNT [Confederación Nacional del Trabajo], but had actually helped to send many of our comrades to prison about two years ago. For the life of me I cannot see what our comrades who did join the united front could expect either from Caballero or the communists.

Besides, if the letter I received from Cultura Proletaria and the article in the last issue of *Vanguard* are to be relied upon, then only the [Angel] Pestaña group [i.e., the Syndicalist Party] joined the united front and participated in the elections. The CNT did not. I cannot believe that our comrades of the Cultura Proletaria would be misinformed. I understand what the CNT did was to organize a number of general strikes in different parts of the [country during the] elections. And that it was really that more than the vote that swung the support of the workers to the left.

Strangely enough, the questions the comrades in Spain are asking are the same I argued by letter with Joe Goldman [in Chicago]. He too insisted that we should join the communists in their fight against war and fascism, forgetting that the communists are only against the war of capitalist countries, while approving Russia's race for armaments. I have said then and I must say now that, with our past experience with socialists and communists, it seems folly to join them. But more important is my firm belief that we would be spitting ourselves in the face, if we approved participation in elections. Fighting ALL POWER AND ALL GOVERNMENT AS WE DO, how can we help [by] putting anyone into positions of power? . . .

No, my dearest Sash, WE SIMPLY CANNOT AND SHOULD NOT MAKE THE PLUNGE. I cannot, anyhow. And I am sure, if you will reflect carefully, you will also not go in for any justification of joining the so-called liberal gang, which is also nothing but reactionary under disguise.

Of course, I do not mean we should censure our comrades in Spain. Every country imposes different methods in certain emergencies. We can only state our own position toward the fundamentals of anarchism. And that has always been opposition to the slick political machine that has ever corrupted the best of people, or has paralyzed their efforts to serve the masses. At least that is my stand. . . .

Dearest, I must close. Love to Emmy and yourself,

E

P.S. Dearie, I had to stop writing and rush to Whitechapel to find someone to sign my application [for a passport renewal].

AB TO EG, March 23, 1936, HOSPITAL PASTEUR, NICE

[On the first page Berkman penciled a marginal instruction: "To be mailed only in the case of my death." It was therefore not sent, for his death came later under circumstances (detailed below) which did not permit him more than a few words of farewell. Emma no doubt found it among the papers that she ultimately deposited in Amsterdam. It appears here out of its chronological place by one day.]

Dearest sailor mine, staunchest chum of a lifetime—

I know how understanding you are—and so you'll forgive me for the wire I had Emmy send you today. It said, "NO OPERATION AT PRESENT," but I am to have my second operation tomorrow morning.

I did not want to worry you, dearest Em. What purpose would it serve? You are about to leave for South Wales to lecture and the news of my operation would worry you fearfully. So, you understand, dear, and forgive.

They have just finished the last tests—day before yesterday for the blood, urine, etc., and now the heart and all is well. I feel comfortable, strong, and everything will be OK.

I could not wait with the operation as I had planned. Dr. Tourtou examined me and said it must be done now.

Well, dearest, I think everything will be OK and I don't feel anxious at all. But there is never any telling and so, in case anything happens, don't grieve too much, dearest. I have lived my life and I am really of the opinion that when one has neither health nor means and cannot work for his ideas, it is time to clear out.

But it is not of this I want to speak now. I just want you to know that my thoughts are with you and I consider our life of work and comradeship and friendship, covering a period of about forty-five years, one of the most beautiful and dearest things in the world.

In this spirit I greet you now, dear immutable sailor girl, and may your work continue to bring light and understanding in this topsy-turvy world of ours. I embrace you with all my heart, you bravest, strongest, and truest woman and comrade I have known in my life. Your old chum, friend, and comrade,

Sasha

P.S. It is understood of course, that anything you want of my things is yours. And my notebooks, mss., etc. I leave to you to do with according to your own judgment.

S

P.S.S. I am happy that you and Emmy have grown to understand each other better. She has been wonderful to me and her devotion limitless. I hope that you will both prove a solace to each other.

S

Send our dear friends Fitzie, Pauline [Turkel], Stella, Mods [Modest Stein], Minna Lowensohn, the [Jeanne and Jay] Leveys, Ben Capes and family, Harry Kelly, Ann Lord, and all others my last thoughts of them.

S

Tell our comrades I send them all my fraternal greetings. May they keep up energetically the work for a brighter and better day and a future of liberty, sanity, and human cooperation.

S

AB TO EG, June 27, 1936, NICE

Dear,

This is your birthday. Sorry I can't be with you. Some other time, I hope.

Nothing new here. Both feeling some better. Will call you up later in the day—it's only 7 A.M. No autobuses yet.

How is everything with you, and the visit of the [Michael] Cohn family?

Got yours of the 25th. Will answer your points by and by.

I hope you have a nice day there (the weather uncertain here today) and enjoy the day.

Affectionately,

S

EG TO AB, June 27, 1936, ST. TROPEZ

My dear,

Whom else should I write on this day but you? Only there is nothing to tell. I keep thinking what a long time to live. For whom? For what? But there is no answer. Useless to rake one's brain.

I have asked Michael and his family to lunch today. One thing, I can still find relief in housework and cooking. Need I tell you that I miss having you on this day? And Emmy, who would have enjoyed the chicken. But if you feel better and are gaining strength, I do not mind the disappointment. Indeed it would have been a grand surprise. And your room so nice and clean and inviting. It looks sad today. Imagine, I had a wire yesterday, you'll never guess from whom. From Demie Coleman, to my birthday. Wonderful that she should remember. She is evidently in England. Cannot make out the name of the town.

Let me hear from you, how you are, Sasha dear. Greetings to Emmy.

Affectionately,

Emma

P.S. Do you want me to send you the Manchester *Guardian* (it comes to me first now) and the *Times Literary* [*Supplement*]? Let me know,

E

Postscript

You have fought so many difficult, nay almost hopeless fights, have stood up for so many lost causes (many of which have now become successful and the staff of life to the Babbitts and Babbittses of radicalism), that you have a right to be proud and cocky and thumb your nose at the Alpes Maritimes and the solid eternities. And you have protected so many of the naked and helpless (physical and spiritual), been a mother to so many and a staunch friend, without asking questions or demanding account, that, even though they or some of them may have forgotten, the great Brahma or whatever the eternal consciousness is in which we don't believe but which inspires us to do noble deeds without hope of return simply because we (and above all you) can't help it, will remember.

HENRY ALSBERG TO EG, June 18, 1929, NEW YORK

AFTER Berkman's death, which is described in heartbroken detail in the "Dear comrades" letter below, Emma still had another revolution to live through. In August comrades called her to Spain. Though she wanted to stay there at their side, she was persuaded to return to England to take charge of the Confederación Nacional del Trabajo (CNT) and the Federación Anarquista Ibérica (FAI) press service and propaganda bureau in London. No individual could have turned the tide of opinion that was running against the Spanish anarchists, but she drew on her incredible energy and tenacity to do what she could. By 1938 the Spanish Revolution had all but joined the others in the long list of her lost causes. What it had meant, its dilemmas and liberating possibilities, she faced with her usual honesty, as shown in these final selections from her correspondence.

As you will recall, in her letter of March 24, 1936, Emma had reaffirmed to Berkman that anarchists could not cooperate with communists in united front action, "knowing as we do that their dictatorship is by no means different than [or from] that of the fascists." Yet the following November, still in Barcelona, she wrote another comrade that keeping the Revolution alive "evidently does justify the most impossible means." But it was only "evidently" so, as she knew in her heart of hearts. The infamous May Days of 1937 realized her worst fears. As she wrote Rudolf Rocker on May 14, 1937,

> the frightful thing has happened, a thing most of us foresaw, only I tried so hard to explain it rather than condemn it at the outset. The pact with Russia in return for a few pieces of arms brought its disastrous results. . . . You will see that the murderous Stalin gang have killed [Camillo] Berneri and another comrade and that they were back of the attempt to disarm the comrades of the CNT-FAI. . . . In other words, it is a repetition of Russia with the identical method of Lenin against the anarchists and social revolu-

tionists. . . . I had hoped against hope that the extermination of our comrades and the emasculation of the Revolution would not come so soon.*

It did not help all that much to reflect that she and Berkman had indeed
foreseen the communists, given the opportunity, playing leading coun-
terrevolutionary roles.

But why did Emma stand by her Catalonian comrades, if they had
already committed themselves to a united front with the communists
against Franco? Her reasons appeared in summary form in a letter she
wrote Vernon Richards before her last visit to Spain. Writing from Paris
on September 10, 1938, she asked her English comrade not to make her
letter public unless "something happens to me":

> Dear Vero, as you know, Spain is not exactly the safest of countries, and
> while I am no alarmist I feel I must be ready to face every emergency. This is
> by way of saying that if something should happen to me, you should make
> known to the comrades through *Spain and the World* [the fortnightly] that
> I will go as I lived believing to the end in the ultimate triumph of our ideas.
> Also you should explain to the comrades that though I disagreed with much
> that our Spanish comrades had done, I stood by them because they were
> fighting so heroically with their backs to the wall against the whole world,
> misunderstood by some of their own comrades and betrayed by the workers
> as well as by every Marxist organization. Whatever verdict future historians
> will give of the struggle of the CNT–FAI, they will be forced to acknowl-
> edge two great actions of our people, their refusal to establish dictatorship
> when they had power, and having been the first to rise against fascism. It
> may seem little now but I am certain it will weigh in the balance in the
> historic appraisement of the Spanish Revolution.

Thus did Emma go an unrepentant revolutionist, still grappling with the
great themes she and Berkman had discussed and had lived for half a
century. And how to bring about needed fundamental changes nonvio-
lently or with a bare minimum of violence remains, in our own times, a
good question, and an increasingly urgent one. It has never been satisfactorily confronted, let alone answered, by the supporters of the nation
state—in fact, nationalists were soon back at their perennial pastime of
remaking the world through war.

It is tempting to speculate on what might have happened to Emmy
Eckstein, Alexander Berkman, and Emma Goldman, had they lived on
into the nazi occupation of France. As Jewish radicals, probably they
would not have lived on long. It is certain that the two old comrades would
have seen in World War II the penultimate apotheosis of the state power
they hated and just as certain that they would have opposed it with the full
weight of their beings. In her letter to Vernon Richards, Emma prophe-

---

* A copy of this letter to Rocker was kindly made available to us by Mollie Steimer.

sied clearly the imminence of war and made clear what her own stand would have been.*

> I have a hunch that the Spanish comrades will support the war against Germany and Italy. They probably will have no choice, for as one Spanish comrade here told me, "we are condemned to death anyway, a World War might help us." It is reasonably certain that the moment war will be declared both France and England will rush supplies to Spain to help get the Germans and Italians out of the country, which would of course mean the end of Franco. In consequence the anti-fascist forces will feel in duty bound to come to the side of France, England, and Russia. But I will not be deceived by that. I know already that all the high sounding slogans of war to crush fascism and nazism will only be used to blind the masses and to strengthen imperialism as well as bolshevism. With my most ardent desire to be of help to our people I could not join them in support of the new World War. I am inclined to think I will stand pretty much alone in my protest against the coming conflagration.

So she would, but it would not have been for the first time.

EG TO COMRADES, *July 12, 1936, ST. TROPEZ*

Dear comrades,

It is only two weeks since our beloved comrade Alexander Berkman passed away, yet it seems an eternity to me. The blow his untimely death struck me has left me completely shattered. I find it difficult to collect my thoughts. But I feel sure you will want to know all about Sasha's end. For have you not loved him all through the years?

Sasha left a note which was found after we returned from his last resting place. It reads:

> I don't want to live a sick man, dependent. Forgive me, Emmy Darling, and you too, Emma. Love to all. Help Emmy.
>
> Sasha

I have two letters from Comrade Berkman dated June 24th and 26th. He wrote that, while he did not feel strong enough to come to St. Tropez the 27th, my sixty-seventh birthday, his condition was not serious and not to worry. On the 27th in the afternoon, Comrade Berkman called me up from Nice, to give me his well-wishes for the day. He said he was feeling better. Comrade Michael Cohn, his family, and a very devoted English

---

* Vernon Richards waited thirty-two years before making Emma's letter public, which he did finally in *Anarchy 114*, X (August 1970), 245–46.

friend were with me. And my thoughts were far away from any danger to my own, old pal.

At 2 A.M. Sunday [the following morning], just two weeks ago, I was awakened by a telephone call from Nice to come at once. I knew at once that our comrade was at the end—but not what kind of an end. "Come at once," from a French village, unless one has one's own auto, that is impossible. As there is no train, no bus, and no taxi to be had, we had to wait three and one-half hours until we could get the first bus out of here and another two and one-half hours to get to Nice.

They were the most tortured hours in the many of my life. On arriving in Sasha's apartment, we found Emmy, his companion of fourteen years, in a collapse, hardly able to tell us what had happened. We finally learned that Sasha had suffered a violent relapse, and while Emmy was trying desperately to get a doctor, Sasha had shot himself in the chest. This Emmy learned only after Sasha had been rushed to a hospital, and she had been dragged off by the police as having killed Sasha. So great was the fortitude of our brave comrade that he did not let Emmy know he had ended his life. Actually she found him in bed, covered up with blankets, so she should not notice his wound.

Getting a doctor in a small town in France is another indication of the backwardness of the country. It took Emmy several hours before the miserable man arrived. He came too late. But when he found the revolver, he notified the police and the hospital, and Sasha was taken away in an ambulance.

We rushed to the hospital. We found Sasha fully conscious, but in terrific pain, so that he could not speak. He did, however, fully recognize us. Michael Cohn and I remained with him until the early afternoon. When we returned at 4 o'clock, Sasha was in a coma. He no longer knew us. And I hope fervently he no longer felt his pain. I stayed with him until 8:30 P.M. planning to return at 11 P.M. and remain with him for the night. But we were notified that he died at 10 o'clock Sunday, June 28th.

In his letters of the 24th and 26th and in his talk with me over the phone on the 27th, Comrade Berkman seemed miles from the thought of ending his life. But his last attack coming on top of the awful pain he had endured for three months, after the second operation, had evidently sapped his strength and brought him to the breaking point.

Comrade Berkman had always maintained that, if ever he would be stricken with suffering beyond his endurance, he would go out of life by his own hand. Perhaps he may not have done it on the fatal evening of the 28th had I or anyone else of our friends been there to help him. But Emmy was desperately trying to get a doctor and there was no one near she could have left with Sasha. She most likely did not realize the gravity of the moment. Anyhow, Sasha remained alone in his apartment and as he always had a revolver with him, in fact since he was released from the living tomb in 1906, Sasha found courage to make an end of his agony. Unfortunately he was not spared another sixteen hours of fiendish agony, for the bullet had perforated his stomach and the lower part of his lungs, and had also paralyzed his legs.

It had always been our comrade's wish to be cremated. This was also my wish and Emmy's. But there is no crematorium in Nice. The next place was Marseilles, and the cost I was told [was] 8,000 francs. Sasha left the *"magnificent"* sum of £80, which the very government that hounded him from pillar to post locked up as soon as Sasha's death became known. No one could get it. I myself have not been blessed with worldly goods, certainly not since I am living in exile. I could, therefore, not carry out the cherished wish of my old pal and comrade. In point of fact, he would have been opposed to such a thing as 8,000 francs for cremation. He would have said, "The living need this money more than the dead."

But it is so characteristic of our damnable system to fleece the living as well as the dead. No one will ever know the humiliation and suffering our comrade went through in France. Four times expelled. Then granted a pittance of three months—then six months. And, irony of ironies, just two weeks before the end, he was given an extension of a year. Just when he might have enjoyed some peace, Alexander Berkman was too harassed by pain and too spent from his operations to live. To cap the climax of persecution, Emmy was dragged off to the police station while Sasha was taken to the hospital. She was charged with having fired the pistol. It was so absurd that one could hardly credit such a thing: Emmy—who had but one world—Sasha. Fortunately a woman neighbor had seen her distractedly run up and down the sidewalk near their flat, waiting for the doctor. She told the police that Emmy was not even in the apartment when Sasha shot himself. But for that it would have been a difficult job to rescue Emmy from the clutches of the police.

During our sojourn in the south of France, we made a few friends, English and American. They are not anarchists but they thought the world of Sasha and they are very fond of me. They came with armfuls of flowers to pay their last tribute to Alexander Berkman. Sholem Asch was also with us and one of his sons and a most devoted French comrade. On June 30th we laid our comrade to rest in the presence of a simple gathering. No greater love, nor more intensely felt devotion, ever followed the dead to the last [resting place in Caucade Cemetery, Nice].

As for myself—the largest part of my life followed our comrade to his grave. Death had robbed me of the chance to be with my lifelong friend until he breathed his last. But it could not prevent me from a few precious moments with him alone in the Death House—moments of serene peace and silence in contemplation of our friendship that had never wavered, our struggles and work for the ideal for which Sasha had suffered so much, and to which he had dedicated his whole life. These moments will remain for me until I myself will breathe the last. And those moments in the House of the Dead will spur me on to continue the work Sasha and I began on August 15, 1889.

I have a double task to perform: I must help Emmy, not only because that was Sasha's last request, but because she has been in his life for fourteen years and has given her all to him.* And I have Sasha's memory to hold high, that it may continue to live in the hearts and minds of those who loved him. That it may inspire the young generation to heroic deeds, even as his own life had been heroic. For had not Sasha died as he had lived? Consistently to the end? I hope fervently [that] I may be as strong as he, if ever I should be stricken beyond endurance. I know how you all feel about our wonderful Sasha. The many cables, wires, and letters I have already received are proof of your devotion and your love. I know you will not deny our dead respect for the method he employed to end his suffering.

Our sorrow is all embracing; our loss beyond mere words.

Let us gather strength to remain true to the flaming spirit of Alexander Berkman. Let us continue the struggle for a new and beautiful world, but let us work for the ultimate triumph of anarchism, the ideal Sasha loved passionately and in which he believed with every fiber of his being. In this way alone can we honor the memory of one of the grandest and bravest comrades in our ranks, ALEXANDER BERKMAN.

[EG]

EG TO JOHN DEWEY, May 3, 1938, LONDON

[This copy appeared under the letterhead of the SIA, or Solidaridad Internacional Antifascita (International Anti-Fascist Solidarity), of which Emma was secretary and Ethel Mannin treasurer; the list of sponsors included W. H. Auden, Havelock Ellis, George Orwell, John Cowper Powys, Herbert Read, Rebecca West, *et al.* Emma described her committee as one more attempt at "resurrecting the dead in England."]

Dear John Dewey,

I am sorry to have neglected answering your letter of February 21st, but I have been so obsessed with Spain and the struggle for the Spanish people that I have had little time for aught else. I was very glad to get your letter

---

* Emma arranged to send Emmy Eckstein twenty-five dollars a month and got a friend to do likewise. She also tried to have her go with Dr. Michael Cohn to America as a governess, but there were difficulties over her passport—primarily because she had been Berkman's companion—and Cohn finally reached the point that he could not stand the difficult young woman. "How could you do it after knowing me for so many years?" he angrily asked Emma. After she sold "Bon Esprit" in 1937, Emma sent Emmy some more money. Following repeated stomach operations and almost a year in a clinic, the unfortunate Emmy died in 1939.

and to read what you have to say about the changes that have taken place in the minds of many of the intelligentsia in the United States regarding the soviet regime and the activities of the Communist Party in America. The trouble with most of these good people is that they have emancipated themselves from one superstition and are again in the throes of another. They are now blaming everything on Stalin, as if he had come to the fore out of nothing, as if he were not merely the dispenser of the legacy left him by Lenin, Trotsky, and the unfortunate group that has been savagely murdered in the last two years. Nothing amuses me so much as the contention that all was well in Russia while Lenin, Zinoviev, and Trotsky were at the helm of state. Actually, the same process of elimination or, to use the Communist Party term, "liquidation," begun by Lenin and his group, took place from the very beginning of the communist ascendancy to power. Already in the early part of 1918, it was Trotsky who liquidated the anarchist headquarters in Moscow by means of machine guns, and it was during that same year that the peasant soviet, consisting of five hundred delegates with Maria Spiridonovna, had been liquidated by sending many of them, including Maria, to the Cheka. Also it was under the regime of Lenin and Trotsky that thousands of people of the intelligentsia, workers, and peasants were liquidated by fire and sword. In other words, it is the communist ideology which has spread the poisonous ideas in the world, first, that the Communist Party has been called upon by history to guide "the social revolution," and second, that the end justifies the means. These notions have created all the evils, including Stalin, that have followed Lenin's death.

As regards Trotsky, I do not know whether you have seen the *New International* of February, March, April, and especially of this month. If you have, you will see that the saying about the leopard changing his spots, but not his nature, applies forcibly to Leon Trotsky. He has learned nothing and forgotten nothing. The usual bolshevik calumny, falsehoods, and misrepresentations have again been dug out from the family closet and hurled at the memory of the Kronstadt sailors. More than that, neither the dead nor the living are exempt from their venomous and scurrilous attacks. The new bête noir for Trotsky are the Spanish anarchists of the CNT and the FAI. Just think of it, at a time when they are fighting with their backs to the wall, when they have been betrayed by the [Léon] Blum Popular Front Government, by the National [Spanish]Government, and by Stalin's regime, Leon Trotsky, who has roused the whole world in his defense, is attacking the heroic people in Spain. This more than anything else merely proves that Trotsky is woven from the same cloth as his archenemy Stalin, and that he hardly deserves the compassion in his present plight which most people entertain for him. Yes, the Communist Party in and out of Russia has done so much harm to the labor and revolutionary movement in the world that it may well take a hundred years to undo. As to the harm they have done in Spain, it is simply incalculable. One thing is already too apparent: Stalin's satraps in Spain, by their methods of undermining the revolutionary achievements of the Spanish people and of keeping up a system of communist favoritism among officers and other military authorities, have worked right into the hands of Franco. I am not exaggerating when I say that the thousands of lives and the rivers of blood shed by Franco's German and Italian hordes must be laid at the feet of Soviet Russia. I realize that the truth will out some day, but the last twenty-odd years have proved that it takes longer to slay a lie.

I am hoping to go to Canada in the late fall, and of course am hoping against hope that a visa to America may again be obtained for me. Strangely enough, I received a letter yesterday from our mutual friend, Carlo Tresca. He kindly offered to help with the campaign for a strong committee of outstanding men and women in the States who might have bearing on the decision in favor of a visa. Should such a committee be launched, I feel sure that you will not refuse to join the others. Thanking you again for your kind letter.

Sincerely,
[EG]

EG TO JOHN COWPER POWYS, n.d. [ca. August 1938], LONDON

[This unsigned copy seems to have been of Emma's final draft for the typist, for there are numerous corrections in her handwriting.]

My dear good friend,

Nearly two months have passed since your letter of June 15th reached me. You are so understanding of prolonged silence that I do not have to go into lengthy explanations of why I have not replied sooner.

It is beautiful of you to want to see my "friends in Catalonia emerge from this war victorious and really at last create an absolutely new experiment in social life and government free from politicians and dictators—a country really free and one that would realize all those hopes that we all had at the beginning of the Revolution in Russia." You will forgive me, I know, my saying that there is a contradiction in this very first paragraph. It is wherein you speak of a "country really free" and yet seem to think that government is necessary to maintain this ideal. Unfortunately freedom and government do not mix harmoniously. At least I know of no government, no matter how democratic or progressive, that has ever granted real freedom.

Another mistake you are making, dear friend, is in your belief in the need of "centralized authority." That is precisely what the Spanish anarchists do not want. Their whole idea is based on federated relations in all walks and purposes of social life and activity. I am taking the liberty of sending you a copy of *Anarcho-Syndicalism: Theory and Practice*, by one of our most brilliant men, Rudolf Rocker. It will explain to you better than I can in a letter that the whole concept of government, centralized authority, and all that go with them in the way of curtailing real freedom, is wrong and inimical to any social system as conceived by anarchist thought and ideology. It will also give you an idea of how far removed the aim of the Spanish anarchists is from the profit element in production and distribution. (The anarchists believe in the necessity of socialization of means of production and distribution—libertarian socialization. Therein lies the great difference between us and the Russian communists. In point of fact, the simplest Spanish peasant has learned over a period of many years of anarchist activity the difference between the brand of communism that Moscow has imposed on the Russians and what he calls Communismo Libertario.)

You are quite right when you say Spain would be the most fertile soil for the experiment as planned by the Spanish anarchists. The explanation for that is that the National Confederation of Labor [CNT] and the Anarchist Federation of Iberia [FAI] have demonstrated by act and example the practical possibilities of anarchist communism. It will interest you to know that I found in some villages four generations steeped in libertarian communism. To them the idea was not merely on paper or in books, but a living force. I am sure it is this that differentiates the Spanish people from the masses elsewhere. They had the good fortune of being saved the corruption of parliamentarism and political intrigue. They relied on direct action and not on those in high places. Over and above [all, it] was the libertarian principle deeply rooted in the workers and peasants which would have no part of dictatorship. They knew perfectly well that once that step is made it is like rolling down a precipice—there is no halting on the way.

This brings me to your point raised on page two of your letter. It is where you say that "I cannot see how they will guard themselves from the tricks of oratorical demagogues and clever, unscrupulous plotters with treacherous 'slogans.' " That is indeed a difficult question, as my Spanish comrades can well testify. They have already paid very dearly for their [being] "sincere and honest and idealistic and so free from those tricky ways that they call '*real* politics.' " But my Spanish comrades felt that it was better to be pricked than to prick. In the last analysis one must make a beginning, if one ever wishes to reach one's goal. The Spanish anarchists could easily, if they wanted to, put the other sectors against the wall, as was done and is being done in Russia. To be sure, the step they had taken in the form of participation in the government [i.e., the acceptance of ministries] was equally inconsistent from the anarchist viewpoint, but it was the lesser of the two evils. As I have repeatedly pointed out to many harsh critics of the CNT–FAI, people living in safety and far removed from the scene of battle, governments can be overthrown, but dictatorship perpetuates its evils by its own crushing momentum.

The fact that my Spanish comrades "have suffered so long and so deeply themselves that perhaps they will find some way of guarding their liberty and their new creation, *and yet* of allowing their *intelligentsia* all the indulgence in the world to criticize," may not prove entirely true, for it is as old as the hills that the slaves of yesterday easily become the tyrants of tomorrow. No, it is not their suffering which will safeguard my comrades from curtailing intellectual freedom the moment they are at the helm of the new social order. Much rather is it their firm conviction that creative work in whatever form is the only security of a rich social culture. (In proof I am sending you the last issue of *Spain and the World,* which contains a report on the "Day of the Book" celebration in Barcelona [on] June 14.) I believe fervently that anarchism is the safest guarantee for intellectual freedom and "all the indulgence in the world to criticize." However, I do not claim infallibility for my Spanish comrades. They, too, may become tyrannical. My one hope is that the liberated masses may soon call the leaders to account. I can assure you of one thing, dear: when the new social order becomes a living reality and [if it then] attempts the curtailment of intellectual freedom, I would cease to be a defender of that experiment.*

Thank you so much, my generous friend, for the fine tribute you are paying me. I hope my comrades will never be foolish enough to consider me "one of the saints and pioneers of the new era." This reminds me of a similar tribute I once received from an interesting English correspondent of mine. Once when I was in a very pessimistic mood, he tried to cheer me up by saying, "Never mind, Emma Goldman. In three hundred years a beautiful cathedral will be built to your name. You will come down from heaven and look through the stained glass windows to see what your followers have made of your teaching and you will say, 'Is this for what I have given my life?' " So you see there is no guarantee to one's immortality after one's followers have realized the ideas and ideals one has propagated.

Yes, I have been cherishing all sorts of plans, the most important being my return to Spain. Unfortunately it has become more difficult than last year to procure visas. More and more the whole world is turned into a frightful fortress from which one can neither get out or to which one can

---

* She had originally typed but then lined out an interesting qualification: She could assure Powys of all this, "if I were still alive" when it came about. The excised condition revealed foreboding that her own end was not far off and her inner fear or conviction that the Spanish cause was lost. Before long many of her Catalonian comrades crowded into the region in the south of France where Emma and Sasha had lived, off and on, since the '20s. After still more years of exile, the Spanish refugees are still there in considerable numbers, eking out miserable existences awaiting word from home which has been a long time coming.

get in. In point of fact, I was to leave for Paris last Saturday and soon after for Spain, but I have been cautioned to try for an English visa first, which some friends are now doing [for me]. The Home Office willing, I may leave some time this week. I am also to go to Amsterdam for a few weeks. The International Institute of Social History in Amsterdam, a very unique and interesting venture, is anxious to acquire the archive of my dear departed comrade and friend, Alexander Berkman. The material has already been shipped to the Institute, but I will have to go there to sort the collection. That will keep me busy until the end of September, when I will return to England for a month or six weeks and then sail for Canada. So you see that you guessed right about my having made all sorts of plans.* However, the work of the CNT and the SIA will go on. My splendid friend, Ethel Mannin, will be in charge of the SIA and other friends will look after the work of the CNT-FAI [in London].

If I thought you an Irishman, I should suspect you of having kissed the Blarney Stone, you say so many nice and flattering things. Still, I am grateful that you think "to have been and to be Emma Goldman is, as our Americans would say, *some* luck in itself." That is going some, as they also say in America. My mail will be forwarded and I will be very glad to hear from you whenever the spirit moves you. With kind greetings,

[EG]

P.S. I am so glad that Llewellyn is "slowly getting *better.*" I am not devout enough to thank the Lord, but I thank whoever has helped him to improve. . . .

---

* *The best-laid plans. . . .* In Paris she fell ill and had to delay going to Spain until mid-September. There the daily bombardment of Barcelona for seven weeks left her unscratched, but on her return to London she fell down a flight of stairs and landed unconscious, with her head bleeding—she said she preferred dying in Spain to living in England, but it was very nearly the other way round. What with one delay and another, she did not get to Amsterdam before the holidays or to Canada until later in 1939. She celebrated her seventieth birthday (June 27, 1939) in Montreal, where she received a greeting from the exiled CNT leader Marino Vasquez, who wrote from Paris in the name of the Spanish Liberation Movement:

> You are the incarnation of the eternal flame of the ideal which you have demonstrated in your life. The Spanish militants admire and revere you, as anarchists should admire and value those of a great heart and abiding humanism for all mankind. . . . We declare you our spiritual mother.

Back in Toronto she overextended herself preventing the deportation of some anti-fascist Italian comrades, suffered a stroke on February 17, 1940, died on May 18—the very anniversary day of Berkman's liberation "from the living tomb"—and finally, still presumably undesirable but now a dead alien, was allowed re-entry to the United States, where she was buried in Chicago's Waldheim Cemetery near the graves of her Haymarket comrades. As she had wished, she went out fighting.

Index

Numbers appearing in *italics* immediately following the name (and identification) indicate letters to or from that individual.